THE ORIGIN OF THE WELFARE STATE IN ENGLAND AND GERMANY, 1850–1914

SOCIAL POLICIES COMPARED

E. P. HENNOCK

University of Liverpool

CAMBRIDGE
UNIVERSITY PRESS

CAMBRIDGE UNIVERSITY PRESS
Cambridge, New York, Melbourne, Madrid, Cape Town, Singapore, São Paulo

Cambridge University Press
The Edinburgh Building, Cambridge CB2 8RU, UK

Published in the United States of America by Cambridge University Press, New York

www.cambridge.org
Information on this title: www.cambridge.org/9780521597708

First published 2007

Printed in the United Kingdom at the University Press, Cambridge

A catalogue record for this publication is available from the British Library

ISBN 978-0-521-59212-3 hardback
ISBN 978-0-521-59770-8 paperback

In memory of E. Z.

Contents

Contents

Plates

Figures

Tables

OTHER TABLES

Acknowledgments

Over the last twelve years I have received help from more people than can be named. Without such collegiality this work would have been impossible. I take this opportunity to thank them all. Certain major debts need to be specifically acknowledged. My thanks go to the Leverhulme Trust for awarding me an emeritus fellowship on my retirement from teaching. Also to the *Historische Kommission zu Berlin*, to Professor Jürgen Kocka's *Arbeitsstelle für vergleichende Gesellschaftsgeschichte* at the Free University, Berlin, and to the *Grossbritannien-Zentrum* at the Humboldt University, Berlin (in particular to Professors Jürgen Schlaeger and Christiane Eisenberg) for hospitality at various stages during the work. I am also greatly indebted to Wolfgang Ayass, Philip Bell, Allan Mitchell and Noel Whiteside who at various times read all or much of the manuscript and substantially contributed to its improvement. Above all, I wish to thank Florian Tennstedt, on whose knowledge I have drawn in almost all the German chapters of the book, as the footnotes testify. He has been unstinting in commenting on the manuscript and in giving me access to his collection of material. Of course none of those mentioned are responsible for any remaining shortcomings. As the author, I alone am responsible for all errors and failings of the work.

Abbreviations

AfS   *Archiv für Sozialgeschichte*
AN   *Amtliche Nachrichten*
ÄVB   (Deutscher) Ärztevereinsbund
Bd   Band (volume)
BPP   British Parliamentary Papers
DV   Deutscher Verein für Armenpflege und Wohltätigkeit
Econ. HR   *Economic History Review*
edn   edition
EHR   *English Historical Review*
GewO   Gewerbeordnung
Hansard   Hansards Parliamentary Debates (preceded by number
             of the series and followed by volume number)
HJ   *Historical Journal*
HZ   *Historische Zeitschrift*
ILO   International Labour Office
Jl Econ. H   *Journal of Economic History*
LGB   Local Government Board
LP   Legislaturperiode
LVA   Landesversicherungsanstalt (pension board)
M   Marks
NF   Neue Folge (new series)
OAV   Ortsarmenverband (Local relief authority)
PRO   Public Records Office
qd   quoted
QS   see below for details
RAS 1885   Reichsarmenstatistik (*Statistik der öffentlichen Armenpflege
             im Jahre 1885. Statistik des Deutschen Reichs*, NF 29 (1887)
RVA   Reichsversicherungsamt (Imperial Insurance Office)
RVO   Reichsversicherungsordnung

SBRT   *Stenographische Berichte des Reichstags*
UWG   Unterstützungswohnsitzgesetz (residential relief system)
VSWG   *Vierteljahrschrift für Sozial- und Wirtschaftsgeschichte*
ZSR   *Zeitschrift für Sozialreform*

QS   *Quellensammlung zur Geschichte der deutschen Sozialpolitik 1867–1914*
QS,E,   *Einführungsband*, K. E. Born, H. Henning and M. Schick (eds.)
QS,I,   *I. Abteilung. Von der Reichsgründungszeit bis zur Kaiserlichen Sozialbotschaft (1867–1881)*

1. volume 1, *Grundfragen staatlicher Sozialpolitik*, Florian Tennstedt and Heidi Winter (eds.) (Stuttgart, 1994)
2. volume 2, *Von der Haftpflichtgesetzgebung zur Ersten Unfallversicherungsvorlage*, Florian Tennstedt and Heidi Winter (eds.) (Stuttgart, 1993)
3. volume 3, *Arbeiterschutz*, Wolfgang Ayass (ed.) (Stuttgart, 1996)
5. volume 5, *Gewerbliche Unterstützungskassen*, Florian Tennstedt and Heidi Winter, with Elmar Roeder and Christian Schmitz (Darmstadt, 2000)
6. volume 6, *Altersversorgungs- und Invalidenkassen*, Florian Tennstedt and Heidi Winter (eds.) (Darmstadt, 2002)
7. volume 7, *Armengesetzgebung und Freizügigkeit*, Christoph Sachsse, Florian Tennstedt and Elmar Roeder (eds.) (Darmstadt, 2000)

QS,II,   *II. Abteilung. Von der Kaiserlichen Sozialbotschaft bis zu den Februarerlassen Wilhelms II. (1881–1890)*

1. volume 1, *Grundfragen der Sozialpolitik*, Wolfgang Ayass, Florian Tennstedt and Heidi Winter (eds.) (Darmstadt, 2003)
2/1. volume 2, Part 1, *Von der zweiten Unfallversicherungsvorlage bis zum Unfallversicherungsgesetz vom 6. Juli 1884*, Florian Tennstedt and Heidi Winter (eds.) (Stuttgart, 1995)

2/2. volume 2, Part 2, *Die Ausdehnungsgesetzgebung und die Praxis der Unfallversicherung*, Wolfgang Ayass (ed.) (Darmstadt, 2001)

3. volume 3, *Arbeiterschutz*, Wolfgang Ayass (ed.) (Darmstadt, 1998)

4. volume 4, *Arbeiterrecht*, Wolfgang Ayass, Karl-Heinz Nickel and Heidi Winter (eds.) (Darmstadt, 1997)

6. volume 6, *Die gesetzliche Invaliditäts- und Altersversicherung*, Ulrike Haerendel (ed.) (Darmstadt, 2004)

Note on British currency

British currency is given throughout in the pounds, shillings and pence (£, s, d) used at the time. Readers may like to be reminded that, prior to decimalisation, the £ contained 20s, and the shilling 12d.

Introduction

What should they know of England
Who only England know!

Rudyard Kipling

This book compares social policies in England and Germany, the two leading industrialising countries in Europe, from roughly the mid-nineteenth century to 1914. It was originally intended as the first volume of a larger project that would have gone to the oil-price crisis of the mid-1970s, the moment when the assumptions about continuous economic growth, which had under-pinned the expansion of the welfare state in both countries since the 1950s, began to be seriously questioned. Those plans have had to be abandoned and this book now stands on its own.

Its structure is thematic, dealing in turn with policies of poor relief and industrial injury, and with policies outside the poor law on sickness, invalidity and old age, and unemployment. These were significant problems in both countries with enough similarity to make for profitable comparison. The focus on these policy areas has resulted from my discovery that time, space and effort were more limited than I had thought. That has led to the omission of public health, housing and labour market policies. A generation ago it had still been usual in Britain to include the first two in the kind of survey that I had in mind.[1] Since then developments in the history of medicine have so transformed the history of public health that it gradually became obvious to me that it would now require a book in its own right. Having completed a study of the policy of vaccination against smallpox focussing on the issues of compulsion and of urban sanitary reform, I was working on bacteriology in public health when I aborted this

---

[1] E.g. Derek Fraser, *The evolution of the British welfare state* (London, 1973); Eric J. Evans (ed.), *Social policy 1830–1914: individualism, collectivism and the origins of the welfare state* (London, 1978); U. Henriques, *Before the welfare state* (London, 1979).

I

part of the project. Housing policy was also discarded, since prior to 1914 it had been so closely linked to public health issues that it would not have made sense on its own. The two completed studies have been published in article form.[2] They are constructed essentially on the same principles as the chapters in this book but represent a mere fragment of what a comparative study of public health policies would have required. The abridged treatment of labour market policies is a matter to which I shall return.

This cutting away has altered the aim of the research. The original intention had been to use a diversity of policies to test the view that there was a fairly consistent difference between the two countries, in particular that policies in Germany were based on compulsion, central bureaucratic control at State level and professionalism; those in England on voluntarism, local initiative and amateurism. I suspected that these stereotypes were based on the difference between the educational system of the two countries, a difference that had greatly influenced ideas of Germany in Britain in the later nineteenth and early twentieth centuries. I believe that they need to be tested against a wider range of evidence. Traces of that agenda can still be found in the book in its final form, but in the necessary process of reducing the range and diversity of subject matter the project has gained greater coherence. It now concentrates on social security and the provision of medical treatment, the two issues that stood at the origin of what is now called the welfare state, and are still considered to form its core.

In this connection it should be emphasised that this book is conceived as a comparative study of social policies. It is not intended to provide a rounded study of the welfare state as a historical phenomenon. It takes the history of State development for granted and it deals only in passing with the consequences of the adoption of new objectives for the structures of domination that characterise the State: the distributing elites, the service bureaucracies and social clienteles.

What should become clear, however, is the intimate connection with the development of modern industrial capitalism in both countries. The State became a welfare state because it increasingly dealt with the social consequences of the way in which modern industrial capitalism was established. These consequences, often described as 'externalities', resulted from the narrow definition of the legal obligations of capitalist entrepreneurs, which contrasted with the obligations imposed on entrepreneurs in the

---

[2] 'Vaccination policy against smallpox, 1835–1914: a comparison of England with Prussia and Imperial Germany', *Social History of Medicine*, 11 (1998), 49–71; 'The urban sanitary reform movement in England and Germany, 1838–1914: a comparison', *Continuity and Change*, 15 (2000), 269–96.

older *corporatist economy*. This emancipation of the entrepreneur was a deliberate act of State, undertaken in the interest of increasing 'the wealth of nations' and therefore the power of states over other states. It undoubtedly had that effect. Enterprise took new and unforeseen forms once it was freed from old regulations. To limit obligations towards workers to the short-term purchase of their labour power, obligations towards the community to the payment of local taxes and to resort to competition without responsibility for those driven out of the market, all this encouraged innovation, increased production and facilitated capital accumulation. But it created problems that resulted from economic decisions while being considered external to the economic process. These, or rather some of these, are the problems that social policies were intended to address. How the State in the two countries did so, is the subject of the book.[3]

The period treated here begins around the mid-nineteenth century with the poor law structures established by the reforms of the 1830s and 1840s both in Prussia and in England and Wales, and with the compulsory insurance introduced in Prussia in the 1840s and 1850s. The latter is contrasted with the voluntary insurance of the friendly societies in England and Wales and their relation to the State. For that purpose it reaches further back, but the focus is on the development among the affiliated orders of a more systematic approach to the insurance function of the movement, and on the role of the Registrar of Friendly Societies from the mid-1840s. The same principle applies to factory regulation, where the turbulent and experimental years of the British factory movement before the 1850s are treated mainly as background.

The year 1914 marks the end of an era for this as for many other aspects of history. The radical changes of the war years make it the inevitable closing date. But the bunching of important legislation, both British and German, in 1911 creates a problem. It has generally been my intention to deal both with the origins of policies and their consequences, but the consequences of insurance systems take time to build up. In the case of the legislation of 1911 it is sometimes only possible to describe the original intentions before radical war-time changes in the value of money, and post-war changes in the nature of unemployment overtook them. In view of the importance of the new structures established so late in the period I have occasionally reached beyond 1914, where that was possible and appropriate. That applies

---

[3] See my entry under 'welfare state – history of' in the *International encyclopedia of the social and behavioral sciences* (Oxford, 2001), pp. 16439–45, for further analysis.

particularly to the Conclusion, which sets out to demonstrate the relevance of the book for the long-term development of social policy.

This is a book of comparative history. That term is open to the objection that all historians rely on comparison. Narrative depends on comparing one time with another, structural exposition frequently on comparing one place or one set of institutions with another. What this book does is to compare one nation-state with another. The choice of the State as the unit of comparison, rather than, say, the region or the city, is deliberate. But for the years before the establishment of the German Empire, which State should it be? For practical and strategic reasons I have concentrated on Prussia. It is impractical to encompass the diversity of the German states, and in relation to poor law, factory regulations and sickness insurance Prussia provided the precedents for the policies adopted by the *Reich*. Such a Prusso-centric approach runs counter to the current trend of German historiography and may seem old-fashioned, but it is justified by the subject-matter.[4] On this side of the North Sea I have concentrated on England and Wales, and on Britain only if the law in Scotland was not significantly different, and the Scottish statistical evidence created no additional problems. In those cases I have referred to Britain; elsewhere I have occasionally used 'English' for 'English and Welsh' merely for the sake of brevity.

These are small matters but they need to be said. The big issues of comparison are methodological. This book owes little to the comparative study of welfare state regimes pursued by empirical quantifying sociologists, nor much to the more theoretical sociological literature on the origins of 'the welfare state'.[5] I do not use comparative studies to test and refine a model of how societies work, whether neo-Marxist or developmental. That is to say that I do not start with the assumption that I already know the crucial questions that a comparative historian of social policy must ask, and that my task consists of filling the blank spaces in a pre-determined framework with the data. My strategy has been different. Historians are used to identifying and analysing different historiographies. An Anglo-German comparison provides the opportunity to confront two of these with one another, to identify their similarities and their

---

[4] Cf. the different approach in my 'The urban sanitary reform movement in England and Germany', where it would not have been appropriate.

[5] For the most influential example of the former see G. Esping-Andersen, *The three worlds of welfare capitalism* (Cambridge, 1990). For a critique see Peter Baldwin, 'Can we define a European welfare state model?' in Bent Grieve (ed.), *Comparative welfare systems: the Scandinavian model in a period of change* (London, 1996); also Christian Toft, 'Jenseits der Dreiweltendiskussion', ZSR, 46 (2000), 68–86. For the latter approach see particularly Peter Flora and Arnold J. Heidenheimer (eds.), *The development of welfare states in Europe and America* (New Brunswick, 1981).

differences. Where the questions posed were basically the same, I needed to obtain the relevant data and to compare the results. Where not, the task was more difficult as well as more rewarding. I needed to ask the questions that had so far not been asked about the one country and became obvious only through comparison with the other. Thus British historiography has proved fruitful for the history of Germany and vice versa. Sometimes it was possible to extract that data from the printed material, secondary and primary, available to me. When not, I have contented myself with drawing attention to a neglected issue that invites archival research. Those occasions may well be among the most valuable contributions of the book.[6]

The scale and range of the book has precluded detailed archival research; it is intended as a synthesis of the existing literature. Few of the monographs and articles on the German side of the story are available in English. For that reason, quite apart from its value as a comparative study, the book should provide a service to English-speaking historians without a reading-knowledge of German. However, even those with a good knowledge of the German literature are likely to find unfamiliar features in this presentation of German social policy. By good fortune the work on the book has coincided with the publication of a bulky series of the documents on German social policy in this period.[7] Most of these had never been available to historians even in manuscript; their publication has added significant evidence and changed the received view of key episodes. That is particularly true of those for the Bismarck era, twelve large volumes of which were published in time to be consulted in the course of the work, providing what is practically an archival dimension to the work.

Nothing similar should be expected of the treatment of British social policy, which will be familiar to specialists. Whatever claim to originality it possesses will be found in the issues raised by the comparison with Germany and the comments that these have required, which, I hope, will throw new light on familiar subjects.

---

[6] E.g. pp. 131–4 and 320–7. For an instance from the comparative studies of public health see 'Vaccination policy against smallpox', 69–71.

[7] *Quellensammlung zur Geschichte der deutschen Sozialpolitik 1867–1914* supported by the Akademie der Wissenschaften und der Literatur, Mainz, to be published in four sections: I (1867–81); II (1881–90), both edited by Florian Tennstedt, III (1890–1904) still to come, IV (1904–14) edited by Karl Erich Born and Hansjoachim Henning. To be referred to as QS. See reviews in *German History*, 13 (1995), 254–5; 16 (1998), 58–74; 21 (2003), 229–38.

The importance of the new German material is one reason why the book differs from Gerhard A. Ritter's work, published in German in 1983 and in a revised English edition in 1986.[8] The other is methodological. Ritter's comparative history consisted of two separate national narratives and left the comparison to a brief final chapter of eight pages. This book treats each of the several social policies comparatively, in addition to providing an overall view in the Conclusion. The original intention to extend the subject beyond Ritter's exclusive concern with social insurance has, however, had to be much curtailed.

In so far as there is a pioneering study that laid out the issues to be considered in a comparative history of social security policies, it was that by G. V. Rimlinger in 1971.[9] There have been few other attempts. Daniel Levine's is primarily an exercise in the history of ideas and only precariously rooted in the study of the relevant institutions.[10] Peter Baldwin, *The politics of social solidarity*, a *tour de force* and an example of versatility across five countries and five languages that few can emulate, compensates for its national breadth by focusing narrowly on pensions policy from one particular point of view.[11] While the early studies by Georg Zacher have now little to contribute of method or substance, the best of W. H. Dawson's work from before 1914 is still worth attention.[12]

My essentially historiographical approach to comparison governs both the individual chapters and the choice of themes. The approach of German and British historians to the subject matter of a history of social policy is not the same, and I believe that each needs to be supplemented by the other. The historiography of German social policy has been overwhelmingly concerned with the history of social insurance. That is partly due to the pioneering role that Germany played in its introduction: compulsory, contributory and State-controlled insurance was their invention. It is also

---

[8] Gerhard A. Ritter, *Sozialversicherung in Deutschland und England. Entstehung und Grundzüge im Vergleich* (Munich, 1983); *Social welfare in Germany and Britain*, trans. Kim Traynor (Leamington Spa, 1986).

[9] G. V. Rimlinger, *Welfare policy and industrialization in Europe, America and Russia* (New York, 1971).

[10] Daniel Levine, *Poverty and society: the growth of the American welfare state in international comparison* (New Brunswick, 1988).

[11] Peter Baldwin, *The politics of social solidarity: class bases of the European welfare state 1875–1975* (Cambridge, 1990). These comments are confined to comparative studies of social security policies. His subsequent and even more ambitious book, *Contagion and the State in Europe 1830–1930* (Cambridge, 1999), is a contribution to the comparative history of public health.

[12] Georg Zacher, *Die Arbeiterversicherung im Ausland*, 5 vols. (Berlin, 1900–8); W. H. Dawson, *Social insurance in Germany 1883–1911: its history, operation, and results, and a comparison with the National Insurance Act 1911* (London, 1912, reprinted Westport, 1979); *Cost of living of the working classes: German towns*, BPP 1908 Cd.4032 CVIII.1; and, less comparative but a major contribution, *Municipal life and government in Germany* (London, 1914).

due to the fact that it plays a particularly important role in the social security system of the German Federal Republic. That is the result of the deliberate rejection of alternative strategies in the period immediately after World War II and the strong support for the traditional German insurance system on the part of the vested interests that had opposed the alternatives.[13]

In 1981 the centenary of the Imperial Message of 17 November 1881, which was held quite wrongly to mark the beginning of the social insurance policy, gave the political establishment of the Federal German Republic an opportunity to celebrate social insurance as quintessentially German, a move that both lawyers and historians were happy to support.[14] Those celebrations were preceded by three international colloquia under the auspices of the Max-Planck Foundation, resulting in prestigious publications which placed the German experience firmly at the centre of international comparison. The final meeting was held in Berlin on 17 November 1981 to coincide with the celebrations by the federal government and the various insurance bodies. The audience was assured that 'the colloquium had demonstrated the vitality of social insurance as an autonomous technique for the establishment of social security'.[15]

The outcome was thus to legitimise the political decisions that had been taken by those opposed to the reform proposals of the Allied Control Commission in 1946–8 and consolidated by the dominant CDU–FDP alliance in the early years of the Federal Republic. By 1981 social security rights had long been recognised as a means of legitimising a regime, and there was in all this an element of confrontation with the different social policy developments in the Soviet zone of occupation and the DDR. There

---

[13] See Hans Günther Hockerts, *Sozialpolitische Entscheidungen im Nachkriegsdeutschland. Alliierte und deutsche Sozialversicherungspolitik 1945 bis 1957* (Stuttgart, 1980), and briefly his 'German post-war social policies against the background of the Beveridge Plan: some observations preparatory to a comparative analysis', in W. J. Mommsen (ed.), *The emergence of the welfare state in Britain and Germany 1850–1950* (London, 1981), pp. 315–39.

[14] On the Imperial Message and the myth around it see pp. 91 and 187–8 below.

[15] Hans Zacher (ed.), *Bedingungen für die Entstehung und Entwicklung von Sozialversicherung. Schriftenreihe für internationales und vergleichendes Sozialrecht*, vol. 3 (Berlin, 1979); Peter Köhler and Hans Zacher (eds.), *Ein Jahrhundert Sozialversicherung in der Bundesrepublik Deutschland, Frankreich, Grossbritannien, Österreich, und der Schweiz. Schriftenreihe . . .*, vol. 6 (Berlin, 1981), translated as *The evolution of social insurance 1881–1981: studies of Germany, France, Great Britain, Austria and Switzerland* (London, 1982); Peter Köhler and Hans Zacher (eds.), *Beiträge zur Geschichte und aktueller Situation der Sozialversicherung. Schriftenreihe . . .*, vol. 8 (Berlin, c. 1983). The quotation is from p. 732 of the third of these publications. The contribution by Gerhard A. Ritter to that colloquium was subsequently expanded to become his Anglo-German comparison, *Sozialversicherung in Deutschland und England* (Munich, 1983).

under the influence of survivors of the Weimar Left, who revived plans first put forward by critics of contributory insurance in the 1920s, the Soviet authorities had introduced a people's insurance financed from general taxation.[16] By the late 1970s pride in the social insurance system of the Federal Republic had become a feature of the ideological climate. It was convenient that the Nazi Labour Front had also once proposed a people's insurance financed from general taxation to replace contributory insurance.[17]

The historiography of British social policy was of course also associated with a political affirmation. Since the late 1940s historians of nineteenth-century Britain had been on the hunt for the history of the collectivism whose triumph was associated with the welfare state reforms of the 1940s.[18] In contrast to the nationalisation of industry, these reforms had by the 1950s become a matter of national unity and pride with which the Conservatives were willing to identify themselves. The nineteenth-century Poor Law as reformed in 1834, once regarded as the extreme repudiation of collective responsibility, underwent historical revision. From a study of his papers Edwin Chadwick, its intellectual progenitor, emerged as someone committed to collectivist as well as individualist policies.[19] Historians revised their view of the practical consequences of the Act of 1834, pointing out that conditions made the more doctrinaire aspects of Chadwick's proposals impossible to carry out in practice and arguing for a more gradual evolution of policy and administration. An intense preoccupation with Poor Law administration on the ground led to a rehabilitation of poor law regimes in the early nineteenth century. Moreover the Poor Law after 1834 came to be presented as an important agency in the evolution of collective provisions in such welfare state areas as education and hospital medicine.[20]

It is not too much to say that the British historiography of what has only gradually come to be described as 'social policy' has been dominated by a preoccupation with the Poor Law. The origin of the institutions character-istic of the post-1945 welfare state has been interpreted as a deliberate revulsion from the 'principles of 1834'. New policies for the elderly, the

---

[16] See Hockerts, *Sozialpolitische Entscheidungen* and 'German post-war social policies'.

[17] R. Smelser, *Robert Ley: Hitler's labor front leader* (Oxford, 1988); Marie-Luise Recker, *Nationalsozialistische Sozialpolitik im Zweiten Weltkrieg* (Munich, 1985).

[18] See the subtitle of Evans, *Social policy*.

[19] S. E. Finer, *The life and times of Sir Edwin Chadwick* (London, 1952).

[20] Derek Fraser (ed.), *The new poor law in the nineteenth century* (London, 1976), see especially contributions by Digby, Duke and Flinn. The reinterpretation of the early nineteenth-century poor law was begun by Mark Blaug's seminal article, 'The myth of the old poor law and the making of the new', Jl Econ. Hist, 23 (1963), 151–84 and the study of parish records is still in full swing.

sick, disabled and the unemployed in the early twentieth century are explained in terms of a determination to remove categories of the deserving poor from the operation of a Poor Law intended to work on principles that had come to be regarded as inappropriate for these groups.[21] The subsequent history of social policy in the twentieth century up to and beyond the reforms of the 1940s is often portrayed as a battle against the Poor Law heritage. For historians of British social policy the Poor Law is therefore central, dominating the subject irrespective of whether its influence was positive or negative.

When they turn to the German history of social policy they are bound to be struck by the lack of interest shown by German historians in that subject. It was an attitude not shared by Americans. Levine had no doubt that 'any account of the development of the welfare state must begin with poor relief', and Rimlinger's comparative study of social security regarded the attitude to poor relief as the first question to be investigated. He did so in detail for England, France and the USA, and dealt with poor relief in Prussia in the period of early industrialisation in so far as the meagre secondary literature available to him permitted.[22]

As a subject, the history of German poor relief was largely ignored by historians and only rescued from neglect by Christoph Sachsse and Florian Tennstedt, two professors of welfare law responsible for the education of students of social work.[23] In 1993 when the American, George Steinmetz, turned his attention to social policy in Imperial Germany he could point to their work as a significant exception to the general neglect of poor relief. He himself made the introduction of 'modern' poor relief an integral element of his book and declared himself puzzled by the neglect of the subject in German histories of the welfare state.[24]

It is significant that the first historian from within the German historical establishment to show interest in linking the introduction of social

---

[21] E.g. Bentley B. Gilbert, *The evolution of national insurance in Great Britain: the origins of the welfare state* (London, 1966); Pat Thane, *The foundations of the welfare state* (London, 1982); Derek Fraser, 'The English poor law and the origins of the British welfare state', in Mommsen (ed.), *Emergence*; E. P. Hennock, *British social reform and German precedent: the case of social insurance 1880–1914* (Oxford, 1987); David Vincent, *Poor citizens: the state and the poor in the twentieth century* (London/New York, 1991).

[22] Levine, *Poverty and society*, p. 40; Rimlinger, *Welfare policy*, pp. 3, 18–63, 93–5.

[23] Christoph Sachsse and Florian Tennstedt, *Geschichte der Armenfürsorge in Deutschland*, 3 vols. (Stuttgart, 1980–92), vol. 1 (enlarged 2nd edn, 1998). Tennstedt's ambitious *Sozialgeschichte der Sozialpolitik in Deutschland* (Göttingen, 1981), the only German history of social policy that pays much attention to poor relief, has not been influential among historians.

[24] George Steinmetz, *Regulating the social: the welfare state and local politics in Imperial Germany* (Princeton, 1993), pp. 42, 110–22.

insurance in the 1880s to poor law policy should have been Gerhard A. Ritter in his history of social welfare in Germany and Britain. That book is probably more important for raising the question than for the answer it provides. In any case more has to be done to change the thrust of German historiography than merely to include a reference to poor relief among the explanation for the origins of social insurance in the 1880s. The subject needs to be treated as an integral part of a full history of German social policy. That is what this book attempts to do.

In that respect, as in others, it has benefited from Tennstedt's recent work as editor for the Bismarck era of the *Quellensammlung zur Geschichte der deutschen Sozialpolitik*. There are now two volumes of documents on the poor relief legislation of the early years of the German Empire. They signal the abandonment of a long tradition of excluding that subject from studies of *Sozialpolitik*.

That tradition had been established by Hans Rothfels, the first historian to be commissioned to undertake an edition of the documents on the social policy of the Bismarck era, in 1919. Surveying the definition of *Sozialpolitik* as it was then understood, he concluded 'that it was generally assumed that poor relief policy was no part of *Sozialpolitik*', and devised his own proposal accordingly.[25] After Rothfels failed to produce his promised work and the project was launched afresh in the 1950s, this time for the *Kaiserreich* as a whole, the new editors followed him in the exclusion of poor relief, although in other respects they opted for a broader concept of *Sozialpolitik* than he had done.[26] Only when Tennstedt joined the editorial team in 1991 with responsibility for the Bismarck era was that policy abandoned. Hence the publication of the first relevant volumes in 2000.

In his introduction to them Tennstedt drew attention to a precedent in 1976, when a section on the development from poor law to modern public assistance (*Sozialhilfe*) was added to a revised edition of the standard text on welfare law.[27] Tennstedt justified his editorial decision in terms more

---

[25] Quoted in *Grundfragen staatlicher Sozialpolitik*, QS,I.1, p. XLI. The fullest modern survey of the history of the concept is F.-X. Kaufmann, 'Der Begriff Sozialpolitik und seine wissenschaftliche Deutung', in *Geschichte der Sozialpolitik in Deutschland seit 1945* published by the Bundesministerium für Arbeit und Sozialordnung und Bundesarchiv, vol. 1 (Baden-Baden, 2001), pp. 7–101.

[26] See Karl Erich Born et al., QS, *Einführungsband* (Wiesbaden, 1966), pp. 11–14.

[27] In view of this and other drastic changes what had been intended as the third revised edition of Gerhard Erdmann's *Die Entwicklung der deutschen Sozialgesetzgebung* (1st edn, Berlin, 1948, 2nd edn, Göttingen, 1957) was published as Michael Stolleis, *Quellen zur Geschichte des Sozialrechts* (Göttingen, 1976). It should be noted that Tennstedt has not followed Stolleis's other innovation, the entire excision of labour law from the scope of his work. For Tennstedt's justification of his innovation see the Introduction to QS,I.7(a), pp. XLV–XLVI.

familiar to British than to German historians, describing the poor law policy of 1842 and 1870 as social policy of the liberal anti-state variety, a *Sozialpolitik* before the *Sozialstaat*, and the introduction of social insurance as a process of *Ausdifferenzierung* (exclusion of particular risks from the poor law). Whereas the British emphasis on the contracting-out of categories of the deserving poor has the merit of suggesting an explanation for the process, the conventional description of the first three branches of social insurance by German historians as forming the 'classic nucleus' of a subsequently expanding system merely begs the question.[28]

Although they ignored poor relief, German historians of social policy have tended to include labour market policies.[29] Even Ritter, whose Anglo-German comparison had on the German side been exclusively about social insurance, was persuaded a few years later to include labour market policies in a wider comparative study.[30]

Should this historiographical tradition be taken on board in an Anglo-German comparison, much as the Anglo-American tradition of including poor relief has been? Statements from British historians in favour of such a step are rare. An exception is Noel Whiteside who has urged us to abandon what she calls the late twentieth-century assumptions which understand industrial relations and social welfare as separate issues and has done so fruitfully in studies of the pre-1914 era and for 1945–60.[31] I believe that there is a *prima facie* case for doing so and had planned a Part IV on 'The State and the Labour Market'. It was to have consisted of two chapters, the first to deal with labour relations policies, the second with policies on employment and unemployment. The case for the second chapter is uncontroversial, for unemployment insurance is an integral part of the history of social insurance and its British origin belongs to the period under examination. But insurance was merely one of several policies for dealing with

---

[28] This idea had first been expounded in 1982 while reviewing the British contribution to an international survey. F. Tennstedt, 'Fortschritte und Defizite in der Sozialversicherungsgeschichtsschreibung – komparative und sonstige Kurzsichtigkeiten nach 100 Jahren "Kaiserliche Botschaft"', AfS, 22 (1982), 653–4. The book reviewed was the German original of Köhler and Zacher, *Evolution of social insurance*. That would suggest that the idea came to him from what he described as 'a survey such as had not previously been available in German'.

[29] See Volker Hentschel, *Geschichte der deutschen Sozialpolitik 1880–1980. Soziale Sicherung und kollektives Arbeitsrecht* (Frankfurt a.M., 1983), p. 7; Ludwig Preller, *Sozialpolitik in der Weimarer Republik* (Stuttgart, 1949, reprint Düsseldorf, 1978).

[30] Gerhard A. Ritter, *Der Sozialstaat. Entstehung und Entwicklung im internationalen Vergleich* (Munich, 1989), pp. XI, 18, 112–29, 159–79, which includes brief contrasts with Britain mainly for the 1920s and the post-1960 period.

[31] N. Whiteside, 'Definir le chômage', in M. Mansfield, R. Salais and N. Whiteside (eds.), *Aux sources du chômage, 1880–1914* (Paris, 1994), pp. 381–412; N. Whiteside, 'Creating the welfare state in Britain, 1945–1960', Jl Soc. Pol., 25 (1996), 83–103.

unemployment. The creation of employment through public works or
counter-cyclical investment and the reduction of unemployment through
labour exchanges belong to the same subject. Other employment policies
debated at the time were minimum wage legislation and the prohibition of
sweated labour. They would have been appropriate under that heading,
although not closely connected with the issue of unemployment.

The first chapter would have dealt with the law on trade unions, which
showed the most striking contrasts between Britain and Germany. The
greater freedom of British trade unions to recruit and intervene in labour
relations can hardly be ignored in any treatment of social policy, not least
because that legal freedom was the key to their industrial and political
effectiveness. It enabled them to exercise their remarkable influence over
the social policy agenda. In short, the effectiveness of organised labour in
the British political process is so basic to the subject that it cannot be
ignored. The choice lies merely between repeated references to the fact or a
systematic exposition of its nature. In a comparison with Germany, where
the position of organised labour was very different, the case for systematic
exposition is overwhelming, not least because the German social policy
agenda was shaped in its turn by the attitude of the political classes to
organised labour in its various ideological forms.

The case for tackling this subject systematically and comparatively may be
overwhelming, but so are the difficulties of the task. The relevant material is
large and complex. It includes not only the histories of the trade union
movements in the two countries and their relation to the political parties. It
also requires an examination of the two legal systems. The official German
response to trade unions was not merely repressive; it led to the establishment
of special labour courts, which had no obvious parallel in Britain. The
traditional explanation for that contrast has emphasised the strength of the
British labour movement and its capacity to solve the problems of British
workers through its own extra-legal procedures. However, since the publication of Willibald Steinmetz's study of the British courts between 1850 and
1925 and their use by workers and employers for the settlement of claims
relating to labour contracts this explanation will no longer serve in its
traditional form.[32] Steinmetz's study of British labour history from the
perspective of someone familiar with the history of German labour courts
is a good example of the value of a comparative perspective for opening up
new ground. Without being fully comparative, it points the way to the use

---

[32] Willibald Steinmetz, *Begegnung vor Gericht. Eine Sozial- und Kulturgeschichte des englischen
Arbeitsrechts (1850–1925)* (Munich, 2002), reviewed by me in *Labour History Review*, 69 (2004), 253–5.

that can be made of the German literature on the origins of that 'juridification' of labour relations that has become a prominent characteristic of the German Federal Republic. While pointing to what might be done, it has, however, revealed the size and complexity of the undertaking. With great reluctance I decided that I had neither the time, the energy nor the space to pursue my original intention.[33] Unlike the omission of public health and housing, which has improved the coherence of the book, this omission has nothing to be said for it except that there is a limit to what one person can achieve. It is a task that will have to be undertaken sooner or later by others, whether singly or in a team, if we are to understand the different paths taken by two of the pioneering welfare states in Europe.[34]

That it cannot be done within the confines of this book is a matter of regret, because it would have made it historiographically more even-handed. Even-handedness is the ideal that I have set before myself. I have tried to write a comparative history that would be equally acceptable to German as to British readers. It is an ideal towards which to strive, but may not be achievable in its entirety. The problem lies less in the misinterpretation or even the disregard of relevant evidence. Any conscientious professional historian should be able to reduce such lapses to a minimum. It is through the choice of the issues considered relevant to the subject that unconscious bias is most likely to creep in. It is my hope that there will have been few such lapses.

With that consideration in mind, something should be said about presentation. That is affected by the readership that I have primarily had in mind. It is a readership with little or no knowledge of German. I have attempted a systematic presentation of both histories but have deliberately presented the German material in greater detail than the British, partly because German concepts and context will be less familiar to most of my readers, partly because detailed studies in English are more readily available even in German libraries. I have usually translated German terms. Where I have not done so I have assumed that the meaning was well known, as in the case of *Reich* and *Reichstag*, or else obvious from the context. I have provided a systematic guide to the system of municipal government at the head of chapter 17, where it is needed, but have not done so for central government.[35]

---

[33] Part IV therefore merely contains two chapters on unemployment policies. The change of title indicates that these deal with the context of that issue but omit other aspects of employment policy from consideration.

[34] A good beginning has been made single-handedly in John Breuilly, *Labour and liberalism in nineteenth-century Europe* (Manchester, 1992), ch. 5.

[35] Those who need more than the explanations provided *en passant* should consult a text-book, such as W. Carr, *History of Germany 1815–1990* (London, 1991), pp. 119–23.

Balance is not the only issue of presentation to be considered in the writing of comparative history. Just as there are different views on how to undertake historical comparisons, so there are different ways of presenting the results. I have deliberately avoided the three-chapter approach that is widespread in the profession, i.e. to have for each period or subject one chapter for country A, one for country B, and a third for comparison. That is orderly, but involves much repetition which can be boring. I have preferred to draw my comparison as soon as the information on both countries has been made available. That often means that it is tacked on to the material on the second country. Such a procedure may offend readers with a passion for system and order, but the logic of the approach should appeal to others. The final chapter consists almost entirely of comparison, but elsewhere the best way to identify the location of explicit comparisons is via the index.

PART I

Public relief of the poor

The national framework

(A) RURAL CHANGE: PRUSSIA

Despite the subsequent preoccupation with urban poverty, the transformation of poor relief in the nineteenth century began in a rural setting. In Prussia as in England it began with drastic change in rural society. In England that change came about in response to market forces and then created a situation that led to the intervention of the State in the form of the Poor Law (Amendment) Act of 1834. In Prussia the intervention of the State did much to promote the changes themselves. From the very start of the subject of comparative social policy we are therefore confronted by one of the significant differences between the two countries: the more ambitious role of the Prussian State in shaping societal change.

That the Prussian State intervened first in rural rather than urban society was also no accident. It stemmed from the long-standing preoccupation of civil servants in the eighteenth century with increasing output and wealth on the Crown's rural estates, a preoccupation that was to be extended to increased agricultural output in the Prince's territory as a whole. As Mack Walker put it in a tone of disapproval, 'the idea that actual social change by legal action could be a useful and feasible program infected the civil servants in the course of their work governing the State's agricultural domains, notably in Prussia but elsewhere too'.[1]

As Mack Walker suggests, systematic land reform was not limited to the eastern provinces of Prussia. I propose, however, to concentrate on these grain-growing areas with their large export potential in a period of European population growth and in consequence with their large revenue-producing potential for a State, heavily burdened since 1806/7 with payments to the French victors and largely dependent for an expansion of its income on the yield of the customs duties. I am implying that the

---

[1] Mack Walker, *German home towns: community, state, general estate, 1648–1871* (Ithaca, 1971), p. 186.

principal reasons for the State initiative that led to the agrarian reforms in the eastern provinces were fiscal. It does not matter greatly that this is an oversimplification, since I am primarily concerned with the process and its consequences for social relations.[2]

Since the sixteenth century the Prussian nobility of these provinces had exercised lordship over the peasantry in a double sense. They exercised justice through their own courts, and they cultivated their estates through enforced labour services, a situation that had disappeared in England by the fifteenth century. The land reforms of the early nineteenth century shifted power over the peasantry from being an exercise of personal lordship to being an act of State authority. At the same time labour relations were transformed from seigneurial dependence to economic domination.[3]

Most peasant farms remained large enough to be economically viable, but the price paid by the peasants was high. By the time they had paid their lord for granting title of ownership for the land that they had previously held from him, and further compensated him for the loss of the labour services that was involved in their so-called emancipation, much land had passed out of their hands into that of their lord. Many of the marginal peasantry joined the already numerous population of those whose holdings were inadequate for the support of their household. They could pay for the use of their cottage and garden only by means of labour services. They shed their former status of legal subordination but their economic position was little changed.

Even these long-term labour contracts were not secure. With population growth that depressed wages and a buoyant demand for grain which kept up prices, estate owners increasingly preferred to hire labour on a short-term basis rather than to agree to long-term labour contracts. The result was a growing population of landless labour at the mercy of the market, such as had been familiar in England for some time.[4]

It used to be thought that, by freeing the peasants from seigneurial control over their lives, land reform permitted earlier marriage and pushed up population. That theory is undermined by our knowledge that the population growth had started well back in the mid-eighteenth century.

---

[2] Hans-Ulrich Wehler, *Deutsche Gesellschaftsgeschichte*, vol. I (Munich, 1987), pp. 412–14 for the motives of the agrarian reforms.

[3] J. J. Sheehan, *German history 1770–1866* (Oxford, 1989), p. 473. That the economic changes had been in preparation some time prior to the intervention of the State is demonstrated in Edgar Melton, 'The decline of Prussian *Gutsherrschaft* and the rise of the Junker as rural patron', *German History*, 12 (1994), 334–50.

[4] Sheehan, *German history*, pp. 474–6; Wehler, *Deutsche Gesellschaftsgeschichte*, vol. I, pp. 417–28.

Table 1.1. *Population growth 1816–64 in selected*
Prussian provinces[a]

West Prussia	119 per cent
Pomerania	110 per cent
East Prussia	99 per cent
Posen	86 per cent
Silesia	85 per cent
Rhineland	76 per cent
Westphalia	56 per cent

Note:
[a] A certain element of this recorded growth may have been due to improvements in the methods of recording.
Source: W. R. Lee (ed.), *European demography and economic growth* (London, 1978), Table 4.1.

There is no doubt about the significant growth in population. In the half-century from 1816 to 1864 the population of Prussia grew by 72 per cent, almost as impressive a figure as the 100 per cent growth of population in England and Wales from 1801 to 1851. The Prussian growth rate was far above that of Bavaria at 32 per cent or Württemberg at 24 per cent, and even within Prussia there were notable regional differences. Apart from Berlin, the highest growth rates were in the eastern grain-growing provinces, which significantly exceeded those for the later industrial heartland of Rhineland/Westphalia and were marginally higher than industrial Silesia.

W. R. Lee has argued that, in contrast to England and Wales, there is no evidence of an increase in nuptuality (lower marriage age or larger percentage of females married), nor in fertility (more children born to a couple), nor in the birth-rate. He suggests that population growth was due rather to a decline in mortality other than that of infants. Life expectancy rose for all ages under fifty-five but especially for the younger age groups. The survival of more women of child-bearing age thus led to population increase and a significant increase in the labour force.[5]

---

[5] W. R. Lee, 'Germany' in Lee, *European demography*, pp. 144–95, esp. pp. 147–50. This view is echoed in Wehler, *Deutsche Gesellschaftsgeschichte*, vol. II (Munich, 1989), pp. 20–4 with specific reference to Lee's work. See E. A. Wrigley and R. S. Schofield, *The population history of England 1541–1871: a reconstruction* (London, 1981), for a contrasting explanation for England and Wales, emphasising changing rates of nuptuality.

Table 1.2. *Eastern Prussian provinces as affected by migration, 1816–71*

	Gain/loss from migration in each period						Elements of change due to migration in	
	1816–25	1826–34	1835–43	1844–52	1853–61	1862–71	numbers	percentages
East Prussia	+73	+1	+62	−9	+14	−28	+113	12.1
West Prussia	+38	+31	+55	+13	+7	−40	+104	14.0
Posen	+40	+71	+17	−12	−11	−109	−4	0.5
Pomerania	+36	+0	+25	−4	−33	−96	−72	8.8
Berlin	+12	+36	+74	+61	+73	+126	+382	60.8
Brandenburg	−9	−7	+44	−13	−48	−44	−77	7.5
Silesia	+75	+37	+162	−7	−25	−59	+183	10.4+

Source: W. Fischer et al., *Sozialgeschichtliches Arbeitsbuch 1815–1870* (Munich, 1982), p. 36.

Between 1816 and 1843 the labour force of the eastern Prussian provinces was swollen also through immigration from neighbouring regions, as Table 1.2 makes clear.

If we ask how that increase in population was not merely sustained but actually accompanied by a reduction in mortality, the answer is to be found in the changes brought about by agrarian reforms. These increased productivity and the demand for labour. From 1816 to 1849 grain production rose in Prussia by 65 per cent, but probably even more important was the introduction of two new crops, potatoes and sugar beet. The potato in particular helped to sustain the population at higher levels of nutrition and thereby probably helped to account for the higher expectation of life. Hence the disastrous effects of the potato-crop failure in 1846–9.

To sum up, land reform had produced structural changes in the agrarian society of Prussia's eastern provinces that generated enormous increases in food production, which sustained a greatly increased population at mortality levels probably lower than in the past.

For the individual in distress, however, the legal and economic changes had eroded the traditional forms of support. These had been of two kinds. One was the obligation of the lord to succour the peasants tied to his estate. This seigneurial obligation had applied to many different status positions but below the peasantry there had always been those, like cotters, for whom the lord had no such obligation and who had to manage otherwise.

There had also been an element of communal protection: for the peasants through the methods of common cultivation, for the cotters through their rights over common land, whether rights of grazing or of fuel. These are familiar to the student of English rural customs. With the abolition of the seigneurial obligation everyone's position became as precarious as that of the cotters, while rights of grazing, fuel etc. were much reduced by the enclosure of the common land.

Much of this is similar to what happened in the corn-growing regions of England, and for a good reason. The bureaucrats largely responsible for the introduction of land reform intended it to sever traditional ties, to make agriculture responsive to market forces and to facilitate the introduction of the new farming methods that were being diffused from north-west Europe, particularly from England and Holland.[6]

In the nature of things the uneven distribution of power led the reforming State to make more concessions to the lords than to the peasants, so that 'the authorities combined welfare for the estate owners with strict *laissez-faire*

[6] Walker, *German home towns*, p. 187.

Table 1.3. *Percentage of the population of Prussia
living in towns*[a]

1816	27.9
1849	28.1
1871	32.5

Note:
[a] These figures refer to towns as defined in contemporary legal terms,
for it is these that are relevant here. For population growth in areas not
then enjoying urban forms of government, but urban according to a
modern geographical definition, see Jürgen Reulecke, *Geschichte der
Urbanisierung in Deutschland* (Frankfurt a.M., 1985).
Source: Fischer et al. *Sozialgeschichtliches Arbeitsbuch 1815–1870*, p. 38.

towards the peasantry'.[7] The success of this new policy depended largely on
migration. People had to be allowed to follow the demand for labour.

(B) URBAN CHANGE: PRUSSIA

The Prussian policy on guild control over handicraft trades is equally
relevant. The process was complex and long drawn-out, with regional
variations even within Prussia, but essentially production was freed from
old forms of control. This involved breaking down the guilds' power to
control trades within the town, and often also the country immediately
surrounding it, and permitting outsiders to settle and pursue a trade. What
was being prised open in the cause of untrammelled enterprise and labour
mobility was not only the town's trade but also the town authorities'
control over settlement. The result was a multiplication of small impoverished masters, of journeymen who had no chance of ever becoming
masters, and of labourers of all kinds.[8]

This opening of the towns to immigration had consequences for urban
population growth. Unable to insulate themselves from rural demographic
change, in the first half of the century the towns participated in it, not
disproportionately as later, but at much the same rate as the countryside.

[7] Erich Jordan, *Die Entstehung der Konservativen Partei und die preussischen Agrarverhältnisse von 1848*
(1914), p. 96, quoted in Sheehan, *German history*, p. 475.
[8] Reinhart Kosellek, *Preussen zwischen Reform und Revolution* (Stuttgart, 1967), pp. 587–608;
K. H. Kaufhold, 'Gewerbefreiheit und gewerbliche Entwicklung im 19. Jahrhundert', *Blätter für
deutsche Landesgeschichte*, 118 (1982), 73–114.

That was almost certainly more than the urban authorities would have permitted, and the expansion of their economy required.[9]

(c) POOR LAW REFORM: PRUSSIA

The commitment of the Prussian State to the freeing of economic enterprise underpinned by labour mobility required an appropriate framework of poor relief. The legislation of 1842, the result of long gestation since 1824 at least, was intended to provide it.[10]

Perhaps the most significant aspect of the new law was the fact that it applied equally to all the provinces of Prussia. Some of its features can be found before 1842, but the variety of provincial laws and the disputes to which this had led were now to be ended. It is important to bear in mind that Prussia had been much enlarged in 1815 and that it consisted of numerous provinces, not necessarily contiguous to each other, strung out from east to west across the breadth of the German Confederation. The Poor Law of 1842 with its claim to override provincial law was an aspect of Prussian State-building.

As of old, the obligation to relieve their members or subordinates was to fall in the first instance on the corporate body or seigneur. But this now applied to an ever smaller proportion of the people. Where it did not apply, the local community was obliged to relieve its members, as it had been before. From being a relief authority for the marginal population, it had become the body with the main responsibility.

The law regulated the community's obligations, and did this in the interests of labour mobility. In practice the power of the communal authorities to restrict the immigration of Prussian subjects had already largely disappeared. What the law did was to restate these conditions of mobility and to accommodate the poor law to them. Towns could deny entry only to persons actually destitute, not to anyone who in the opinion of the authorities might become a liability in the future.[11] It made claims to poor relief independent of the various grades of community membership and dependent on nothing more than normally living in the place over a

---

[9] See Walker, *Home towns*, pp. 332–3, for the far lower population growth recorded in urban areas of Germany where this control had not been removed.

[10] Harald Schinkel, 'Armenpflege und Freizügigkeit in der preussischen Gesetzgebung vom Jahre 1842', VSWG, 50 (1963), 459–79; Kosellek, *Preussen*, pp. 631–4.

[11] There were three laws all closely connected and all passed on 31 December 1842. One defined Prussian citizenship, one dealt with the admission of immigrants, and one dealt with the obligations of poor relief. QS,I,7(b), Appendices 2, 3 and 4; Sachsse and Tennstedt, *Geschichte der Armenfürsorge*, vol. I, pp. 195–203 and 276–80.

stated period of time. Householders automatically acquired the right to relief; others did so after three years' normal residence, if they had kept clear of the need for poor relief. Normal residence did not mean uninterrupted residence. Convicted felons could, however, still be denied the right of residence. Under § 32 anyone employed on a regular basis (*in einem festen Dienstverhältnis*) as a servant, and that included journeymen craftsmen, had to be supported by the community of residence when ill until they had recovered. There was no right to reimbursement from the community of origin or from any other.

There were, as always, ways to avoid the burden of the law, and three years' normal residence could be made difficult by short tenancy and service arrangements.[12] But freedom of movement in search of employment was significantly facilitated by providing those who wished to settle elsewhere with the essential conditions under which they could do so. And it was entirely in the spirit of this policy that a further law in 1843 tightened and elaborated measures for the control of vagrancy.

Since these rights were extended to all Prussian citizens, the concept of citizenship had to be defined as had not been the case in the past.[13] The migrant poor, unless Prussian citizens, could be expelled once they became destitute, or at least they became the financial liability of their State of origin. Until German unification this was a matter that was regulated by a series of bilateral treaties with other German states.

Prussian subjects lost their resident status and right to relief after three years' absence. This meant that they could lose the status without necessarily having acquired the right to poor relief in another community. Such people became the responsibility of a larger poor law authority that normally covered the whole province, the so-called *Landarmenverband*. This body was also responsible for providing such institutions as houses of correction for vagrants and asylums for the blind and sick. But the vast majority became the responsibility of the local communal authorities, who exercised the functions of a local poor law authority (*Ortsarmenverband* or OAV).[14]

The government was, however, under political pressure from the communes at the receiving end of the wave of migration. In 1855 it produced an amendment of the Poor Law that made no more than minimum

[12] On this point see Sachsse and Tennstedt, *Geschichte der Armenfürsorge*, vol. I, pp. 200–2; also Koselleck, *Preussen*, p. 633, who emphasises the element of compromise and the survival of 'outdated methods' in what is usually regarded as a progressive piece of legislation.

[13] R. Brubaker, *Citizenship and nationhood in France and Germany* (Cambridge, MA, 1992), ch. 3.

[14] For a calculation of the actual proportions see the more detailed discussion of the role of the *Landarmenverband* on p. 37 below.

concessions to them. The new Law made all entitlement to relief from local funds subject to one year's residence. For that year it reimposed the obligation to provide relief on the commune of previous residence. After three months it also allowed relief authorities to claim reimbursement of the cost of maintaining sick servants from other relief authorities elsewhere.[15] These reversals of the policy of 1842 were regarded as modest enough not to act as a brake on migration.

In several other German states legislation after 1850 tended in much the same direction, making it difficult for immigrants to be excluded and facilitating the acquisition of a right to relief. But in contrast to Prussia this right, the so-called *Heimatrecht*, was lost only when it was acquired elsewhere.[16] Otherwise migrants could be returned to the community where they still enjoyed the *Heimatrecht*, i.e. the right to relief, regardless of the length of time that they had been absent. That did not happen in Prussia, where, with the exception of the one-year concession just referred to, communities of former residence had no obligation after the expiry of three years. Thereafter destitute persons were relieved in the place in which they lived. The only question to be resolved was whose legal responsibility it was. If they had acquired a residential right of relief (*Unterstützungswohnsitz*) in the local community, that was where the responsibility lay. If they had failed to do so, the state authority in the province accepted responsibility instead. For that purpose it operated through the *Landarmenverband*.

In this matter the Prussian law was untypical, being followed only in the principality of Waldeck. But it was the principle of the Prussian law that became the basis of the law for the whole North German Confederation, and soon after for most of the Empire. It was modified slightly by reducing the waiting period for the acquisition as well as the loss of resident status and right to relief from three years to two, and by permitting relief authorities to claim reimbursement for the maintenance of sick servants after six weeks. By 1873 it applied everywhere with the exception of Bavaria and Alsace-Lorraine.[17]

---

[15] Jürgen Reulecke, *Geschichte der Urbanisierung in Deutschland* (Frankfurt, 1985), pp. 36–7; Heinrich Volkmann, *Die Arbeiterfrage im preussischen Abgeordnetenhaus 1848–1869* (Berlin, 1968), p. 81; QS,I,7(2), Appendix 7.

[16] For the struggle over the terms on which *Heimatrecht* could be acquired in certain areas of south-west Germany see Walker, *German home towns*, ch. 12.

[17] The important legislation was the North German Confederation Law of November 1867 on *Freizügigkeit*, and the Law of June 1870 on the *Unterstützungswohnsitz*. Alsace-Lorraine, which had originally operated on the French system, came into line in 1910; Bavaria in 1916. See QS,I,7(1), pp. XIX–XXXV, for details.

The years 1867–73 therefore saw a major reform of poor relief in most of the non-Prussian parts of Germany and in the territories newly annexed by Prussia. Even within the older parts of Prussia the legislation of this period introduced significant changes through the shortening of the qualifying period of residence from three to two years. Nor was that the only innovation. All subjects of the Empire, irrespective of their state citizenship, were now entitled to equal treatment. German unification thus found its expression in the treatment of the German citizen migrating within the bounds of the Empire, always with the reservation that things were done differently in Bavaria and in the former French territories of Alsace-Lorraine.

(D) POOR LAW REFORM: ENGLAND

Anyone familiar with the English Poor Law will be struck by the narrow range of matters which were dealt with by the Prussian law. The 1834 Poor Law Amendment Act had given the central government in England and Wales powers for the compulsory creation of Poor Law Unions and had carefully prescribed the constitution of the elected Boards of Guardians, the authorities responsible for the administration of poor relief. It had established a Central Poor Law Commission with powers to issue Orders regulating the conditions of relief across the country, with its own staff of Assistant Commissioners or Inspectors.

Before the 1834 Act poor relief in England had been the responsibility of the parish or in the northern counties of the township. There were some 15,500 of these poor law authorities varying greatly in population and in their constitution. Some of these had been formed from unions of parishes, a procedure permitted under special Local Acts of Parliament and encouraged by a permissive general Act of 1782 (Gilbert's Act), but the vast majority were no more than single parishes or townships. The Act of 1834 led to the merging of these parishes or townships into Poor Law Unions, a process that was 95 per cent complete by 1839.[18] Poor law authorities established by special legislation prior to 1834, whether by the Act of 1782 or by a local Act, were not covered by the Act of 1834 with its prescription for the constitution, procedures and powers of poor law authorities. It required persistent pressure from central government and

---

[18] Sidney Webb and Beatrice Webb, *English poor law history*. Part II, *The last 100 years* (London, 1929), vol. I, pp. 81 and 119.

some amending legislation before the last of them was finally absorbed into the reformed system in 1868.[19]

The Boards of Guardians of these Unions created by the Act of 1834 were elected under a plural franchise that favoured owners and occupiers of large property among the large ratepayers. After 1844 owners had anything up to six votes, as did occupiers. Owner-occupiers of heavily rated property therefore disposed of twelve times as many votes as the lowest ratepayer. The weighting of the Boards of Guardians in favour of property was further increased by a property qualification for all Guardians and by the fact that the local justices of the peace were members of the Board *ex officio*.[20]

These Boards assumed the duties that had previously been exercised in each parish by the vestry and the overseers of the poor. Vestries had been in most cases assemblies of all householders. Overseers had been householders obliged to give unpaid citizen service on a rota basis, although it was not uncommon for the wealthier householders to pay a substitute. An important change brought about by the Act of 1834 was the supersession of this unpaid citizen service. The Act required the Guardians to administer poor relief through full-time salaried relieving officers.[21] The duties of parish overseers were reduced to dealing with the removal of paupers to their parish of settlement and to the levying of the parish rates.

No such wide-ranging rationalisation occurred in Prussia. Communes were permitted to unite to establish a common OAV, but these optional powers were relatively rarely invoked. In town and country the commune (*Gemeinde*) usually remained the basic unit of relief.[22] In some rural areas, where something like the old manorial administration had been preserved and the lord of the manor exercised authority on behalf of the State, he was responsible for poor relief, but few such manorial districts (*Gutsbezirke*) were found outside the north and east of Germany by 1885.[23] In that year there were over 47,000 local relief authorities in Prussia and close on 71,000 in the German Empire as a whole, compared with 647 Unions in

---

[19] Webb and Webb, *Poor law history*, Part II, vol. I, pp. 119 and 226.
[20] This situation continued until 1894, when the *ex officio* element was abolished, a single-vote ratepayers' franchise was introduced and the property qualification for Guardians was abolished. B. Keith-Lucas, *The English local government franchise: a short history* (Oxford, 1952).
[21] Sidney Webb and Beatrice Webb, *Statutory authorities for special purposes* (London, 1922), pp. 454–7.
[22] The main exceptions were the 4,477 mixed OAVs, made up from a combination of different communes (6 per cent of the total) and the twenty-eight unions established on a voluntary basis in Saxony. The latter were not unlike the English Unions.
[23] Kaiserliches Statistisches Amt, *Statistik der öffentlichen Armenpflege im Jahre 1885, Statistik des Deutschen Reichs*, NF 29 (1887), Table 1 (to be referred to below as RAS 1885).

England and Wales. Even allowing for the difference in total population, there were over thirty times as many local relief authorities in Germany as in England and Wales.[24] Even disregarding the manorial district (*Gutsbezirk*), whose population was often tiny, local relief authorities varied enormously from little village communes with a population of under 100 to large city communes.[25] Of these Berlin with 1.3 million stood very much on its own, but there were three others with over 250,000 (Hamburg, Breslau and Munich).[26]

Much of this is reminiscent of England and Wales prior to the New Poor Law, but the contrast with the subsequent situation is striking. In 1881 there were no Poor Law authorities with less than 2,000 inhabitants and only nine with less than 5,000. At the other end of the scale things were not so different, however. Although no English Union was as large as Berlin, four had a population of over 250,000.[27]

What is true of size applies also to the constitution of the local relief authorities. The communes themselves were regulated by laws that determined the nature of the franchise and of the governing bodies. But how they organised their administration of poor relief could greatly vary. No common pattern would have been equally suited to a small village and a large city.

This lack of interest in creating comparable authorities across Prussia, not to mention the Empire, is paralleled by a lack of interest in the methods and policies applied to the granting of poor relief. There was no equivalent in Prussia to the Poor Law Commission, and its successors, the Poor Law

---

[24] RAS 1885, Table 1; *Return of paupers relieved, January 1885*, BPP 1886 (58B) LVI, 59. The corrected total for England and Wales would have been 2,267 Unions. The German total was 31.3 times that figure.

[25] In 1885 the only attempt at providing poor relief statistics for the German Empire drew the line at returning the details of all 70,949 OAVs individually. It grouped them by each *Kreis*, the administrative unit above the commune and below the district. For these it recorded the average population per OAV. Of these groupings of rural OAVs, thirty-two had an average population of less than 250. They consisted of 4,069 OAVs. The extreme cases were in East Prussia, where thirty-two OAVs in *Kreis* Niederung had an average population of seventy-nine. Calculated from RAS 1885, Tables 1 and I.A.a.1. It should be noted that this 4,069 does not represent the total of OAVs with less than 250 inhabitants. Some of them would have exceeded the average in their grouping, whereas other *Kreis* groupings, whose average exceeded 250, would have included some OAVs with less than 250 inhabitants.

[26] RAS 1885, Table 20. This chaotic situation was not tackled until after the Weimar Republic's legislation of 1923, which left the detailed decisions, however, to the *Länder*, the successors of the states under the Empire. In 1925 the *Kreis*, as well as any town that had the status of a *Kreis*, became the basic unit for the OAV in Prussia. Other *Länder* also regulated the basis of the OAVs anew. Sachsse and Tennstedt, *Geschichte der Armenfürsorge in Deutschland*, vol. II, pp. 146–7.

[27] West Derby (in Liverpool), Islington, Chorlton (in Manchester) and Lambeth. *Return of paupers relieved, January 1885*. For details of the position in 1831 see Mark Blaug, 'The poor law re-examined', Jl Econ. H, 24 (1964), 244.

Board of 1848–71 and the Local Government Board of 1871–1918, with their Orders designed to regulate the relief policies of whole categories of authorities across the whole of England and Wales. Nor were there any central government inspectors. There was no requirement on the local or on the provincial relief authorities to provide information on their work; there was no interest in the regular provision of statistics. In all these matters the Prussian poor law authorities did as they chose. They raised taxes when needed under legal authority that they enjoyed in any case, and they did without them if possible.

In practice the control exercised by the central authority for England and Wales was never as effective as intended. The Orders that were supposed to lay down permissible forms of relief could not be fully enforced. The statistical returns that the central authority required as a means of monitoring the compliance of the Unions were not to be greatly relied upon. Male able-bodied paupers, for instance, continued to receive outdoor relief in rural Unions in defiance of the central authority's Outdoor Relief Prohibitory Order. They merely appeared in the statistics as among the sick and infirm, as no doubt in many respects they were.[28]

The Poor Law Inspectorate was too small to keep the 647 Boards of Guardians under effective surveillance, and lacked the range of powers needed to impose policy on the localities. The central authority could not directly require Unions to undertake matters that it desired, such as the building or enlarging of workhouses. As long as Boards of Guardians did not wish to raise additional capital, they could ignore the suggestions of the inspectors or the central authority. But when they approached that authority for permission to raise capital for purposes of their own choice, they became vulnerable to pressure from the centre. The history of the English poor law is full of such instances, when recommendations of the central authority that had been ignored for years were carried out as the price to be paid for permission to raise a loan. It was its loan-sanctioning powers that provided the central authority with the leverage to make its views felt in the localities, but only after much negotiation and procrastination. The voluminous correspondence between the central and the local poor law authorities is testimony both to the centre's ability to insist that local authorities give an account of themselves and to the limited powers of command that it possessed.[29]

---

[28] Anne Digby, 'The labour market and the continuity of social policy after 1834: the case of the eastern counties', Econ. HR, 2nd ser., 28 (1975), 69–83, esp. 70–4. On the statistics see also pp. 40–1 below.

[29] Christine Bellamy, *Administering central–local relations 1871–1919: the local government board in its fiscal and cultural context* (Manchester, 1988).

Since the central authority in Prussia never even tried to implement such policies, the circumscribed and limited attempts in England and Wales acquire significance after all, a significance that revisionist historians of the English Poor Law intent on demolishing the inflated claims of English poor law ideology have ignored.[30] Why should the central authority in England and Wales have wanted to do this, when its counterpart in Prussia did not?

Any answer to that question must take account of the similarity in the intentions behind the poor relief legislation of the two countries. In both cases it was designed to break down existing obstacles to the creation of a labour market responsive to entrepreneurial initiatives. In Prussia that was achieved by the legislation for land reform and freedom from guild control. It was underpinned by legislation on the right of residence and the entitlement to poor relief in the place of normal residence.

In England, where guilds had long ago ceased to control the labour market and where the magistrates' powers to fix wages had fallen into disuse, the Poor Law had become the principal instrument for regulating the conditions of labour. That was particularly the case in the rural corn-growing counties, where high population growth had led to serious under-employment, and where the introduction of new forms of cultivation after 1815 accentuated seasonal fluctuations in labour demand just when enclosure of commons made the poor more than ever dependent on wage labour.[31] Control of poor relief enabled the principal farmers of the parish to maintain the under-employed population in the periods when labour demand was relatively low. This was done by methods that subsidised the employment of relatively unproductive labourers.[32]

The result had been a steep increase in the cost of poor relief in absolute terms. Little attention was paid to the fact that it was not in excess of population growth. But there was an outcry against the burden on the rates and the alleged demoralisation of the labourers, voiced by the property

---

[30] Since the OAV was not responsible for institutional relief and therefore had few reasons for capital investment, it was largely unaffected by the loan-sanctioning powers of the Prussian State authorities.

[31] The population of fourteen agricultural counties in the mainly corn-growing areas increased from 1801 to 1831 by 41 per cent. Calculated from Phyllis Deane and W. A. Cole, *British economic growth 1688–1959* (Cambridge, 1964), Table 24, p. 103. For changes in cultivation see K. D. M. Snell, *Annals of the labouring poor: social change and agrarian England 1660–1900* (Cambridge, 1985), ch. 4.

[32] *Ibid.*, ch. 3. For an excellent exposition of the rationality of the pre-1834 poor law in German see Thomas Sokoll, '"Alte Armut". Unterstützungspraxis und Formen lebenszyklischer Armut unter dem Alten Armenrecht, 1780–1834', in Bernd Weisbrod (ed.), *'Victorian values': Arm und Reich im Viktorianischen England* (Bochum, 1988), pp. 13–64.

owners represented in Parliament. The Royal Commission on the Poor Laws of 1834, appointed to find an answer to both these problems, was convinced, rightly or wrongly, that this subsidy from the poor rates feather-bedded large farmers at the expense of their smaller competitors, discouraged the productive use of labour and diverted resources that could otherwise be used for investment to generate more labour demand. It recommended that methods of relief be controlled so that they were not used to subsidise and distort the labour market. Since it was impossible to cut off poor relief altogether without endangering the public peace, relief was to be clearly separated from wages. This was to be achieved by the refusal to relieve able-bodied males except in a workhouse, where conditions were to be less 'eligible' than those of the poorest labourer dependent on the labour market.

It was this policy that pointed to the need to regulate the conditions on which relief was granted, to provide appropriate workhouses and to regulate the conditions under which they operated. The twin dogmas of the workhouse test for the able-bodied and of less eligibility, the mistaken assumption that existing parish workhouses could be adapted to the purpose, the subsequent realisation that the proposed policy would be impossible to carry out without substantial capital investment in new institutions, these are familiar aspects of the history of the English Poor Law.[33] What matters for our purposes is less the gradual realisation that the intended policy was deeply flawed than the fact that it was thought to require the supervision of relief by a central authority committed to it.

Once the decision had been taken that institutional forms of relief were to play a major role, the small size and low population levels of the average parish became identified as a major problem. Hence the need to unite parishes into larger Unions, at least for the provision of institutional relief. In Prussia too institutional relief became the responsibility of larger unions, the provincial relief authorities, but since institutions were not accorded the same prominent role, these bodies remained marginal to the Prussian scene.[34]

The nationwide creation of Unions was the most significant of all the exercises of central authority to which the Act of 1834 gave rise. It removed the administration of poor relief in the localities from the control of parish vestries composed of all householders, and placed it into the hands of

---

[33] M. A. Crowther, *The workhouse system 1834–1929* (London, 1981); S. E. Finer, *The life and times of Sir Edwin Chadwick* (London, 1952).
[34] See Table 1.4 below.

Boards of Guardians, elected by a franchise that gave power to large ratepayers. The inclusion of all justices of the peace (JPs) *ex officio* on the Board of Guardians gave landowners in general a very strong say on these bodies, but it deprived individual JPs of the appellate role that they had exercised over parish poor relief under the old system. The result was greater uniformity in policy across the Union as a whole. Individual JPs now had less influence than before, and individual parishes were brought to heel by the majority on a Board elected from all the parishes.

Once these measures had confirmed the power of the local notables over this essential area of local administration, they wanted to exercise it according to their own preferences and resisted the other centralising demands contained in the law. The changes of 1834 were therefore more effective in centralising power at Union and county level than in centralising it in London. The preferences of local notables mostly included deterrence and the reduction of the rates. Recent historians have emphasised the widespread acceptance of the new political economy among the English upper classes.[35]

The differences between poor relief in the two countries have frequently been exaggerated. In Germany poor relief was also frequently meant to be a deterrent. Workhouses in Germany were indeed far more of a deterrent than in England, for in practice English workhouses were full of the aged and infirm, whereas the German workhouses (*Armenarbeitshäuser*) were full of the work-shy. German poor relief was accompanied by loss of civic rights and was in that respect no different from its English counterpart.

What we do not find, however, is anything like the ideological programme of reform that characterised England, particularly in the 1830s and 1840s. Those institutions of the English Poor Law with which we have been concerned – the Union, the central authority, the Inspectorate, the regulatory Orders, the annual statistical returns – were fashioned in those decades with the intention of putting that programme into effect. Once established, they adapted themselves to political realities that seriously circumscribed their effectiveness, but they did not disappear. They became

---

[35] Peter Mandler, 'The making of the new poor law *redivivus*', *Past & Present*, 117 (1987), 131; Mandler, 'Tories and paupers: political economy and the making of the new poor law', HJ, 33 (1990), 81; Anthony Brundage, *The making of the new poor law: the politics of inquiry, enactment and implementation, 1832–1839* (London, 1978). Though differing in other matters, these two scholars are in agreement on the substance of this paragraph. See their respective contributions to the debate in *Past & Present*, 127 (1990). See also P. Harling, 'The power of persuasion: central authority, local bureaucracy and the new poor law', EHR, 107 (1992), 30.

vested interests and generated their own momentum, concerned to survive and, if possible, to expand.

(E) SETTLEMENT LAW: ENGLAND

So far we have been considering those features of the English legislation that had no parallel in that of Prussia. How did the English law deal with the issue on which the Prussian law focused to the exclusion of everything else, the connection between the right of residence and that of poor relief?

The right of residence caused few problems in England. There was no requirement to register with the police on arrival at a new place, and hence no control over immigration. After 1795 immigrants could be returned to their parish of settlement only when they actually applied for poor relief.[36]

At first there was great reluctance to permit the immigrant to acquire a settlement in the technical sense of a right to relief. From the 1840s onwards, however, the law developed along similar lines to Prussia. In 1846 five years of continuous residence gave persons the right to relief in the parish where they resided. That compared badly with the three years required by the Prussian Law of 1842, but the principle was the same. The same Act laid down that those who applied for relief merely on account of temporary sickness or accidents were protected from being sent back to their parish of settlement.[37] That was similar to the situation in Prussia. In 1861 the period of residence that gave protection from removal was reduced to three years, as in Prussia. It was reduced in 1865 to only one year, compared with the two years required by the Law of 1870, first for the North German Confederation and then for the greater part of the Empire.[38]

So in one sense the legislation of the two countries was similar, but only if one ignores the important changes taking place concurrently in the relationship between parish and Union. In retrospect the combination of parishes into Unions emerges as one of the most significant achievements of the 1834 Poor Law Amendment Act, for it redefined the concept of community. That took time, but an Act of 1865 converted the Union into a genuine financial unit, with the cost of all poor relief paid for by a uniform

---

[36] Before then it had been legal for magistrates to return persons occupying accommodation rated at less than £10 p.a. to their parish of settlement, i.e. that in which they enjoyed the right to relief, on the mere suspicion that they might one day apply for poor relief.

[37] Webb and Webb, *Poor law history*, part II, vol. 1, p. 422.

[38] *Ibid.*, pp. 430–1; M. E. Rose, 'Settlement, removal and the new poor law', in Derek Fraser (ed.), *The new poor law in the nineteenth century* (London, 1976), pp. 30–1.

assessment on the rateable value across the Union as a whole. To make the
Union the real unit of support in this sense had been the aim of those who
had drafted the 1834 Bill and of the officials of the central authority ever
since, but community loyalty as expressed in Parliament had been to the
parish. Although the Union took thirty years to become fully accepted,
after 1865 it rather than the parish can be regarded as the real community
for purposes of relief. This change of sentiment received confirmation in
1876 when three years' continuous residence in the Union, irrespective of
any move from one constituent parish to another, became a qualification
for settlement.[39]

The roughly similar timing of the English and the Prussian legislation
on the right of settlement is not what one should have expected. England's
economic development had after all been far ahead of that of Prussia, and
labour mobility had played a crucial part in it for a long time. One would
have expected England to have taken the lead in adapting its Poor Law
accordingly. Many distinguished people, from Adam Smith onwards,
condemned the Law of Settlement on economic grounds of this kind,
but there is no evidence that in practice it acted as a significant obstacle to
labour mobility. It was common for parish officers to issue departing
parishioners with certificates stating that the parish would accept liability
for the cost of poor relief, and these were willingly accepted by the authorities at the receiving end of the migration. Even in the absence of certificates arrangements between parishes were common.

These facts make one wonder whether Prussian policy makers were right
to regard the residential right to relief as the essential pre-condition for
labour mobility. As far as I am aware no one has ever investigated whether
the alternative provision, the *Heimatrecht* which operated in several other
parts of Germany before 1870, did actually act as an obstacle to
migration.[40]

Although no obstacle to economic growth, the state of the law was
undoubtedly a source of hardship to individuals, to women in particular.
Another group that should be mentioned in this context are the Irish, for
whom being sent back home was so dire a prospect that it was frequently
used as an effective threat. Experts believed that it deterred many of the

---

[39] Rose, 'Settlement', pp. 29–31.
[40] On this point see the all too brief discussion in Sachsse and Tennstedt, *Armenfürsorge*, vol. I, p. 203.
For the distinction between the Prussian residential relief system and the *Heimatrecht*, see p. 25
above.

Irish from applying for poor relief more effectively and more cheaply than the workhouse test would have done.[41]

(F) THE LANDARMENVERBAND

I propose to conclude this comparison of the two systems by looking more closely at the German provincial relief authority, or *Landarmenverband*.[42] Originally a Prussian device, it was introduced elsewhere only in the 1870s. It represents the element of innovation and made the system workable. It dealt with two of its shortcomings in particular.

In the first place it took responsibility for those who had lost their former residential right to relief without having acquired a new one and thus plugged a crucial gap in the system. Secondly, it provided the institutional poor relief that could not have been undertaken by most of the local relief authorities on account of their inadequate size. They lacked the resources for the necessary capital investment and enough persons to fill an institution of their own. These had been the reasons for the creation of Unions in England. The same constraints applied to most German local relief authorities.

There was a further disadvantage from which the smaller authorities were liable to suffer. Communities of perhaps thirty households were in no position to meet the costs of anything out of the ordinary, particularly if it had to be paid in cash. An urban authority claiming reimbursement of medical care for one or two villagers temporarily living there could spell financial disaster for a small rural relief authority. In Prussia such authorities could receive subsidies from the provincial body, but with a few exceptions the amount was not large. The arrangement, which might have been the basis of a regular subsidy from the State had it been further developed, was of little significance.[43]

The provincial relief authority was not not merely a larger version of the local relief authority. The latter was an aspect of the local commune, which possessed its own form of representative government and legally established autonomy. The former was an aspect of State administration,

---

[41] Webb and Webb, *Poor law history*, part I, pp. 328–49; Rose, 'Settlement', pp. 31–40; David Ashforth, 'The urban poor law', in Fraser (ed.), *The new poor law*, pp. 145–6.

[42] I have used this term to translate *Landarmenverband* since in Prussia it was usually coterminous with the province, although not in the province of East Prussia. In a few large towns it coincided with the commune. For this and for other states, see 'Einleitung', RAS 1885, p. 5.

[43] F. von Reitzenstein (ed.), *Die ländliche Armenpflege und ihre Reform* (Freiburg, 1887), *Allgemeiner Teil*, p. 131, *Spezieller Teil*, pp. 48–9.

exercised at the provincial level, not another form of representative government. It is common in the German literature to find the Law of 1842 and its
successors represented as the intervention of the State in the affairs of the
communes, obliging the latter to admit persons to the circle of those
benefiting from membership of the community, whom they would have
preferred to exclude. The provincial relief authority was a creation of that
State policy, and the relation between local and provincial relief authorities
continued to be marked by the conflict between community preferences
and considerations of State, which characterised the history of poor relief in
nineteenth-century Germany.[44]

Small local relief authorities, in which the financial burden of even a
single extra pauper family was most acutely felt, were notorious for the
expedients they employed to prevent labouring families from acquiring a
resident's right to relief. This could be done by refusing to employ any non-
settled person for the two years needed to acquire the right. The reduction
of the qualifying period from three to two years, it is often said, led to
parallel reductions in the normal period of continuous employment in
the eastern Prussian provinces. It was not unknown for the commune
to threaten house-owners with fines if they failed to remove tenants
before they acquired a right of settlement. Cases were reported from
Württemberg of labourers lodged in a neighbouring community just
long enough to be disqualified for the rights of a resident, and then brought
back to their former lodging. This was a relatively mild treatment of the
labourers in question. More frequent was the permanent ejection of such
families, who had to take to the road to find employment elsewhere.

These devices were just part of the constant effort that went into
reducing the local liability for poor relief. From the community's point
of view it did not matter whether this led to the acquisition of a residential
right elsewhere, perhaps in some place where the letting of accommodation
was less easy to monitor, or whether they created a claim on the provincial
funds. These devices could cause great suffering through homelessness,
throwing people on the poor relief system who would otherwise not have
had recourse to it.

But many observers were convinced that claims on the provincial relief
authority were frequently established with the tacit connivance of those
who might have been regarded as the victims of the chicanery, the so-called
Landarme. Unlike the poor person with a claim on the commune, the
Ortsarme, the *Landarme* imposed no burden on local funds, since the cost

---

[44] On this theme outside Prussia see Walker, *Home towns*, passim.

of relief was reimbursed by the provincial relief authority from State funds. As long as they did not threaten to change their status, they were acceptable to local inhabitants, providing labour without liability. They were therefore not treated with the hard-hearted parsimony for which the small rural communes in the poorer parts of the Empire were notorious. Their rate of relief was assessed not by the canny local headman and elders of the village, but by some official sitting in the provincial capital, who was frequently unaware of how meanly the irreducible needs of the poor in distant villages were being assessed, or unwilling to screw relief down to levels that the village elders found acceptable. The status of *Landarme* could therefore be desirable. The result was a conspiracy of the village community with the local poor at the expense of the State.[45]

These are the difference between the German provincial relief authority and the English Union. The similarity lies in their responsibility for capital-intensive institutional provision and in little else.

The provincial relief authority is significant as a device created by the state to permit the survival of communally based poor relief. The alternative would have been what happened in England, the transfer of poor relief functions from the traditional local authority to a newly created body designed specifically for that purpose. The Union might conceivably have become the new basis of local government in general, but, despite a few steps in that direction, that did not happen. It was the borough, reformed and enlarged after the 1835 Municipal Corporations Act, and the sanitary authority established after 1848, that became the basis for representative local government in general.[46] The Union and the Board of Guardians remained cut off from that development, with serious negative consequences.

In Germany that fatal divide between the Poor Law administration and all other local administration was avoided. The commune remained the

---

[45] Evidence for these two paragraphs comes from Reitzenstein, *Ländliche Armenpflege, Allgemeiner Teil*, pp. 164–7, and *Spezieller Teil*, pp. 21 and 201. It should, however, be pointed out that some of the claims that OAVs were deliberately creating *Landarme* came from Pomerania, a province that had altogether only ninety-seven *Landarme* in 1885. The actual percentage of *Landarme* revealed in the statistics suggests that the matter could not have been of much significance anywhere but in East Prussia (9.5 per cent) and Posen (5 per cent) among the Prussian provinces, and perhaps in Württemberg (2.9 per cent) and Baden (2.5 per cent) in the south. Calculated from RAS 1885, pp. 134 and 136. Reitzenstein is an excellent source for the perception of a small minority of officials concerned over the state of poor relief, and its anecdotal evidence is valuable. But it does not provide a balanced view.

[46] E. P. Hennock, 'The creation of an urban local government system in England and Wales', in H. Naunin (ed.), *Städteordnungen des 19. Jahrhunderts* (Institut für vergleichende Städtegeschichte, Münster), vol. 19 (Bohlau, Cologne and Vienna, 1984), pp. 19–32.

Table 1.4. *Relief authorities in the area of the residential relief system*

	Local	Provincial
Percentage of paupers maintained by	97	3
Percentage of total expenditure	90	10

Source: RAS 1885, pp. 28*, 50*.

predominant organ for dealing with the problems of poverty. Some crude picture of the relative importance of the local and the provincial relief authorities is provided in the statistical returns of 1885. See Table 1.4.

The provincial relief authorities thus dealt with only 3 per cent of all paupers. The fact that they provided 10 per cent of total expenditure was due to their responsibility for the more expensive institutional services.

It would be a mistake to regard the provincial relief authority as a means of State supervision or control. It administered its own responsibilities in the localities and did not do it very well, because there was so little contact between the administrative centre of the province and the local relief authorities strung out across its territory. It also acted as an instance for complaints against the local relief authorities by the poor, a process that did not often occur, and for which it used the normal quasi-legal procedures. What was lacking was an inspectorate. 'Why should there not be poor relief inspectors just as there are building inspectors at provincial level?' asked one Prussian civil servant during the course of an inquiry into the operation of the provincial relief system. There was never an answer.[47] Neither in the supervision of relief practices nor in the collection of statistics did the provincial relief authority act as an instrument of the central State.

(G) GERMAN REFORM PROPOSALS 1871–81

The national framework of poor relief remained largely unchanged until the end of the Empire, except for the adherence of Alsace-Lorraine and Bavaria in 1910 and 1916 respectively. But the redistribution of the burden of poor relief effected by the Law on relief rights of 1870 was not easily accepted by those who felt themselves disadvantaged by the change. Debates over possible reforms of the law rumbled on for the next decade,

---

[47] Emil Münsterberg, *Das Landarmenwesen. Schriften des deutschen Vereins für Armenpflege und Wohlthätigkeit*, 10. Heft (Leipzig, 1890), p. 25.

focusing on the unequal financial burden imposed on local poor law authorities, and especially pitting the interests of the towns over those of the countryside.[48] In 1881 the demand for a reform of the residential relief system once more gained enough political leverage to require government attention.

On that occasion the officials in the ministry came to the conclusion that these demands for allegedly greater justice in the distribution of the burdens between local communities were no more than a symptom of the malaise that actually required attention. Its real cause lay in the excessive burden placed on the local communities as such. They argued that, having established labour mobility by legislation for the sake of its overall economic benefit, the *Reich* had a responsibility to mitigate the financial consequences for local communities. Partly they were arguing for greater deterrence, partly for shifting the burden of support more on to employers in line with traditional social obligations, and partly for shifting some of the remaining burden to larger territorial units, including the member states and the *Reich*.

At the time that this was suggested, the government was already committed to compulsory accident and sickness insurance. This diagnosis of the problems of the poor law cannot account therefore for the new social policy. The redistribution of the burdens of ordinary poor relief to larger units up to and including the individual states (not, however, to the *Reich*) obtained Bismarck's strong support. A bill along those lines was drafted in February 1882 but never introduced, as the attention of the government and the time of the *Reichstag* were taken up by the conflict over accident insurance to a far greater extent than had been expected.[49] The reform of the poor law had actually formed part of the legislative programme to be announced in the Imperial Message of November 1881, but was removed from the speech in the course of later revision.[50]

(H) STATISTICAL COMPARISON

So much for the two systems. What results did they produce in terms of people relieved or resources expended? Anyone who wants an answer to

---

[48] For an example of the former see the article by Adickes, mayor of Altona, cited in Ritter, *Social welfare in Germany and Britain: origins and development* (Leamington Spa, 1986), p. 41, n. 72. More generally Münsterberg, *Die deutsche Armengesetzgebung*, pp. 183–210 and 320–75.

[49] QS,I,7(1), pp. XXXVIII–XL, 633, n. 10.

[50] F. Tennstedt and H. Winter, 'Neues zur Kaiserlichen Sozialbotschaft vom 17. November 1881', ZSR, 48 (2002), 644f.

those questions is faced with major problems. Neither in Prussia nor in the German Empire was the State particularly interested in regularly gathering information on performance. There is a Prussian statistical survey of 1849 that is considered by German specialists to be of no great value. It lends itself to a comparison of expenditure per 100 of population and has been used for that purpose.[51] It was not repeated until 1881, when the Imperial authorities decided to initiate an inquiry across the Empire as a whole. This seems to have been in part a response to demands for a revision of the law on the residential relief system, but the prominence of questions on accident-related poverty suggests that it was also related to the contemporary preoccupation with accident insurance. Despite a concurrent compilation of imperial accident statistics, it was 'more a survey of poor relief accident statistics than of actual poor relief', to quote a contemporary. Yet the inquiry was a failure, largely because the authorities had been given inadequate notice to organise it properly. The results were not published, but it was decided to repeat the exercise in 1885 in an amended form. On that occasion the interest in accidents as a cause of poverty was still in evidence, although not in the same detail.[52]

For 1885 we therefore have wide-ranging and comprehensive information on the state of German poor relief. Yet the exercise was never repeated during the life of the Empire, which is a telling comment on the importance that the authorities attached to it. By the time it was published, it was presumably of no further interest for the planning of accident insurance, which was now beginning to generate its own information. For the purpose of monitoring the operation of the highly contentious residential relief system, the data were inadequate, as was pointed out at the time.[53] By 1885 the debate over the reform of the law of settlement had been pushed aside by other priorities, of which accident insurance had been the first.

For England and Wales we have an annual statistical series. It is therefore possible to produce figures for 1885 for both countries. But whereas the special investigation in Germany was conceived on ambitious lines, the regular English statistical series provided information already generated by the administrative process and requiring the minimum of expenditure in

---

[51] See the Appendix to this chapter, Table 1.9, note c, p. 48 below. The best statistical series on poor relief are those for Oldenburg and Bavaria. The former is too small to be significant for our purpose; the latter was thoroughly untypical of the Empire. For details see Emil Münsterberg, *Die deutsche Armengesetzgebung und das Material zu ihrer Reform* (Leipzig, 1887), pp. 32–50.

[52] Emil Münsterberg, 'Die Armenstatistik', *Conrads Jahrbücher für Nationalökonomie und Statistik*, NF 12 (1886), 395, 408.

[53] Münsterberg, *Die deutsche Armengesetzgebung*, pp. 42–3.

time and effort. The German inquiry dealt with a full calendar year and was based on an individual record for every pauper relieved during the course of it. No such laborious procedure underlay the regular English returns, which only recorded paupers relieved on a single day every six months, on 1 January and 1 July. They were suited to recording change over a series of years, and that was the purpose for which they were used. They tell us nothing about what happened in any particular year, and are incompatible with the German material. What is true of the English pauper totals is even truer of the categories into which these were divided. The serious short-comings of this classification have been repeatedly pointed out.[54] Its only justification was that this is how the administrative records were kept. It was inappropriate for the purpose of description and is therefore largely useless even for comparison of changes over time. It should be ignored by historians.

This then is the problem: on the one hand the German Empire with information on only a single year, and, on the other hand, England and Wales with a regular series, whose overall figures are informative within narrow limits on the process of historical change. No numerical comparison is possible between a single-day count and a whole-year count. The proce-dures used to construct tables of comparable figures in spite of this, and the detailed calculations that result, can be found in the Appendix to this chapter.

In the year ending 25 March 1885 paupers accounted for **6.6** per cent of the total population in England and Wales. They accounted for **3.4** per cent in the German Empire in the year 1885 and for the same percentage in the area of the residential relief system (UWG). This difference must have been even greater, as explained in the Appendix, since the German figures included the inmates of certain institutions not counted in the English poor law statistics. The total percentage of people in receipt of relief in England and Wales would therefore have been *at least twice as large as in Germany, and probably more.*

Before commenting on these results we shall look at comparative expenditure. By taking the area of the UWG we can exclude not merely all capital expenditure but all expenditure on maintenance of buildings and salaries and thus compare expenditure on poor relief alone. That is useful, particularly since salary costs in England and Wales were much greater than in Germany.[55] On that basis expenditure on poor relief per pauper in

---

[54] P. F. Aschrott, *The English poor law system: past and present* (London, 1902), Appendix II; Webb and Webb, *English poor law history*, Part II, vol. II, Appendix II.

[55] Aschrott, *English poor law system*, p. 193.

England and Wales was £3.3s.2d; that in the German Empire (in the UWG) was £1.14s.6d.

Expenditure can be expected to be somewhat lower in Germany. In many rural areas householders still took it in turn to accommodate and feed a pauper for a limited period. Unlike other provision in kind, this was not recorded as expenditure. The German statistics also included those living rent-free in alms-houses, and those given mere shelter without subsistence in *Ortsarmenhäusern* (poor-houses), although in neither case would any expenditure be incurred. That reduced the figure for expenditure per pauper. But, even so, the difference (3.5 times the German figure per 100 of population and 1.8 times that per pauper) is too large to be explained away by such considerations.[56]

Part of the explanation might be found in differences in the proportion of those receiving institutional relief, for which the cost was very much higher than for outdoor relief. After adjusting the figures for England and Wales so as to remove this difference, expenditure per 100 of population is £19.1s.6d; per pauper it is £2.18.1d.[57] That leaves expenditure per 100 of population still *3.2 times* as much as in Germany. Expenditure per pauper would be *1.9 times* as much. It is clear that the explanation for the greater part of the differences between the two countries must be sought elsewhere. Nor can it be found in differences in the proportion of the elderly, the section of the population that would have imposed the greatest burden on the poor law. Those aged over 65 made up 4.7 per cent of the population in Germany in 1880 and 4.6 per cent in England and Wales in 1881.[58]

---

[56] For his wide-ranging international comparison Peter Lindert drew the German figures for 1885 from a report to the British Royal Commission on the Poor Laws of 1909, where they were cited without detailed explanation. He confessed that he did not know whether the figures for paupers related to a single-year or a one-day count, but nevertheless treated them as comparable with those for England and Wales in 1880. English relief expenditure per pauper in his Table 2 is consequently shown as 3.5 times greater than in Germany, not 1.8 times as is correct. This error had consequences for his calculation of the ratio of benefit per pauper to national income per non-pauper in the same table, which he calls R. He did not use these figures for his book, but used figures of expenditure per head of population and as a share of national product. Those expenditure figures also suffer from his lack of access to the explanatory notes in the German original but probably not to any serious extent in the context of his overall thesis. Peter H. Lindert, 'Poor relief before the welfare state: Britain versus the Continent, 1780–1880', Europ. Rev. Econ. Hist., 2 (1998), 101–40, Tables 1 and 2; Peter H. Lindert, *Growing public* (Cambridge, 2004), vol. 1, Figures 3.1 and 3.2.

[57] On account of the unreliability of these figures, such an adjustment would actually be an over-correction. The admission of the head of the household to an institution led to the whole family being counted as indoor paupers.

[58] Hohorst, *Sozialgeschichtliches Arbeitsbuch*, vol. 2, p. 24; Mitchell, *Historical statistics*, p. 12.

German experts on poor relief appear to have been unaware of this marked difference. In 1886 Viktor Böhmert, probably the person most interested in the statistics of German poor relief, published a comparative table of paupers per population in which the figures for England and Wales were drawn from the Local Government Board's single-day count. They appeared to be in the same range as those for several of the German states, which were, however, based on whole-year counts.[59]

Aschrott, the German expert on the English Poor Law system, who certainly knew his way around the English statistics and who might have been expected to notice the discrepancy, deliberately decided to make no use of them for comparative purposes. That may have been because his work was done before the 1885 *Reichsarmenstatistik* was available, but he showed no interest subsequently in using it for purposes of comparison.[60]

Nor did the officials of the Imperial Statistical Office responsible for the 1885 *Reichsarmenstatistik* attempt to add an international dimension to their investigation, a decision which they justified by reference to the diversity of the foreign statistics.[61]

Large differences in expenditure per pauper and per population were not a peculiarity of international comparison. There were differences of this kind between different parts of Germany, not just between town and country but also between different rural areas.[62] This was a matter on which contemporary German experts frequently commented. They pointed out that even within the same region it was the fertile areas that showed the greater expenditure compared with the infertile ones, and those in which property was held in large units compared with those where very small holdings predominated. Far from suggesting that higher expenditure was accompanied by greater destitution, they explained the contrast by suggesting that relief tends to be given more easily and in larger amounts where the standard of living was higher.[63]

This observation could suggest an explanation for the Anglo-German contrast, and it prompts questions about the relative national income of the two countries. The figure for the nett domestic product (NDP) (at factor

---

[59] C. V. Böhmert, *Das Armenwesen in 77 deutschen Städten und einigen Landarmenverbänden* (Dresden, 1886), *Allgemeiner Teil*, p. 20.

[60] Aschrott, *English poor law system* (2nd edn, 1902). The original German version was published in 1886.

[61] M. Schumann, 'Die Armenlast im deutschen Reich', *Conrads Jahrbücher für Nationalökonomie und Statistik*, NF 16 (1887), 600.

[62] See the maps at the end of the RAS 1885.

[63] M. Schumann, 'Die Armenlast im deutschen Reich', pp. 617–18. See RAS 1885, p. 62*, for similar comments.

cost) of the German Empire in 1885 has been calculated as 337 M or £16.85 per head of population and £30 for the United Kingdom.[64]

On the basis of those figures the expenditure on poor relief per head of population in the area of the UWG was 0.35 per cent of per capita NDP, based on calculations done for the German Empire. The parallel expenditure in England and Wales was 0.69 per cent, as calculated for the United Kingdom as a whole. There are no figures of NDP for England and Wales alone. If we follow Phyllis Deane in dividing the UK figure according to population, poor law expenditure per head of population as a percentage of per capita NDP in England and Wales would have been roughly twice as high as in the area of the UWG. In other words, they did not merely pay more; they paid substantially more in relation to their economic resources.

If Lindert's survey of poor relief in Britain, Belgium, the Netherlands, France and Scandinavia between 1780 and 1880 is at all reliable, the same had originally been true in all these countries with the exception of the Netherlands. But it had become less and less true over time. According to Lindert England had by 1880 been overtaken by Denmark, the Netherlands and Norway, and almost matched by Sweden. As a share of national product Germany's poor relief expenditure was below that of all these countries and exceeded only that of Belgium and Finland.[65]

Returning to an Anglo-German comparison for the 1880s, we find therefore that, far from living up to its image as the land of the deterrent Poor Law, England together with Wales, with a generally higher standard of living and consequentially higher expectations, was the land where relief was more easily granted and at higher levels per pauper than in Germany, a country that at this stage still had a markedly lower standard of living.

If that result is a surprise, it may not be the only one. That the German Empire, as a federal structure, left a great deal of control over administration to its constituent states is only to be expected. But that Prussia should not have exercised the degree of state control over poor relief that was found in England may surprise readers who are not specialists in Prussian history. Yet it did not collect statistics of poor relief on a regular basis, had no poor law inspectorate and issued no regulations on the

---

[64] Flora *et al.*, *State, economy and society*, vol. 2, pp. 351, 367. The rate of exchange used is once again 1 Mark = 1 shilling.

[65] Lindert, 'Poor relief', p. 127 and Table 2; Lindert, *Growing public*, vol. I, pp. 45–8; Phyllis Deane, 'New estimates for the gross national product of the United Kingdom, 1830–1914' *Review of Income and Wealth*, 14 (1968), 2. I have no means of assessing the reliability of these figures except those for Germany. On these see n. 56 above.

methods of relief. Nor had it rationalised the multiplicity of relief authorities as drastically as had been done in England with the replacement of
the parish by the Union. In matters of poor relief it was England not Prussia
that was the centralised State with ambitions to supervise and to control.

APPENDIX: COMPARATIVE POOR LAW STATISTICS

It is possible to convert the English figures for a single day into figures for the
year. There were two occasions (1892 and 1907) on which the English authorities were persuaded to undertake a whole-year count as part of a special
investigation. Since the regular one-day count continued to be available, it is
possible to calculate a conversion factor from one-day to whole-year figures.
In 1892 that factor for the single-day count on 1 January was 2.24. In 1907 it
was 2.22, which would suggest that the ratio in 1892 was reasonably reliable.
I shall apply the detailed ratios for 1892, 2.19 for outdoor paupers and 2.38 for
indoor paupers, to the figures for 1885.[66] That is the least unsatisfactory way to
obtain data that can be compared with those for Germany.

What other aspects of the two forms of information gathering, or of the
two relief systems, might impair the comparability of the two sets of
figures? The German statistics probably returned a larger proportion of
the country's total of sick poor, since they included patients on poor relief
treated in the municipal hospital. The English statistics would have
returned patients in Poor Law infirmaries or patients specifically sent by
the Poor Law authority to other hospitals, but not other poor patients
in the large urban hospitals, which were counted as charitable bodies.
Similarly, the English statistics took no notice of the beneficiaries of
endowed charities, such as almshouses, whereas the German records
included them. That suggests an under-recording of the English pauper
total when compared with the German one.

While detailing the many quirks of the English Poor Law statistics, Sidney
and Beatrice Webb came to the conclusion that 'in such a large aggregate as a
million or so, these sources of error are of little consequence'.[67] It is in that
spirit that this investigation is undertaken. Only very considerable differences will be considered relevant. Here are the actual figures.

---

[66] *22nd Report of the Local Government Board 1892–3*, p. lix, BPP 1893 C.7180 XLIII.1; *Royal Commission
on the poor law, Statistical appendix*, Part IV, pp. 5577–67, BPP 1910 Cd.5077 LIII; *Return of numbers
of paupers relieved 1 January 1907 and 1 July 1907*, p. iii, BPP 1907 (108) LXXII, 155.
[67] Webb and Webb, *English poor law history*, Part II, vol. 2, p. 1044.

Paupers as a percentage of population

Table 1.5. *Calculation of paupers as a percentage of population, England and Wales, 1885*

January 1885	
Paupers on outdoor relief	594,199
Paupers on indoor relief	194,703[a]
Year ended 25 March 1885, applying the 1892 ratios	
Estimated number of paupers on outdoor relief	1,302,955
Estimated number of paupers on indoor relief	463,929
Estimated pauper total	1,766,884
Estimated population mid-year 1884	26,922,000[b]
Paupers on outdoor relief as percentage of population	4.8 per cent
Paupers on indoor relief as percentage of population	1.7 per cent
Pauper total as percentage of population	6.6 per cent[c]

Notes:

[a] Local Government Board, *Report for 1885–6*, Appendix D, Table 36, pp. 136–7, BPP 1886 C.4844 XXXI. The figures given in that table include 119 persons returned as both indoor and outdoor paupers. So as not to inflate the total these 119 have been subtracted from the indoor and outdoor figures according to the indoor/outdoor ratio, i.e. 29 and 90.

[b] Mitchell, *Historical statistics*, p. 9. This is less than the estimate used by the LGB report of 1885–6 (see note a above). The percentage has therefore been calculated afresh and not taken from the text of the report.

[c] All percentages in these tables are calculated to the first decimal point.

Table 1.6. *Calculation of paupers as a percentage of population, German Empire, 1885*

Paupers on outdoor relief	1,269,320
Paupers on indoor relief	323,066[a]
Pauper total	1,592,386
Population (1885 Census)	46,855,704[b]
Paupers on outdoor relief as percentage of population	2.7 per cent
Paupers on indoor relief as percentage of population	0.7 per cent
Pauper total as percentage of population	3.4 per cent[c]

Notes:

[a] RAS 1885, Table 4, p. 35*.
[b] RAS 1885, Table 1, p. 26*.
[c] RAS 1885, p. 28*.

Table 1.7. *Calculation of paupers as a percentage of population, German Empire, area of the residential relief system only, 1885*

Paupers on outdoor relief	1,078,921
Paupers on indoor relief	288,426[a]
Pauper total	1,367,347[a]
Population (1885 Census)	39,871,150[b]
Paupers on outdoor relief as percentage of population	2.7 per cent[b]
Paupers on indoor relief as percentage of population	0.7 per cent
Pauper total as percentage of population	3.4 per cent[c]

Notes:
[a] RAS 1885, Table 4, p. 35*.
[b] RAS 1885, Table 1, p. 26*.
[c] RAS 1885, p. 28*.

Since Bavaria and Alsace-Lorraine operated a different system, their statistical returns are not always comparable with the rest of Germany, where the residential relief system operated. Since we shall need to refer to the figures for that area for the purpose of later calculations, it will be useful to provide them at this stage. It should be noted that on this occasion the percentages are actually identical for the two territories.[68]

No conversion factor is required for a comparison of expenditure. Like that for Germany, the English expenditure figures relate to the whole year, but in the English case not to the calendar year but that beginning on Lady-day (25 March). By excluding Bavaria and Alsace-Lorraine and concentrating on the area of the residential relief system, it is possible to exclude all capital expenditure and all expenditure on maintenance of buildings and salaries and to compare expenditure on poor relief alone. That is useful, particularly since salary costs in England and Wales were much greater than in Germany.[69]

---

[68] It was often asserted at the time that the introduction of the residential relief system with provincial relief authorities acting as fall-back relief authorities tended to increase the total burden of poor relief. Insofar as the frequent calls for a restoration of the *Heimatrecht* were intended to reduce the total burden of poor relief rather than merely to redistribute it among local authorities, they can be seen to have been based on false assumptions. For the debate and reform proposals see Münsterberg, *Deutsche Armengesetzgebung*, pp. 183–210 and 320–75.

[69] Aschrott, *English poor law system*, p. 193.

Poor relief expenditure

Table 1.8. *Poor relief expenditure, German Empire, area of the residential relief system only, 1885*

Total poor relief expenditure	47,289,181 M[a]
Population (1885 Census)	39,871,150[b]
Expenditure on relief per 100 of population	118.605 M
On the basis of 1 Mark = 1 shilling	£5.930 (i.e. £5.18s.7d)
Number of paupers	1,367,347[c]
Expenditure on relief per pauper	34.585 M
On the basis of 1 Mark = 1 shilling	£1.729 (i.e. £1.14s.6d)

Notes:
[a] RAS 1885, Table 14, p. 51*.
[b] RAS 1885, Table 1, p. 26*.
[c] RAS 1885, p. 28*.

Table 1.9. *Poor relief expenditure, England and Wales, year ended 25 March 1885*

Total poor relief expenditure	£5,579,445[a]
Estimated population mid-1884	26,922,000[b]
Expenditure per 100 of population	£20.724 (i.e. £20.14.6d)[c]
Estimated number of paupers	1,766,884
Expenditure on relief per pauper	£3.158 (i.e. £3.3s.2d)

Notes:
[a] LGB Report 1885–6, p. 108. This includes expenditure of £1,188,012 on lunatics in asylums and licensed houses. Although it is only that paid to the relevant institutions for patients, it is likely to include a contribution to the cost of salaries and maintenance of the institution, and is therefore probably somewhat higher than what would be spent on mere maintenance of the patient. But much the same objection applies to the German figures. Münsterberg, 'Armenstatistik', pp. 426–7.
[b] Mitchell, *Historical statistics*, p. 9.
[c] For 1849 the English figures are £21.714 compared with £5.27 for Prussia. The Prussian expenditure figure is calculated from the 5,706296 Thaler, given in the table reproduced in C. B. A. Emminghaus, *Das Armenwesen und die Armengesetzgebung in Europäischen Staaten* (Berlin, 1870), p. 63, col. 3. The figures in the comparative Table B in the same publication are useless.

Table 1.10. *Poor relief expenditure, England and Wales, corrected for proportion of indoor to outdoor paupers*

Total poor relief expenditure after correcting for the difference between England and Wales and UWG in the proportion of indoor to outdoor paupers	£5,135,299.5
Expenditure on relief per 100 of population. Instead of £20.724, it is £19.075, i.e.	**£19.1s.6d**
Expenditure on relief per pauper. Instead of £3.158, it is £2.906, i.e.	**£2.18s.1d**

2

The urban poor law

(A) THE 'DEUTSCHE VEREIN'

In the absence of inspectors to comment and advise, and of a central authority to disseminate information on best practice through its annual reports, and of regularly published statistics to measure and compare performance, how did those responsible for administering poor relief in Germany actually manage? They did what energetic persons in the nineteenth century usually did in the absence of provision from the State. In 1880 they founded an association for their common needs, the *Deutsche Verein für Armenpflege und Wohltätigkeit*, often referred to as the *Deutsche Verein* (DV).[1] Like similar associations in Britain and Germany, it was run by a chairman and steering committee and held meetings annually in different places to read and discuss papers of common interest. Although in this period not particularly influential in government circles, the DV was intellectually an altogether more impressive body than its English counterpart, the Poor Law Conferences.[2] Over the years there were few subjects of importance that it did not investigate and debate. Its published papers and proceedings form the most accessible source of information on the practice of poor relief and kindred matters in Imperial Germany.

The DV concerned itself early on with the provision of statistics. At its second congress in 1881 it established a statistical commission and

---

[1] For the best introduction to this body see Florian Tennstedt, 'Fürsorgegeschichte und Vereinsgeschichte. 100 Jahre Deutscher Verein in der Geschichte der deutschen Fürsorge', ZSR, 27 (1981), 72–100. For the work and publications of the first twenty-five years see Emil Münsterberg, *Generalbericht über die Tätigkeit des deutschen Vereins für Armenpflege und Wohltätigkeit während der ersten 25 Jahre seines Bestehens 1880–1905, nebst Verzeichnissen der Vereinsschriften und alphabetischen Register zu den Vereinsschriften. Schriften des deutschen Vereins*, vol. 72 (Leipzig, 1905). See also Hans Muthesius (ed.), *Beiträge zur Entwicklung der deutschen Fürsorge. 75 Jahre Deutscher Verein* (Cologne and Berlin, 1955); Eberhardt Orthband, *Der Deutsche Verein in der Geschichte der deutschen Fürsorge* (Frankfurt, 1980).

[2] District Conferences dated from 1868; the Central Poor Law Conferences from 1871.

embarked on a survey of poor relief using individual index cards. This was published in 1886.[3] Compared to the almost contemporary *Reichsarmenstatistik*, this survey had all the strengths and weaknesses of voluntarism. Its range of questions were more extensive and flexible, carefully designed to produce information on the contentious UWG system. It was, however, limited to authorities with links to the DV, i.e. to a tiny fraction of mostly urban authorities.

During the 1890s the DV turned its attention to establishing common procedures for the presentation of information on expenditure for poor relief. It was in no position to do this for the whole Empire, but in 1902 it published a survey of financial statistics for 108 towns with a population of over 25,000. That exercise was repeated in 1908, by which time the number of participating towns had risen to 130. Although an impressive achievement, it covered less than a quarter of the population of the Empire.[4] It is some indication of the remoteness of the small rural relief authorities that, when the DV sent out invitations to its second conference in 1881, it did not know how to communicate even indirectly with the rural authorities outside Prussia.[5] Its membership never encompassed the world of the village headman and elders; it studied it as a phenomenon, but did so from afar.[6]

The establishment of common procedures and the publication of statistics were intended to diagnose practical shortcomings. It was part of the DV's long-standing aim to identify best practice and to disseminate information on it. This found its most prominent expression in the repeated attention paid to the methods of poor relief associated with Elberfeld. Although the so-called Elberfeld system had received some publicity since 1858 at least, it was largely through the DV that it acquired its subsequent prominence.[7]

[3] C. V. Böhmert, *Das Armenwesen in 77 deutschen Städten und einigen Landarmenverbänden. Allgemeiner Theil* (Dresden, 1886).

[4] H. Silbergleit (ed.), *Finanzstatistik der Armenverwaltungen von 108 deutschen Städten. Schriften des deutschen Vereins für Armenpflege und Wohlthätigkeit*, Heft 61 (Leipzig, 1902); H. Silbergleit (ed.), *Finanzstatistik der Armenverwaltungen von 130 deutschen Städten 1901–1905. Schriften des deutschen Vereins für Armenpflege und Wohltätigkeit*, Heft 78 (Leipzig, 1908).

[5] Münsterberg, *Generalbericht*, p. 8.

[6] See comments in chapter 1, n. 45.

[7] There are descriptions of the Elberfeld system in C. B. A. Emminghaus (ed.), *Das Armenwesen und die Armengesetzgebung in den europäischen Staaten* (Berlin, 1870), translated and abridged as *Poor relief in different parts of Europe* (London, 1873). A report first given in 1858 at a Church congress in Hamburg was to be reprinted together with other material on Elberfeld in C. V. Böhmert, *Das Armenwesen. Allgemeiner Theil* (Dresden, 1886), *Specieller Theil, 2. Abtheilung* (Dresden, 1888). See also Karl Kayser, *Die Stellung der ehrenamtlichen Organe in der Armenpflege, Schriften des deutschen Vereins*, vol. 49 (Leipzig, 1900); Emil Münsterberg, *Das Elberfelder System. Schriften des Deutschen Vereins*, vol. 63 (Leipzig, 1903). Later publications include Elsa Schlaudraff, *Ein Vergleich zwischen dem Elberfelder, dem*

(B) THE ELBERFELD SYSTEM

The Elberfeld system is practically the only aspect of German poor relief that is at all widely known. Together with neighbouring Barmen, Elberfeld was one of the earliest centres of industrialisation in Germany. Its expanding textile industry attracted a large labour force, and like some English textile towns it diversified via textile machinery into engineering in general. Its population expanded enormously in consequence.

The former Duchy of Berg, to which Elberfeld belonged and which was incorporated into Prussia in 1815, was an area of Calvinistic Protestantism. Its textile towns produced many examples of the classic bourgeoisie, combining a strong work ethic and strict inner discipline with a commitment to social and moral improvement. It was an area in which communal responsibility for the poor, introduced during the French occupation, was for much of the first half of the century opposed by the churches, who regarded poor relief, i.e. charity, as one of their essential functions. They only relinquished this claim reluctantly because of insufficient means. A communal poor relief authority established in 1841 found itself overwhelmed by the crisis conditions of the late 1840s. In 1851 in reaction to rapidly rising costs and what they regarded as indiscriminate administration, the churches declared their determination to resume control of relief. The Lutherans, who were few and well-to-do, persevered until 1854, but the Calvinists and the Catholics realised within a year that this was beyond their means. The introduction of a new system of communal poor relief in 1853 was, however, strongly influenced by the determination of the

Table 2.1. *Population of Elberfeld*

1819	22,000
1850	39,000
1870	71,000
1910	170,000

Source: J. Reulecke, *Geschichte der Urbanisierung in Deutschland* (Frankfurt a.M., 1985), Table 3.

Strassburger und dem Frankfurter System in der Armenpflege (Nürnberg-Zirndorf, 1932); *Hilfe von Mensch zu Mensch, 100 Jahre Elberfelder Armenpflegesystem 1853–1953*, Stadtverwaltung Wuppertal (ed.) (Wuppertal-Elberfeld, 1953); Giovanna Berger, *Die ehrenamtliche Tätigkeit in der Sozialarbeit. Motive, Tendenzen, Probleme, dargestellt am Beispiel des Elberfelder Systems* (Frankfurt, Bern and Las Vegas, 1979).

Calvinist or Reformed congregation to play a larger role in these matters. Indeed it was regarded by them originally as no more than a temporary expedient. In better times they expected to be able to return to the abortive attempt of 1851.[8]

It is useful to bear in mind what was not new in 1853. The old system had relied on honorary service, it had divided the town into districts and the districts in turn into areas. Each area had been served by a visitor, and each district had been under a superintendent.

The new system differed from its predecessor in increasing the number of visitors so as to reduce their case-load, and in decentralising decision-making. Previously there had been fifty honorary visitors, whose function had been merely that of investigation and report. All decisions on relief were taken by the twenty-three members of the central authority. They too served in an honorary capacity. The ten districts with their superintendent were each to be divided into fifteen areas, thereby reducing the case-load of each visitor to no more than four families. At the same time as their work was made more manageable, it was made more interesting. It was the visitors for each district, meeting under the chairmanship of their superintendent, who were responsible for decision-making. The superintendents in turn reported back to the central authority, who controlled finance.

The function of the visitors now extended well beyond investigation. They became responsible for the oversight of the poor, and, since relief was given only for a fortnight at a time, they could exercise a firm control over them. That individual oversight and control aimed to ensure 'responsible' conduct and restore the poor rapidly to the labour market. No more effective form of disciplining the poor in the values of the new society could have been devised. The visitors were officially urged to combine love with firmness. Those at the receiving end no doubt responded to the intrusion of these 'Pottkieker' (cooking-pot snoopers) with equally mixed feelings.[9] Those who would not co-operate found themselves excluded from out-relief and handed over to the corrective powers of the police.

---

[8] Berger, *Ehrenamtliche Tätigkeit*, pp. 33–4; Bernd Weisbrod, 'Wohltätigkeit und "symbolische Gewalt" in der Frühindustrialisierung. Städtische Armut und Armenpolitik im Wuppertal', in H. Mommsen und W. Schulze (eds.), *Vom Elend der Handarbeit. Probleme historischer Unterschichtenforschung* (Stuttgart, 1981), pp. 334–57; Barbara Lube, 'Mythos und Wirklichkeit des Elberfelder Systems', in Karl-Hermann Beeck (ed.), *Gründerzeit. Versuch einer Grenzbestimmung in Wuppertal* (Cologne, 1984), pp. 158–84.

[9] For the slang term see J. Reulecke, 'Das "Elberfelder System" als Reiseziel – Johann Hinrich Wichern (1857), William Rathbone (1871), Andrew Doyle (1871)', in *Reisen im Bergischen Land*, vol. II (Neustadt an der Aisch, 1984), p. 226.

Like all German towns Elberfeld had relied on the honorary service of its citizens already before 1853. German citizens were legally obliged to serve for at least three years, if called upon to do so, and were subject to severe fines if they refused. The new system greatly increased the demands on the citizen body, while at the same time making the work highly responsible. The authors of the scheme were prominent bankers and industrialists who were also prominent church leaders, and the churches rose to the challenge to imbue the poor with their own values. The church councils nominated respectable and reliable citizens for the various offices and their proposals were confirmed by the civic authorities.[10] With powerful and respected leaders deeply committed to the system, with a call couched in terms of Christian service – an expression of 'love from man to man', as the slogan had it – the 160 citizens were forthcoming.[11] The close scrutiny of applicants for relief, the determination to enforce the law on the financial obligations of relatives,[12] and the active supervision of those in receipt of relief soon resulted in striking reductions in total expenditure. At the same time expenditure per pauper rose as part of a policy to provide adequately for the basic needs of the deserving.

By 1861 all thought of returning poor relief to the churches had been dropped. A revised ordinance (*Armenordnung*) increased the number of districts to eighteen and of areas in the care of a single visitor to 252. The 'Instructions' laid down in great detail the duties of visitors, superintendents and central poor relief authority, the procedures, the tariff for relief and other matters of this kind. As the population expanded, so did the number of visitors. By 1886 there were 364 visitors; by 1900 there were 518 with an average case-load of two.[13]

At first observers doubted whether the system could be sustained once the dominant influence of the founders, exceptionally dedicated individuals who combined economic, social and religious leadership, had passed. The subsequent expansion of the system put such doubts to rest. Attracted by its remarkable financial success and the prospects of effective social control that it held out, other Rhineland towns with similar economic and

---

[10] Berger, *Ehrenamtliche Tätigkeit*, p. 52.

[11] For an English example of the response of religious idealism to the transfer of functions from church to local government see the role played by certain Nonconformist churches in the recruitment of prominent business people to the Birmingham Town Council in the age of the 'Municipal Gospel'. E. P. Hennock, *Fit and proper persons: ideal and reality in nineteenth-century urban government* (London, 1973), Book I, Part II.

[12] This applied to a wider circle of relatives than in England. Andrew Doyle, *The poor law system of Elberfeld: first report of the Local Government Board*, Appendix, p. 250. BPP 1872 C.516 XXVIII, 1.

[13] See the table in Berger, *Ehrenamtliche Tätigkeit*, p. 58.

social structures began to introduce the system, beginning with Barmen and Krefeld in 1862/3. In the 1870s it spread beyond the Rhineland, and after 1880 this process accelerated under the influence of the DV.[14]

By then the structural changes associated with the growth of cities made the strict imitation of a form of administration designed for medium-sized towns somewhat problematic. Many cities, particularly larger ones, adopted what may be described as modifications of the original model, while nevertheless claiming to be in the true line of descent from what had become prestigious and successful. Sometimes the power of the district chairman was enhanced by allocating all visitors to the district as a whole, not each to an individual area. It was left to the chairman, to whom all applications went in the first instance, to appoint a suitable visitor to each case. A further modification of the decentralisation of decision-taking that had characterised the original model occurred where the district committee was confined to making recommendations, while the decision on relief was left to the central body. Whatever the modifications, recruitment of honorary visitors in numbers large enough to facilitate a small case-load remained a feature of all reforms that claimed to be descended from the Elberfeld system.[15] The diffusion of this feature suggests that this form of administration with its heavy demand on honorary service was no longer dependent on its original link with a particular kind of religious commitment. It was able to appeal successfully to a sense of civic solidarity and in turn to foster such sentiments.[16]

There is no indication of how long the churches in Elberfeld acted as recruiting agencies for the visitors and superintendents. A report of 1871 referred to nominations being made in each district.[17] Many of those originally recruited for the obligatory three years continued in office voluntarily for far longer terms.[18] The social class from which this formidable body of visitors was drawn is a matter of the greatest interest to

[14] George Steinmetz, *Regulating the social: the welfare state and local politics in Imperial Germany* (Princeton, NJ, 1993), p. 159, for a select chronological list of towns adopting the Elberfeld system.

[15] Kayser, *Stellung*, pp. 34–44; Sachsse and Tennstedt, *Geschichte der Armenfürsorge in Deutschland*, vol. 2 (Stuttgart, 1988), pp. 23–5. For a modification of the system by the employment of salaried officials without in any way reducing the need for honorary visitors, see pp. 61–2 below.

[16] J. Reulecke, 'Formen bürgerlich-sozialen Engagement in Deutschland und England im 19. Jahrhundert', in J. Kocka (ed.), *Arbeiter und Bürger im 19. Jahrhundert* (Munich, 1986), pp. 264–6, drawing on evidence from Böhmert, *Das Armenwesen*, published in 1886 under the auspices of the DV.

[17] Andrew Doyle, *The poor law system of Elberfeld*, in *First report of the Local Government Board*, Appendix, p. 246, BPP 1872 C.516 XXVIII, 1.

[18] Kayser, *Stellung*, p. 19. This study of the system in German towns in general, dated 1900, referred to some visitors serving as much as twenty-five to forty-five years in office.

historians. Descriptions suggest a spectrum that included the professional and business classes, white-collar workers and master craftsmen. I know of no information on the relative proportions for any period earlier than 1903. In that year 25 per cent of Dresden's 795 honorary poor relief officials were drawn from the professions, 25 per cent from artisans and tradesmen (*Handwerker und Gewerbetreibende*), 20 per cent from commercial occupations (*Handels-Gewerbetreibende*). In what was not much of an industrial city, only 8 per cent were industrial entrepreneurs and manufacturers (*Unternehmer und Fabrikanten*).[19] These figures testify to the attraction of this kind of service for the lower middle classes, both the traditional class of master craftsmen and the new class of white-collar workers.

Dresden's total of 2,846 honorary offices indicates the importance of honorary public service in urban Germany. Those participating in tax assessment outnumbered even those in poor relief.

(C) HONORARY V. SALARIED SERVICE: ENGLAND AND WALES

Perhaps the biggest difference between the Elberfeld system and the administration of the urban Poor Law in England and Wales lay in the role that the large number of visitors played in the German administration of relief. The labour-intensive nature of the German system was only possible because it was able to call on the unpaid obligatory service of its citizens. Such a tradition of unpaid obligatory service by householders had once also existed in England, for instance the obligatory service by the overseers of the poor in well over 15,000 parishes before 1834. That was, however, condemned as wayward and inefficient, and the practice was deliberately replaced in 1834 by the use of salaried full-time officials, appointed by and accountable to elected bodies.

What had been abolished in the administration of poor relief was obligatory honorary (i.e. unpaid) service; what took its place was the voluntary honorary service of the elected Guardians. It was voluntary honorary service by elected persons that sustained not only the Poor Law authorities but numerous other local authorities in the nineteenth century.

---

[19] Table in Wolfgang Hofmann, 'Aufgaben und Struktur der kommunalen Selbstverwaltung in der Zeit der Hochindustrialisierung', in Kurt G. A. Jeserich, Hans Pohl, Georg-Christoph von Unruh (eds.), *Deutsche Verwaltungsgeschichte*, vol. 3 (Stuttgart, 1984), p. 618. This does not take into account the further 342 honorary offices concerned with the care of orphans. Kayser, *Stellung*, p. 13, provides a table for Elberfeld and a separate and more detailed table for thirteen other towns, but these do not distinguish between industrialists and master craftsmen, or between different status levels among the commercial occupations. Nor does the table in Münsterberg, *Elberfelder System*, p. 25.

The Guardians were in some respects like the German district committees of visitors, for both made the decisions on the relief to be granted to applicants. But in marked contrast to Germany, the Guardians were required to interpose a full-time salaried official between themselves and the poor.[20]

Faced with unreliable and inefficient citizens rendering obligatory honorary service, German reformers of urban poor relief had taken the opposite road. They had devised forms of supervision and control and had spread the load to make the job more manageable. The result was a huge expansion of honorary service in the course of the nineteenth century, as population grew and the number of those with some margin of time and energy to spare from the task of earning a living also increased. Far from withering away, honorary citizen service became a characteristic feature of German civic culture.

The English insistence on salaried professionalism had economic consequences. On that basis poor law administration could not be labour-intensive without being ruinously expensive. The introduction of elected Boards of Guardians based on a ratepayers' franchise ensured, moreover, that poor law administration was governed by considerations of economy. Unions kept their staff small, and the relieving officers responsible for outdoor relief were grossly overworked. In 1871 the Liverpool poor law authority employed 14½ officers for the administration of outdoor relief – six relieving officers, three assistants, one full-time and one part-time medical visitor, two warrant officers and two cross-visitors to check consistency across the districts. They cost £1,538 in salaries. The relieving officers' case-load in the six districts ranged from 372 to 846.[21] In 1868 the national average case load per relieving officer was 250–300.

The relieving officer was expected to investigate all applications, to sit with the Guardians in order to report and advise while they made their decisions, to pay all allowances, to visit those in receipt of outdoor relief at proper intervals and to report if their circumstances changed.[22] Faced with such a case-load even the most conscientious officer had to skimp on investigation and resort to largely indiscriminate methods of relief.

One of the first English descriptions of the Elberfeld system commented on the plight of the relieving officers and the impossibility of informed

---

[20] In the exercise of their responsibility for the indoor paupers they also had to act through a full-time salaried official, the workhouse master.
[21] Rathbone Papers, University of Liverpool, IX.9.21. Press cuttings of Liverpool Select Vestry meetings 1873.
[22] Aschrott, *English poor law system*, pp. 224–7.

recommendations. Twenty years later a Poor Law inspector drew the same contrast between the two countries.[23] When the English authorities investigated the Elberfeld system, they concluded that it belonged to a different world from their own. Of the district meetings Inspector Doyle wrote in 1871:

There is no corresponding administrative body in our poor law system. The counterpart to it with us would be a meeting of fourteen relieving officers, unpaid, each with a district comprising not more than four cases, bound to administer relief in accordance with certain fixed and very stringent rules, each responsible to the majority of his fellows, and all responsible to the higher administrative tribunal, the town administration.

Turning to the fact that there was no workhouse test, he explained that the inquiry preceding the granting of outdoor relief was 'so close and searching, so absolutely inquisitorial, that no man who could possibly escape from it would submit to it'. He gave details from the questionnaire that visitors had to use for the inquiry, adding that among the 'minute regulations' with which the granting of relief was 'fenced round' was the keeping of a wages book with information on earnings entered by the employer. The close scrutiny constantly exercised by the visitors resulted in 60 per cent of cases coming off relief within the course of a month. He summed up his impressions:

I am satisfied . . . that in Elberfeld and the few other towns that have adopted it, this part of the system works with complete success. Possibly, however, in England it might be less difficult to reconcile the poor to such a system than it would be to find among the well-to-do middle-class families fit and willing agents for its administration.[24]

Seventeen years later, Inspector Davy wrote:

The attempt to introduce the machinery of unpaid visitors alone into the constitution of an English union, except perhaps as a subsidiary to the investigations of the relieving officers, would almost certainly fail.[25]

---

[23] C. B. P. Bosanquet, *London: some account of its growth, charitable agencies and wants* (London, 1868), pp. 197–9 and 216–22; J. S. Davy, *Report on the Elberfeld system of poor law relief in some German towns*, in *Reports on the Elberfeld poor law system*, p. 42. BPP 1888 C.5341 LXXX, 313.

[24] Doyle, *The poor law system of Elberfeld*, pp. 247, 253–4, 256 and 265.

[25] J. S. Davy, *Report on the Elberfeld system of poor law relief in some German towns*, in *Reports on the Elberfeld poor law system and German workmen's colonies*, pp. 23, 25 and 41–2. BPP 1888 C.5341 LXXX, 313.

No one contemplated replacing the relieving officer. Hence there was no prospect of reviving the old obligation of unpaid service within the reformed Poor Law.

The ideal of a rational philanthropy based on individual investigation, on suiting the gift to the circumstances of the individual and thereby using the power that alms-giving gave to influence the conduct of the poor, was as much part of British as of German culture. In the absence of general compulsion it found expression through voluntary service. Hence those most interested in the Elberfeld system were not Poor Law administrators but people who wished to harness the powerful tradition of voluntary charitable work to the case-work ideal. The societies which they hoped to found or had already founded were intended to do what, as everyone agreed, the Poor Law could not possibly achieve.[26]

(D) HONORARY V. SALARIED SERVICE: GERMANY

It is surely remarkable that in the Germany of the turn of the twentieth century, characterised by increasing reliance on professional expertise in many areas of life, including that of municipal administration, the principle of honorary citizen service should have survived for public poor relief. What had been ancient even in the 1850s, but had been imbued with new life by religious commitment and civic pride, could have been expected to decline and fail with the increased mobility of population and the great expansion of towns that marked the period 1890–1914.

Indeed in Berlin, far and away the largest of the OAVs, where poor relief had been organised on the basis of honorary service well before the reforms in Elberfeld, the system began to decline under the impact of industrialisation, immigration and party politics from the 1860s onwards.[27] In the later part of the century Berlin served British commentators as an example of the inappropriateness of the Elberfeld system for the impersonal conditions of large cities. But, in 1903, it was reorganised under Emil Münsterberg, a strong advocate of Elberfeld principles, to take account of the growth of the

---

[26] For the interest shown in the Elberfeld system in Britain for over half a century see E. P. Hennock, 'German models for British social reform: compulsory insurance and the Elberfeld system of poor relief', in R. Muhs, J. Paulmann and W. Steinmetz (eds.), *Aneignung und Abwehr. Interkultureller Transfer zwischen Deutschland und Grossbritannien im 19. Jahrhundert. Veröffentlichung Nr. 32 des Arbeitskreises Deutsche England-Forschung* (Bodenheim, 1998), pp. 127–42.

[27] On Berlin prior to 1903 see Ludovica Scarpa, *Gemeinwohl und Lokale Macht. Honorationen und Gemeindewesen in der Luisenstadt im 19. Jahrhundert* (Munich, 1995); Böhmert, *Das Armenwesen, Specieller Teil*, Part I. On the post-1903 administration see n. 29 below.

city. An intermediate layer of committees, drawn partly from the district
committees and partly from the central body, restored the effectiveness of
central control.[28] The reform demonstrated that with flexibility the main
principles of the Elberfeld system could still be applied even in the biggest
city of the Empire. But there were difficulties in recruiting 'visitors',
especially in the newer areas of the city. In 1908 Berlin had close on
4,000 'visitors', but Münsterberg admitted that ideally it required
8–9,000 and that there was no possibility of recruiting such large numbers.
In consequence cases were not revisited as often as was desirable to maintain strict control.[29] Berlin with its population in 1910 of over two million
was, however, the exception, not the rule.

Hamburg, which with a population of 931,000 was then the second-
largest city of the Empire, had reformed its poor relief administration as
late as 1893 with conspicuous success, increasing the number of its honorary
visitors fourfold. In 1902 it stood at 1,560 with a ratio of 5.8 cases per
visitor.[30] Leipzig, Munich, Dresden, the next largest German cities, all
relied on honorary visitors for their poor relief administration, which,
without being identical in all its features with that in Elberfeld, was
organised on similar principles.[31]

That is not to say that the administration of poor relief was totally
insulated from the trend towards the growing power of salaried officials
that characterised many other areas of municipal administration.[32] Salaried
officials, previously merely messengers or clerks engaged in keeping
records, began to be employed in a number of towns to back up the
work of visitors, undertaking investigations, supervising certain cases or
issuing orders for medical treatment. The mobility of the poor in large
cities and the possibility that applicants for relief might be entitled to
benefit under compulsory insurance had made the investigation of circumstances more complicated. Cutting as it did across the deeply held belief in
the virtue of honorary service, the employment of salaried officials was
passionately debated at meetings of the DV and monitored with suspicion.

---

[28] The same principle had been effectively applied in Hamburg in 1893: *Foreign and Colonial Systems of Poor Relief, Royal Commission on the Poor Laws*, Appendix, vol. XXXIII, pp. 111 and 122–3, BPP 1910 Cd.5441 LV.

[29] *Foreign and colonial systems of poor relief, Royal Commission on the Poor Laws*, Appendix, vol. XXXIII, pp. 112–24, BPP 1910 Cd.5441 LV, but especially Münsterberg in *Minutes of evidence, Royal Commission on the Poor Laws*, Appendix, vol. IX, QQ.100300–590, BPP 1910 Cd.5068 XLIX.

[30] Münsterberg, *Elberfelder System*, p. 43; Münsterberg, Evidence to Royal Commission on the Poor Laws, Q.100300(6).

[31] Kayser, *Stellung*, pp. 34–7.

[32] Hofmann, 'Aufgaben und Struktur der kommunalen Selbstverwaltung'.

Directors of poor relief knew that to employ officials for anything but strictly auxiliary purposes was to invite conflict with those on whom the system basically relied.[33] They proceeded mostly with the greatest caution.

There was one important exception. Bold innovation came, as it often does, from the frontier region between two cultures, in this case from Strassburg (with a population of 179,000 in 1910). Alsace-Lorraine, of which it was the principal town, had been under French administration prior to 1871 and that implied a very different approach to poor relief. Until 1910 it was therefore treated as a special case and excluded from the operation of the UWG. Situated between two cultures, the French reliance on officials and their dislike of tax-provided poor relief, the German determination that the way in which their taxes were spent on the poor should be under citizen control. Strassburg had every incentive to approach its problems in its own way.

Since the middle of the century Strassburg had relied on a small number of honorary *inspecteurs des pauvres*, each responsible for the investigation of applications for poor relief in his district. They submitted their recommendations to a central poor relief authority that made the decisions in accordance with a closely defined set of instructions. By Elberfeld standards the honorary inspectors had an excessive case-load even in normal times. In times of special distress they were regularly supplemented by salaried officials from the central office. This niggardly use of honorary citizen service meant that investigation and supervision was inadequate and recommendations less discriminating than they should have been. In the 1880s it was decided to organise the outer suburbs on the Elberfeld system, but that also proved unsatisfactory.[34]

The break with the past came in 1906 under the direction of Rudolf Schwander, its recently appointed *Armendirektor*.[35] The new regime was characterised by a bold acceptance of salaried officials and a clear division between their duties and those of honorary visitors. The former were to be employed for the work of investigation, leaving honorary visitors with the work of supervision and advice. The whole city was divided into a small number of districts each under a district commission chaired by a member of the central poor relief authority. Each district was intended to have no more than 600 cases, and a large number of visitors, anything up to 200,

---

[33] Kayser, *Stellung*, pp. 44–50. See also Münsterberg's comment in his evidence to the Royal Commission on the Poor Laws, Q.100300(6).

[34] Wilhelm Steinhilber, '25 Jahre Strassburger System', *Deutsche Zeitschrift für Wohlfahrtspflege*, 7(2) (May 1931), 61–7.

[35] For Schwander see also p. 323 below.

were attached to it. Eight of these were nominated by the central authority
to constitute the district commission. Each district also had a full-time
salaried official attached to it and working from the *Armenamt*, the office of
the central relief authority. All applications for relief went to him for
investigation and it was on his recommendation that decisions were
made by the district commission. It was then left to the district commission
to appoint a visitor of their choice to supervise the case. For short-term
cases or for hardened paupers, who might require stronger discipline, the
salaried official could be left in charge. No visitor was supposed to have
more than three cases in his care. Once appointed to a case, he became the
sole channel of communication between the pauper and the office, but had
no powers of decision. These rested with the commission on the advice of
the salaried official.[36]

First introduced in 1906, the Strassburg system redefined the role of full-
time salaried officers and part-time honorary visitors, the two components
of the Elberfeld system, and was to be of great influence in the post-war
period.[37]

(E) WORKERS' INSURANCE

One reason why investigations by full-time salaried officials became more
important in the cities after the 1880s was the possibility that applicants for
poor relief might be entitled to social insurance benefits. There was no
sharp distinction between the clientele of social insurance and poor relief
and this immediately complicated the administrative task of relief authorities.[38] One merit of the redefinition of the roles of salaried officers and
honorary visitors, which characterised the Strassburg system, was that it
accommodated itself to that development.

The 1890s saw the beginning of an interest in the effect of social
insurance on German poor relief, and particularly in the extent to which
it had reduced its financial burden. An investigation by the DV in 1894 was

---

[36] For the Strassburg system, apart from Steinhilber, see Elsa Schlaudraff, *Ein Vergleich zwischen dem
Elberfelder, dem Strassburger und dem Frankfurter System in der Armenpflege* (Nürnberg-Zirndorf,
1932); Christoph Sachsse, *Mütterlichkeit als Beruf. Sozialarbeit, Sozialreform und Frauenbewegung
1871–1929* (Frankfurt, 1986), pp. 42–7, largely echoed in Sachsse and Tennstedt, *Geschichte der
Armenfürsorge in Deutschland*, vol. 2 (Stuttgart, 1988), pp. 25–7.

[37] Sachsse sees the Strassburg system as providing a model for the later distinction between administrators and social workers. Sachsse, *Mütterlichkeit*, pp. 43–4 and 46–7.

[38] For the contrast with the intention of the British legislation of the period 1908–13 and the way in
which that was, however, rapidly subverted by war-time inflation, see p. 225 and n. 33, below.

followed in 1895 by another from the Imperial Statistical Office.[39] Neither of them provided comprehensive statistical evidence; they were mainly content to collect the opinions of relief authorities. But by the end of our period the continuing interest in these matters had produced some relevant if limited figures.

Since the victims of industrial accidents and their dependants would not previously have been dependent on poor relief, there was no comprehensive source of information on the extent to which accident insurance relieved the authorities from expenditure. What could be done was to monitor any temporary relief granted while they waited for the relevant authorities to decide on their case. The impact of sickness insurance on the expenditure of relief authorities was cushioned in many localities by the existence of compulsory insurance well before 1883. The fullest figures were those for the impact of invalidity and old age pensions on poor relief expenditure for the aged and infirm. This was where pensions had most frequently to be supplemented by poor relief on account of their inadequacy, particularly in the early years.[40] Thus in Berlin 16 per cent of male and 20 per cent of female invalidity pensioners of the local pensions board needed to have their pension supplemented in 1910. For old-age pensioners the figures were 8 per cent of males and 19 per cent of females. Berlin was considered to have been an extreme case; other areas produced totals for both kinds of pensioners of 8–12 per cent.[41] These figures still suggest considerable savings on a major category of paupers.

Despite this evidence and a widely held opinion that social insurance had indeed reduced the burden on relief authorities, the expenditure totals actually increased. There was no sign that poor law authorities were able or willing to reduce the excessive financial burden of which they had complained for years. Totals increased not only absolutely but relative to population. No one appears to have measured these against the increase in the cost of living. But where we have per capita figures the increase was so great that it is unnecessary to agonise over the most appropriate way in which rises in living-costs should be measured.

In Bavaria poor relief expenditure per capita increased by 20 per cent from 1901 to 1907; in towns of over 20,000 inhabitants by 29 per cent.

---

[39] R. Freund, *Armenpflege und Arbeiterversicherung. Schriften des Deutschen Vereins für Armenpflege und Wohltätigkeit*, Heft 21 (Leipzig, 1895); *Vierteljahrshefte z. Statistik des Deutschen Reichs* (1897), vol. II.

[40] For these pensions in general see chapter 10, section (iv), pp. 191–3 below.

[41] Christoph Conrad, *Vom Greis zum Rentner. Der Strukturwandel des Alters in Deutschland zwischen 1830 und 1930* (Göttingen, 1994), pp. 296–7; F. Zahn, 'Arbeiterversicherung und Armenwesen in Deutschland', *Zeitschrift d. Königl. Bayerischen Statistischen Landesamts*, 43(1) (1911), 11.

A table of six large cities (population over 100,000 in 1910), which gives per capita expenditure for 1885–1908/9, shows in one case a 14 per cent increase, while that of the remaining five ranged from 66 per cent to 110 per cent.[42]

What explanations are there for this paradoxical development? There is some evidence that the operation of insurance made new forms of expenditure inevitable. Sickness benefit for patients admitted to hospital could leave dependants inadequately provided for, and the limited period for which it was available left those not yet able to return to work dependent on poor relief.[43]

The greater familiarity with the value of medical treatment that increased the uptake of sickness insurance was not limited to insurance contributors. This 'medicalisation of the working class', as it has been called, would have had implications for the dependants of the insured and have acted as an example to their neighbours. The effect would have been a rising demand for the medical services of the poor law. The spread of antiseptic and aseptic methods in surgery, and the innovations in medical diagnosis, both of which made hospitals more acceptable, would also have driven up the cost of medical relief, particularly in cities.

There were more general ways in which insurance acted as a stimulus. A clear example is provided by the Bavarian poor law regulation of 1899, which laid down that, whenever insurance pensioners applied for supplementation, half their pension should be disregarded in setting the level of relief. From 1904 Munich sanctioned the same levels of support for anyone over seventy, insurance pensioners or not.[44] In this particular matter Munich may have been exceptional, but greater generosity in setting levels of relief was common.[45]

There was also a growing interest in prevention, which led to the identification of new needs and the willingness to undertake new tasks. It blurred the distinction between the duties of urban local government in general and of urban poor relief in particular, and ultimately led to the reorganisation of welfare policy into municipal departments

---

[42] Zahn, 'Arbeiterversicherung und Armenwesen', pp. 15–7. In addition Cologne recorded a 54 per cent increase from 1890 to 1908.

[43] For the gap in insurance benefit between sickness insurance and invalidity insurance see pp. 234–5 below.

[44] Their maximum relief had been increased by 50 per cent already in 1893. W. Rudloff, *Die Wohlfahrtsstadt. Kommunale Ernährungs-, Fürsorge- und Wohnungspolitik am Beispiel Münchens 1910–1933* (Göttingen, 1998), pp. 610–11.

[45] Freund, *Armenpflege und Armenversicherung*, pp. 100–1; Zahn, *Arbeiterversicherung und Armenwesen*, p. 20.

(*Ämter*). These dealt each with a particular sphere such as housing, health, youth-work and unemployment, and provided a common administrative focus in which traditional poor relief was merged and the distinction between the relief authority and municipal provision (*Fürsorge*) in general was abolished. This development became general in the early Weimar years, but could be found already before 1914 in a number of cities.[46]

For our purpose the most relevant aspect was the care of orphans. While the poor relief authority was responsible for their support, a special court appointed guardians and usually did so via the municipal authority. In 1900 the Prussian law on the care and education of minors added duties for the care of neglected (*verwahrloste*) children, whether orphans or not, to those of the police authority. That was the background to the reorganisation of poor relief in Frankfurt in 1900, when municipal responsibility for local orphans and neglected children was vested in the poor law authority (*Armenamt*), which already paid for the maintenance of children in orphanages and foster-families. These responsibilities were underpinned by costly new administrative structures and by the appointment of a new type of female social worker, of which there were seven by 1908. Until the establishment of an approriate municipal department in 1914 the cost of these innovations fell on the budget of the poor law authority.[47] Few other cities, where these functions were also consolidated, were any quicker to remove the extra costs from the poor relief budget by establishing a municipal *Jugendamt*.[48]

Other initiatives followed the co-ordination of the work of public and voluntary bodies, such as subsidies towards the building of old peoples' homes and widowers' homes by the voluntary sector, and the provision of special funds for work among the physically or mentally handicapped.[49]

How does this picture of German urban poor relief, responding to the introduction of social insurance and the growing tax-base of the cities in an expanding economy with higher relief levels and embarking on new initiatives, compare with the contemporary situation in England and Wales? There is some similarity. Prevention rather than mere relief of destitution was proclaimed as the aim of the future, which ignited a debate

[46] Sachsse and Tennstedt, *Geschichte*, vol. 2, pp. 27–38.
[47] C. Sachsse, 'Frühformen der Leistungsverwaltung: die kommunale Armenfürsorge im deutschen Kaiserreich', *Jahrbuch für europ. Verwaltungsgeschichte*, 5 (1993), 1–20, esp. 11–16.
[48] Rudloff, *Wohlfahrtsstadt*, pp. 105–7.
[49] Sachsse, 'Frühformen', p. 20; H. Boettcher, *Fürsorge in Lübeck, vor und nach dem ersten Weltkrieg* (Lübeck, 1988), p. 45.

on its implications for the relation between the poor law and the other local authority services. But more striking are the differences.

For one thing there was no new money. Old age pensions did not effectively come on stream until 1911 nor national insurance benefits before 1913.[50] Until then Boards of Guardians found themselves struggling to cope with the rising cost of the aged and infirm and other traditional pauper categories. The biggest new development was the provision of poor law infirmaries in place of the infirmary wards of the workhouse, and attempts to upgrade standards. These could not but compare unfavourably with those of the voluntary hospitals at a time when they were in turn developing new services. All of which produced practically unlimited demands for capital expenditure and staffing salaries. German hospitals experienced the same wave of innovation and expansion, but public sector hospitals were the responsibility of the municipalities or universities. There were no separate poor law hospitals as in England.[51]

That brings us to the other big difference. The expansion of preventive services with their demands for new professional personnel and bureaucratic infrastructures, which the German historical literature has begun to record, can certainly be found in Britain, particularly in the public health services. But public health was the responsibility of municipal corporations, not Boards of Guardians. In Britain the existence of separate Poor Law Unions and Boards of Guardians, separately elected and administering areas that did not coincide with municipal boundaries, isolated them from these developments. The Royal Commission on the Poor Laws of 1905–9 provided an opportunity for a major debate on the appropriateness of two such separate authorities. Their duties, it could be argued, needed to be merged. That was similar to developments in the most active German cities. But in the debate on this issue, generated by the rival reports of the Royal Commission, the vested interest of numerous Boards of Guardians were at stake. These could not be overthrown.[52] In consequence the merging of functions organised under municipal departments, that had begun in Germany before 1914 and was accelerated by new war-time and post-war needs, did not happen in Britain until 1929. That was when the

---

[50] See p. 270 below.
[51] M. A. Crowther, *The workhouse system 1834–1929* (London, 1983); Brian Abel Smith, *The hospitals, 1800–1948* (London, 1964); A. Labisch and R. Spree (eds.), *Krankenhaus-Report 19. Jahrhundert* (Frankfurt a.M., 2001).
[52] *Royal Commission on the poor laws and relief of distress: report*, BPP 1909 Cd.4499, XXXVII, 1; McBriar, *An Edwardian mixed doubles.*

Boards of Guardians were finally abolished and their functions transferred to counties and county boroughs.

(F) WOMEN IN ADMINISTRATION

Home visits to assess need and to accompany relief with advice on attitudes and conduct were common to both countries. In Germany they were a feature of the administration of statutory poor relief; in England they were confined to the voluntary sector. English district visiting societies relied heavily on the work of women throughout the nineteenth century. Women did not merely have the necessary leisure; they were considered to have a special aptitude for the work, 'as they can freely enter the homes in which few men are ever found, except when confined by illness'. Everyone agreed that female volunteers moved more easily among wives and mothers and were more sympathetic to their problems.[53]

Voluntary societies that used women for domestic visiting among the poor were not unknown in Germany, but until almost the end of the century the domestic visiting, which played a central role in Germany in connection with public relief, was monopolised by men. The fact that the households which they visited were overwhelmingly headed by women made no difference to the view that this was a man's job. The adequate supply of men for what was regarded as honourable citizens' service meant that for a long time there was no need to reconsider these matters.[54]

The first German town to appoint women as official visitors was Ratibor (Upper Silesia) in 1874. In 1881 Kassel was the first large German city to follow suit, and the same year saw the subject up for debate at the meeting of the DV. It was to return to the subject in 1896. The arguments put forward in support of women visitors were those familiar from discussions in England, and won the support of the majority of the DV. Nevertheless the recruitment of women was slow and accompanied by much opposition in one town after another, including the threat of mass resignations. By 1911, in eighty-eight towns for which Steinmetz had information, women

---

[53] Frank Prochaska, *Women and philanthropy in nineteenth-century England* (Oxford, 1980), chapter 4. The quotation on p. 110 dates from the 1860s, but Prochaska makes it clear that women had been engaged in the organised visiting of the poor throughout the century, not to mention the unorganised visiting that had been a traditional aspect of women's lives. See also Anne Summers, 'A home from home – Women's philanthropic work in the nineteenth century', in Sandra Burman (ed.), *Fit work for women* (London, 1979).

[54] Steinmetz, *Regulating the social*, pp. 163–4, for figures on the ratio of women to men among those on long-term out-relief. See also Sachsse and Tennstedt, *Armenfürsorge*, pp. 290–301, for a district in Frankfurt in 1887, where the ratio of female to male heads of household was 25:8.

constituted a mere 10 per cent of municipal visitors, their proportions varying from city to city between nil and over 50 per cent.[55]

There was more at stake here than would have been the case with voluntary charity, for under the Elberfeld system domestic visiting was an exercise of public authority. Visitors exercised the most important aspect of this authority, the decision on the relief to be granted, not as individuals but collectively within the district committees.

For these reasons the real English parallel is not the role of women in voluntary societies, nor even their work as voluntary workhouse visitors, but as elected members of the Board of Guardians.[56] Here the situation was remarkably similar in both countries. The first recorded election of a woman Guardian was in 1875, but it was not until the 1880s that they were elected in any numbers. The legal qualifications for the exercise of the office laid down that Guardians had to be ratepayers, i.e. heads of households, and that tended to exclude the two most desirable categories of women: married women, who were experienced in household-management, and unmarried daughters living at home, who had the necessary leisure. The property qualification was substantial, and, since married women could not be ratepayers for the married home even with the consent of their husbands, they qualified only if they owned and paid rates on some other property. In addition, the complexity of the voting system and the technical chicanery that characterised these elections meant that technical advice from a professional was another essential pre-condition for success. Hence the importance of the establishment in 1881 of the Women Guardian Society, an integral component of the national women's movement, who knew how to cope with the technicalities. In practice they recruited the candidates. A firm foothold had been gained by 1893; there were forty women Guardians in London and 119 in the provinces. Thereafter the situation was fundamentally transformed by the Local Government Act of 1894. By abolishing plural voting and the property qualification, it opened the gates to women, and by making working-class candidatures possible even added some working-class women to the solid phalanx of ladies. The Women's Co-operative Guild played an important

[55] Steinmetz, *Regulating the social*, pp. 167–8. Also Emil Münsterberg's evidence before the Royal Commission on the Poor Laws, QQ.100300(6), 100492–5. The success of the ambitious reorganisation in Hamburg in 1893 and Strassburg in 1906 owed much to the acceptance of women as visitors there. Steinhilber, *Strassburger System*, p. 73.

[56] For the workhouse lady visitors and their lack of authority over the Poor Law administrators see Patricia Hollis, *Ladies elect: women in English local government 1865–1914* (Oxford, 1987), pp. 198–200.

role in training and backing these working-class women. By 1895 the number of women Guardians had risen to eighty-six in London and 789 in the provinces.[57]

The process of election may well have made it easier for women to break into what had been a male preserve in both countries, than if they had had to rely on the good-will of those responsible for nominations, as was the case in Germany. To break into this traditional male preserve, women in England had to win elections; in Germany they had to be co-opted by the existing visitors. Election may well have been the easier route. Certainly the entrenched attitudes of those who had come to regard these bodies as a male club, with its own mores and forms of consensus, formed a major obstacle in both countries. Nor was the transition helped by the fact that both German district committees and English Boards of Guardians contained a high proportion of men drawn from a lower class than the ladies who now claimed to sit alongside them. As we have seen, there was a large proportion of master-artisans and white-collar workers among the honorary visitors in German towns.[58] English Boards of Guardians tended to be recruited from farmers, small shopkeepers and the middle ranks of business. They objected to what they regarded as bossy ladies, as did their officials, and yielded only slowly to the women's demands for places on the more important committees. Indeed, the aspect of poor law administration over which women had least influence was the administration of outdoor relief.[59]

The impact of the women's movement on the administration of statutory poor relief is strikingly similar in both countries, despite superficial differences of law and practice. In both countries the innovation was justified by the special domestic and motherly gifts that women were considered to bring to the work; in both countries these qualities were regarded with suspicion by men long accustomed to conducting business in their own ways. In England there might be fear that excessive womanly sympathy would increase the rates, but there could equally well be objection to the narrow temperance and Charity Organisation Society views among many of the newcomers. By 1914–15 the number of women Guardians had risen to 1,546. They constituted 6.3 per cent of the total.[60] If that is set against the 10 per cent calculated by Steinmetz for his eighty-

[57] Patricia Hollis, *Ladies elect*, chapter 4 and Appendix B.   [58] See p. 55 above.
[59] Hollis, *Ladies elect*, pp. 209–11, 219–21 and 286–7. For the numbers and the treatment of women on outdoor relief see Pat Thane, 'Women and the poor law in Victorian and Edwardian England', *History Workshop Jl*, 6 (Autumn 1978), 29–51.
[60] Hollis, *Ladies elect*, pp. 203, 212, 296, Appendix B; *Statistics relating to England and Wales, Royal Commission on the Poor Laws*, Appendix vol. XXV, p. 651, BPP 1910 Cd.5077 LIII.

eight German towns, it has to be remembered that these are drawn from a sample and are not strictly comparable.

(G) CONCLUSION

This treatment of the urban poor law has been deliberately selective. It has focused on the administration of out-relief and in particular on honorary citizen service and salaried full-time officials. What conclusions should be drawn from it? I want to mention two.

1. The role of visitors in the German urban poor law administration calls into question the distinction between voluntary action and legal compulsion, a distinction that looms large in several of the subsequent chapters. The recruitment of visitors in the German towns was undoubtedly based on legal compulsion. Yet there is ample evidence that in practice the length of service rendered by them greatly exceeded the requirements of the law. In such cases legal obligation served as the basis for voluntary action in a way that, except for education, was not much understood in England until the introduction of National Insurance in 1911.[61]

2. When dealing with the relative roles of full-time salaried officers and part-time amateurs we have been faced once more, as in the previous chapter, with the reversal of a stereotype. The reliance on amateurs in contrast to professionals is supposed to have been a characteristic of nineteenth-century and indeed of twentieth-century England, whereas in numerous statements Germany has been identified as the land of the professionals. Such a picture does not fit the administration of poor relief in either case.

---

[61] In the case of education voluntary school attendance was often over and above the years for which attendance was compulsory. Similarly under the National Insurance Act a minimum contribution was compulsory, but arrangements allowed for voluntary contributions over and above the minimum.

PART II

The state and industrial injury

At the heart of this section is a comparison of German accident insurance and its nearest British equivalent, workmen's compensation. It occupies such a prominent place in the book because of its importance in the history of social policy in Germany. Although accident insurance is now the least significant of the various branches of social insurance and quite uncontroversial, it was around this issue that the workers' insurance system of the German Empire was originally constructed. Accident insurance was the most prominent and the most controversial of its branches, and it was only because it was so controversial that it was not the first to become law.

Of the various ways to deal with the consequences of industrial methods of production and its associated human costs, two have been of particular significance – prevention and compensation. The most important preventive policies were established by factory legislation. Claims for compensation for industrial accidents were pursued through the courts in cases where negligence by the employer could be shown. Reforms of the law of employers' liability, designed to make access to the courts easier for injured workers or their dependants, were considered in both countries. There was, however, an alternative approach to compensation, which it was hoped would eliminate or at least much reduce the need for litigation. That was to establish rights to compensation regardless of negligence. These three policies – prevention through factory legislation and inspection, compensation through the courts, and no-fault compensation – were closely connected with one another in both countries, but in different ways.

3

Factory legislation to 1878

(A) ENGLAND AND WALES

We begin with factory legislation in England and Wales. That always dealt with more than the prevention of accidents at work, although that was to become an important component. English factory legislation, as it was constructed in the crucial decades 1833–53, was the outcome of conflicting impulses.[1] First and foremost it was a response to the agitation by workers in the textile districts of Lancashire and Yorkshire for a limitation of the hours of labour in factories. The workers demanded a standard twelve-hour working day. This 'short-time movement' had produced evidence of the harmful effect of long hours of labour on the children, whose work was an integral part of the labour process. But in 1833, instead of accepting the demand for a statutory limitation of the hours of labour for all, Parliament prohibited the work of children under eight altogether, while limiting the hours of older children and young persons in such a way as to leave employers free to demand longer hours from adults. Thus the semblance of a free contractual relation between adults bargaining in the labour market, which was a prominent feature of the new economic theory, was preserved.

The Factory Act of 1833 was merely one stage in the conflict over the terms on which the factory production of textiles should be permitted. In 1844 the hours of labour for women were limited in the same way as those for young persons. In 1847 the working day for all but adult men was limited to ten hours per day. This legislation was difficult to enforce as long as there were no restrictions on the length of time that machinery could

---

[1] I shall refer to English factory legislation even when it is the same for Scotland. The principal authorities for the history of English factory legislation are Robert Gray, *The factory question in industrial England, 1830–1860* (Cambridge, 1996); M. W. Thomas, *The early factory legislation* (Leigh-on-Sea, 1948); B. L. Hutchins and A. Harrison, *A history of factory legislation* (2nd edn, London, 1911).

run. In 1850 a standard working day of twelve hours was therefore imposed, within which the labour of women and young persons were to be limited to 10½ hours. This standard working day was what the male workers' short-time committees had been demanding all along, for it necessarily also limited the length of their own working day. An Act of 1853 included the hours worked by children within this standard working day and so finally put an end to the relay-system, i.e. the flexible use of children at any time that employers found convenient. The early factory movement was therefore primarily concerned with the protection of the labour force through the limitation of working hours, and in the case of children with supplementing work with school.

Factory inspectors were, however, soon drawing attention to the accidents caused by machinery. In 1840 under the chairmanship of Lord Ashley (soon to become Lord Shaftesbury) the Select Committee to inquire into the operation of the Factory Act took up the issue of accident prevention. After further investigation and conflict, an Act of 1844 prohibited the cleaning of machinery whilst in motion by any child or young person. It also made regulations for the fencing of moving parts of machinery. Injuries that prevented the worker in question from resuming work before 9 a.m. on the following day were to be reported to the certifying surgeon. He in turn was to investigate the nature and causes of the injury and report the facts to the sub-inspector. This greatly enhanced the role of the surgeon, who had previously been merely expected to certify the age of the children to be employed. His reports followed a standard form in all districts and provided the data for detailed accident statistics on a national and comparative basis. That was to be an important form of evidence.

In practice these safety clauses proved difficult to enforce and little was done until the mid-1850s, when attempts at enforcement led to the so-called fencing controversy. In 1856 a new Act exempted moving shafts situated more than 7 ft from the floor from being compulsorily fenced, with exceptions on which it was in practice too difficult to insist.

None of this added up to effective supervision for the prevention of accidents. Factory inspectors, of whom there were nineteen in 1856, were too few, and after 1844 they lacked powers to impose penalties on their own. For this they were dependent on local magistrates, who were often themselves employers and reluctant to convict. Even when they did so, in about 75 per cent of convictions the fine imposed was at the minimum permitted level. In such a situation the inspectors soon decided that their best course lay in explaining the law to employers and attempting to secure their co-operation. After an initial burst the number of prosecutions for breaches of the safety clauses therefore dropped sharply. By 1849 they were on a declining trend and by the 1860s had become numerically insignificant.[2] Nevertheless the reserve power to prosecute strengthened the hands of the inspectors in what has been described as a process of negotiating compliance.[3]

This protective legislation was originally limited to textile factories. When Parliament after 1845 tentatively began to extend legislation to industries allied to textiles, the chief preoccupation was once more with restricting the hours of labour. Indeed the Lace Work Act of 1861 contained no safety clauses at all. But in the 1860s what had been a tentative extension of legislation to industries allied to textiles acquired a new dynamic from the investigations of a Royal Commission of Enquiry into children's employment in industries not already regulated by the law. Its report recommended the regulation of all factories and workshops and in 1867 led to two Acts. The Factory Acts Extension Act applied the clauses of the previous Factory Acts on hours of labour, fencing of machinery and schooling to a large number of previously unregulated industries. That was no straightforward process. There were many exceptions and modifications of the original clauses, which had after all been specifically designed for textile production. Secondly, the Workshops Regulation Act placed establishments employing fewer than fifty workers under the inspection of local sanitary authorities.

The legislation of 1867 marked a significant breakthrough. The limitations on the use of labour had once been fiercely contested in principle and justified by the special conditions of factory production of textiles. They were now regarded as applicable to all forms of industrial production, whether mechanical or handicrafts. Yet this success brought new problems in its wake.

The number of factories to be inspected increased from 8,000 to over 29,000.[4] But that was nothing compared to the implications of applying the law to workshops. Instead of being concentrated in factory districts, these were widely scattered across the country and difficult to locate. In

[2] P. W. J. Bartrip and P. T. Fenn, 'The administration of safety: the enforcement policy of the early factory inspectorate, 1844–1864', *Public Administration* 58 (1980), 87–107. The figures are from pp. 95 and 97. See also, more generally, P. W. J. Bartrip, 'British government inspection, 1832–1875: some observations', Hist. Jl 25 (1982), 605–25. Number of inspectors from Jill Pellew, *The Home Office 1848–1914* (London, 1982), Appendix E.

[3] P. W. J. Bartrip and P. T. Fenn, 'The evolution of the regulatory style in the nineteenth century British factory inspectorate', *Journal of Law and Society* 10 (1983), 218.

[4] *Report, Royal Commission on factory and workshops acts*, Appendix D (93), p. 187, BPP 1876 C.1443 XXIX.

theory local sanitary authorities already had the duty of inspecting all premises in their area, and it was suggested that their inspectors required only the necessary additional powers to control the conditions of employment in workshops. In practice this was far from being the case. Enforcement of the Workshops Regulation Act was left to the discretion of sanitary authorities, and these were most reluctant to exercise their new powers. The number of sanitary inspectors was almost everywhere inadequate even for the administration of the Public Health Acts. Parliament had produced no financial incentive to appoint additional numbers to deal with these new regulations. The local councils elected by their ratepayers included small local employers. They were in any case reluctant to interfere with local trade. A marked interest in inspection and enforcement was likely to bring electoral retribution in its wake. In all these respects the factory inspectors directly responsible to the Home Office were in a different position. Unfortunately they lacked both the numbers and the requisite local knowledge. The evidence that the regulation of workshops was being neglected by local authorities was, however, so irrefutable that in 1871 factory inspectors were given responsibility for their enforcement. Sanitary inspectors were merely left with responsibility for the enforcement of the sanitary regulations.

This change of the law added enormously to the responsibility of the factory inspectorate. Their numbers, now forty-three, had roughly doubled since 1863, whereas the number of factories had quadrupled. The new responsibilities prompted the creation of a junior grade of inspector. By 1874 a staff of fifty-five was responsible for over 29,000 factories and 87,000 workshops.[5] The operation of the Factory and Workshop Acts was investigated by a royal commission in 1876, which found much to criticise in the state of the law, and in 1878 a new Act simplified and codified the legislation that had been superimposed one upon another over the previous forty-five years.

The years 1867–78 may be regarded as a prolonged period of experimentation with the practical consequences of the expansion of industrial regulation that had now been accepted in principle. In the absence of workable alternatives the factory inspectorate assumed a far greater task than the State was in practice prepared to finance in those years of Gladstonian parsimony and strict Treasury control of expenditure.

[5] *Ibid.*

(B) PRUSSIA AND GERMANY

(i) From 1839 to 1870

Under the *Regulativ* of 1839 legislation in Prussia also prohibited the labour of young children in factories and limited the working hours of older children. The law was amended in 1853, raising the minimum age to twelve, reducing the hours of work for those under fourteen to six plus three hours of school, while limiting them to ten for young persons of fourteen to sixteen. As before, night-work was forbidden for children and young persons, as was work on Sundays and public holidays.[6]

In 1839 enforcement had been the duty of the police authorities. They were local organs of the State and under the supervision of the State administration at district level (*Regierungsbezirk*). Even so, they were too close to the local community to be effective instruments of enforcement, as was only too apparent from enquiries made in 1851. In the preparation of the Act of 1853 interest had been expressed in the English factory inspectors, and under the Act it was possible for the heads of the district administration to request the appointment of special factory inspectors for their district. This was done for three of the most industrialised districts in the Prussian Rhineland, Düsseldorf, Aachen and Arnsberg, but on the death of the inspector for Arnsberg in 1860 his post was left unfilled. These Prussian inspectors were essentially policemen with special duties and drawn from the same class of men. They were expected to call on the local police for support. In all this they differed markedly from the English factory inspectors, who were gentlemen and who had no significant contact with the local constables at either municipal or county level.[7]

There are many differences of detail between the legislation in the two countries. Not all need concern us, but some do. By 1855 the age below which the work of children in factories under Prussian legislation was prohibited was twelve; in England it was ten in the textile industry and eight in other industries. That is a very significant difference. In England this prohibition applied, however, to all work; in Prussia it applied only to 'regular' work, and in practice this greatly added to the difficulty of

---

[6] The standard work is Günther K. Anton, *Geschichte der preussischen Fabrikgesetzgebung bis zu ihrer Aufnahme durch die Reichsgewerbeordnung* (new edition with introduction by H. Bülter, Berlin-Ost, 1953), a revised edition of the work originally published in Leipzig, 1891, from which this and the next four paragraphs are drawn (unless otherwise specified).

[7] Michael Karl, *Fabrikinspektoren in Preussen. Das Personal der Gewerbeaufsicht 1854–1945* (Opladen, 1993), pp. 57–74.

enforcement. The hours of work of children under fourteen were limited in Prussia to six per day; in England they were limited to either six per day in textiles (6½ in other branches) or to ten, if the children worked on alternate days. The limitation to ten hours and the prohibition of night-work for young persons applied in Prussia only to those under sixteen; in England the ten hours in textiles (10½ hours in other branches) and the prohibition of night-work applied to all under eighteen. In England it also applied to women, whose hours were not regulated at all in Prussia. Work on Sundays was specifically prohibited in Prussia, but it was also in practice unknown in England. If we consider merely those under sixteen and disregard the question of enforcement, the law was therefore considerably stricter in Prussia than in England.

In addition to these differences of detail, there were differences in the considerations that had put the subject on the political agenda. In the Prussia of the 1830s there had been no pressure from below. The legislation of 1839 had originated from the inability of the authorities in the industrial districts of the Rhineland to enforce school attendance as laid down by law in 1825. After struggling to use their existing powers, they had reluctantly recognised the need to strengthen the hand of the local police authorities by what was originally described as a *Fabrikschulgesetz*, a law to deal with the school attendance of factory children.[8] In England the enforcement of schooling for factory children had been an afterthought, a means to prevent the shortening of working hours from leading them into mischief. In Prussia it was the central purpose.

In both countries attention had been drawn to the effect of factory labour on the physical development of the children. But the existence of military conscription in Prussia gave the State a direct interest in the matter that was not found in England. When the army had complained in 1828 of the declining quality of recruits from the industrial districts, the government took up the subject, although at that stage nothing was done.

There were no safety clauses in the Prussian Factory Acts, which brings us to a further difference. Beginning with quite limited objectives restricted to textile production in factories, the English Factory Acts gradually added more and more powers over the conditions of production across most of the economy, in workshops as well as factories. By 1878 that process of accretion had reached such an extent as to require codification.[9] Although in the sixteenth and seventeenth centuries English legislation to control

---

[8] Adolf Meyer, *Schule und Kinderarbeit* (Hamburg, 1971).
[9] There was a parallel expansion in the scope of the Mines Acts after 1842.

industrial production had been extensive, those laws had lapsed and been repealed in the early nineteenth century. Hence the importance of the Factory Acts as the vehicle for the development of State control in this sphere.

In Prussia, where guilds had originally been less under State control than in England, control was increasingly asserted in the eighteenth century. The reduction in the power of guilds to control production, which Germans called *Gewerbefreiheit*, was itself an act of State and certainly did not signal an abdication from its claim to regulate economic life. In 1845 this claim was enshrined in a codification of the relevant laws, known as the *Gewerbeordnung* (GewO), a code to apply uniformly across the Prussian territory.[10]

The GewO of 1845 demanded proper consideration for the health and morals of journeymen, assistants and apprentices. That was a sentiment unaccompanied by any specific requirements. It also provided for the protection of neighbouring property owners and the public at large from danger and inconvenience by making the erection and equipment of certain industrial establishments dependent on permission from the local police authority.[11] That clause was not originally concerned with the protection of workers, but in 1869 the GewO for the North German Confederation, which in 1871 became that for the Empire, included this consideration in its wording (clause 18). The licence was, however, issued once and for all. Clause 107 'required every industrial employer, insofar as consideration for the special conditions of the industry and the work-place permitted, to provide at his own cost and to maintain all equipment necessary for the effective protection of the workers against dangers to life and health'.[12] Here was a principle that would one day form the basis for specific safety regulations, but not yet. The legislature refused power to issue regulations, and in their absence, in view of the reservations built into the clause, it was of no practical use.

More immediately important was the incorporation of the Prussian Law of 1853 into the GewO. That made it applicable to Saxony, which had previously known no regulation of child labour at all. It also brought the other states up to the Prussian standard. Enforcement was left to the discretion of each state. In 1872 Saxony added the duty of monitoring compliance with the limitations of the labour of children and young

---

[10] 'Gewerbegesetzgebung' in *Handwörterbuch der Staatswissenschaften*, vol. 4 (3rd edn, Jena, 1909–11).
[11] Clauses 13b and 26.
[12] QS,I.3, pp. XXI, 85–6. This work provides the best overall introduction to the subject.

persons to those of its four inspectors of steam boilers. None followed
Prussia in establishing special inspectors for the purpose.

The GewO for 1869 is mainly remarkable for its reluctance to intervene
between employers and their workforce. In England the relative prosperity
of industry in the 1860s had been taken as a sign that restrictions imposed
on textile employers in the previous two decades had not harmed production. It was this reassurance that permitted restrictions to be extended to
industry in general. Because German industrialisation had begun later, the
1860s saw an overriding preoccupation with industrial development and a
determination by those in authority that nothing should hinder the process. The contrast and its implications for the history of state regulation of
industry could scarcely be greater.

(ii) The 1870s

The following decade was crucial for the history of factory legislation and
its enforcement in the German Empire. After a vigorous initial drive all
efforts came to a stop. They were succeeded in the 1880s by measures for the
benefit of workers that were of a totally different kind.[13] The process of
factory legislation was not revived until the 1890s.

The impetus for this initial drive came from the Prussian Ministry of
Trade and Industry and in particular from Theodor Lohmann, who had
been recruited to its staff of senior officials in 1871. From his correspondence we know a great deal about his views on the nature and purpose of
social policy, which he pursued with remarkable determination. He was a
native of Hanover and actively engaged in the affairs of its established
church at the time of the kingdom's annexation by Prussia in 1866. His
political and social ideas were shaped by the struggle of the church for
liberty from total State control and its claims for freedom in its own sphere.
In doctrinal matters he identified with majority opinion in the Hanoverian
church in opposition to liberal and rationalist trends. His priority was the
development of the individual as a moral person and he considered it the
duty of the state to establish laws that would foster and protect associations
within which the individual could realise his potential. Among these he
included trade unions. Moral development was possible only if membership was freely chosen; by precluding choice compulsion destroyed the
moral significance of action. Compulsion was certainly necessary, but only
to prevent things that endangered the capacity of others to live truly human

---

[13] In addition to QS,I.3 see also QS,I.1, pp. XXX–XXXVIII.

lives.[14] For this reason Lohmann gave high priority to factory legislation and to its proper enforcement.

In 1872 he persuaded the Minister to issue strict instructions to include considerations of workers' safety in the licensing procedure required for the erection of certain factories, and to insist on the enforcement of the clauses of the GewO referring to the health and safety of workers. The post of factory inspector in the district of Arnsberg, vacant since 1860, was filled. Meanwhile an inquiry into the enforcement of restrictions on the work of children and juveniles in other parts of Prussia was initiated. When this produced evidence of widespread neglect, Lohmann was able to begin the systematic expansion of the inspectorate, from two in 1871 to twenty by 1879.

Nor were changes merely quantitative. The inspectors' remit was extended to include matters of safety. That required an altogether new type of inspector, not the ex-policemen or former non-commissioned officers who had been considered appropriate for enforcing the child labour law, but technically or scientifically schooled experts able to discuss safety requirements for a range of industrial processes with employers. Like the English factory inspectors, who were Lohmann's model, they were not to wear uniform, and were to cultivate a good understanding with employers and their senior technical staff. They were to advise them, resorting to prosecution only as a last resort. In England the inspectors were gentlemen who had acquired their expertise on the job; in Prussia, with its different culture, the new type of inspector required academic qualifications as a prerequisite for appointment.[15]

The publication of the annual reports of the new Prussian inspectorate produced shocking information on the conditions of industrial production. It rapidly created a public opinion sympathetic to vigorous state intervention. In 1876 Lohmann produced proposals for the reform of the law with particular emphasis on the enforcement of safety measures. They included the obligatory reporting of accidents at work, 'on the model of the English legislation', and the appointment of inspectors in all the states of

---

[14] L. Machtan, 'Der Gesellschaftsreformer Theodor Lohmann. Grundanschauung und Programm', in I. Marssolek and T. Schelz-Brandenburg (eds.), *Soziale Demokratie und sozialistische Theorie. Festschrift für Hans-Josef Steinberg* (Bremen, 1996), pp. 30–8; F. Tennstedt, 'Sozialreform als Mission. Anmerkungen zum politischen Handeln Theodor Lohmanns', in J. Kocka, H.-J. Puhle, K. Tenfelde (eds.), *Von der Arbeiterbewegung zum modernen Sozialstaat. Festschrift für Gerhard A. Ritter zum 65. Geburtstag* (Munich, 1994), pp. 538–59; H. Rothfels, *Theodor Lohmann und die Kampfjahre der staatlichen Sozialpolitik (1871–1905)* (Berlin, 1927); Renate Litt, *Zwischen innerer Mission und staatlicher Sozialpolitik. Der protestantische Sozialreformer Theodor Lohmann (1831–1905)* (Heidelberg, 1997).

[15] Karl, *Fabrikinspektoren in Preussen*, pp. 90–125 and Appendices.

the German Empire. He also proposed to exclude women from working at night or on Sundays, and to restrict the working hours of girls aged sixteen to eighteen to ten per day.

At this point he met with resistance that was to prove fatal to most of his endeavours. On receiving these proposals, Bismarck reacted most unfavourably. He regarded any further factory legislation as an infringement of the freedom of action of workers, and considered bureaucratic interference in matters of safety as harmful to economic development. More inspectors, he was convinced, would increase the opportunities for corruption. He was soon to experience the impact of safety inspection on the saw-mill on his own estate. Bismarck was furious when the recently appointed inspector insisted on protective shields for the blades of circular saws. Although much has been made of this incident to explain his hostility to factory inspection, it should be noted that he had already made his hostile comments before.[16] In a formal memorandum Bismarck declared his opposition to all legislative measures that would hinder production at this difficult economic juncture unless urgently justified. He then argued at length against restrictions on women's work and the extension of existing ones for children and young people. Finally he ordered the adjournment of the whole matter. Bismarck was therefore surprised to be presented with as many as three draft bills in the following year and angrily stopped all further work on them.[17]

Those few clauses to which he did not object were incorporated into a new GewO, which was laid before the *Reichstag* in 1878. It contained only minor changes to the regulations on hours of labour,[18] no restrictions on women's work, no requirement to report accidents and no obligatory appointment of inspectors in all the states of the Empire. Lohmann, however, was not so easily stopped. He wrote anonymous newspaper articles in support of his original proposals and secretly provided the Centre Party opposition with the text of amendments to the very bill that he was responsible for defending in the *Reichstag*. It was in this way that factory inspection across the Empire became law. 'Statesmen in disguise' is how the activities of such zealots for social reform among

---

[16] L. Machtan, 'Von Kreissägen und anderen "Gefahren die das menschliche Leben überall bedrohen". Eine vielzitierte Quelle zur Bismarckschen Sozialpolitik in neueren Licht', in Karsten Linne und Thomas Wohlleben (eds.), *Patient Geschichte. Für Karl Heinz Roth* (Frankfurt, 1993), pp. 141–65; QS,I.3, pp. XXXIII and XXXV.

[17] W. Ayass, 'Bismarck und der Arbeiterschutz', VSWG, 89 (2002), 400–26, a systematic exposition of Bismarck's attitude by the editor of the volumes on *Arbeiterschutz* in the QS series.

[18] Children under twelve were barred from even occasional work in factories, mines, foundries and stamping-mills.

civil servants such as Edwin Chadwick, John Simon and James Kay-Shuttleworth have been described in British historiography. The British distinction between civil servants and ministers is not found in quite that form in Prussia, but by the standards expected from Prussian officials Lohmann's behaviour was quite astonishing. He was indeed a 'statesman in disguise'.[19]

With the GewO of 1878 we have reached the end of the development of factory legislation in Germany for the next thirteen years and the point at which some general comparative comments are appropriate.

A survey of factory legislation in the several European states, compiled by Lohmann and published in 1878, identifies the 1870s as the decade in which it was greatly extended or, in the case of some of the less industrialised countries, introduced for the first time. In addition to Great Britain, the first group included Hungary (1872), France (1874, 1875 and 1877), Switzerland (1877) and Austria, where new legislation was then under discussion; the second group Denmark (1873) and the Netherlands (1874). Only Belgium among the important industrial countries had failed to introduce any factory legislation. The most ambitious of these laws was that for Switzerland, where earlier cantonal legislation had just been superseded by a federal law. Switzerland provided the federal German Empire with a model that was more appropriate than England's, both on account of its federal structure and because of the peculiar complexity of the English law at this particular moment just prior to the codification of 1878.

The conclusion that Lohmann drew from the survey was that, except in comparison with the recent Swiss law, German legislation was not generally backward. On the contrary, the restrictions on the labour of children and young persons were greater than in England or France. Only in two ways did it fall significantly below the standards of these two countries: by the absence of any restrictions on the labour of women over sixteen and in respect of systems of enforcement.[20]

Before dealing with the issues raised by enforcement, there are some fundamental differences to be considered in the nature of legislation. 'One should not overlook the fact that English law is constructed totally

---

[19] Tennstedt, 'Sozialreform als Mission'; G. Kitson Clark, 'Statesmen in disguise: reflection on the history of the neutrality of the civil service', HJ, 2 (1959), 19–39.

[20] T. Lohmann (ed.), *Die Fabrik-Gesetzgebungen der Staaten des europäischen Kontinents* (Berlin, 1878). This had already been preceded in 1876 by a publication of the English legislation in translation, on which Lohmann drew for his systematic comparison. *Die Englischen Fabrik- und Werkstätten-Gesetze*, Auf Veranlassung des Kgl. Preussischen Ministeriums für Handel, Gewerbe etc. in Deutscher Übersetzung herausgegeben von V. v. Bojanowski, Kais. Deutsch. Wirkl. Legations-Rath, General-Konsul (Berlin, 1876).

differently from the German and is resistant to comparison. An industrial code on the pattern of the continent has never been known in England', wrote Victor von Bojanowski, the German consul-general in London, in 1877.[21] This presentation has taken that difference into account, but it needs to be underlined. The focus in English history on factory legislation, which alone furnished the legal basis for the regulation of labour, should be contrasted with the far less specific general obligations that the law in Prussia and subsequently in Germany imposed on employers and the police.

The general safety clauses of the GewO of 1869 are a case in point; so is the even more general concern for the life and health of the public enumerated as among the duties of the police in a Prussian Police Law of 1850.[22] Such general duties could be ignored, as they usually were, or they could occasionally serve as the legal basis for more specific regulations. These in turn could be ignored, lost in the mass of other duties of the local police, or else occasionally monitored or enforced. Even the vague appeal to masters to consider the health and morals of their journeymen, assistants and apprentices, contained in the GewO of 1845, could be made the legal basis of protective regulation. In 1854 the Ministry issued regulations to reduce the risk to health involved in the manufacture of mercury mirrors, in 1857 it did the same for phosphorus matches, in 1865 for aniline dyes.[23]

Whereas English history is about the passing of carefully defined and limited legislation to curtail the general freedom of entrepreneurs, Prussian and subsequently German experience is about the filling in of broadly defined powers by means of more specific regulations. Such regulations could be confined to certain administrative areas, with their particular industrial conditions, and in this way they might resemble the focus of English statutes on specific industries. It was this process of filling in for which Lohmann was vainly pleading in the 1870s.

On the few occasions that the enforcement of any of these regulations was investigated, as in the case of child labour in 1851–2 or more generally in 1873, it emerged that most, if not all of them, were a dead letter. Hence the appointment of factory inspectors. The English factory inspectorate served

---

[21] V. v. Bojanowski, *Unternehmer und Arbeiter nach englischem Recht* (Stuttgart, 1877), p. vi. This study of the English law on employers and workers was published in the wake of an apparently unproductive official inquiry into the conditions of German workers in workshops and factories, commissioned by the *Bundesrat* in 1875.

[22] QS,I.3, p. XXI.

[23] Arne Andersen, 'Arbeiterschutz in Deutschland im 19. und frühen 20. Jahrhundert', AfS, 31 (1991), 65. Andersen indicates, however, that the last of these was about environmental protection and not the safety of the workers.

both in the 1850s and 1870s as the model for the introduction of factory inspectors in Prussia. German historians have freely acknowledged this debt. Yet a comparative historian needs also to be aware of the differences between the two countries, which are much less commonly acknowledged.

Unlike England, Prussia was systematically covered by enforcement agencies under the authority of the State. The local police were expected to enforce a broad range of regulations, including those on school attendance. It was therefore natural to assume that no special provisions were required. That was not the case in England. Before 1833 justices of the peace in quarter session had been empowered to appoint two of their own members to visit (i.e. inspect) textile mills. They had no officers at their disposal and, although the expedient had been used before in the case of prisons, it was no more suitable to the one than to the other. The only alternative was to rely on common informers.[24] In 1833 there were no local police officers comparable to anything that would have been recognised as such in Prussia. The establishment of salaried inspectors under the Home Office to enforce the Act was done in circumstances when there was no alternative machinery at hand.

The establishment of factory inspectors in Prussia was quite different. It was the supplementation of general police officers by specialists. Once there were specialists, their qualifications could be adapted to their changing duties, as happened in the 1870s. Thus in Prussia the choice of methods for enforcement lay between generalists and specialists, either of whom were accountable to the state, not to representative local government.

In England the choice lay between enforcement either by central or by local government. Not in the 1830s, but when the issue of enforcement was raised once again in the late 1860s, there were elected local authorities available with their own force of inspectors. The issue hinged on the suitability of elected local authorities for the task.

---

[24] Hutchins and Harrison, *History*, p. 36, for reliance on common informers. In the early 1830s the workers' 'short-time committees' had demanded the imposition by law of a 'standard working-day', which would have made it easy to identify factories that were over-running the permitted time. They did not ask for outside inspectors but regarded the common informer as the proper means to lay evidence before the magistrates, a form of community empowerment. Gray, *The factory question*, pp. 62 and 94. For visiting justices see S. Webb and B. Webb, *English prisons under local government* (London, 1922), pp. 29 and 79.

4

German accident insurance

Faced with Bismarck's veto on any further state regulation of working conditions, Lohmann looked for alternative means to obtain his objectives. He found them in the reform of the law of employers' liability.[1]

Employers' liability was based on a law of 1871. This had made employers of labour in mines, quarries and factories liable to pay compensation for injury or death at work caused by their own negligence or that of their supervisory staff, but not that of other workers. In these occupations the law had expanded the traditional principle of liability for negligence beyond that of the employer personally in recognition of the delegated authority characteristic of larger undertakings. For railway companies it had, however, taken over the principles of the Prussian Railway Law of 1838 and made them liable for all injury or death unless this could be proved to have been the victim's own fault or else not due to negligence at all, i.e. an 'act of God'. The difference between railways and the other undertakings was that in railway accidents the victims usually included members of the public, whose claims were based on the contract created by the purchase of a ticket; in the other kinds of accidents they tended to be confined to workers. The Law of 1871 went beyond the Prussian Railway Law in that liability could not be contractually disclaimed or modified, but it strictly confined this presumption of liability to injury caused while the train was in motion, thereby excluding those sustained by railway workers while loading and unloading. In all cases insurance payments were allowed to count towards the sum awarded, provided that the employer had paid at least one-third of the contribution.

---

[1] The best treatment is Florian Tennstedt and Heidi Winter, '"Der Staat hat wenig Liebe – activ wie passiv". Die Anfänge des Sozialstaats im Deutschen Reich von 1871, Teil 1', ZSR, 38 (1993), 362–92, based on the documents in and expanding the introduction to QS,I.2.

Except for railway workers in circumstances under which they were treated on equal terms with injured passengers, the law placed injured workers or their dependants in an almost impossible position. They had to fight their employers in court at a time when they were least able to bear the financial and mental strain involved. German trade unions, unlike British ones, were at the time rarely in a position to take on the role of champion in the courts. Throughout the 1870s major accidents, particularly in mining but also on building sites, which were not even covered by the Law of 1871, drew the attention of the public to the inadequate rights of injured workers.

If the law could be reformed so that employers could not escape paying for the cost of accidents, they would have an incentive to ensure the maximum possible safety of their workers. Here was a way of circumventing Bismarck's veto on any further safety legislation and inspection, and one that could draw strength from the widespread public condemnation of the existing state of the law. Lohmann turned his attention to this matter early in 1878. By 1879 he had reached the conclusion that employers' liability to compensate their injured workers need not be based on grounds of negligence, however widely interpreted. It might be regarded merely as part of the cost of production or operation, an inevitable risk for which financial provision should be made. Legislation along these lines would give employers an incentive to insure themselves against the risk and to ensure that they and their workers adopted appropriate safety measures. Lohmann proposed to encourage the establishment of mutual insurance associations on a trade basis with contributions from both workers and employers. In exchange for their contributions workers would have the right to participate in the administration of the insurance funds. This emphasis on voluntary association to meet common interests created by the demands of the law, and on the role of the state to encourage co-operation between both sides of industry, was characteristic of Lohmann's priorities in social policy.

An initiative in the *Reichstag* gave him his opportunity. It came from the Conservative deputy Carl Ferdinand Stumm, the most important employer in mining and the iron and steel industries in the Saarland. Mining had had a corporate organisation with compulsory membership since the sixteenth century, the *Knappschaften*. These provided insurance against invalidity and old age, financed from contributions by both workers and employers. When mining ceased to be a state monopoly and was opened to private enterprise, as happened in Prussia between 1854 and 1865, compulsory insurance had been retained. Stumm's proposal to extend the principle to all industrial workers was supported by the *Reichstag* in so far as factory production was concerned. It was passed on to the Chancellor and from there to the states for comment; in Prussia it was in turn passed on to the district administrations and accompanied by searching questions from Lohmann's pen.

Stumm's proposal was just the kind of heavy-handed State compulsion of which Lohmann disapproved. It would preclude voluntary associations and require a sheaf of detailed regulations from above. When the expected sceptical replies arrived from the districts, he submitted his own very different proposals for the consideration of his recently appointed minister, Karl Hofmann. Hofmann himself preferred Stumm's proposals and, in debate with his stubborn subordinate, found support from another prominent industrialist, Louis Baare, director-general of the coal and steel combine *Bochumer Verein* in the Ruhr, whom he persuaded to submit his views in writing. Baare was critical of the 1871 law on employer's liability because of the constant need to determine to whose negligence any particular injury could be ascribed. The uncertainty that this created made any rational financial planning impossible. He would rather pay a limited sum in all cases of accidents, and proposed the establishment of compulsory insurance funds for every firm with contributions from both workers and employers. Neither Baare nor Lohmann was much interested in Stumm's grandiose plans to provide for invalidity and old age; both wanted to concentrate on compensation for accidents, which they wished to be considered part of the normal cost of production. They proposed to repeal the law of 1871 and to introduce insurance, but disagreed over whether it should be done by compulsion.

Nevertheless the man who mattered was Hofmann. He allowed himself to be persuaded by Lohmann in favour of incentives rather than compulsion, but he was convinced that the reform of the 1871 Law proposed by both his advisers went too far and would be unacceptable to Bismarck. In a cautious inquiry whether Stumm's proposals might be dropped in favour of reforming the law of employers' liability, which he submitted to Bismarck in July 1880, he sketched out the sort of reform that he had in mind. He made no mention of accidents as part of the cost of production but suggested that, like railway companies, employers should be liable for the consequences of all accidents unless they were due to the victim's own fault or an 'act of God'.

His inquiry was not well received. 'I shall fight such proposals with every means at my disposal', was Bismarck's reply, and he promptly dismissed Hofmann from office. The latter's suppression of the argument in favour of considering all accidents part of the cost of production, which freed the whole matter from any suggestion of guilt, had been a mistake. The law of 1871, as it applied to railways, was based on the allocation of fault; it made employers liable for the fault of anybody in their employ except for the victim himself. To apply this presumption of guilt to employers generally struck Bismarck as grossly unjust. Furthermore, to make it easier for workers to start a law suit against their employer, he believed, was to poison relations between the two sides of industry and would offer trade unions the role of workers' champions. Such proposals, he added, were both ruinous for industry and useless for the revival of handicraft production.

Before leaving office Hofmann defended himself against that accusation. On the contrary, he pointed out, as prominent an industrialist as Baare wanted to go further in assuming responsibility for compensation. He referred Bismarck to the memorandum in his possession. Bismarck had taken temporary charge of the strategically important ministry himself and was interested. He noticed that Baare's proposals were open to neither of his two objections. Hofmann's proposals seemed to him an idealistically motivated interference with industrial production; what Baare offered him was a reform to avoid industrial and political conflict, bringing greater productivity and political stabilty in its wake.

On the basis of Baare's memorandum Bismarck now formulated his own policy: no enlargement of employers' liability for injuries through accidents for which they were not to blame, but provision through insurance, covering almost all cases of accidental injury but limiting the amount of individual compensation.

He departed from Baare's ideas by ruling out the use of private insurance and proposed a *Reich* insurance of some kind. There were at least three reasons for that choice. In public he objected to profit being made out of misfortune with the risk of an insurance company going bankrupt. He was also aware of the criticism that their customers levied against the sharp practices of insurance companies and had taken an interest in a possible nationalisation of life insurance.[2] The statesman in him was attracted by the prospect of a *Reich* insurance analogous to the *Reich* bank and postal service, both established since 1871 to enhance the powers of the Imperial government.[3]

---

[2] Otto Pflanze, *Bismarck and the development of Germany*, vol. III (Princeton, 1990), pp. 162–4. See also the article in favour of the nationalisation of insurance by one of his close advisers at the time, Adolph Wagner, 'Der Staat und das Versicherungswesen', *Zeitschrift für die gesamte Staatswissenschaft*, 37 (1881), 102–72.

[3] Florian Tennstedt, '"Nur nicht privat mit Dividende und Konkurs". Der deutsche Weg zum Sozialstaat – auch eine Folge von Bismarcks Ansichten über private Unfallversicherungsgesellschaften', in M. Heinze and Jochem Schmitt (eds.), *Festschrift für Wolfgang Gitter* (Wiesbaden, 1995), pp. 993–1004.

Baare had suggested that the cost of insurance be carried by employers, workers and the State in equal part. Bismarck's plan was for equal contributions from employers and the higher-paid workers, but for lower-paid workers to be excused contributions altogether. Two-thirds of these were to come from the employer and one-third from public funds, thereby casting the *Reich* in the role of provider for those in need.[4]

In the words of two recent historians, Bismarck thus turned a legal technical problem into a part of his wider programme of *innere Reichsgründung*, the process of establishing the *Reich* as a fact of domestic and not merely of external politics.[5] That may do justice to Bismarck, but for Lohmann the reform of the law had also been more than merely a legal technical problem. It had been a means towards his wider project of social reform for the sake of the well-being of the workers and their integration into the national community.

These original proposals are important for estimating the distance between Bismarck's intentions and his actual achievement. He may have wished to enhance the power of the Imperial government, but for that very reason his proposal for the *Reich* to carry the insurance was unacceptable to the defenders of the interests of the individual states. It weathered criticism in the *Bundesrat*, but was rejected by the *Reichstag*.

Nor was this the only obstacle that he encountered. Before the *Reich* with its narrow tax-base could assume the role of Lady Bountiful to the lower-paid, it had to find the money. Bismarck thought it reasonable for this to be provided by the poor law authorities, who would otherwise have had to support the disabled. But he quickly ran into opposition and unsurmountable technical difficulties, since the community of residence responsible for maintenance and that of employment did not necessarily coincide. His second proposal, that the money should come either from the states or from the *Reich*, was rejected by the *Reichstag*. By June 1881 Bismarck's draft legislation had been so drastically amended that he recommended its withdrawal. His next proposal, that the *Reich* should have a monopoly on the sale of tobacco and pay for both old age and accident insurance out of the profits, was aired in the *Reichstag* elections and overwhelmingly rejected in the autumn of 1881, the most disastrous election for Bismarck since the birth of the Empire.

Far from accepting failure, Bismarck renewed the struggle with all the resources at his disposal. He wrote a speech for the Emperor to deliver at the opening of the new *Reichstag*, which committed the government to

---

[4] The lower limit for liability for contributions was an annual income of 750 M.
[5] Tennstedt and Winter, "'Der Staat hat wenig Liebe'", p. 379.

insurance against accidents and sickness, adding that those unable to work on account of old age or invalidity also had a well-founded claim on the community for a higher measure of public support than they had so far received. Since the Emperor was unwell, Bismarck read it on his behalf. This was the Imperial Message of 17 November 1881, which, although issued well over a year after the initiation of Bismarck's policy, has come to be regarded as the founding document of the German welfare state.[6]

The Liberals, whose numbers in the *Reichstag* had been swollen by the elections, now took the initiative and produced a draft bill of their own. They accepted the principle of no-fault compensation and proposed that the necessary insurance should be carried by mutual indemnity associations or commercial insurance companies, as each employer chose, under regulations to be decided upon. Those were to include (i) the prohibition of any discrimination against individual firms, i.e. all firms in the particular trade or district were to be accepted, (ii) the deposit of adequate capital reserves for all pensions when awarded, and (iii) evidence of financial security to be submitted to a supervisory authority set up by each state. Here was the outline of a system of approved societies that made the direct state insurance, recently rejected by the *Reichstag*, unnecessary. It offered Bismarck the opportunity to work with the parties towards a mutually acceptable compromise. That was certainly Lohmann's view at the time, who more than anyone knew the technical problems that would have to be solved.[7]

Instead Bismarck did his best to destroy the proposal at birth, and within a few weeks he produced a second bill of his own. This bill of February 1882 would be succeeded by a third, which in turn underwent crucial alterations before finally becoming law in July 1884. To understand the principal features of the final version some attention will have to be paid to the political process from which they emerged.

---

[6] F. Tennstedt, 'Vorgeschichte und Entstehung der Kaiserlichen Botschaft vom 7. November 1881', ZSR, 27 (1981), 663–710. For the period between the Imperial Message and the passing of the accident insurance law the best treatment is Florian Tennstedt and Heidi Winter, '"Jeder Tag hat seine eigenen Sorgen, und es ist nicht weise, die Sorgen der Zukunft freiwillig auf die Gegenwart zu übernehmen". (Bismarck) Die Anfänge des Sozialstaats im Deutschen Reich von 1871', Teil 2, ZSR, 41 (1995), 671–706, based on the documents and expanding the introduction to QS,II.2/1. The publication of QS,I.1, I.2 and II.2/1 has made all previous treatments of the subject in need of revision. For the background to the documentary series and its implications see E. P. Hennock, 'Social policy under the Empire – myths and evidence', *German History*, 16 (1998), 58–74.

[7] Tennstedt, '"Nur nicht privat"', p. 998.

(B) THE CARRIERS OF THE INSURANCE

Insurance was to be carried for each trade by mutual associations with compulsory membership (*Berufsgenossenschaften*). These would have the power to levy contributions on their members to cover the cost of compensation and to lay down safety conditions as they considered appropriate. The role of the *Reich* would be reduced to providing an Insurance Office with supervisory powers and the right to settle disputes.

Although he succeeded in killing the Liberal bill, the claims of commercial insurance and voluntary mutual indemnity associations refused to go away. Their wish to participate in accident insurance in some form or other was upheld by the *Reichstag* in committee. By the end of the session there was every indication that this disagreement would be fatal to the Bill.

Bismarck's determined opposition to anything that would dilute the monopoly of his proposed *Berufsgenossenschaften* was based on more than hostility to the Liberals and suspicion of commercial insurance companies.[8] Since the *Reichstag* had refused to sanction a state subsidy, the money would have to come mainly from employers. At one point he thought that the lack of a state subsidy would be fatal to the scheme by imposing a burden on employers that German industry would be unable to bear.[9] But he discovered that fully inclusive *Berufsgenossenschaften* would not need to accumulate capital reserves to cover all their future liabilities. Like regular state institutions they would be able to operate on the pay-as-you-go principle, meeting their obligations each year by raising the necessary contribution from their members in the year after. Since liabilities would accumulate only gradually, this arrangement reduced costs in the early years and made the proposed levels of compensation feasible after all. Although this would be achieved at the price of piling up problems in the future, it allowed any consideration of state subsidies to be put off for the moment.[10]

The *Reich* would therefore impose compulsory payment on both sides of industry, but make no significant contribution of its own.[11]

---

[8] His personal animus was boosted in December 1882, when the insurance on his estate was steeply increased at a time when the company in question was recording rising profits. Pflanze, *Bismarck*, vol. III, pp. 166–71. That coincided with his determined opposition to giving the companies any role whatever in the proposed scheme, as described below.

[9] This had been his main reason for withdrawing his first bill in the summer of 1880.

[10] Tennstedt, "'Nur nicht privat'", pp. 998–1000.

[11] It would at best provide some administrative support and act as short-term lender to facilitate the pay-as-you-go arrangements.

Originally it had been expected to provide insurance cover and part of the premium too. Now insurance was to be carried by mutual trade associations and the premium by the two sides of industry, with the employers paying the lion's share. The role of the *Reich* as provider had been replaced by that of the *Reich* as enforcer.

Although no part of the original conception, comprehensive and therefore compulsory *Berufsgenossenschaften* thus soon became a necessary part of the policy. Moreover, they assumed an additional importance in Bismarck's mind that altogether transcended the sphere of accident insurance.

Since his break with the Liberals in 1878/9, Bismarck's position in the *Reichstag* had been most precarious, resting as it did on a shifting conjunction of parties. This had served to reinforce his critical view of party politicians, as people whose mostly academic education rendered them doctrinaire and impractical. He began to think about alternative representative institutions based not on party but on common economic interests. The year 1880 saw the creation of a Prussian *Volkswirtschaftsrat* (Economic Council), composed of the representatives of different economic interests. It was intended as the precursor of a similar body for the *Reich*, but the *Reichstag* refused to provide the necessary funds so that the project remained confined to Prussia.

Comprehensive *Berufsgenossenschaften* appeared to provide a form of economic representation across the Empire as a whole. In 1883 Bismarck went so far as to say to Lohmann in the context of their disagreement over compulsory membership that he valued them primarily as a means to supplement or even to provide an alternative to the *Reichstag* – in the last resort, he added, through a *coup d'état*. Accident insurance was of secondary importance. Some historians have attached great importance to this remark. Its significance is lessened, however, by the fact that within a few months he was prepared to drop the separate representation of workers in the *Berufsgenossenschaften*, a change that entirely destroyed their value as representative institutions.[12]

Indeed, Bismarck's preferences were one thing, what was acceptable to the *Reichstag* was quite another. He would never have got his way, and the bill would have fallen at this hurdle, but for the skill with which he played off his political opponents against each other. Basically, the Centre party hated the Liberals even more than they hated Bismarck. When it appeared that there might be a rapprochement between their enemies, with all that

---

[12] QS,II.1, pp. 381 and XXIX–XXXI.

this implied for the Catholic Church, the Centre party entered into negotiations with the government and with the Conservatives who supported it. Faced with the choice, Bismarck dropped his plans for *Berufsgenossenschaften* as an alternative form of representation so as to gain the support of the Centre Party and thereby a majority for a bill that made no concessions to commercial insurance companies or voluntary associations.[13]

(c) THE IMPORTANCE OF THE SOCIALISTS

The long battle over accident insurance thus ended with a Liberal defeat. That was consistent with the origins of the policy. For Bismarck's initiative in 1880 must be understood against the background of the political events of 1878–9. Those years had seen three major innovations: the Anti-Socialist Law of 1878, the introduction of protective tariffs, and the break with his Liberal supporters. These matters were inter-dependent; even the Anti-Socialist Law is now interpreted primarily as a move to weaken the Liberals.[14]

What were their implications for social policy in the 1880s? The break with the Liberals had made it possible to embark on a social policy that was highly distasteful to them. The introduction of protective tariffs had at one time seemed to provide the *Reich* with a large new source of revenue. In the end it did nothing of the kind and still left Bismarck looking for means to overcome its financial weakness.

What implications did the Anti-Socialist Law have? Workers' insurance has traditionally been viewed as a way to balance repression of the Socialists with a positive policy to appeal to non-ideological workers and to ensure their loyalty to the *Reich*. '*Zuckerbrot und Peitsche*', the German version of 'stick and carrot', describes this view of the relation between the two policies, a formula first coined by the Social Democrats as a justification for their distrust of these dubious benefits. Workers' insurance undoubtedly appealed to some people on these grounds, and the connection was explicitly made in government statements to recommend the legislation. But it should be noted that the connection was not made by Bismarck until long after all the crucial decisions had been taken.

---

[13] Tennstedt, '"Jeder Tag"', pp. 686ff in full. More briefly, Tennstedt, '"Nur nicht privat"', pp. 1001–4. Further information in K. O. von Aretin, *Franckenstein* (Stuttgart, 2003), pp. 177–82.

[14] Lothar Gall, *Bismarck, the white revolutionary* (London, 1986), vol. 2, pp. 82–116.

Social reform as part of a deliberate 'double strategy' linked to the repression of the Socialists had its advocates in government circles as early as 1878, but it was rejected by Bismarck at the time.[15] It was Lohmann who first used the argument in support of accident insurance. He did so in the opening paragraph of the draft *Begründung*, the memorandum in support of the bill, which he submitted to Bismarck in December 1880. That is how Bismarck seems to have come across the idea, and thereafter he increasingly adopted the argument as his own. It formed part of his report to the Emperor, asking permission to submit the bill to the *Bundesrat*. It has been suggested that it became a favourite argument for use with the Emperor, whose injury from the assassination attempt in 1878, often but quite wrongly attributed to a Social Democrat, made him tolerant of anything that would weaken the movement. Standing at the head of the *Begründung* of the bill, it featured prominently in the public debates. It proved a popular argument and contributed to the acceptance of highly contentious proposals. When it was over, Bismarck could comment ironically on the value of the Social Democrats. But for the fear that they inspired in many people, he told the *Reichstag* four months after the acceptance of the Law, the modest progress that had been made in social reform would not have happened.[16]

By December 1880 the draft bill was, however, already in its fourth version. Every decision that might be thought to have originated in a wish to find a complement to the Anti-Socialist Law had been taken. What followed were administrative details, political concessions and little else. There is therefore no documentary evidence that this connection was in Bismarck's mind when he embarked upon the insurance policy.[17] He believed that the revolutionary wing of the Social Democratic party could be isolated and put down by police action. He was far more

[15] QS,I.1, Nos. 153–8. Robert Bosse, advisor to the Deputy Chancellor Stolberg-Wernigerode and the initiator of these suggestions, subsequently became a colleague and confidant of Lohmann. F. Tennstedt, '"Bismarcks Arbeiterversicherung" zwischen Absicherung der Arbeiterexistenz und Abwehr der Arbeiterbewegung', in H. Matthöfer *et al.* (eds.), *Bismarck und die Soziale Frage im 19. Jahrhundert* (Friedrichsruh, 2001), pp. 83–5. This matter is more fully covered below on pp. 187–8, and the accompanying footnote.

[16] Speech of 26 November 1884, quoted in H. Matthöfer, W. Mühlhausen and F. Tennstedt (eds.), *Bismarck und die soziale Frage im 19. Jahrhundert* (Friedrichsruh, 2001), pp. 86–7.

[17] The relevant documents, it should be remembered, were not published until 1993. An influential view of Bismarck's policy as part of a deliberate double strategy can be found in the work of Hans Rothfels, and has been repeated in every treatment of the subject until recently. Hans Rothfels, 'Bismarcks Staatsanschauung', in Hans Rothfels, *Otto von Bismarck, Deutscher Staat* (Munich, 1925), p. xliv, and his *Theodor Lohmann und die Kampfjahre der staatlichen Sozialpolitik (1871–1905)* (Berlin, 1927). Rothfels, who had read the unpublished documents, appears to have deliberately misled his readers. See QS,I.1, XXXV and nn. 44 and 48.

concerned to further the industrial development of Germany and the power of the *Reich*.[18]

(D) INDUSTRY

If the Social Democrats hardly entered Bismarck's original calculations, the leaders of heavy industry certainly did. The fundamental principle of a no-fault insurance for the victims of industrial accidents had been proposed by Baare, although it should be borne in mind that it was one that, unknown to Bismarck, Lohmann also held. Bismarck asked Baare to consult with other industrialists and to come back with proposals for a draft bill.

At the same time the experienced officials under Lohmann were hard at work, and it was their draft bill that became the basis of all subsequent discussion. Baare rapidly found himself by-passed. A mere three months after he had submitted his own draft bill, he regarded the level of compensation proposed by the government as ruinous to industry, declaring that he would rather put up with a reform of the law of employer's liability. That kind of language is not unusual when an interest group is trying to influence government legislation. Baare was to recommend acceptance of the final version of the bill to his fellow-industrialists in the Central Association of German Industrialists as one that, for all its failings, could be expected to work satisfactorily. Suggestions by some historians that heavy industry was shaping the provisions of the legislation are not borne out by the recently discovered Baare correspondence. It was certainly intended to operate in the interest of industrial employers, but their wishes were far from paramount.[19]

(E) THE WORKERS

Something more should be said about the role of workers in this insurance, both their contribution to the cost and their representation in the scheme. To understand the first, we need to look outside the organisation of accident insurance itself. For the first thirteen weeks sickness insurance

---

[18] QS,I.1, XXIX.
[19] See also Hennock, 'Social policy under the Empire', pp. 65–66, which corrects M. Breger, 'Der Anteil der deutschen Grossindustriellen an der Konzeptualisierung der Bismarckschen Sozialgesetzgebung', in Lothar Machtan (ed.), *Bismarcks Sozialstaat* (Frankfurt and New York, 1994), pp. 25–60. Also useful in English, H.-P. Ullmann, 'German industry and Bismarck's social security system', in W. J. Mommsen (ed.), *The emergence of the welfare state in Britain and Germany* (London, 1981), pp. 133–49.

funds were to care for the victims of accidents. Workers' contributions to these provided 17 per cent of the total cost of accident insurance. The administrative input from sickness insurance funds was also important. In 1908 78.5 per cent of all illness was caused by accidents lasting no more than thirteen weeks. By taking responsibility for this period the sickness funds saved employers' associations the hassle of dealing with large numbers of temporary claims.[20] Their role in providing financial and medical assistance in the immediate aftermath of an accident was widely regarded as essential for the functioning of the scheme.

The original proposals had envisaged only four weeks. The *Reichstag* had wanted to reduce this to fourteen days, a proposal to which Bismarck had no objection. The decision to extend the period to thirteen weeks was Lohmann's, at a time when illness had forced Bismarck to take his eye off the details of the bill. It naturally pleased the employers, but Lohmann's initiative owed nothing to a desire to reduce their costs. He had ignored Bismarck's agreement to the *Reichstag* proposal in order to ensure that a nationwide extension of sickness insurance would be a necessary part of the reforms. And he had increased the period for which the workers were required to provide two-thirds of the finance because he believed that only by paying would they have the right to a voice in the administration. As a social reformer his priority was to guarantee workers a legitimate voice in the institutions that governed the relations between capital and labour.[21]

How were workers represented in the insurance based on mutual trade associations? Both Bismarck and Lohmann, for different reasons, had wished to require a distinct workers' committee in every association. It would have to be consulted over safety regulations and would nominate workers to serve on appeal tribunals. But an independent workers' voice was unacceptable to the interests represented in the *Reichstag*. As part of the final compromise separate workers' committees were replaced by workers' representatives on the larger executive committee, where their views could be more easily overridden. Despite some half-hearted concessions to workers' representation accident insurance emerged as an employer-dominated scheme.[22]

---

[20] F. C. Schwedtman and J. A. Emery, *Accident prevention and relief: an investigation of the subject in Europe with special attention to England and Germany* (New York, 1911), pp. 52 and 58.

[21] Tennstedt and Winter, "'Jeder Tag'", pp. 681–2, 683 and 684. See chapter 8 below for a full treatment of the Sickness Insurance Law.

[22] Complaints against the operation of its appeal tribunals were so widespread that they were replaced in 1900 by tribunals organised on a local authority basis and modelled on those established meanwhile to deal with invalidity. Ernst Wickenhagen, *Geschichte der gewerblichen Unfallversicherung. Anlageband* (Munich, 1980), pp. 84–5 and 95–6.

(F) ACCIDENT PREVENTION

One further sphere of action was envisaged for the *Berufsgenossenschaften*. Since they were to bear the cost of injuries caused by accidents at work in their branch of industry, they could be expected to have an interest in safety measures. The Law of 1884 authorised them to issue safety regulations which their members had to observe. If they wished, they could appoint their own inspectors to check that records were properly kept and safety regulations adhered to. This was Bismarck's answer to the proposals made in 1877–8 for the State to fill out the general requirement of the GewO with specific safety regulations for individual industries and to enforce these through State inspection. Whereas other countries, including Great Britain, relied on the State and its inspectors, Germany was now intended to rely primarily on associations of employers. Not until Bismarck's fall did the State inspectorate acquire an importance comparable to that of other countries.

This aspect of the work of the *Berufsgenossenschaften* was not obligatory, but the Imperial Insurance Office made it its task to chivvy the associations into taking action. By 1889 about 70 per cent had issued some sort of safety regulations. Ten years later it had risen to 95 per cent. It was a further ten years before the last of the associations fell into line. In 1890 forty-one associations had appointed a total of 146 salaried inspectors. Many of these had nothing more than clerical duties and qualifications. Others had some technical qualifications or experience, but nothing comparable with those of the factory inspectorate. They were employed by the employers' association and could not be expected to act independently of it. Indeed they had no authority of their own; their duty was to report infringements to the management of the association, which alone could take measures to enforce the regulations. By 1900 their numbers had risen to 232 in fifty-four associations, but since many of them were expected to check the books, it is impossible to tell how much time they spent on safety inspections. By 1913 the distinction between clerical and technical supervision becomes easier to make; there were 386 inspectors responsible for the latter.[23]

By leaving safety requirements to the discretion of trade associations, the legislation of 1884 ensured that employers would not be subjected to pressure from outside authority. Pressure was intended to be generated instead by a

---

[23] Rolf Simons, *Staatliche Gewerbeaufsicht und gewerbliche Berufsgenossenschaften: Entstehung und Entwicklung des dualen Aufsichtssystems im Arbeitsschutz in Deutschland von den Anfängen bis zum Ende der Weimarer Republik* (Frankfurt a.M., 1984). The figures come from pp. 82–4, 135, 137, 169 and 171.

desire to reduce the cost of compensation. Safety measures whose costs could not be justified by clearly foreseeable savings in compensation payments were ruled out from the beginning. It is therefore important that what has been regarded by at least one scholar as Bismarck's original intention to subordinate the existing factory inspectorate to the *Berufsgenossenschaften* was not pursued by him, and that proposals from the *Berufsgenossenschaften* in 1891 along those lines were rejected by the *Reichstag*.[24]

(G) LOHMANN VERSUS BISMARCK

If Baare and his friends were not in control of the policy-making process, neither in the end was Lohmann, who had at first acted as Bismarck's most trusted and indispensable adviser. But Lohmann's desire to foster voluntary institutions through legislative incentives was of little interest to Bismarck. Illness prevented Bismarck from taking much interest in the details of sickness insurance which became law in 1883. There Lohmann largely had his way, with important implications, as noted even for the details of accident insurance, of which it formed an integral part. But the funding of accident insurance on the pay-as-you-go principle and the establishment of *Berufsgenossenschaften* with compulsory membership were suggested to Bismarck by other advisers. They were opposed by Lohmann in every possible way, until he was relieved of further work on the bill in October 1883. He was highly critical of compulsory *Berufsgenossenschaften*. 'Not the common interest of its members but the mere fiat of the law has brought individuals into these associations', he wrote in words that might have come from an English Liberal.[25]

Lohmann is important for any Anglo-German comparison. He was at heart a liberal who regarded workers as citizens to be reconciled through social reform, whereas Bismarck was a conservative who regarded them as subjects to be attached to the existing order. It is no accident that it was sickness insurance, which incorporated Lohmann's priorities, that was to provide British Liberal legislators between 1908 and 1911 with precedents that they could use and adapt.

He represents the course not taken, and the course that, but for Bismarck, could well have been taken. He provides therefore some

---

[24] Simons, *Staatliche Gewerbeaufsicht*, pp. 87, 192 (for Bismarck's presumed intentions) and 100–5 (for the debates in 1891). On the former point I am, however, informed by Wolfgang Ayass, the editor of the relevant volume of QS, that the archives contain no evidence of any such suggestion by Bismarck.

[25] Anonymous, undated article quoted in Rothfels, *Theodor Lohmann*, p. 73.

measure of Bismarck's personal influence. Bismarck's obstruction of factory legislation along the lines of other European States was to be no more than temporary. But compulsory insurance for the new nation, and not just at the discretion of a few municipalities, was his lasting contribution. True, there were important differences between his original concept and that which became law in 1884. That should not hide the fact that nothing along these lines would ever have been done but for his bold departure from precedent and his determination to make concessions to circumvent all obstacles. After 1884 invalidity and old age insurance would depart even further from anything that Bismarck had intended. But it was deeply influenced by what his perseverance and ingenuity had achieved.

(H) EXPANSION

Between 1884 and 1887 the law, which had originally been limited mainly to wage-earners in mines, salt-works, quarries, factories, ship-building yards, smelting works and building sites, was extended to further categories of building workers as well as to sailors, state employees and even workers in agriculture and forestry. In the latter two cases it was left to each individual state to issue its own legislation, thereby watering down what had originally been one of the attractions of the insurance legislation, namely its uniformity across the *Reich*.

Further amendments in 1900 and 1911 did little to extend the circle of the insured, which still excluded handicrafts and other small trades, home work, and commerce.[26] The number of *Berufsgenossenschaften* rose from 57 in 1885 to 117 in 1914, the number of the insured from 7 per cent of total population in 1885 to just on 40 per cent in 1914.[27]

This is not the place to describe the levels of compensation. They will be found on pp. 112–13 below as part of the comparison with those available under the British Workmen's Compensation Acts.

---

[26] For the full list of occupations see W. H. Dawson, *Social insurance in Germany* (London, 1912), ch. 4. This is the best description in English and is based on the state of the law in 1911. It has the additional advantage of making detailed comparisons with the law in Britain. For the legislation to expand the circle of the insured and the latest and fullest description of the working of the system see QS,II.2/2.

[27] Figures for 1885 from Reichsversicherungsamt, *Statistik der Arbeiterversicherung des Deutschen Reichs 1885–1904* (Berlin, 1906), Tables 1 and 3; for 1914 calculated from QS,E, Table II.1 and P. Flora *et al.* (eds.), *State, economy and society in western Europe 1815–1975: a data handbook* (Frankfurt, London and Chicago, 1987), vol. 2, p. 58.

5

British workmen's compensation

(A) BACKGROUND

In Britain as in Germany no-fault compensation for the consequences of industrial accidents was introduced to block a reform of the law of employers' liability that would have made it easier for workers to obtain compensation through the courts. But whereas the German proposals on employers' liability were provoked by government hostility to factory legislation and inspection, that was not the case in Great Britain. On the contrary the contentious proposals of 1893 to reform the law of employers' liability, which quickly led to the introduction of no-fault compensation for industrial injuries, were the work of Herbert Asquith, the Liberal Home Secretary, who was an active advocate of factory inspection. In Britain the concentration on alternative forms of compensation for injury that characterised the years 1893–7 had no connection with any hostility towards the expansion of factory legislation and inspection.

There is a further difference that we have met before and that we shall encounter repeatedly when comparing the genesis of social reforms in Germany with those in Britain. The German initiatives had originated from government officials. The British initiative was a response to pressure from organised labour.

The genesis of German accident insurance has been presented in some detail, since it is based on evidence only recently made available and provides almost certainly the first up-to-date version in English. The genesis of British workmen's compensation will be kept briefer, since it largely draws on the version of events presented in a previous study published in 1987.[1]

---

[1] E. P. Hennock, *British social reform and German precedents: the case of social insurance, 1880–1914* (Oxford, 1987), Part I.

In common law masters had been responsible both for their own negligence and that of their servants. Thus a master had to compensate a victim of his coachman's negligence. But in 1837 a legal judgment laid down that masters were not liable for the negligence of their servant if the injured person was also in their employ, for instance if their valet were injured by the negligence of their coachman. This 'defence of common employment' meant in practice that an employee had a claim only if there had been negligence on the part of the master personally. By the 1850s this dubious interpretation of the law had become the dominant one in the English courts and was applied in the widest possible terms. In the case of large undertakings in which the owner was remote from the actual running of the business, such as mines and railways, that left the workman with no claim that he could in practice pursue.[2]

In such cases it was impossible to use the civil law to bring home to owners their responsibility for safety provisions and procedures. Whether the matter was regarded from the point of view of safeguarding lives, of the moral claims of the victim, or of the workers' own benefit funds, the state of the law was bound to be a grievance in an accident-prone industry such as coal mining. That was already so when the Miners' National Union was founded in 1863, but it was the extension of the franchise in 1867 and the creation of the Parliamentary Committee of the Trade Union Congress (TUC) in 1871, chaired by Alexander Macdonald, the miners' leader, that gave the miners a voice in Parliament.

The Amalgamated Society of Railway Servants (ASRS), founded in 1871, was equally opposed to the law. Unlike mining disasters, railway disasters affect passengers as well as workers. Injured passengers could sue the company for the negligence of its officials, while the doctrine of common employment meant that railway workers injured on the same occasion could not. Such a grievance had a particular appeal to the TUC, which was then campaigning against the legal discrimination suffered by workers compared with ordinary citizens under the Masters and Servants Acts. When its agitation against the Criminal Law Amendment Act of 1871 and the Masters and Servants Acts had been brought to a successful conclusion in 1875, the reform of the law of employers' liability became the Parliamentary Committee's principal objective.

Coal mining and railways were to dominate the history of British legislation on employers' liability and workmen's compensation from the

---

[2] For a detailed exposition of the law see P. W. J. Bartrip and S. B. Burman, *The wounded soldiers of industry: industrial compensation policy 1833–1897* (Oxford, 1983).

1870s to the 1890s, as they had not done in Germany. Coal miners in Germany had their own separate and more comprehensive provision for sickness and invalidity in the *Knappschaften*. This had provided Stumm with his precedent in 1879 when he suggested extending comprehensive invalidity and old age insurance to the whole of factory production.[3] It was this proposal that Lohmann had been able to quash. The importance of coal mining thus lay in providing the precedent that was ignored in the course of accident insurance legislation. That legislation was discussed mainly in terms of the iron-producing and processing industries.[4] Railways had also enjoyed a special status, in Prussia since 1838 and in Germany since the law of employers' liability of 1871. That law also served as a precedent for an initiative that was quashed, Lohmann's proposal to amend the law of employers' liability in 1880. Whatever similarities there were in principle, the fact remains that railways no more than mining had set the terms of the policy debate in Germany, as they did in Britain.

That is not to suggest that the differences between the policies pursued in the two countries can be fully accounted for in this way. What differed were the political forces that had to be considered: in Germany the iron and steel industry organised in the Central Association of German Industrialists (CDI), in Britain the coal and railway unions organised in the TUC and the owners organised in the Mining Association and the Railway Association respectively.[5]

The second half of the 1870s saw several bills introduced into Parliament on behalf of the miners or the railwaymen, and the House of Commons responded by setting up a Select Committee. By 1878, when yet another bill was before the House, no one was defending the existing state of the law, but further delay ensured that no action had been taken by the time of the general election of 1880. The general election of 1874 had returned two miners as MPs to Parliament, of whom Alexander Macdonald was one. More significant still had been the willingness of trade unionists to make their support of the traditional parties dependent on pledges in support of labour legislation. This pattern was repeated in 1880 with the difference

---

[3] See p. 87 above.

[4] A point made in Dietrich Milles, 'Medical opinion and socio-political control in the case of occupational diseases in the late nineteenth century', *Dynamis*, 13 (1993), 141.

[5] It should be added that, in the preparation of the Workmen's Compensation Bill of 1897, Joseph Chamberlain consulted mainly ironmasters and engineering firms, with a sprinkling of building contractors and textile manufacturers. His list of contacts included only two coal-owners and one chemical manufacturer. That probably reflected his own connections as a former screw manufacturer in the West Midlands. See memo, 'Workmen's Accident Compensation. *Confidential*', dated 17 February 1897, in Joseph Chamberlain Papers, University of Birmingham Library, JC6/3/3/18.

that the Liberal candidates had taken warning from their poor performance in 1874. The ASRS was particularly effective in mobilising its branches in support of its bill, obtaining pledges from 300 of the successful candidates, most of whom were Liberals. Four of these became members of the Liberal cabinet under Gladstone, which made the ASRS bill the basis of its legislation.

As it finally emerged from Parliament, the Act of 1880 made employers liable for the negligence of their supervisory staff, but not of those ordinarily engaged in manual labour. In the case of the railways negligence by train drivers, signalmen and those responsible for setting the points was explicitly included. The Act did not abolish the defence of common employment, it tried to take account of the fact that in many firms supervision and its responsibilities were delegated through a chain of command.[6] It was roughly similar in this to the German law of 1871, except in the case of railways for which the latter was more inclusive.

These changes filled mine owners with apprehension. Unlike railway directors they were not often sued for damages caused by accidents to the general public. They were now to be liable for the numerous accidents ranging from great disasters to the loss of life or limb by individuals that were common in mining. Their liability extended far beyond any measures they could personally take, since they were to be liable for the negligence of their subordinate supervisors even if these ignored explicit regulations.

Some employers responded to the Act by insuring themselves against the new risks. The Employers' Liability Assurance Corporation was founded in 1880 for just that purpose and was soon followed by similar commercial companies. Others established a mutual insurance association. Still others took a step that had been given prominence during the parliamentary debates. In exchange for a contribution to their benefit fund, workers were persuaded to waive their right of legal action under the Act. Once taken, the decision became a condition of employment in the firm.

This 'contracting out of the Act' was not widespread and was hardly known outside the mining industry and the railways. In mining it was confined to certain collieries in Lancashire, Cheshire, the Midlands and North Wales; among railways to the London and North Western Railway Company. In South Wales contracting out was not a condition of employment, merely a condition of membership of the benefit fund, and much the same was true of the London, Brighton and South Coast Railway Company, whose benefit fund was particularly generously subsidised. By

---

[6] Hennock, *British social reform*, pp. 40–7; Bartrip and Burman, *Wounded soldiers*, pp. 126–57.

the late 1880s roughly 20 per cent of colliery workers had contracted out of the Act in exchange for membership of a subsidised accident fund, and of these roughly half had done so as a condition of employment. But in the areas where the practice existed, and these were the most dangerous, its impact was far greater than these figures would suggest. The employers' contributions in the mining districts amounted to a mere 20–25 per cent of the miners' own subscriptions; the railway companies were more generous.

The objection of trade union leaders to the practice was immediate and vehement. They looked on the Employers' Liability Act with its penalties for negligence as a measure that would prevent accidents, and regarded contracting out as a means of avoiding the penalties of carelessness. The view that mutual insurance fostered neglect was passionately held even after 1893, when the Home Office informed the Royal Commission on Labour that its analysis of the accident statistics lent no support to it. In any case there were other grounds for the objections of the trade union movement. Unions used their funds both to support victims of accidents, sickness or unemployment, and to support strikes. A fund subsidised by the employer and directed specifically to compensation for injury weakened their appeal and hampered their freedom of action. They saw it as an insidious attempt to undermine the foundations of their trade associations. Another objection was that the organisation of benefit funds on the basis of a firm, or even of a district, could tie a man to a job which otherwise he might have preferred to leave, and thus gave additional power to employers.[7]

As early as 1881 both the TUC and the ASRS sponsored bills to make contracting out illegal, and in the following year they combined their efforts in a single bill. After the election of 1885 had provided an opportunity to put pressure on MPs, the Commons set up a Select Committee on the operation of the Employers' Liability Act. It is some indication of the extent to which organised labour's views had gained a hearing in the Liberal party, that the Committee divided evenly on party lines over a proposal to forbid all contracting out of the Act. Only the chairman's casting vote ensured its defeat. The Conservatives were keen to defend the use of benefit funds as an alternative to the Act of 1880 by making it proof against abuse. In fact there was wide support, well beyond the vested interests of mine owners and railway directors, for the view that insurance funds were to be preferred to litigation. They made for co-operation and good feelings between masters and men, it was said, whereas litigation cast a trade union official or solicitor as the workers' champion in a conflict in which

---

[7] Hennock, *British social reform*, pp. 47–9; Bartrip and Burman, *Wounded soldiers*, pp. 158–73.

the employer was the enemy. It would be costly in lawyers' fees and in good relations at the workplace.

The recommendations of the Select Committee became the basis of two abortive bills introduced by the Conservative Government in 1888 and 1890. Since both were bitterly opposed by the parliamentary spokesmen of organised labour, the bills, intended as a gesture to meet labour grievances, were withdrawn. Labour's unyielding opposition owed much to the close links that it had forged with the Liberals. By 1891 the TUC's proposals on employers' liability had become part of the Liberal party programme and organised labour looked forward confidently to the time when their demands, on the defence of common employment as well as on contracting out, would be met in full by a Liberal majority in the Commons.

With the general election of 1892 that moment had arrived. In the following year Asquith, as Liberal Home Secretary, introduced an Employers' Liability Bill that proposed to abolish the doctrine of common employment, to remove the upper limit of compensation in cases of death, thereby leaving the courts free to award what compensation they thought fit, and to prohibit contracting out. On the first two issues opinion had moved rapidly since the Conservative bill of 1890 and there was little prospect that the compromise proposed in that measure could be revived. The ensuing conflict was to be over the legitimacy of contracting out. It was so bitter that in 1894 the government's proposals were rejected by the Conservative majority in the House of Lords and the bill was abandoned by the government.[8]

(B) NO-FAULT COMPENSATION

This deadlock over the reform of the law of employers' liability created the conditions for compensation for all injuries caused by accidents at work. That was enacted by the Workmen's Compensation Act of 1897. The principle that compensation for injury should be reckoned as part of the cost of production was explicitly borrowed from the German legislation of 1884. The proposal had originated with Sir John Gorst, British delegate to the International Labour Conference held in Berlin in 1890, and was taken up by Joseph Chamberlain, who introduced it as an amendment on the Second Reading of the Liberal bill in 1893. The trade union spokesmen in

---

[8] Bartrip and Burman, *Wounded soldiers*, pp. 190–8. D. G. Hanes, *The first British Workmen's Compensation Act 1897* (New Haven, 1968) provides a fuller account of the parliamentary debates on the 1893 Bill and the 1897 Act, but lacks a sense of context.

Parliament decided to oppose it. In view of this, Asquith, although not opposed to general compensation in principle, stuck to his original proposals. Chamberlain thereupon withdrew his amendment, but not before his proposals had received the widespread attention that he had desired.

Chamberlain had been a Liberal cabinet minister until the party split in 1886 over Home Rule for Ireland. He was now a Liberal Unionist uneasily poised between the two main parties and tentatively moving towards an understanding with the Conservatives. That gave him the independence needed for what was in effect a drastic break with the policies of both parties. He was scornful of the political spokesmen of organised labour and thought that he knew what was in the interests of the working-class electorate at least as well. His proposals removed the common ground on which the parties had engaged in conflict, namely the extension of the law of liability for negligence. By 1894 there had been three attempts to reform the Act of 1880 and all had failed. No one defended the law as it stood. It gave the workers a grievance for which they blamed the Conservatives. That grievance would persist if a future Conservative government were to enact a new Employers' Liability Act that retained contracting out. Such a measure would attach organised labour even more closely to the Liberals, who would be bound to try to abolish contracting out once they were back in office.

In 1895 the Liberal Unionists joined a government under Lord Salisbury, the Conservative leader. Chamberlain had been offered the Home Office, the key post for legislation on employers' liability. Although he turned it down in favour of the Colonial Office, it was he who took responsibility for the subsequent Workmen's Compensation Act. It was his personal achievement. Only someone as dynamic as Chamberlain could have dragged a reluctant Home Secretary and an even more reluctant Conservative party in a direction of which they were deeply suspicious.[9]

The ministers called their measure a Workmen's Compensation Bill, and emphasised that it was as a compensation bill that it should be judged. From that point of view their proposals were greatly superior to any reform of the law of employers' liability. Chamberlain calculated with the help of the German accident statistics that 43 per cent of recorded accidents would not have qualified for compensation even if the defence of common employment were abolished. If the House wanted to add to the existing arrangements for the prevention of accidents, he argued, it would have to do so through factory legislation or by

---

[9] Hennock, *British social reform*, pp. 52–79.

tightening the criminal law on negligence. It was a mistake to believe that by punishing employers and making them pay it was possible to prevent the majority of accidents from happening.[10] Yet that had been the traditional view, not least in the ranks of organised labour. Despite Chamberlain's attempt to shift the focus of attention to matters of compensation for hardship, or perhaps because this was seen as illegitimate, the debate tended to return repeatedly to the effect of workmen's compensation on accident prevention.

In their study, *The wounded soldiers of industry*, Bartrip and Burman have played down the difference between the policy of 1880–93 and that of 1897. Referring to statements by which Chamberlain countered objections that his policy would lead to increased accidents and argued that insurance companies could be relied upon to penalise employers with a bad accident record by increasing their premiums, they turned statements intended to ward off objections into a major objective of policy. Their view that 'improvement of safety was the fundamental reason for introducing . . . both the Employers' Liability Act of 1880 and the Workmen's Compensation Act of 1897' cannot be accepted. Neither this evidence nor the few statements quoted from factory inspectors, while admitting that these made no attempt to influence policy in that direction, justifies their view that 'both the Employers' Liability Act and the Workmen's Compensation Acts were moves away from the pursuit of industrial safety by means of regulation and inspection (though these strategies continued to exist)'. Such an interpretation, which blurs the contrast between the British policy and that of Bismarck, cannot be sustained.[11]

Although British policy, as embodied in the Act of 1897 and its successor, the Workmen's Compensation Act of 1906, had borrowed from the German law the principle of compensation for all injuries caused by accidents at work (excepting serious and wilful misconduct on the part of the workman himself), together with a limitation on the sum to be paid, there were important differences between the law in the two countries.

1. In Germany the obligation had been laid on a corporate body, the *Berufsgenossenschaft*, established for the purpose, membership of which

---

[10]   4 *Hansard* 48 (3 May 1897) 1461–5.

[11]   Bartrip and Burman, *Wounded soldiers*, pp. 67–8, 95, 168, 213 and 218. Their description of Chamberlain's policy as one of insurance blurs the distinction between the presentation of his case in 1893, when he expected that all employers would insure themselves and said that he had no objection to legislation to compel them to do so, and 1897, when he thought that most employers would carry the risk themselves and opposed all suggestions for compulsory insurance. 4 *Hansard* 8 (29 February 1893) 1969; 4 *Hansard* 48 (3 May 1897) 1463, 1467.

was compulsory and which had powers of financial levy and safety regulation over its members. In Great Britain the obligation fell on the employer himself, who was free to make any arrangements that he considered appropriate.

2. In Germany accident insurance was associated with sickness insurance for workers in general, which took medical, financial and administrative responsibility for the first thirteen weeks. In Britain that was the case only with the few schemes that had contracted out of the Act of 1880.

3. The Imperial Insurance Office (*Reichsversicherungsamt*) exercised a vigorous oversight over the bodies that administered the German insurance system and acted as a court of appeal. In Britain responsibility was distributed over several departments of state, and the normal courts dealt with legal disputes. The lack of a single supervising authority was to be identified as a weakness in 1920, but the appointment of a Commissioner, as recommended by a departmental committee in that year, was never made.

(c) COMPULSION TO INSURE

The House of Commons was well aware of the first of these differences. Referring to what had been done in Germany, Chamberlain explained with the approbation of the House that 'the elaboration of the system, its bureaucratic tendency, and the arbitrary interference of officials are all matters which are so objectionable to English people . . . that it is absolutely impossible and absolutely impracticable to attempt any system of operation of that kind'. The Home Secretary admitted that under the British law there was a risk that after a major accident a bankrupt employer might not be able to meet the claims of his workmen, but added that 'it was hardly to be expected that the Government could have proposed any scheme of compulsory trade responsibility or insurance. Anyone who has studied the details of the German system will feel that it could never be introduced into this country.' He expressed the hope that in practice employers would choose to form trade associations or make similar mutual arrangements between cognate trades. 'Such arrangements', he added, 'made voluntarily, as is the custom in this country, will be far more effective and economical and in accordance with English feeling than any compulsory system.'[12]

The view that compulsory trade associations were quite out of the question was never challenged in the House. But the problem of the

---

[12] 4 *Hansard* 49 (17 May 1897) 699–700, quoted in Hennock, *British social reform*, pp. 74–5.

bankrupt employer, unable to meet his legal obligations to his injured workmen or their dependants, continued to cause concern. It was considered in detail in 1904, when the system was under investigation by a departmental committee. 'No amendment of the Act', its report concluded, 'would be satisfactory unless Parliament was prepared to contemplate compulsory insurance.' Despite greatly extending the range of occupations covered by the law, and thereby greatly increasing the number of small employers unlikely to assume the expense of insurance, the Act of 1906 made no such provision. Yet the amount of concern expressed during the parliamentary debates was such that the government promised an inquiry into the matter 'either that year or the next'. Other issues supervened and no further notice was taken of the matter before 1919. Even then the recommendation of a Departmental Committee for the introduction of compulsory insurance was ignored until after the Second World War except for the special case of coal mining.[13]

In the absence of prescribed machinery there was little certainty how the numerous individual firms would choose to act, whether after 1897 or after 1906. There were four courses open to them. They could associate with other employers to share the risk by means of a mutual indemnity fund; they could insure with a commercial company; they could carry their own risk without insurance; or they could induce their workers to take part in a jointly financed benefit fund in exchange for contracting out of the rights guaranteed them by employers' liability and workmen's compensation laws. This right to contract out had been retained by the Conservatives in 1897 as a sop to party consistency, but the alternative scheme had to be at least as favourable to the workmen and as costly to the employer as the provisions made under the Act. That requirement deprived the fund of any attraction for employers. By 1906 contracting out had ceased to be a grievance. The Liberals did not trouble to abolish it but left it to wither on the vine. By 1920 there were only twenty such schemes, covering 63,000 workers out of an estimated total of 15 million.[14]

In so far as one can tell from the defective evidence available, employers' mutual indemnity associations were widespread and favoured by industries, such as shipping and mining, that were particularly liable to accidents. But unlike *Berufsgenossenschaften*, which were legally responsible for compensation payments and could not escape the obligation, British mutual indemnity associations tended to cover only exceptionally heavy

---

[13] Hennock, *British social reform*, pp. 82–94. Quotations on pp. 83 and 87.
[14] Hennock, *British social reform*, p. 95.

liabilities, leaving it to their members to shoulder ordinary risks. That blurs the distinction between mutual insurance and self-insurance or non-insurance.[15] Being merely off-loading expedients with an incomplete membership and a limited commitment, the British associations did little to develop provisions for medical rehabilitation and even less in the matter of safety. It was this absence of collective responsibility and compulsory membership that was the crucial difference between the two countries. It largely accounts for the less dynamic role that the British associations played in the development of services.

Next in importance to mutual indemnity associations were the commercial insurance companies, whose opposite numbers had been altogether excluded from the scheme in Germany. The British authorities did little to regulate their role in the scheme, beyond requiring them in 1907 to deposit a sum as surety and in 1909 to file their revenue accounts with the Board of Trade, which published them. That was more than was required from the mutual indemnity associations. Although the Board published the accounts of insurance companies, it took no interest in the information provided. Only in 1923 did the Home Office begin to monitor company profits and negotiate an agreement to limit these.[16]

Two kinds of employers did not insure themselves at all. There were large companies, such as railway companies, whose reserves were adequate to cover any liabilities. At the other end of the scale there were numerous small employers too careless or too improvident to cover themselves. In 1920 it was estimated on the basis of very inadequate statistics that the latter amounted at the very least to a quarter of a million.[17] That emphasises the importance of compulsion. It casts doubt on Lohmann's objection in 1882–3 to the compulsory membership of *Berufsgenossenschaften*, although it should be added that, unlike the subsequent British legislation, Lohmann had intended the law to provide employers with strong incentives to organise themselves in suitable associations. The experience of the coal industry in the 1930s demonstrates that the problem of the bankrupt employer was not limited to small employers, but until then it was usually associated with them. Their existence could lead to workers or their dependants being denied their legal right of compensation altogether; more often these were

[15] The statistical information is in Hennock, *British social reform*, pp. 96–8. For a discussion of the consequences of partial insurance for the coal industry between the wars, see *ibid.*, p. 93.

[16] W. A. Dinsdale, *History of accident insurance in Great Britain* (London, 1959), p. 154; Hennock, *British social reform*, p. 104; Wilson and Levy, *Workmen's compensation*, vol. I, pp. 164–7.

[17] Wilson and Levy, *Workmen's compensation*, vol. I, pp. 160–2.

induced by the threat of bankruptcy to accept smaller sums than were their due.[18]

Both the German and the British legislation had strictly limited the categories of occupations covered in the first instance but, as in Germany, once agreement had been reached on a system, pressure built up quickly to extend it to further occupations. The first British extension of the law was passed in 1900 and covered all employers of agricultural labour. In 1904 a departmental committee advised against extending the law to all forms of employment and proposed including no more than a few specified occupations. Its views were swept aside in 1906 by the incoming Liberal government, which paid more attention to the wishes of trade unions than to the cautious recommendation of the committee. Their bill applied to employers generally, excluding only some particularly difficult categories. The most important of these were included before the bill reached the statute book. Even after the extension of German accident insurance in 1911, certain categories of workers, such as domestic servants, workers in the retail trades and in small handicraft workshops, were covered by the British but not the German law.[19] This difference is not surprising: the British law had no organisational implications of any kind.

(D) FINANCIAL COMPENSATION

For the vast majority of workers who were covered in both countries what mattered most was the level of compensation. Here the German law provided significantly more. British workers, if totally disabled, received half their average weekly earnings calculated over the previous twelve months up to a maximum of £1 per week. That meant that earnings over £2 per week were disregarded, which could have implications for skilled men. German workers, if totally disabled, received two-thirds of the previous yearly earnings, but only one-third for earnings above 1,500 M (1,800 M after 1912). These were very high earnings limits. Even then the German law was more generous. If the injured was dependent on outside care and nursing, the German law required the pension to be adequate for the purpose and it could be increased up to the full yearly wage. For partial incapacity the German scheme laid down a tariff according to the nature of the incapacity. The British law was less specific, but generally intended to

---

[18] *Ibid.*, pp. 160–2.
[19] A list of categories of occupations covered in Germany can be found in Dawson, *Social insurance*, pp. 103–5.

take account of the difference between the original average weekly earnings and those able to be earned afterwards. The departmental committee in 1920 compared the two methods and preferred the German one, but matters continued as before.[20]

In Germany, in the case of death, a widow received a pension of 20 per cent of her late husband's yearly earnings until her death or remarriage. Each orphan under fifteen and other necessitous dependants received 20 per cent up to a total of 60 per cent. On remarriage the widow received a lump sum of two-thirds of her late husband's previous yearly earnings. British dependants usually received not a pension but a lump sum of between £150 and £300. If partially dependent, they received less, and only if there were no dependants was there a grant for medical and funeral expenses of £10 at most. The German funeral grant of one-fifteenth of yearly earnings with at least 50 M or £2.50 (30 M or £1.50 before 1900) was automatic. There are obvious problems in comparing a regular pension with a lump sum payment, but all British experts were agreed in condemning the manner in which in practice the lump sum system worked to the detriment of the widow. That was because they regarded the lump sum as a substitute for a regular pension. But unless she was quite old, a widow without dependent children was likely to be earning and therefore not entitled to a pension in any case. A German study has suggested that younger widows with dependent children were likely to marry again and indeed needed to do so. In that situation their entitlement to a lump sum was an important asset and placed them in a better position to choose their future provider. The lump sum on remarriage, it has been suggested, was perhaps the most practical and realistic benefit for the widow to be provided by the system.[21] If such an argument can be transferred to the situation of British widows, the British lump sum available to the widow as a dowry would have been a greater asset still. But that would be one of the few circumstances under which the British compensation was not significantly worse than what was its German counterpart.[22]

[20] Wilson and Levy, *Workmen's compensation*, vol. I, pp. 187–9. These German pensions had originally come into effect only after the thirteenth week, but from 1911 they were made available from the fourth week onward. In the initial period the injured received the much lower sickness benefits provided by the sickness insurance funds. Dawson, *Social insurance*, pp. 112–13.

[21] Wolfgang Schröder, 'Subjekt oder Objekt der Sozialpolitik? Zur Wirkung der Sozialgesetzgebung auf die Addressaten', in Lothar Machtan (ed.), *Bismarcks Sozialstaat* (Frankfurt, 1994), pp. 150–3.

[22] For Germany with some comparison with England see Dawson, *Social insurance*, pp. 111–22. For England see also Wilson and Levy, *Workmen's compensation*, vol. I. chs. 9–11.

(E) MEDICAL REHABILITATION

The biggest difference between the benefits under the two systems lay in the provision of medical treatment under the German scheme and its total absence under British workmen's compensation law. Not until the introduction of National Health Insurance in 1911 were any steps taken to give the British injured worker a right to the treatment that he would have needed. Of course, there were charitable hospitals as well as Poor Law infirmaries to which the victims of accidents could be taken, but that is meagre when compared with the hospital provision and the provision of medical treatment after discharge to which German sickness insurance gave entitlement. German accident insurance was part of a system of medical provision; British workmen's compensation law was not.

In both countries those who had to pay pensions to the long-term injured had an interest in speeding their recovery and restoring their earning capacity. In both countries insurance bodies exercised their right to have claimants examined by doctors of their own choosing, a practice that created a sense of unfair treatment among injured workers. But unlike British insurers, even mutual associations, German *Berufsgenossenschaften* developed an active interest in the rehabilitation of the injured. Between 1885 and 1892 they went beyond the letter of the law and with the approval of the Imperial Insurance Office in many cases they assumed medical and financial responsibility for the treatment of serious injury already in the first thirteen weeks. This practice was legalised in 1892 in the first amendment of the Sickness Insurance Law. and they were given the right to insist on taking such action irrespective of the views of the sickness funds.[23]

Furthermore they sponsored the manufacture of artificial limbs and established their own rehabilitation clinics. The rehabilitation clinics would have been more acceptable to their patients, who had no choice but to attend them if they wished to retain their pension rights, had they not been so closely identified with the financial interests of the *Berufsgenossenschaften*. Foreign observers and official descriptions presented them as one of the positive achievements of the German insurance system. But they had a bad reputation among workers as *Rentenquetschen*,

---

[23] Wickenhagen, *Geschichte*, vol. I, pp. 74–80 and 104. The guidelines issued in 1911 by the Imperial Insurance Office suggest that this power had led to friction with the sickness fund doctors, whose authority and remuneration were threatened thereby. C. Kaufmann, 'Vergleichende Übersicht über den gegenwärtigen Stand der Unfallgesetzgebung in den verschiedenen Ländern mit Berücksichtigung der die ärztliche Tätigkeit berührenden Verhältnisse', in *Verhandlungen des III. internationalen medizinischen Unfallkongresses zu Düsseldorf 1912* (Düsseldorf, 1912), pp. 79–85.

places for the reduction of pensions, not least because decisions on the success achieved by the treatment were made by the doctors whose salaries depended on the effectiveness of their clinic.[24]

There was no British parallel to this German initiative until the later 1930s and the post-war years. British social policy had moved from emphasising prevention to adding a further emphasis on financial compensation. German social security in the Wilhelmine era was about more than financial compensation. It was also about rehabilitation with the aim of maintaining and augmenting human labour as national capital.[25]

(f) INDUSTRIAL DISEASES

There is a further difference to be considered: the inclusion of compensation for injury from certain specified industrial diseases in the 1906 Workmen's Compensation Act. The Act itself specified six diseases but gave the Home Secretary power to add to the list at any time. Injury from anthrax, one of those specifically included in the Act, had been ruled in 1905 by the House of Lords to be an accidental injury in the case of a wool-sorter who had caught the disease from handling infected wool. That had raised the whole question of the inclusion of industrial diseases. Yet by including diseases clearly caused by exposure to industrial processes but whose onset could not be identified with a particular accidental event, the Act of 1906 introduced a new principle. Another eighteen industrial diseases were added in 1907, while the investigations of a specially appointed departmental committee led to the addition of a further number in 1908. By 1913 the list stood at twenty-five.[26] This development had not been envisaged in 1897. It resulted from the sustained attention paid by the factory inspectorate since the 1890s to diseases caused by a particular industrial process. This is a matter to which we shall return when dealing with factory legislation and inspection in that period.

---

[24] For the official view see Wickenhagen, *Geschichte*, vol. I, pp. 118–24; for that of the workers, Schröder, 'Subjekt oder Objekt', pp. 145–9. See Greg Eghigian, *Making security social: disability, insurance, and the birth of the social entitlement state in Germany* (Ann Arbor, 2000), pp. 127–50, for a detailed description.

[25] Eghigian, *Making security social*, ch. 4.

[26] P. W. J. Bartrip, *Workmen's compensation in the twentieth century in Britain* (Aldershot, 1987), pp. 53, 59 and 71–2; Wilson and Levy, *Workmen's compensation*, pp. 106–7; *Statistics of compensation and proceedings under the Workmen's Compensation Act of 1906 ... during the year 1913*, Table 6, BPP 1914–16 Cd.7669 LXI, p. 991.

In Germany there was also interest in the right to compensation for the consequences of industrial diseases. Since the law contained no definition of an accident, it had been left to the Imperial Insurance Office in its judicial capacity to decide what kind of injury should be compensated. It had defined an accident as a sudden event and ruled out injury from industrial diseases that developed gradually.[27] During the *Reichstag* debates on the consolidating legislation of 1911, the SPD proposed that occupational diseases developing over time should be treated for purposes of compensation in the same way as sudden accidents. On the other hand the Centre Party proposed that the *Bundesrat* be empowered to schedule certain specific occupational diseases as qualifying for compensation under accident insurance. That was similar to the powers given to the British Home Secretary. The SPD proposal was rejected as opening the door to endless disputes as to what qualified as an occupational disease, and the SPD thereupon supported the Centre Party's proposal. Between them these parties were able to override government opposition and obtain a *Reichstag* majority for the inclusion of this clause in the Law. All now depended on whether the *Bundesrat* would make use of its powers. It made no use of them before 1925.[28]

There would appear to be two reasons for this difference. One was the attitude of the governments. In 1911 the German government had resisted the proposals of the two parties that spoke for their respective trade union movements. In Britain a Conservative government bill in 1905 had made no mention of the inclusion of industrial diseases, a proposal that had been rejected by a departmental committee in 1904. But after the massive Conservative defeat at the 1906 general election the incoming Liberal government was acutely conscious of the fifty-four labour representatives, some belonging to their own party, others to the new Labour party. They regarded their bill from the outset as what the Prime Minister called a 'sop to Labour' and included the clause on industrial diseases.[29] The speed with which the Liberal Home Secretary moved to act on the discretion vested in him also indicated the government's responsiveness to labour concerns. The German government

---

[27] Note the case of a victim of phosphorus necrosis in 1887 in QS,II.2/2, No. 306.

[28] J. S. Hohmann, *Berufskrankheiten in der Unfallversicherung* (Cologne, 1984), pp. 134–48.

[29] Hennock, *British social reform*, p. 85. The Parliamentary Committee of the TUC had drawn up their own workmen's compensation bill before they knew the content of the government measure. They withdrew it and at a conference between their representatives and the government ministers the government bill was examined in detail. Bartrip, *Workmen's compensation*, p. 52.

showed no such responsiveness. The new Law came into force at the beginning of 1913, but when the Centre party asked in the *Reichstag* on 21 March whether any preparations had yet been made to decide to what extent occupational diseases should be incorporated within accident insurance, the government spokesman admitted that nothing had been done. He added that no rapid action should be expected.[30] This negative attitude should be seen in the light of the concessions over other branches of insurance that had recently been made, which are treated in chapter 4, section (a), and chapter 9. It was determined to have a pause in this kind of social policy.

That attitude was easier to maintain than such an attitude would have been in Britain, since disability, whether from industrial diseases or not, whether total or partial, attracted a pension under German invalidity insurance. The issue at stake over scheduling industrial diseases under accident insurance was less absolute, although real enough. It was the level of the pension received by the workers and the proportion of it to be paid by the employers. There was also the question of safety.

(G) LITIGATION

In both countries those who initiated the legislation wished to construct a system that would replace litigation by administration. In neither country did this happen. The existence of arbitration tribunals, manned equally by employers and workmen with a neutral chairman, did not prevent the *Berufsgenossenschaften* from testing the scope and meaning of the law on numerous occasions before the Imperial Insurance Office (RVA). Nor were workers always content to abide by the decision of the tribunals. The extent of this conflict obliged the RVA to establish a large body of case law and precedent based on its decisions. The records of the RVA contain numerous statements by workers struggling to translate their experience of pain and suffering into language appropriate for pursuing claims for compensation in a bureaucratic system. That was no easy task nor did the appropriate conventions lie easily to hand. It has also demonstrated that the RVA officials were able to distance themselves from the production-oriented considerations of the employer organisations and to draw on their legal training to adjudicate between the conflicting parties. This was of course just what Bismarck had

---

[30] Hohmann, *Berufskrankheiten*, pp. 116–25.

intended to avoid when he turned from factory legislation to accident insurance.[31]

In Britain the Workmen's Compensation Acts gave rise to even more litigation. Not only did the wording of the British Acts give rise to numerous court cases, but the refusal of the trade unions outside the Durham and Northumberland coal-fields to co-operate in setting up joint arbitration tribunals on the German pattern, as had been envisaged in the Act, made the county courts the arbiters of every dispute. The adversarial system within which British unions were accustomed to operate and the litigious attitude of the insurance bodies between them created a climate of litigation which operated especially to the disadvantage of those working in trades that were not strongly unionised.[32]

This comparison has been sparing in the use of statistics. Whereas statistical information on German accident insurance is detailed and comprehensive, that on British workmen's compensation is incomplete and is defective in many other ways.[33] Although, for instance, there can be no doubt that the total amount spent on compensation payments was significantly higher in Germany than in Britain, it is impossible to use the British figures for the purpose of comparison. Returns were only required from industries that were already under some form of state regulation or were so concentrated that it was easy to collect the information. That ignored more than half the employers to whom the law applied.[34] Whereas the Germans had created an organisation responsible for accident insurance, the British had merely passed a law imposing additional obligations on employers. The Imperial Insurance Office under Tonio Bödiker, its energetic first President, supervised the several aspects of the scheme and provided an efficient statistical overview. In Britain there was no such centre. Employers could meet their legal obligations in a variety of ways. Of these some generated statistical information while others did not. There was no overview.

'Germany ... is organised not only for war but for peace. We are organised for nothing except party politics.'[35] There are many reasons to

[31] Eghigian, *Making security social*, ch. 3. One needs to remember that the material on which it draws provides access to the mentality of only a minority of workers. This ambitious example of history from below has at present nothing comparable among studies of British workmen's compensation. It cries out for imitation, if appropriate records can be discovered.

[32] Bartrip, *Workmen's compensation*, pp. 22–7 and 59–63; Hennock, *British social reform*, p. 80.

[33] There are critical overviews of the British statistics in Schwedtman and Emery, *Accident prevention and relief*, pp. 173–4; and Wilson and Levy, *Workmen's compensation*, vol. I, pp. 307–15.

[34] Hennock, *British social reform*, pp. 95–6.

[35] W. S. Churchill to H. H. Asquith, 29 December 1908, in R. S. Churchill (ed.), *Winston S. Churchill*, vol. II, *Companion*, Part 2 (London, 1967), p. 863.

qualify the extravagant contrast that Winston Churchill famously drew in 1908.[36] Yet it seems particularly appropriate to compensation for industrial injury. Government and parliament were soon to turn to the needs of the elderly, the unemployed, the sick and the disabled by setting up new forms of organisation. Workmen's compensation remained a disorganised backwater of social policy for another thirty years.

---

[36] See for one instance E. P. Hennock, 'The urban sanitary movement in England and Germany, 1838–1914: a comparison', *Continuity and Change*, 15 (2000), 269–96.

6

Factory legislation to 1914

(A) GERMANY

In Germany compensation for industrial injury had sprung from Bismarck's determination to block any further development of prevention through regulation and inspection. But as Austria was quick to demonstrate, the two policies did not have to be alternatives. There the amendment of the *Gewerbeordnung* modelled on England and Switzerland, the two most advanced countries in the regulation of working conditions, was practically contemporaneous with the introduction of accident insurance modelled on the German law. In the Austria of the 1880s social insurance and workers' protection were components of one and the same programme. As a historian of social policy has put it, 'social reformers . . . would have considered the postponement of workers' protection, as opposed to social insurance – a feature of Bismarck's social legislation – an untenable inconsistency'.[1] Great Britain in the 1890s also demonstrated that, even where factory regulation and inspection were accepted policy, problems with the law of employers' liability could propel governments towards a broader basis for compensation.

In Germany the two policies had been alternatives only because of Bismarck's hostility to the one and his creative commitment to the other. As long as Bismarck was in charge, the repeated attempts in the *Reichstag* throughout the 1880s to expand the regulation of working conditions, sometimes with the secret connivance of Lohmann in the ministry, were futile. They were blocked both in the *Reichstag* and, when necessary, in the *Bundesrat*, where Prussia, while lacking an absolute majority of votes, in

[1] Herbert Hofmeister, 'Austria', in Peter A. Köhler and Hans F. Zacher (eds.), *The evolution of social insurance 1881–1981: studies of Germany, France, Great Britain, Austria and Switzerland* (London and New York, 1982), p. 280.

practice controlled the decision-making process. But after much original disagreement over priorities, by 1888 the parties had hammered out a common set of legislative proposals. In that sense these seemingly barren years prepared a fertile ground for a subsequent harvest.[2]

In 1888 with the accession of William II at the age of twenty-eight, the position of the Chancellor began to look uncertain. 'I shall give the old man six months' grace and then I shall do the ruling', was one of several similar remarks reported by contemporaries.[3] In fact Bismarck remained in control for another twenty months, but he knew that he was fighting for survival and did so with all the ingenuity at his disposal. Lothar Gall has provided an interpretation of the last two years of Bismarck's chancellorship that treats every one of his often startling hints and proposals as mere tactics, thereby casting doubt on his actual commitment to any of them, be it the renewal of the Anti-Socialist Law on stricter terms or the possible abrogation of the constitution.[4]

The same kind of uncertainty does not apply to William's statements at the time. These were impulsive rather than calculated, giving rise to uncertainty of a different kind. How far did he understand the implications of what he was saying, and how far could he be relied upon to stand by his declared aims? Their disagreement over foreign policy need not concern us. In domestic matters William declared that he wanted to be the Emperor of his whole people. He identified with those who wished to heal the breach with the working-class movements by turning away from the politics of confrontation towards removal of legitimate grievances, particularly over conditions at work. The outbreak of a nationwide miners' strike had in any case focused attention on matters of this kind.

The good intentions that William had imbibed from his tutor were given substance with the help of new advisers, and were announced by William to his Prussian ministers on 24 January 1890. A version, edited by Bismarck himself, was published on 4 February as two imperial edicts. They envisaged additional regulation of hours and conditions of work, workers' representation on bodies for the settlement of industrial disputes, and reform of the Prussian mining industry. They also required the Chancellor to convene an international labour conference to limit working

---

[2] See Introduction to QS,II.3 for details.
[3] Gall, *Bismarck*, vol. II, p. 196.
[4] For the crisis of 1889–90 in its social policy aspect Gall, *Bismarck*, should be complemented by Hans-Jörg von Berlepsch, *'Neuer Kurs' im Kaiserreich? Die Arbeiterpolitik des Freiherrn v. Berlepsch 1890–1896* (Bonn, 1987). This is the most authoritative study of German social policy in the period 1890–6 and, where no other source is given, forms the basis for what follows.

hours on an international basis. Because the wording of these edicts was actually Bismarck's and they were said to have been signed by William without much attention to detail, their significance is distinctly Janus-faced. They have been interpreted as part of the tactical manoeuvring between Bismarck and the Emperor. But they were also generally regarded then and since as a public declaration of the Emperor's intention to embark on a social policy which would reverse that of the previous era both in principle and in detail.

Bismarck had reacted to the Emperor's announcement by suggesting the appointment of Hans von Berlepsch to the post of Prussian minister of trade and industry that Bismarck had held since 1880. Berlepsch, the president of the Rhine province, had gained a reputation for promoting conciliation in labour matters. He was the only person of any standing whom the Emperor was believed to have consulted, and Bismarck wished to tie him down with the responsibility of office.[5] Like other manoeuvres at the time this did not work as Bismarck had expected. On 18 March, three days into the International Labour Conference, Bismarck was forced to resign and was replaced as Chancellor by Leo von Caprivi. Berlepsch remained at the Prussian ministry of trade. Behind Berlepsch stood Lohmann, who could now return to the agenda that he was forced to shelve in 1879, and who now became the most influential of his advisers.

The Anti-Socialist Law was allowed to lapse later in 1890, more from inability to agree on the terms of its extension than from any considered decision to seek reconciliation with the Social Democrats. In the Bismarck era all power had been concentrated in his own hands, and no conflict between political repression and social policy had been allowed to arise. Under William II these two aspects of policy were to be the responsibility of different people. Which of them would dictate priorities at any given time depended on the particular constellation of power in the government of the *Reich* and of Prussia. In the years immediately after Bismarck's fall, social reform had priority and focused on matters that Bismarck had previously blocked. It was an aspect of the new direction (*Neue Kurs*) in which Germany ventured under Caprivi's chancellorship.

The International Labour Conference was held in Berlin after the Swiss had been persuaded to withdraw their earlier invitation to a conference in Berne. Foreign governments were puzzled how to interpret this German

---

[5] Bismarck was deliberately misled about William's principal advisers in order to protect Paul Kayser, specialist on international labour matters and civil servant in the Foreign Office. Berlepsch, *'Neuer Kurs'*, pp. 20, 25 and 48.

initiative. The British government's attitude to previous suggestions for such international conferences had been cool; it did not wish to be pressured to restrict economic freedom unless required by domestic considerations. However, since they did not wish to offer a slight to the German Emperor, they sent a government minister, Sir John Gorst, albeit one who, as Under-Secretary of State for India, had no responsibility for the matters to be discussed and could not be expected to commit himself to any proposals.[6]

The conference achieved some limited success in that it was able to pass resolutions recommending banning industrial work by children under twelve, limiting the hours of older children to six per day, and those of young people under sixteen to ten, while totally banning their work at night and on Sundays. But any hope that these resolutions would be binding international commitments were dashed. They therefore did nothing to fulfil the hopes of its German sponsors that they would safeguard German industry from being placed at a competitive disadvantage. Yet the publicity certainly reaffirmed the Emperor's commitment to the further regulation of working conditions.

That was done in the following year by amendments to the GewO, which in this respect had remained unchanged since 1878.[7] In 1878 Lohmann had tried to introduce restrictions on the work of adult women, in particular the prohibition of work at night and on Sundays, but had been stopped by Bismarck. The employment of women underground in coal-mines had been forbidden in Prussia and Saxony since 1867 and 1868 respectively, a prohibition reiterated in 1878 in the GewO. The only new concession that the *Reichstag* had obtained in 1878 was a clause to empower the *Bundesrat* to exclude women from employment in certain dangerous trades, a power that was very sparingly used. It had also insisted on some modest restrictions on the employment of women after childbirth.[8] In general, however, only children and young persons had been considered to need legislative protection, although the regulation of women's work was common in other European countries. Limitation of the hours of adult women date back in England to 1844; in Switzerland to 1877, and in Austria to 1884.[9]

---

[6] Gorst's attendance provides a good example of the indirect benefits that such international exchanges could have. For the interest in the German approach to accident insurance and old age pensions that he acquired on that occasion, and his role in disseminating these ideas in British political circles, see Hennock, *British social reform and German precedents*, pp. 52–8.

[7] There had been amendments in 1881 and 1883.   [8] Berlepsch, 'Neuer Kurs', pp. 250–8.

[9] Hutchins and Harrison, *Factory legislation*, p. 85; Lohmann, *Fabrikgesetzgebung*, p. 76; Hofmeister, 'Austria', p. 291.

In 1891 Germany finally accepted the principle that the hours of work for women were a proper sphere for state regulation. Night work and Sunday work were prohibited, a maximum working day of eleven hours was laid down with ten on Saturdays, as was a midday break of at least one hour, with the right of those with household responsibilities to demand an hour and a half. The ban on the employment of women after childbirth was extended from three weeks to six. None of these measures was at all controversial in principle; agreement had been reached well before.[10]

These regulations were to cover workshops as well as factories, and the remit of the inspectorate was extended accordingly, a process that was to be taken further in 1908. To reflect this broadening of their sphere of action, factory inspectors were to be known as *Gewerbe* inspectors and their numbers increased. They were given somewhat greater independence from the higher state authorities, but in contrast to Britain they continued to have to rely on the police to undertake the actual prosecutions.[11]

These restrictions on working hours, roughly similar to those in Britain, are too marginal to the subject of industrial injury to call for detailed comparison with Britain or assessment of their impact in practice.

An exception may be made over the prohibition of the employment of women after child-birth. This was a policy without parallel in Britain, and it presented many problems in practice. Having been first introduced in 1878 for three weeks, it was now extended to six weeks or to four weeks on the production of an appropriate medical certificate. No doubt this enabled those who wished to take this time off to do so without being penalised, but there is much evidence that women regarded the prohibition as a hardship. Since 1883 they had been entitled to sickness insurance benefit, but even this amounted to only half their normal wage. However, those who wished to return to work earlier than the law permitted usually found it possible to do so. The obligation was on the employer not to re-employ them in the prescribed period; all they had to do was to find employment where their recent pregnancy was not known.

Nevertheless, it was a policy that appealed to the legislators. The period was increased to eight weeks in 1908 in such a way as to include part of the pregnancy. Since prior to 1914 there was no right to insurance benefit for

[10] Wolfgang Ayass, "'Der Übel grösstes". Das Verbot der Nachtarbeit von Arbeiterinnen in Deutschland (1891–1992)', *Zeitschrift für Sozialreform*, 46 (2000), 189–220, for the widespread and highly moralistic condemnation of night-work for women. See also Sabine Schmitt, *Der Arbeiterinnenschutz im deutschen Kaiserreich. Zur Konstruktion der schutzbedürftigen Arbeiterin* (Stuttgart, 1995), p. 107.

[11] Simons, *Staatliche Gewerbeaufsicht*, pp. 99–100, 104–5 and 107.

this longer period, it is unlikely that this was much appreciated.[12] There was no such policy in Britain at any time in this period, perhaps because before 1912 the absence of universal health insurance which could replace the lost salary would have made such measures even more oppressive and nugatory than in Germany.

The willingness to restrict the working day for women contrasts with a refusal to introduce the eleven-hour maximum working day for adult men, as demanded by the SPD.[13] The International Labour Conference had made it clear that neither the British nor the Belgians were prepared to limit the hours of work of adult men. Not that an eleven-hour day was an issue in Britain; there the demand of part of the labour movement was rather for a maximum of eight hours. Berlepsch was quick to point to the British experience to suggest that a similar reduction in the hours of work could be expected to occur gradually in Germany, but that ignored the difference in the legal rights and actual strength of trade unions in the two countries at the time. In industries with a large female labour force men were to benefit from the adjustments required, and these tended to be the ones with the longest hours of work.

But much could be done by means of § 120 of the GewO, which permitted the *Bundesrat* to regulate conditions of work in the interests of life and safety. On three occasions it had issued regulations even in the unfavourable 1880s: for the use of white phosphorus in the manufacture of matches (1884), for the manufacture of lead paints and lead acetate (1886), and for the manufacture of hand-rolled cigars (1888). Of these, the first two processes were toxic and caused serious dangers to health, but were not accidents in the sense of the accident insurance law. These regulations were intended to protect the health of the work-force. So was the third which regulated the employment of large numbers of women in ill-ventilated rooms under insanitary conditions. They required the provision of toilets, washing facilities and changing rooms. They also prohibited sub-contracting, which was regarded as a threat to the morality of the women. Both health and decency were thus at stake.[14]

---

[12] Marlene Ellerkamp, *Industriearbeit, Krankheit und Geschlecht. Zu den Kosten der Industrialisierung: Bremer Textilarbeiterinnen 1870–1914* (Göttingen, 1991), pp. 176–81; Schmitt, *Arbeiterinnenschutz*, pp. 99, 106 and 125–6.

[13] In the 1860s and 1870s this had had the support of the Conservatives, but they increasingly distanced themselves from it once the SPD had made it their cause. Berlepsch, 'Neuer Kurs', pp. 192, 195 and 198.

[14] The other manufacturing process notorious at the time for its effect on the health of the work-force, the manufacture of mercury-coated mirrors, was not subject to any federal regulations. Regulations of various kinds had, however, been issued by Prussia, Bavaria and Baden, and these were harmonised with each other. Berlepsch, 'Neuer Kurs', p. 185; QS,II.3, Nos. 187, 43, 121 and 170.

In 1891 § 120 was amended so as to give the *Bundesrat* the right to introduce regulations limiting the hours of work in any trade where it considered the health of the workers to be endangered by excessive hours. In the words of the committee of the *Reichstag*, 'without prejudging the appropriateness of a maximum working-day for all, this proposal creates the possibility of removing the scandalous abuses in this respect that exist according to the reports of the factory inspectors in certain trades'. The way was thus opened for restrictions on the working hours of adult men. However, before appropriate regulations could be drawn up more needed to be known of what happened in various trades than could be obtained from the reports of the factory inspectors.

That was the task of another of Berlepsch's innovations, an Imperial Commission for Labour Statistics established in 1892. The name is misleading; we are really dealing here with the creation of a body to undertake investigations into the condition of labour, reminiscent of such British Royal Commissions as those of the 1840s and 1860s into childrens' employment. Like these it was expected to make recommendations for legislation on the regulation of labour, if necessary.[15]

Its first investigations dealt with conditions of work in the bakery trade, first brought to the attention of the public in 1889–90 by the Social Democrats. This was a trade in which organised labour was particularly weak. It was characterised by long hours of work, much of it at night, in rooms that were badly ventilated and badly lit, and by the ruthless exploitation of the apprenticeship system. The publication of the Commission's final report in 1894 indicated that here was an appropriate field for restriction on the work of young workers and the hours of labour generally. The trade consisted mostly of small businesses organised into bakers' guilds, against whose loud and well-organised protests Berlepsch had to fight for his policy. The issue was debated in a political atmosphere far removed from that of 1890–2. Chancellor Caprivi had been replaced by the Conservative Chlodwig von Hohenlohe. The Emperor had changed his domestic political priorities and was now calling for a 'fight against revolution' and the 'conjunction of all the forces supporting the State in opposition to Social Democracy', the so-called *Sammlungspolitik*. This implied a reliance on the political support of the *Mittelstand* and placed the bakers' guilds in a strong political position. Support from other government ministers was at best lukewarm. Only by threatening to resign and

[15] Berlepsch, *'Neuer Kurs'*, pp. 190–200.

making several concessions to the trade did he finally obtain the Emperor's grudging support.[16]

Berlepsch was to score another success before the political basis of his policy was altogether destroyed. In 1893 and 1895 the Commission produced two reports on the retail trades. These trades had already been investigated in 1876. Excessively long hours and conditions detrimental to health had been uncovered, but no action had been taken. The new investigation revealed that hours were now even longer. This was an area in which trade unionism had made no inroads. Without protection or rights, the workers were for good or ill entirely at the mercy of the decisions of their employer.[17] Under regulations issued in 1896 shops were to be open for a maximum of 13½ hours per day and not between 8 p.m. and 5 a.m.

Both regulations, those for bakers and confectioners and those for the retail trades, were issued under the powers of § 120 of the GewO. They did not have to be debated in the *Reichstag*. The true extent of the opposition to them only emerged when they came to be enforced. The 'maximum working day on grounds of health' had at first been supported by the Conservatives. Under the concerted pressure of bakers and retailers, respected members of the *Mittelstand*, they now withdrew their support in the *Reichstag* and left Berlepsch's policy backed by only the SPD and the Centre party. That made his position impossible unless he had the full support of the other ministers. When that was not forthcoming, he resigned in June 1896. In a bitter parting speech he defended his policy and accused the Conservatives of betrayal. It was the end of the period of reform.[18]

Such periods tend not to last long. They are the result of a rare political conjunction of forces, which disintegrates under the opposition of the vested interests affected. But in this case, more fundamental still was the change in the priorities of the Emperor. When he failed to stand firm, no one else could do so. *Sammlungspolitik* had replaced the *Neue Kurs*, and workers mattered less than small masters.

In the long run the restriction of working hours would be extended to other sectors of the economy. In 1897, when *Gewerbe* inspectors were asked

---

[16] *Ibid.*, pp. 206–15. [17] *Ibid.*, p. 216.

[18] There were other aspects of Berlepsch's reform programme, but these were less successful. Mention should be made, however, of the law of 1891 empowering local authorities to set up so-called Labour Courts, for which employers and workers provided an assessor each. In practice these courts had very limited powers, but were important for extending the principle of equal representation first established for appeal tribunals of the insurance system. It should be added that the 8 p.m. closing time for shops did not survive Berlepsch's fall, but in 1900 a revised *Gewerbeordnung* laid down a 9 p.m. closing time, a midday break of 1½ hours and a break between shifts of at least ten hours. Berlepsch, 'Neuer Kurs', pp. 84–126 and 225.

to indicate industries in which hours of work were detrimental to health, they named a total of fifty. Of these a small number were subsequently regulated. For women the maximum working day was reduced to ten in 1908. But the statutory maximum working day for all, as demanded by the Social Democrats, had to wait until 1919.[19]

(B) ENGLAND AND WALES

It was no more than a coincidence that the early 1890s were also a period of expansion and innovation in the regulation of working conditions in Britain. The consolidated Factory and Workshop Act of 1878 had been the climax of one period of legislative innovation and of an increase in the size of the inspectorate. It was followed by stagnation. The chief inspector, Alexander Redgrave, had been recruited in the distant 1840s and was of a conservative temper. Despite his opposition, the trade union movement obtained the appointment of junior inspectors drawn from the working class, a sign of the increased attention paid by Liberal governments in particular to organised labour, and of the fact that the labour movement had become converted to state inspection. Ten junior inspectors were appointed between 1881 and 1886, but they were not used in any capacity in which their previous work experience would have been of value. The number of other inspectors did not increase at all between 1878 and 1891.

Redgrave's retirement in 1891, rapidly followed in 1892 by the appointment of Asquith as Home Secretary, began a new era of expansion and reform. With the support of a sympathetic Chancellor of the Exchequer, the inspectorate was increased by a further twenty, of whom only five were inspectors' assistants, as the working-class junior inspectors were now called. The administration was decentralised by the establishment of seventeen regional offices. Two of the new inspectors were women, a significant innovation that had long been opposed by Redgrave but had the firm support of his successor. This women's branch was directly under the control of the chief inspector. The 'lady inspectors' were well educated and dedicated pioneers in their new role. They proved such a success that by 1914 their numbers had increased to twenty-two.[20] A similar development occurred in Germany. From 1897 a few women were appointed in the smaller states and Prussia following suit in 1900. By 1914 there were altogether forty. Except for a solitary inspector in Baden

---

[19] Berlepsch, *'Neuer Kurs'*, pp. 217–25; Schmitt, *Arbeiterinnenschutz*, pp. 120–1.
[20] M. D. McFeely, *Lady inspectors* (Oxford, 1988), vividly conveys the pioneering ethos.

these German women, in contrast to those in Britain, were appointed as mere assistants.[21]

In 1894 a general overhaul of the statistical service of the Home Office produced improved factory statistics. Then, within a few months of the fall of the Liberal government, the appointment of Thomas Whitelegge as chief inspector provided another boost. Whitelegge was a doctor and a former county medical officer, an outsider whose appointment was a recognition of the importance of the impact of working conditions on health. He provided capable leadership for the next twenty-one years.[22]

In Britain official concern over occupational diseases went back to the 1850s. It owed much to John Simon, Medical Officer at the Privy Council. Simon obtained the appointment of Dr Edward Greenhow to a lectureship in public health at St Thomas's Hospital, the first post of this kind in Britain. Greenhow began to analyse the Registrar General's mortality returns to identify occupation as the possible causes of differences in death-rates. Simon thereupon commissioned him to investigate respiratory diseases in industrial centres. That was followed by an investigation of industries using toxic substances, such as arsenic, phosphorus, lead and mercury. It was to facilitate the correlation of mortality statistics with occupations working with particular materials that the occupation tables of the census were revised in 1861.[23] The response to the evidence on the dangers of dust and toxic fumes was to require ventilation, first generally in 1864, and more specifically in 1867 with the installation of mechanical fans. Where workers were at risk from work with white lead, the employment of children and women under eighteen was prohibited and so was the consumption of food in work-rooms.

There is no reason to think that this legislation, again culminating in the Act of 1878, had much practical effect any more than the Prussian regulations mentioned above. It was neither specific enough, nor could it be adequately enforced by the inspectorate of the 1880s.[24] It is significant that the first attempt to lay down detailed measures, in 1883, was not the result of accumulated experience by the inspectorate, but of the insistence of two backbench MPs connected with the trade union movement. John Broadhurst and John Burt drew their knowledge of the fatal nature of

---

[21] Simons, *Staatliche Gewerbeaufsicht*, pp. 119–20. Figures from Stephan Poerschke, *Die Entwicklung der Gewerbeaufsicht in Deutschland* (2nd edn, Jena, 1913), Tables I–VI.

[22] Pellew, *Home Office*, pp. 151–58.

[23] Edward Higgs, 'The struggle for the occupational census, 1841–1911', in Roy MacLeod (ed.), *Government and expertise* (Cambridge, 1988), pp. 77–9.

[24] A. S. Wohl, *Endangered lives* (London, 1983), pp. 261–4 and 270–1.

lead poisoning from newspaper coverage of coroners' reports. Their persistence led the Home Office to commission an inquiry by Redgrave. When that produced proposals that failed to satisfy them, the Home Office commissioned a more thorough one. This proposed to compel manufacturers to provide a range of safety measures and was adopted in the Factory and Workshops Amendment Act of 1883, also referred to as the White Lead Act. It was the first legislative attempt to suppress an industrial disease by measures specifically devised for the conditions of that industry. The publicity that had surrounded it in turn prompted the *Bundesrat* to issue its own regulations in 1886. Like other legislative landmarks, its practical effect should be regarded with scepticism; it was neither adequately enforced nor were the regulations based on a full appreciation of the cause of the disease. But it provided the model for further regulations in the 1890s specifically directed at other dangerous trades.[25]

After 1891 the Home Secretary could certify any manufacturing trade as dangerous and injurious to health. He could propose a set of special rules, but the employers had the right to object and, if necessary, to insist on arbitration. This was a procedure that caused much delay, and the right to arbitration was therefore abolished in 1901.[26] The practice was to appoint a departmental committee to investigate a particular trade before issuing special rules. The first, in 1893, investigated the various lead industries and proposed a tightening of the regulations issued under the Act of 1883. Others soon followed, dealing with previously neglected trades. Compulsory notification of certain industrial diseases in 1895, although far from reliable, provided a statistical basis for investigation that was less chancy than the figures previously collected from hospitals. Under Whitelegge departmental committees of this kind multiplied and generated specialist knowledge that influenced policy-making. By 1914 at least a further forty subjects had been investigated and numerous special rules issued.[27] The appointment of a medically qualified inspector in 1898 resulted from this interest in occupational disease. By 1913 there were two, as well as two specialist inspectors of dangerous trades.[28]

---

[25] P. W. J. Bartrip, *The Home Office and the dangerous trades* (Amsterdam and New York, 2002), ch. 3. For the German regulations see p. 124 above.

[26] Peter Bartrip, 'Too little, too late? The Home Office and the Asbestos Industry Regulations 1931', *Medical History*, 42 (1998), 428.

[27] Thomas Oliver (ed.), *Dangerous trades*, pp. 24–44 and 827–64; and *Dangerous trades: action taken by the Home Office under the Factory and Workshop Acts, 1891, 1895 and 1901*, BPP 1906, Cd.3037, CX, 119.

[28] Pellew, *The Home Office*, p. 158.

From 1891 to 1914 Britain therefore regulated dangerous trades by special rules, designed for the specific circumstances of a constantly increasing number of industries, and adapted the inspectorate accordingly. After an initial delay, during which the restriction of working hours had topped the agenda, German policy-makers also turned their attention in the same direction. In 1891 § 120 of the GewO, which laid down the employers' obligation to safeguard his workers against dangers to life and health, had been expanded to include references to the provision of adequate light and air, the removal of dust, fumes and gases, the protection from contact with machinery and the avoidance of fires. But these general requirements were not enforceable unless accompanied by specific regulations. Their purpose was merely to provide a legal basis for them. They could be issued by an inspector for an individual establishment on the occasion of an inspection, or by the *Bundesrat* for a particular industry across the Empire. Failing the latter they could also be issued by the authorities in any of the federated states for their own territory. Apart from reissuing the regulations already made in the 1880s, the *Bundesrat* took no further action until 1897, when it regulated printing works and the manufacture of alkaline chromates. But after 1900 it produced a steady stream of regulations, extending them to further industries and increasing the demands on industries already regulated.[29]

After 1900 the two countries were therefore fairly similar in this respect. In 1911 the International Labour Office listed twenty-four industries under special regulations in Germany and twenty-eight in the UK.[30] Unfortunately the state of the existing historiography makes it impossible to compare the scope of regulations in detail or to assess the degree to which these were actually enforced. What is striking is the marked difference between the historiography on dangerous trades in the two countries.

The British historiography consists of studies of specific occupational diseases in their industrial setting, much of it fuelled by a critical interest in the operation of regulatory regimes, the production of scientific knowledge and its dependence on funded research. It is no accident that they mostly date from the period when policy-makers in Britain turned away from public ownership towards a reliance on the regulation of private enterprise. At the same time they required scientists to rely less on public funding and

---

[29] Berlepsch, 'Neuer Kurs', pp. 185–90; F. Syrup and O. Neuloh, *Hundert Jahre staatliche Sozialpolitik 1839–1939* (Stuttgart, 1957), pp. 93–6, lists fifteen such regulations issued between 1900 and 1914. There is no indication in any of these monographs of the extent to which individual states made use of their reserve powers to issue regulations.

[30] ILO, *First comparative report on the administration of labour laws: inspection in Europe* (London, 1911), pp. 17–18.

to go into the market-place for the funding of their research. Since in these matters British policy has followed American precedents, this historiography has been significantly influenced by studies in America.[31]

Most of the British studies deal with policy after 1914.[32] But there are at least four exceptions. These deal with white lead and arsenic in a number of industrial processes, with white phosphorus in the manufacture of matches, and with anthrax in the textile industry.[33] They relativise the role of the inspectorate and of routine inspection by drawing attention to initiatives taken by coroners, local trades councils, MPs, local authorities and their medical officers of health, but in particular by pressure groups and press campaigns. Mortimer and Melling's work on the Bradford-based Anthrax Investigation Board provides an early example of the use of research bodies financed by the industry in question to control the research agenda in the interest of employers.[34]

On the other hand, there exists an extensive German literature that emphasises the way in which the intellectual dominance of a scientific model of causation in conjunction with the operation of accident insurance shaped the priorities of a new body of experts in industrial hygiene.[35] The

---

[31] Peter Bartrip and R. M. Hartwell, 'Profit and virtue: economic theory and the regulation of occupational health in nineteenth and twentieth century Britain', in, Keith Hawkins (ed.), *The human face of law: essays in honour of Donald Harris* (Oxford, 1997), pp. 45–63, for an explicit acknowledgment of the first of these influences. For the second see the influential study by David Rosner and Gerald Markovitz, *Deadly dust: silicosis and the politics of occupational disease in twentieth century America* (Princeton, 1987).

[32] G. Tweedale and P. Hansen, 'Protecting the workers: the medical board and the asbestos industry, 1930s–60s', *Medical History*, 42 (1998), 439–57; Bartrip, 'Too little, too late?'; G. Tweedale, *From magic mineral to killer dust: Turner & Newall and the asbestos hazard* (Oxford, 2000). For subjects other than asbestos see the pioneering collection of conference papers, P. Weindling (ed.), *The social history of occupational health* (Croom Helm, 1985).

[33] P. W. J. Bartrip, *The Home Office and the dangerous trades* (Amsterdam and New York, 2002); Clare Hollingworth, *Potters' rot and plumbism: occupational health in the North Staffordshire Potteries, 1890–1914* (unpublished PhD thesis, University of Liverpool, 1995); Carolyn Malone, 'The gendering of dangerous trades: government regulation of womens' work in the white lead trade in England, 1892–1918', *Jl of Women's History*, 8 (1996), 15–35; Lowell J. Satre, 'After the match girls' strike: Bryant and May in the 1890s', *Victorian Studies*, 26 (1982), 7–31; I. Mortimer and J. Melling, 'The contest between commerce and trade, on the one side, and human life on the other: British government policies for the regulation of anthrax infection and the wool textile industries, 1880–1939', *Textile History*, 31 (2000), 222–36.

[34] Mortimer and Melling, 'Contest' pp. 224–6.

[35] Dietrich Milles, 'Zur Dethematisierung arbeitsbedingter Krankheiten durch die Gutachtermedizin in der Geschichte der Sozialversicherung' and 'Pathologie des Defektes oder Ökonomie der Arbeitsfähigkeit. Zur Dethematisierung arbeitsbedingter Krankheiten in der Soziogenese der Arbeitsmedizin', in Rainer Müller and Dietrich Milles (eds.), *Beiträge zur Geschichte der Arbeiterkrankheiten und der Arbeitsmedizin in Deutschland* (Dortmund, 1984), pp. 534–50 and 123–79. Likewise D. Milles, 'From worker's diseases to occupational diseases: the impact of experts' concepts on workers' attitudes', in Weindling, *Social history of occupational health*, pp. 55–77;

scientific model diverted attention away from the deterioration of health caused by industrial labour as such, which was considered a normal consequence of work, to the so-called occupational diseases that could be proved to have been caused principally by the conditions of work in a particular trade, i.e. to the dangerous trades. Compensation under the accident insurance law was governed by the legal definition of an accident as an injury demonstrably caused by a sudden event, and excluded all forms of illness that did not fall within this tight definition. It thus excluded the occupational diseases.

This double exclusion pushed the study of industrial hygiene towards a preoccupation with the establishment of claims for compensation by individual workers. This is where in practice there was a demand for the new experts, as referees at the service of the *Berufsgenossenschaften*. There was little if any demand for studies that focused on the prevention of ill-health through changes in industrial processes. The freedom of choice that the *Berufsgenossenschaften* enjoyed in the selection of referees largely placed the medical experts at their mercy and inevitably discouraged them from raising wider questions about the implications of industrial processes for the health of workers. There was nothing to be hoped from employment by the state. The *Gewerbe* inspectorate was recruited from graduates in mechanical engineering or chemistry. All attempts from within the profession to persuade the Prussian authorities to appoint medically qualified inspectors failed prior to 1921. Only Baden and Bavaria made a medical appointment, in 1906 and 1909 respectively.[36] Numerically that was not so different from Great Britain, even if the first British appointment had taken place a decade earlier. But the argument is that their influence was minimal, and that could not have been said of Britain at the time.[37]

D. Milles and R. Müller, 'Zur Dethematisierung sozialpolitischer Aufgaben am Beispiel des Gesundheitsschutzes für Arbeiter in historischen Rückblick', in F.-X. Kaufmann (ed.), *Staat, intermediäre Instanzen und Selbsthilfe. Bedingungen sozialpolitischer Intervention* (Munich, 1987); D. Milles, 'Industrial hygiene: a state obligation? Industrial pathology as a problem in German social policy', in W. R. Lee and E. Rosenhaft (eds.), *The state and social change in Germany, 1880–1980* (Oxford, 1990), pp. 161–99; D. Milles, 'Medical opinion and sociopolitical control in the case of occupational diseases in the late nineteenth century', *Dynamis*, 13 (1993), 139–53.

[36] T. Sommerfeld, *Der Gewerbearzt* (Jena, 1905); Rainer Müller, 'German occupational health statistics', in Weindling (ed.), *Social history of occupational health*, p. 130. Although not mentioned by Milles or Müller, Württemberg also made a similar appointment in 1905 but on a part-time basis. Stephan Poerschke, *Die Entwicklung der Gewerbeaufsicht in Deutschland* (2nd edn, Jena, 1913), Table IV.

[37] In his report to the Labor Statistics Bureau of the US Department of Labor (Bulletin No. 142), George M. Price points out that Britain and Belgium were the only countries with separate medical divisions in their factory inspection departments and attaches considerable importance to this fact in his Anglo-German comparison. *The administration of labor laws and factory inspection in certain European countries* (Washington, 1914), p. 15.

The acceptance of the deterioration of health caused by normal industrial labour as unproblematic, and the focus of attention on diseases that
could be proved to have been principally caused by the conditions of work
in a particular trade was common to both countries.[38] But the preoccupation with the history of insurance, even when it leads to thoroughly
negative conclusions, is a peculiarity of German historiography. In view
of the failure before 1925 to bring compensation for injury from occupational diseases within the scope of accident insurance, and the restriction of
the technical inspectors of the *Berufsgenossenschaften* to the prevention of
accidents, one would have expected historians interested in occupational
diseases to have paid some attention to the enforcement of the regulations
issued by the *Bundesrat*. Yet this is not so. In their preoccupation with the
double exclusion identified by them, they do not seem to have noticed that
they have added a further exclusion. There appear to be no historical
studies of the regulatory process such as there are for Britain.[39]

Before these contrasting historiographies can be used for a comparative
history of policy on occupational diseases, systematic research is required at
a level that cannot be attempted here. What can be done is to draw
attention to this need.[40]

In the absence of detailed studies of the control of particular industries,
any comparison of the regulatory work of the inspectorate is bound to
be crude. The most obvious differences were structural. In Germany there
were several bodies of inspectors. One consisted of the *Gewerbe* inspectors,
who operated separately in each of the states of the Empire but derived
their powers from the imperial GewO. Another consisted of the technical
inspectors under the control of the numerous *Berufsgenossenschaften* with
responsibility for a particular industry across the whole Empire, who
derived their powers from the Accident Insurance Law.[41] Yet a third

---

[38] See Barbara Harrison, *Not only the 'dangerous trades': women's work and health in Britain, 1880–1914*
(London, 1996), for a British study that refuses to be bound by this convention. Unfortunately by
consistently ignoring the situation of men she makes it impossible to assess the relative significance of
her evidence on women's employment.

[39] This is a conclusion reached after consulting Dr Milles.

[40] Vicki May und Katherine Bird, 'Berufskrankheiten in England und Deutschland. Historische
Entwicklungen und Forschungsfragen', in D. Milles (ed.), *Gesundheitsrisiken, Industriegesellschaft
und soziale Sicherungen in der Geschichte* (Bremerhaven, 1993), pp. 389–415, is a preliminary sketch
for a comparative research project that was aborted for lack of funding, according to information
from Dr Milles. It contributes little to the subject.

[41] The term was introduced only in 1900 to distinguish these inspectors from those engaged in
inspecting the books. It had at first been customary to use the same staff for the two purposes, a
practice that was still permitted even after the change in nomenclature. Simons, *Staatliche
Gewerbeaufsicht*, p. 162.

consisted of the police whose problematic relationship to the *Gewerbe* inspectors is a matter to which we shall return, after paying some attention to the relationship between the first two.

Neither in 1891, when the scope of the inspectorate was greatly enlarged by the new GewO, nor subsequently was a clear division established between the responsibilities of these two bodies. As long as the appointment of inspectors by the *Berufsgenossenschaften* was not mandatory it was impossible to exclude the state inspectorate from responsibility for measures in the interest of life and safety. Although the *Berufsgenossenschaften* that had appointed technical inspectors by the early 1900s were numerous, they were under no legal requirement to do so.[42] In the absence of a clear division, there was overlapping, friction and a failure of communication. These problems increased as the work of the *Berufsgenossenschaften* grew, although after 1900 the two sets of inspectors were at least no longer able to impose contradictory requirements on the same firm.[43] The German literature, both contemporary and historical, is much preoccupied with the disadvantages of this dualism. It pays surprisingly little attention to the possible advantage gained from the increase in inspections which must have resulted from it.

Even to leave aside the dual system in Germany and to concentrate on the factory inspectorate and its immediate German parallel does not dispel the impression that Germany was the land of diversity and Britain that of centralised control. That was partly due to the responsibility of the individual states and the directly administered imperial territory (*Reichsland*) of Alsace-Lorraine for inspection in their own territory. That alone meant twenty-six different inspectorates, with a variety of additional duties over and above those required by imperial legislation, and no attempts at setting common standards on the part of the *Bundesrat*. Such diversity had good aspects as well as bad. It enabled a small state like Baden to set an example and create a model service. Unlike other spheres, however, there was no professional organisation to compensate for the lack of action from the centralised administration by facilitating or publicising best practice. There was no association of German *Gewerbe* inspectors prior to 1919.[44]

---

[42] Only to issue safety regulations, and before 1911 even that requirement was at the discretion of the Imperial Insurance Office. Simons, *Staatliche Gewerbeaufsicht*, pp. 161–2 and 182.

[43] Simons, *Staatliche Gewerbeaufsicht*, for details pp. 141–59, 163 and 175–7, for a summary pp. 187–90.

[44] Simons, *Staatliche Gewerbeaufsicht*, pp. 108–11 and 114; W. Bocks, *Die badische Fabrikinspektion. Arbeiterschutz, Arbeitsverhältnisse und Arbeiterbewegung in Baden 1879 bis 1914* (Freiburg, 1978), pp. 20 and 48. In the early years the inspectors in Baden did at least have some contact with the Prussian ones through attending Prussian training courses.

Even Prussia, whose inspectorate of 328 in 1912 was by far the biggest of these, had no chief inspector. The individual principal inspectors enjoyed wide discretion within each of the state's thirty-three administrative districts (*Regierungsbezirk*), and even within the 187 inspection districts created specifically by the service. That contrasts sharply with the centralisation of the service in Britain under a chief inspector in London, and with the centralisation of such specialist services as the medical inspectorate and the women's branch. In Britain the provincial offices were principally bureaucratic devices for speeding up the flow of information between the centre and the sixty inspection districts that existed by 1914; they had no devolved discretion. Two international comparisons both emphasise the absence of central control and the markedly greater discretion enjoyed by German inspectors.[45]

As in the case of poor relief, Prussia emerges as the less centralised state, compared this time not only with England and Wales but even with Great Britain as a whole. In this matter Prussia was at the extreme end of the scale as far as the principal German states were concerned. At the other end was Baden whose far smaller territory was highly centralised under a chief inspector. Bavaria was less so and Saxony still less so.[46]

Such discretion as was exercised by the Prussian inspectors would have been impossible but for their high standards of technical training, 'the most highly technically trained men in inspection work in Europe'.[47] Even at the end of the period the formal entrance qualification to the British inspectorate reflected the tradition of recruiting men with a general education and required no more science than any educated man could acquire. But in practice a large proportion of British inspectors did have technical training as engineers, chemists or sanitary inspectors, while others had been managers of businesses.[48] The greater discretion allowed in Prussia had probably more to do with contrasting legal traditions and with the fact that in Prussia inspection had from the first been the responsibility of the district not the central administration.

The Anglo-German difference in the form and nature of their legislation has already been mentioned in the context of the 1870s and before.[49] After 1890 the German practice of providing a general framework of legal obligations, but one that had to be supplemented by specific regulations

---

[45] Price, *Administration of labor laws*, p. 22; International Labour Office, *Factory inspection: historical development and present organisation in certain countries* (Zurich, 1923), p. 9.
[46] Simons, *Staatliche Gewerbeaufsicht*, pp. 112–16; Price, *Administration of labor laws*, p. 13.
[47] Price, *Administration of labor laws*, pp. 18 and 22.
[48] Pellew, *Home Office*, p. 159.   [49] See pp. 83–5 above.

before they could be enforced, finds some parallel in the discretionary powers contained, for instance, in the British Factory and Workshop Act of 1891. This authorised the Home Secretary to schedule a list of dangerous trades and issue special rules for their regulation. But important differences still remained. These discretionary powers were granted solely to the Secretary of State, not as in Germany to the *Bundesrat* in the first instance and, failing action there, to the lower authorities at the level of state governments and police authority. The British inspectors were subject to no more than one authority; they were not expected to operate under the patchwork of regulations that characterised the situation in Germany.

In Britain the only matter faintly resembling this lack of co-ordination was the responsibility of local authorities for the sanitary inspection of workshops, which had survived the abolition of the full local authority responsibility for the inspection of workshops that existed from 1868 to 1878. But local sanitary inspectors were increasingly obliged to report their actions to the factory inspectorate, to whom they were increasingly subordinated.[50]

To complete the picture for Germany we need to deal with the role of the police. What was said of the German inspectorate in the 1850s[51] remained true, despite a rapid increase in numbers from 1891 to 1914. They were now easily distinguished from police officers by their status and expertise, but they were still essentially specialists intended to supplement the police in the tasks for which the latter were not adequate. The police continued to have a general responsibility for enforcing the law, including the GewO, in its more straightforward aspects. These included the proper display of regulations, the inspection of records of employment, and the observation of the prohibition of Sunday work. Such matters were more easily monitored than more technical ones.[52] German policemen did some of the work that was done in Britain by assistant inspectors (or junior inspectors as they were called before 1893) recruited from the working-class. They were also frequently employed on follow-up inspections to check on compliance with recommendations originally made by the inspectors. The whole relationship in Germany between local police authorities and the inspectorate was of a kind that had no parallel in Britain, where inspectors were directly under the Home Office and undertook their own prosecution of offenders. In Germany inspectors could only recommend prosecution; the decision to do so and the conduct of such cases rested with the police authorities. The time spent by British inspectors in court should therefore

---

[50] H. A. Mess, *Factory legislation and its administration 1891–1924* (London, 1926), passim.
[51] See pp. 84–5 above.   [52] Simons, *Staatliche Gewerbeaufsicht*, pp. 126–7.

be set against that spent by German ones on corresponding with the police authorities over details, and the frustration and bureaucratic delay that this involved.[53]

These structural differences hardly touch on the question of comparative effectiveness. By 1913 there were 217 inspectors in Britain including twenty-two women inspectors and working-class assistant inspectors. In Germany, in addition to the 386 technical inspectors of the *Berufsgenossenschaften*, there were 565 inspectors including forty women assistants, one woman inspector and some working-class assistants. That was the highest total in any European country.[54] For purposes of comparison these figures need to be converted into ratios. One relevant measure would be the frequency with which the registered firms in each country were inspected. Figures of this kind are available for both countries, but in such complicated and different ways that it is impossible to reach any conclusion, however tentative.[55] It looks at first sight as if British firms were inspected more frequently, even when the work of technical inspectors of the *Berufsgenossenschaften* is included. But the lack of information on inspections by the police renders such a conclusion unreliable.[56] Since no other evidence on relative effectiveness is available, this question must reluctantly be left unanswered.

Here is a serious obstacle to any final assessment of the Anglo-German differences that have emerged in these four chapters. To put Bismarck's accident insurance into its historical setting reveals it as a deliberate move to block the development of German factory legislation and inspection along the lines and up to the standard that had become accepted in other comparable European countries. It implies the replacement of prevention

---

[53] Shortly before 1914 in Hamburg, Saxony and Prussia inspectors were given at least the decision-making power. Simons, *Staatliche Gewerbeaufsicht*, pp. 115–16.

[54] Prussia had consistently refused to appoint working-class assistants. These were from the southern states, and from Saxony, Hesse and Bremen. Annual Report of the *Chief Inspector of Factories and Workshops*, BPP 1914 Cd.7491 XXIX, 541, Table 23; Simons, *Staatliche Gewerbeaufsicht*, pp. 117–18, 122 and 171. The total of women was for 1911. Poerschke, *Entwicklung*, Tables I–VI.

[55] For Germany Poerschke, *Entwicklung*, provides tables based on information extracted from the annual reports issued by the various states and *Berufsgenossenschaften*. For Britain the information is presented in a table on the Administration of the Factory Acts in the Annual Reports of the Chief Inspector for Factories and Workshops in the BPP, and for the years 1905–9 in the *Report of the Departmental Committee on factory accidents*, p. 51. BPP 1911 Cd.5535 XXIII.

[56] The International Labour Office provides figures for 1909 which, while being very much higher for the UK than for Germany, are also unuseable in view of the different methods on which they are based. According to a later study there are no statistics showing the extent to which the German police authorities assisted in factory inspection. ILO, *First comparative report*, Table I and p. 5; ILO, *Factory inspection: historical development and present organisation in certain countries* (Geneva, 1923), p. 86.

by compensation. Alongside the traditional literature that celebrates the establishment of insurance, there is now one that presents it as marginalising the protection of the work-force. As Lothar Machtan has put it, 'The material security that was gained through social insurance seems relatively small when compared with the burden of risk concurrently imposed on the workers in the interest of employers.'[57] In that critical historiography Britain provides one of the models despite the shortcomings of its workmen's compensation. Machtan writes of 'that peculiarity of the German welfare state at the end of the nineteenth century that, instead of prevention of injury being elevated to the leading principle and the residue of risk left to be dealt with by compensation – as for instance in England – on the contrary, compensation was erected on a narrow, too narrow base of protective measures of prevention.' Was there necessarily a trade-off between compensation and prevention, as Machtan appears to suggest? When he writes that 'the historical progressiveness of German workers' insurance was bought at the cost of chronic backwardness in the regulation of conditions of work for the protection of the work-force', he is commenting on the implications of Bismarck's policy for the longer term.[58] Yet how chronic was this backwardness? Was it a temporary setback that could be put right after his fall and had been largely overcome by 1914? Or have we been observing a shift in priorities that could not be altered?

This presentation has tended towards the first line of argument. Bismarck undoubtedly meant to prevent state interference with production. The control by *Berufsgenossenschaften* over safety was merely an option that they could adopt, if they wished, to cut their costs. The Imperial Insurance Office, however, strongly encouraged them to develop safety regulation and inspection both quantitatively and qualitatively. In any case the regulation of working conditions was never monopolised by the *Berufsgenossenschaften* with their narrow concerns with safety regimes that would pay for themselves by reducing compensation payments. After 1890 state regulation and state inspection acquired a dynamic, which, while greater in some years than in others, could not be reversed or checked. The untidiness of the dual system

---

[57] Lothar Machtan, 'Risikoversicherung statt Gesundheitsschutz für Arbeiter. Zur Entstehung der Unfallversicherungsgesetzgebung im Bismarck-Reich', *Leviathan*, 13 (1985), 420–41, quotation on p. 41. Machtan, Milles and Müller, all from the University of Bremen, are the leading exponents of this critical school.

[58] Lothar Machtan, 'Der Arbeiterschutz als sozialpolitisches Problem im Zeitalter der Industrialisierung', in Hans Pohl (ed.), *Staatliche, städtische, betriebliche und kirchliche Sozialpolitik vom Mittelalter bis zur Gegenwart*. VSWG, Beiheft 95 (Stuttgart, 1991), 111–36, both quotations on p. 136.

of inspection, described and deplored by Simons, ensured that the public interest was allowed to intrude into the economic priorities of industry. 'To catch up with international standards' is how Machtan describes the policy of 1890–1914 and that probably settles the matter for the purpose of comparison, even if he himself would have preferred Germany to have had the pioneering role.[59] It justifies my own decision not to differentiate sharply in this matter between the two countries.[60] After all, modern historians who have studied the effectiveness of factory regulation and inspection in either country are equally critical.[61] The significant difference between the two countries may well lie not here but, as Machtan perceptively suggests, in the ability of British trade unions to insist on some degree of control over working practices. That undoubtedly influenced working hours and thereby probably also increased safety. Other practices on which the unions were able to insist might well have had the same effect.

[59] Machtan, 'Arbeiterschutz', p. 136.

[60] Since this chapter was written much the same conclusion has been reached in W. Ayass, 'Bismarck und der Arbeiterschutz'.

[61] 'Inadequate, although imposing in international comparison': Simons, *Staatliche Gerbeaufsicht*. 'There seems little justification for holding up the early British factory legislation as an example of effective regulation': P. W. J. Bartrip and P. T. Fenn, 'Factory fatalities and regulation in Britain, 1878–1913', *Explorations in Economic History*, 25 (1988), 60–74, quotation on p. 73.

PART III

Sickness, invalidity and old age

This Part deals with a combination of three distinct subjects: public provision for temporary sickness, invalidity and old age. There are two reasons for treating these three together in a comparative study, not under two separate headings as is usual when no Anglo-German comparison is involved. In the German legislation, invalidity was dealt with in conjunction with old age; in the British legislation, in conjunction with temporary sickness. Secondly, in Germany the sickness insurance law of 1883 was a necessary complement to accident insurance, which was enacted in the following year. In Britain health and disablement benefits, provided in the National Insurance Act of 1911, were a necessary complement to the Old Age Pensions Act of 1908. That means that, in order to understand the provision made for invalidity (or disablement as it was called in England at the time), we have to consider the provisions made by Part I of the National Insurance Act that dealt with health insurance but also those of the German Law on Invalidity and Old Age Insurance of 1889. Yet to understand the circumstances which led to the legislation, we have to look at the consequences of German sickness legislation and of the British Old Age Pensions Act. The legal provisions pull one way; the politics pull the other way. Only as a triad can this history be adequately compared.

Two further points should be borne in mind. In Germany we shall be dealing with the events of the 1880s; in England with those of twenty-five years later. But in neither country was the relevant legislation inscribed on a *tabula rasa*. It dealt with institutions of long standing, the Prussian *Krankenkassen* and the English friendly societies. The policies that had shaped these went back in Prussia to the 1840s and in England even further. We first need to compare these institutions and these policies.

Although the institutions met some of the same needs, they were the outcome of very different processes. In England and Wales working people chose to associate for the purposes of fellowship that expressed itself in mutual support in times of need. This aspect became increasingly routinised with a growing emphasis on calculability, so that it becomes possible to speak of insurance. The government's response to this pheno-menon took the form of registration and regulation, in order to facilitate and guide what was regarded as potentially a highly desirable development. But registration and regulation were constrained by the knowledge that what people had chosen to do they could choose also not to do. When studying government policy in this sphere we are watching government in a liberal society experimenting with forms of action designed to preserve and foster rather than to abrogate the voluntary impulse towards mutual support.

The German circumstances could hardly be different. They involved a society in which people were traditionally obliged to belong to corpora-tions whose rules and customs governed what they could do and on which they could rely for mutual support. Government policy in the nineteenth century was to assert the supremacy of the State over these corporations, to decide which of the traditional forms of regulation and constraint to dismantle and which to reshape under its own control. Faced with the problems of a working population, which in times of sickness threatened to become an unacceptable burden to the communal taxpayer, it resorted to the reshaping and extension of the institutions of compulsion familiar from the past. In Prussia and subsequently in the German Empire government was experimenting with forms of compulsory mutual support and with the conditions under which it was possible to institute and control them. Liberal ideas in favour of voluntary action were not unknown and they occasionally impinged on government policy. But they were marginal to it, just as the voluntary institutions of mutual support that also existed were marginal to the available provision.

The support provided for individuals in times of need is capable of comparison, in so far as administration under such different conditions generated evidence in a comparable form. So is the extent to which the working population of the two countries was included in the networks of mutual support. Until the introduction of National Insurance in 1911, however, government policy hardly lends itself to anything but contrast.

7

The friendly societies of England and Wales

We shall start with England and Wales and its friendly societies.[1] Friendly societies belong to the category of working-class associations. Indeed they were the most successful example of the kind. In 1904 there were 5.6 million members of registered friendly societies of various kinds in the UK compared with 2 million trade unionists.[2] Their growth should be regarded as an aspect of ordinary working men's capacity to organise themselves to meet their needs as they themselves identified them.

An important contribution that public policy made to the growth of the movement was through the deterrence that largely characterised the Poor Law after 1834. That was intended as an incentive for those who could do so to ensure their independence through mutual help, and it seems to have had that effect. The extent to which the rapid increase in membership and in the number of societies recorded between 1835 and 1845 was a reaction to the change in Poor Law policy rather than to other causes is uncertain.[3] However, the determination of most working men to remain independent

[1] General surveys are P. H. J. H. Gosden, *Friendly societies in England 1815–1875* (London, 1961); P. H. J. H. Gosden, *Self-help: voluntary associations in Great Britain* (London, 1973); David Neave, 'Friendly societies in Great Britain', in Marcel van der Linden (ed.), *Social security mutualism* (Berne, 1996), pp. 41–64; and Simon Cordery, *British friendly societies, 1750–1914* (Basingstoke, 2003). This chapter, originally written in 1995, has been revised in the light of later publications, where these provide new evidence and perspectives.

[2] Gosden, *Self-help*, p. 91; B. R. Mitchell and P. Deane, *Abstract of British historical statistics* (Cambridge, 1962), p. 68. The figures used in the subsequent tables are on the more selective basis required by the focus on sickness insurance and are limited to England and Wales. For the difference between friendly societies and trade unions see pp. 149–50 below.

[3] The view that this growth in a period of adverse economic conditions was only explicable as a response to the changes in the Poor Law, originally put forward by Gosden, is supported by Neave, even after making allowance for other influences suggested by recent historians. Gosden, *Friendly societies*, pp. 205–9; Neave, 'Friendly societies', pp. 46–8. For this debate see also David Neave, *Mutual aid in the Victorian countryside: friendly societies in the rural East Riding 1830–1914* (Hull, 1991), pp. 17–21; J. O'Neill, 'Friendly societies in Nottinghamshire 1724–1912' (unpublished PhD thesis, University of Nottingham, Trent, 1992), pp. 37 and 40; J. J. Turner, 'Friendly societies in South Durham and North Yorkshire c.1790–1914: studies in development, membership characteristics, and behaviour' (unpublished PhD thesis, Teesside Polytechnic, 1992), pp. 97–109.

of the Poor Law is well attested. For English working men friendly society membership became a status matter; the regular payment of contributions was both a means and a sign of that status.

Not that the treatment of lapsed friendly society members by the local Boards of Guardians was always as deterrent as in theory it was supposed to be. In practice members who had to turn to the Poor Law in old age were often treated less harshly than other paupers. Knowledge of that fact could also serve as an incentive to membership.

The most significant aspect of the history of English friendly societies is their development into regional and ultimately national groupings, the so-called affiliated orders. In 1877 there were 163 of these federations. Five years earlier thirty-four of them had a membership of over 1,000 each and a total membership of just on 1.3 million. The largest and most influential of the affiliated orders were the Manchester Unity of Oddfellows with over 426,600 members, and the Ancient Order of Foresters with over 388,800.

As its name suggests, the Manchester Unity of Oddfellows began in Manchester. It spread outwards from an original 'lodge', as the societies were called, by establishing similar lodges within the Manchester district. These provided sickness benefit out of their own individual funds but pooled their resources for the payment of funeral benefit. By the 1820s the Order had spread into Yorkshire and the Potteries, forming lodges grouped into districts with a common funeral fund and individual sickness funds. By 1827 the Manchester Unity had established the basic pattern of its federal form of representative government: a central Board of Directors under a Grand Master. The history of the Ancient Order of Foresters is similar, except that it originated in Leeds and its federal structure gave somewhat less authority to the Executive Council under its High Chief Ranger.[4]

The history of these affiliated orders is one of tension between central-ising tendencies emanating from the Board of Directors and Executive Council respectively and the fierce independence of the lodges, courts and districts. This led to secessions, a fact that accounts for the large number of affiliated orders in existence by the 1870s, many with similar names.[5] By the 1840s their position was secure and they had begun to expand well beyond their industrial heartland to become bodies of a national character.

[4] Gosden, *Self-help*, pp. 28–30 and 44–6.
[5] E.g. Grand United Order of Oddfellows, Bolton Unity of Oddfellows, London Unity of Oddfellows, National Independent Order of Oddfellows, Nottingham Ancient Imperial Order of Oddfellows. In 1877 there were thirty-four different Orders of Oddfellows, five of Foresters, eleven of Druids, ten of Ancient Britons and four of Rechabites: Gosden, *Friendly societies*, p. 47.

Individual societies continued to exist in large numbers, but the pace of development was set by the larger of the affiliated orders. Behind their centralising thrust lay concern for the financial viability of the individual lodges. It led the central body to insist on the provision of information on sickness claims. By 1840 the Manchester Unity was able to compile a table of probability based on the actual experience of its members. The knowledge required to levy premiums adequate to meet liabilities existed by 1850. Since individual societies, lodges etc. had been levying merely a customary rate of contributions, the task of bringing custom in line with actuarial demands began. Its pace varied greatly, with the Manchester Unity in the lead. As late as 1890 there were still smaller orders which had not introduced graduated scales, and many others, which on adopting the new scales had imposed them on new members only. The failure of the great majority even of the affiliated orders fully to cover their potential liabilities evoked critical comment for well over half a century, only to be remedied at a stroke in 1911 by the National Insurance Act, when the State took over the financing of most of these liabilities.[6]

In the reforms of the mid-century more was at stake than the size of the weekly contribution. The demands of rational calculation impinged on customary conduct, where sociability and mutual support in times of misfortune had always been intertwined. Club nights always had two components, a business meeting followed by a social function.[7] In 1845 the Manchester Unity ordered its lodges to establish a separate fund for all expenses other than sickness and funeral benefits. The drink consumed at the weekly meetings, which was how landlords were often paid for the use of a room, the annual feast and all other forms of sociability were not to impinge on the lodge's ability to meet its commitment to the financial security of its members.[8]

What was the relationship of the State to the societies? The authorities hoped that working-class mutual thrift would reduce the burden of the poor rates. On several occasions between the 1790s and the 1820s Parliament considered proposals for *compelling* the poor to belong to provident funds under the control of the parish. From a comparative

[6] Wilkinson, *Mutual thrift*, pp. 248–51; B. B. Gilbert, *The evolution of national insurance in Great Britain: the origins of the welfare state* (London, 1966), pp. 340–1.

[7] Cordery, *Friendly societies*, p. 34. Cordery is particularly valuable for his attention to the element of sociability, structured by ritual and characterised by 'carefully controlled rowdy enjoyment'. Much of his book is structured around the tension between sociability and financial calculation.

[8] Gosden, *Self-help*, p. 54. Readers of Cordery need to be reminded that the growing emphasis on bureaucratic norms and calculability did not come merely from the State but was part of a larger cultural change.

perspective the important point is that nothing came of these proposals. Parliament concentrated instead on the encouragement and supervision of *voluntary* societies. By legislation in 1793, 1817 and 1819 it offered societies willing to register with the county magistrates certain privileges. Some were financial, i.e. exemption from stamp duty and favourable rates of interest, some legal, i.e. the right to sue and be sued and therefore to protect themselves against defrauding office-holders.

The financial dangers that members ran sprang less from fraud than from their inability to estimate risk and to match contributions to benefit entitlement. Beginning in 1819 Parliament tried to discriminate between financially sound and unsound societies, but after investigation in 1825 and 1827 it reached the conclusion that the necessary knowledge was not available.

Legislation in 1829 and 1834 dismantled many of the former paternalistic controls. Policy came to reflect the liberal views of the reform era of the 1830s. The State was envisaged not as a controlling mechanism, intent on protecting the public interest or that of society members, but as an instrument to make relevant information available, leaving it to society members and the public to draw their own conclusions. Nevertheless, the element of control could not be entirely discarded. Since registered societies still enjoyed some financial and legal privileges, their rules were scrutinised to see whether they fulfilled the requirements of the law. But these financial privileges were being deliberately reduced, while the purposes for which lawful associations could be formed were in any case progressively expanded. Certification, the process of scrutiny, was taken out of the hands of the county magistrates, who had been erratic in the exercise of their powers, and became the responsibility of an official based in London. In 1846 he acquired the title of Registrar of Friendly Societies. He received a regular salary instead of fees, an establishment of clerks and office expenses. In 1857 he began to issue annual reports.

This State policy cannot be called a success. The more information the State insisted on receiving from societies applying for certification, and the fewer privileges it offered in return, the less willing these were to submit to public scrutiny. If the State wished to obtain at least some of the relevant information, it had to lower the barriers that prevented societies from co-operating, but even that brought only limited success. In 1874 it was estimated that only about two-thirds of the existing societies had registered, and of these only just over half sent in their accounts.[9]

[9] Gosden, *Friendly societies*, p. 194.

There are two further reasons why the State should not be credited with much of a role in encouraging the growth of the friendly society movement. In 1853–4 the Registrar commissioned an actuarial table of sickness, which he recommended for use by the societies. It was a sound enough calculation, based on a rigorous definition of sickness that excluded chronic ailments and disablement. Unfortunately it bore no relation to the actual world of friendly societies, where members suffering from those conditions would certainly have qualified for benefit. 'The government tables', as they were called, thus made it more difficult for societies to calculate their liabilities, and they undercut the effect of the revised tables issued by the Manchester Unity three years earlier.[10]

But the supreme irony is that the affiliated orders, the fastest growing and most progressive sector of the movement, was the one that received least encouragement from the State. Until 1850 their structure and constitution made them illegal under the Corresponding Societies Act of 1801, and even after that date the orders as such were ignored by the Registrar, who insisted on all lodges registering as individual societies. The consequence was widespread non-cooperation. This unsatisfactory situation changed only after 1875.[11]

Between 1871 and 1874 a royal commission investigated the whole friendly society phenomenon. This inquiry was followed in 1875 by legislation. What emerged was essentially a reaffirmation of the principles established since the 1830s. State policy was 'to provide managers of societies with information useful to them, and to require societies to provide the public with such information as would enable intelligent persons to judge the position of a society for themselves, but otherwise to leave them as free as possible to follow any course they pleased'.[12]

As we shall see, this was in marked contrast to the almost contemporaneous German Law of 1876, which narrowly defined the objects of registered funds and the way that they were run. The British left scope for the invention of new kinds of bodies capable of adapting to changing social conditions. The wisdom of this was demonstrated towards the end of the century, when alternative leisure pursuits had become available, by the rapid growth of centralised societies without local branches and conviviality.[13]

---

[10] *Ibid.*, pp. 102–4.   [11] Gosden, *Self-help*, pp. 72–3 and 98–104.   [12] *Ibid.*, p. 80.
[13] E. W. Brabrook, *Provident societies and industrial welfare* (London, 1898), pp. 67–9; Paul Johnson, *Saving and spending: the working-class economy in Britain 1870–1939* (Oxford, 1985), pp. 61–2.

Registered societies had to submit accounts audited annually in a stand-ardised form. Every five years they had to submit a valuation of their assets and liabilities. Returns of sickness and mortality proved too much to expect and after 1881 they were no longer required. The Act laid down penalties for non-compliance.[14]

The office of Registrar was strengthened. There was now a Chief Registrar with Assistant Registrars for Scotland, Ireland and England (with Wales). He could cancel or suspend a registration, appoint inspectors or call a society's officers to a meeting to discuss any problems of which he was aware. In dire circumstances he could order the dissolution of a society at the request of a minority of its members. None of this amounted to much, but the power of temporary suspension proved a useful threat, inducing some societies, who would otherwise not have bothered, to make valuations of their assets and to submit regular returns. The other powers were invoked only on rare occasions; their mere existence probably did something to encourage compliance.

Societies were still under no compulsion to register. It was hoped that the advantages offered by registration would by themselves achieve the desired result. But 'if the society chooses to exist without those privileges, this is a free country and I should let them do it', said the Chief Registrar in 1906. He estimated the ratio of members of unregistered to registered societies in 1892 for England and Wales as 300:386, not far short of half the total friendly society membership.[15]

When one compares these English societies with the provident funds in Prussia, one is struck by some major differences. The most obvious relates to State policy. In view of the Prussian history of compulsion, which we shall examine in the next chapter, the British decision to confine the role of the State to enforcing the publication of information, and even then to rely on voluntary compliance, is highly significant.

Another is the emphasis placed on creating district and national struc-tures. This has a parallel in the German trade union funds, but none before the 1880s in the State-supervised funds in Prussia or Imperial Germany.

A third is the English preoccupation with the problem of adjusting contributions to liabilities. This is largely missing in Prussia and Imperial Germany. The difference arose from the fact that the financial problems of

---

[14] J. M. Baernreither, *English associations of working men* (London, 1889), p. 318.

[15] *Royal Commission on the Poor Laws*, Appendix, vol. III, Minutes of Evidence, Q.34331, BPP 1909 Cd.4755, XI, 541. For similar views expressed by his predecessor see Select Committee on National Provident Insurance, Minutes of Evidence, Q.1483, BPP 1884–5, (270) X. For 1892 see Gosden, *Self-help*, p. 91.

a voluntary society were different from one whose membership was compulsory. The latter could expect to continue to recruit young members, which was important since liability to sickness increases with age. For a voluntary society it was not enough merely to fix a standard contribution adequate to cover the annual benefits paid out, unless it was certain that young members would always be recruited in adequate numbers to cover the needs of those that were older. That could not be assumed on the basis of voluntary membership. Friendly societies therefore needed to accumulate a reserve to meet the higher claims inevitable at a later time. The size of this reserve largely depended on its age structure and posed a considerable challenge to the determination and actuarial sophistication of those who ran it.

For these reasons the introduction of rates of contributions that differed according to age was a significant development in the history of friendly societies. Differentiation of contributions by income was uncommon. But since different societies had different levels of contributions and benefits, they recruited their members accordingly.[16] There was certainly no compulsion to link the level of contribution to the level of wages, as was the case in certain Prussian funds in the 1870s and increasingly under the Imperial legislation of the 1880s.

Furthermore there were no contributions from employers on a compulsory basis. Most of the societies to which reference has so far been made were deliberately not confined to one particular occupation, nor to one particular firm. Within the limits imposed by the local employment structure, societies made a point of recruiting from as many occupations as possible. That made their income less vulnerable to disruption from temporary difficulties experienced by a trade or the failure of a particular firm.[17]

After 1825, when combination in restraint of trade ceased to be a criminal offence, friendly societies limited to a particular trade tended to use their accumulated funds for whatever purposes seemed most urgent for the defence of their trade interests. By registering under the Trade Union Act of 1871 they obtained recognition as legal associations. Since registration under the Friendly Society Act of 1875 required societies to submit their accounts in a form that separated benefit funds from other kinds of expenditure, they did not register as friendly societies. Despite their

---

[16] Sir George Young, *Report to the Royal Commission on Friendly Societies*, p. 2, BPP 1874 C.997, XIII Part II.
[17] Gosden, *Friendly societies*, pp. 71–2; Young, *Report*, p. 19.

names such bodies as the Friendly Society of Ironfounders and the Friendly
Society of Operative Stonemasons had the status not of friendly societies
but of trade unions. They undoubtedly provided sickness benefit and are
included in the statistical Appendix to chapter 9, in so far as it is possible to
identify them. But the legal distinction had significant implications for
their members' entitlement to sickness benefit.[18]

Naturally employers did not contribute to the sickness provisions of
trade unions not under their control. However, there were mutual benefit
societies to which they did make contributions. The most important of
these, which were briefly mentioned in chapter 3, were in mining and
railways. They received special treatment in both countries and can be
mentioned here only in passing before we turn our attention to Prussia.[19]

---

[18] For the role of trade unions as associations of mutual insurance, see S. Webb and B. Webb, *Industrial
democracy* (London, 1920 edn), Part II, ch. 1. The best recent study is in French, Noel Whiteside, 'La
protection du métier: l'organisation industrielle et les services des syndicats dans l'Angleterre de la fin
du dix-neuvième siècle', *Les cahiers d'histoire de l'institut de recherches marxistes*, 51 (1993), 29–51.

[19] For the provision of medical treatment and the societies' relation to the medical profession see
pp. 233 and 245 below.

8

From Prussian Hilfskassen to German Krankenkassen

(A) LEGISLATION FOR PRUSSIA

Friendly societies were part of the free associational life of the English working class. The vast majority of Prussian provident funds (*Hülfskassen*) were not. As already indicated, they originated from the compulsory organisation of the artisan trades through guilds. Their history is the product of the impact of State policy on guild organisation. We are dealing here with something quite different from voluntarism, a compulsory organisation unknown in England since the early eighteenth century. One of its aspects was the journeymen provident fund (*Gesellenladen*), membership of which was compulsory for all journeymen in the trade. In the course of the nineteenth century the German states dismantled the monopoly powers of the guilds over admission to the trade, a process in which Prussia was particularly to the fore. However, they enhanced their powers in some other respects, including assistance to journeymen in time of need, associated as this was with the disciplining of the labour force.[1] As membership of guilds ceased to be compulsory and masters were able to practise their trade and employ journeymen outside guild control, the State stepped in. In Prussia the industrial code (*Gewerbeordnung*) of 1845 authorised local authorities, if they wished, to reimpose the requirement on all journeymen in the trade to belong to the journeymen funds. In that case it was to scrutinise and sanction their rules. In 1849 the Prussian Ministry of Trade and Industry published model rules for their guidance.

The German working class did develop its own autonomous institutions for insurance against various contingencies including sickness, but, on account of the action of the State, they did so in a very different context

---

[1] Christiane Eisenberg, *Deutsche und englische Gewerkschaften. Entstehung und Entwicklung bis 1878 im Vergleich* (Göttingen, 1986), p. 257.

from that in England and a less favourable one. Their growth was confined to the interstices left by the State.[2]

It is useful to set the 1845 initiative against the background of the Prussian Poor Law legislation of 1842. That had imposed the duty of poor relief in the first instance on the corporate body to which a person belonged, but in the absence of corporate obligation on the local communal poor law authority (*Ortsarmenverband*) of the place of residence.[3] Communes could no longer assume that all journeymen, when reduced to distress by illness, would be supported by the guild. *Gewerbefreiheit*, freedom of occupation, increasingly drove them to rely on the commune. But any commune threatened by this process was free to adopt the powers granted in 1845 to protect itself.[4]

The local insistence on compulsory membership of provident funds, widely regarded as the forerunner of the insurance legislation of the Bismarck era, is often presented as a defensive reaction to the political threat of the proletariat in 1848. The policy of the 1880s could thus be presented as a repetition of the same political tactics of repression softened by palliative social policy measures.[5] Quite apart from the doubts that have now been cast on the view that this was the original reason for Bismarck's introduction of workers' insurance, one should note that the legislation on provident funds predates the events of 1848. It was initially a reaction to the distress widespread among artisans in the 1840s and to the changes in the poor law that had been introduced in the interest of labour mobility. The conventional interpretation is unravelling from both ends.

Further measures along the same lines as in 1845 followed after 1848. They were again commended on the grounds that they saved local communal authorities from an unsupportable burden of poor relief. To that consideration was now added the further one, that they would help to supervise the politically suspect journeymen funds and to protect the existing social order from a recurrence of major distress.[6]

---

[2] Gunnar Stollberg, '*Hilfskassen* in Nineteenth-Century Germany', in Marcel van der Linden (ed.), *Social security mutualism* (Berne, 1996), pp. 309–28, for a survey of them in English.

[3] See chapter 1 above.

[4] Wilfried Reininghaus, 'Das erste staatlich beaufsichtigte System von Krankenkassen: Preussen 1845–1869. Das Beispiel der Regierungsbezirke Arnsberg und Minden', ZSR, 29 (1983), 272–3.

[5] E.g. Gerhard A. Ritter, *Social welfare in Britain and Germany*, pp. 20 and 33–4; Heinrich Volkmann, *Die Arbeiterfrage im preussischen Abgeordnetenhaus 1848–1869* (Berlin, 1968), p. 39.

[6] We know from a study of Düsseldorf that journeymen associations of various kinds and various degrees of independence from their masters had developed by 1849. These were suppressed by the authorities and forced to adopt rules that confined them strictly to the business of a provident fund. In Westphalia similar bodies with a social life and regular meetings like that of English societies also

So much for the artisans. But economic development outside the ring-fence of the guild controls was not confined to the handicraft trades. By the 1840s factory workers could hardly be ignored in discussions of the social problem. The novelty of the changes taking place in the textile industry ensured that, if anything, factory workers gained attention out of all proportion to their contribution to the manual labour force or to the extent of dire poverty. The prominence of factory labour increased in the 1850s with the growth of the iron and steel industry.

The Industrial Code had mentioned factory workers in 1845, allowing them to join newly established provident funds. But no one took any action. Then the so-called Emergency Ordinance (*Notverordnung*) of 1849 laid down that the communal authorities could compel them to belong to provident funds. Factory owners could be compelled to make a financial contribution.

This State interest in provident funds for factory workers was an attempt to deal with them by institutions similar to those already provided for artisans. Just as existing artisan funds were placed under local authority supervision and supplemented by newly established funds for trades that had not had them before, so the benefit funds that factory owners had established for their workers were placed under similar supervision. Factory workers who had no fund were obliged to join funds under local authority supervision either jointly with artisans or established specifically for them. In this way all workers engaged in manufacture in a particular district could be made to belong to a local fund at the behest of the local authority. As the historian of this development explains, 'the primary consideration was the relief of the public poor law funds'.[7] Anxiety for poor law finance runs like a thread through the history of provident-fund legislation.

The communes were not much interested, however, in taking advantage of this protection. By the beginning of 1854 a mere 226 local authorities had adopted local compulsion, and of these no more than fifty-eight had required contributions from employers.[8] One explanation widely

---

failed to survive the years of reaction. Margaret Asmuth, *Gewerbliche Unterstützungskassen in Düsseldorf* (Cologne, 1984); Wilfried Reininghaus, 'Die Unterstützungskassen der Handwerkgesellen und Fabrikarbeiter in Westfalen und Lippe (1800–1850)', *Westfälische Forschungen*, 35 (1985), 130–63.

7 Reininghaus, 'Krankenkassen, p. 273. Similar views are expressed in Paul Honigmann, 'Zur Arbeiterkrankenversicherungsfrage', *Jahrbücher für Nationalökonomiee und Statistik*, NF 6 (1883), 97 and 259; Ute Frevert, *Krankheit als politisches Problem 1770–1880* (Göttingen, 1984), pp. 171–2; Heinrich Volkmann, *Die Arbeiterfrage im preussischen Abgeordnetenhaus 1848–1869* (Berlin, 1968), pp. 65 and 134.

8 *Die unter staatlicher Aufsicht stehenden gewerblichen Hülfskassen für Arbeitnehmer ... im preussischen Staate. Bearbeitet im Auftrage des Ministers für Handel, Gewerbe und öffentliche Arbeiten* (Berlin, 1878), p. II (to be cited as *Hülfskassen*).

canvassed at the time, particularly by the officials in the Ministry, was that the political influence of employers prevented local authorities from pursuing their own best interests. What should the State do? Should it respect the autonomy of local representative institutions or impose action on them for their own good? In this matter the authoritarian instincts of the Prussian bureaucracy won out.

In 1854, in addition to the local communes, State officials at district level (*Regierungsbezirk*) were authorised to establish provident funds with compulsory membership in any locality considered suitable. 'The protection of the communes from the impoverishment of this numerous class of inhabitants' stood once more at the forefront of the official justification of the law.[9]

This law was closely linked to the politics of poor relief. Whereas the government wanted the burden on the communes reduced through compulsory provident funds with employer contributions, the communes most severely affected by immigration had different priorities. In 1853 they petitioned for powers to limit freedom of movement so as to prevent what they saw as the increasing pauperisation of their locality.[10] That was unacceptable to the government, which remained committed to labour mobility.[11]

It responded to the political pressure under which it found itself by introducing two Laws: the Law on Provident Funds in 1854 and the amendment of the Poor Law (*Armenrechtsnovelle*) in 1855, referred to in chapter 1 above. The latter was no more than a minimum concession to the communes at the receiving end of the wave of migration. It made entitlement to relief from local funds subject to one year's residence. For that year it laid the obligation to pay for relief on the commune of previous residence.[12] Although a reversal of the policy of 1842, it was too slight to act as a brake on migration. Taken together the Laws of 1854 and 1855 demonstrate that the government preferred to invade the cherished autonomy of elected local government to acquiescing in a sharp reversal of its policy on labour mobility.

[9] Gesetz betr. die Gewerblichen Unterstützungskassen vom 3. April 1854, § 3 in *Hülfskassen*, p. 252.
[10] Jürgen Reulecke, *Geschichte der Urbanisierung in Deutschland* (Frankfurt, 1985), pp. 36–7, for the petitions to the Upper Chamber.
[11] Denkschrift zu dem Gesetz-Entwurf zur Ergänzung des Gesetzes vom 31. Dezember 1842 über die Verpflichtung zur Armenpflege, quoted in Volkmann, *Arbeiterfrage*, p. 81.
[12] Christoph Sachsse and Florian Tennstedt, *Geschichte der Armenfürsorge*, vol. 1, p. 203.

The legislation of 1854 was followed by a rapid increase in provident funds.[13] In the 1860s, however, as the political influence of the Liberals increased, so State compulsion received a setback. Trade unions were founded under Liberal influence, which established their own mutual benefit funds on the British pattern. These were soon followed by trade unions under Social Democratic influence with similar structures. Like the compulsory funds established by Prussian law, these trade union funds were organised on the basis of a single trade. But, unlike them, they were rarely organised exclusively on a local basis. Rather they mirrored the structure of the unions themselves with local branches and a nationwide organisation. More important still, the mutual insurance funds of the trade unions were based on the principles of freedom: freedom from employer control and consequently from employer contributions, freedom from state control, and (at least formally) freedom to join or not to join. Both Liberals and Socialists saw insurance funds as a valuable means of recruitment to trade unions, and in particular as a means to retain members' loyalty once the excitement of wage grievances and strike action had subsided. But the state of the law made it difficult to recruit among workers who were already compulsorily enrolled in state-supervised funds. On grounds of finance as well as of principle trade unions were firmly opposed to the only role that the law permitted them to play in the provision of insurance, namely levying contributions among their members over and above those that they already had to pay. Even that was at the discretion of the authorities without whose permission no association of any kind was lawful.

(B) LEGISLATION FOR THE NORTH GERMAN CONFEDERATION AND EMPIRE

These grievances would have been less serious but for the constitutional changes of those years. The North German Confederation introduced universal male suffrage in 1867 for elections to the *Reichstag*. That gave the workers a voice that could not be ignored. Social policy became a matter of party political differences, as it had not been in the Prussian Chamber.

Nor could the Prussian law be left in its existing state. It needed to be extended to the Prussian territories annexed in 1866 and fitted into a new Industrial Code for the North German Confederation as a whole. When

---

[13] Reininghaus, 'Das erste staatlich beaufsichtigte System', pp. 279–81 and 295–6; Volkmann, *Arbeiterfrage*, p. 76. Also QS,I.5, p. XXV. For the period 1867–1881 this source, and particularly the Introduction, provides the most authoritative treatment of the subject.

that Industrial Code was before the *Reichstag*, Socialists and Left Liberals co-operated in the interests of trade union benefit funds. An amendment permitted the requirement to join a provident fund to be met by membership of one of the 'free', i.e. voluntary, funds. To the annoyance of the government this was accepted by a narrow majority.

This § 141.2 of the Industrial Code was expected to encourage the growth of trade unionism by facilitating benefit funds on the British model. In practice the courts made difficulties over its interpretation, and the effect on the growth of trade unionism was probably slight.[14] But there is no doubt of its effect on provident funds. The snap amendment had left the law in a form that was far from clear. Contradictory decisions by the courts in various localities caused much confusion. The authorities thereupon stopped insisting on the establishment of further compulsory funds, leaving scope for the spread of free funds of whatever kind. Between 1868 and 1874 the number of officially supervised provident funds for artisans actually fell, while the total of all officially supervised funds rose by no more than 4 per cent.[15]

Even so, the government was in no hurry to amend the law, despite a request from the *Reichstag* for clarification. It judged the existing situation to be no real threat and the lesser evil to opening what it regarded as a can of worms. Ministers would gladly have restored the *status quo*. They had to admit, however, that this was politically out of the question.

There was no possibility of restoring the powers to direct workers to a particular fund, but nothing had yet been done to abandon compulsory insurance as such. Regulations were needed to ensure that voluntary funds offered benefits comparable to the established funds and were not merely an expedient to avoid paying contributions at the level required by the law. This was achieved by the Law on Provident Funds of 1876.

The Law created the status of registered funds, which could be either voluntary or compulsory, and laid down the qualifications for registration. They had to shed all their other features and confine their object to insurance against sickness and death, providing assistance for such minimum periods and at such minimum levels as were laid down. This transformation of the former *Hilfskassen* into mere *Krankenkassen* meant strict separation from all bodies with other purposes. In a move directed against the use of benefit funds for trade union recruitment, membership of other

---

[14] Eisenberg, *Gewerkschaften*, pp. 184–91.
[15] *Hülfskassen*, pp. IV–VII. An increase of 179 since 1868. In addition the government sources estimated around 6–700 voluntary funds. Frevert, *Krankheit*, p. 177.

societies as a condition for membership of the fund was strictly controlled. Nor could fund members be obliged to undertake or desist from any action unconnected with the purpose of the fund, such as a strike. It became illegal to invest the reserves of factory sickness funds in the firm, thus removing one of their attractions for employers in the past. In the same year an amendment of the Industrial Code specified that members of funds that failed to meet these conditions for registration had to belong to a registered fund as well, i.e. unregistered funds could offer their members no more than supplementary insurance.[16]

The double legislation of 1876 proved to be remarkably short-lived. Within five years, work had begun on a new law to overturn the principle of local selectivity on which compulsory sickness insurance had previously been based. This became the Sickness Insurance Law of 1883, the first of the workers' insurance laws of the Bismarck era to reach the statute book. That priority had not been intended. Originally the sickness insurance provisions had formed part of the accident insurance law, but for the sake of simplicity they were subsequently turned into a separate bill. In the 1882–3 session of the *Reichstag* the accident insurance law ran once more into serious opposition, but the sickness insurance law was less controversial and was passed ahead of its companion. It was nevertheless an essential part of the accident insurance legislation, for responsibility for all victims of accidents was to be carried by sickness insurance in the first place. Since accident insurance was to be compulsory across the whole Empire, sickness insurance could no longer be left to local discretion; it too had to be compulsory across the Empire as a whole.[17] The reason for this momentous departure from the principle of local selectivity was not therefore that the needs of local poor law authorities were interpreted differently from before. It was that sickness insurance was now governed by new considerations. It was no longer primarily an aspect of poor law policy, providing communal authorities in industrial areas with an option to protect themselves in an era

---

[16] *Gesetz über die eingeschriebenen Hilfskassen vom 7. April 1876* especially §§ 13, 7, 11, 14 and 6. The text of the two laws is printed in QS,I,5, Nos. 164 and 165. For comments see the Introduction to that volume and Frevert, *Krankheit*, p. 178. Existing funds had until 1885 to bring themselves up to the standards laid down for registration. Since most of them left it until the last moment, there were few registered funds in 1883 when the law was once more revised.

[17] Sickness insurance which presupposed the existence of a regular employer withholding a proportion of wages as insurance contributions was, however, considered inappropriate for casual workers. For that reason the overlap between accident insurance and sickness insurance was not total, and special provisions were made for such cases. 'Begründung des Entwurfes eines Gesetzes, betr. die Krankenversicherung der Arbeiter' in SBRT, 5. Legislaturperiode, II Session 1882/83, vol. 5, pp. 140 and 141.

of labour mobility. It had become a prerequisite for a policy designed to mitigate the consequences of industrial methods of production in ways that interfered less with the autonomy of employers than either state regulation of working conditions or reform of the law of employers' liability.

Except for the need to deal with accidents, the admitted shortcomings of the reform of 1876 would not have qualified for such rapid attention, as Bismarck admitted at the time. For Lohmann this was an opportunity to further his own priorities. It was widely accepted that the immediate needs of the injured for medical and financial support were best dealt with by the small local sickness funds that normally consisted of workers in the same trade. These were well placed to deal with the many cases in which injury was merely temporary and to prevent malingering. In 1881 the accident insurance bill had proposed that they be responsible for the first four weeks, but Bismarck had accepted a suggestion from the *Reichstag* to reduce this to only two weeks.[18] In the 1882 version this was actually extended to the first thirteen weeks, the same period for which funds were legally required to provide support in all cases of sickness. Having thereby ensured an indispensable role for sickness funds in the new system, Lohmann seized the opportunity to introduce other reforms. He revised the cumbersome administrative requirements laid down in 1876 and increased minimum benefits.

The Law of 1883 recognised seven categories of sickness funds.

1. *Local funds*, each consisting of one or possibly more trades, established and supervised by the local authority.
2. *Factory funds* established by employers but with regulations that had to be sanctioned by the local authority. Their name was changed to *Betriebskassen* (works funds), but I propose to follow Dawson's example and continue to refer to them as factory funds. The law permitted a firm to establish a single fund for more than one factory under its control.
3. *Miners' funds* (*Knappschaftskassen*). The long-standing provisions for miners operated under their own laws and have not been included in Tables 8.2 to 8.4.
4. *Building-trade funds* for building workers too mobile to be organised through a local fund.
5. *Guild funds* for journeymen and apprentices of members of artisan guilds.
6. *Registered voluntary funds* meeting the requirements of the imperial Law of 1876 or of the legislation of one of the individual states. Membership

---

[18] QS,II.2(1), p. XXVII.

of these was to be an adequate substitute for membership of a compulsory fund.

7. Any worker liable to compulsory sickness insurance who did not fit into these categories had to belong to a residual category, called a *parish fund*, which offered a minimal form of insurance underwritten by the parish.

Only the fourth and the last of these were new, and in the latter case the explanatory memorandum went out of its way to claim that it could be regarded as a development from Bavarian precedents. The guiding principle of the law had been to incorporate the existing institutions into a comprehensive system.[19]

The level of cash benefits will be considered in chapter 9. Now that insurance against sickness was declared to be 'one of the most important measures for the improvement of the position of the workers',[20] and not merely looked upon as an alternative to poor relief, these were judged by new standards. One consequence of general compulsion across the Empire can be mentioned already. Workers were now able to change their jobs while continuing to enjoy the uninterrupted benefit of insurance. Previously, even if there were sick funds in the parish or the factory to which they had moved (a matter that could not have been taken for granted), workers were unable to join without paying a special entrance fee and fulfilling a waiting period before qualifying for benefit. These requirements now became illegal, since it was assumed that in a world of universal provision gains and losses from labour mobility would be cancelled out.

It is impossible to say how policy would have developed but for the new priorities. Lohmann claimed that the Law of 1876 had been a failure and had led to a numerical decline in sick funds and their membership, but he used figures for his base-line that were inflated by the inclusion of mere burial funds.[21] He was obviously anxious to justify further reform and was far from sure that the accident insurance law would be accepted. Membership of funds had actually increased but it is impossible to tell by how much.

[19] Begründung, SBRT, 5. Legislaturperiode, II Session 1882–3, vol. 5, Anlagen, pp. 140–5 and 147. For the Bavarian precedent see also briefly QS,I.7(1), pp. XLIII–IV and QS,I.7(2), No. 194. For this and similar arrangements for compulsory hospital insurance in other South German states see R. Spree, 'Krankenhausentwicklung und Sozialpolitik in Deutschland während des 19. Jahrhunderts', HZ, 260 (1995), 95–102; A. Labisch and R. Spree (eds.), *Krankenhaus-Report 19. Jahrhundert* (Frankfurt a.M., 2001).
[20] *Begründung*, p. 140.   [21] Cf. *Begründung*, p. 141 with figures in QS,I,5, Table 14.

Table 8.1. *Membership of German voluntary sickness funds*

Date	Numbers	As percentage of insured population
1880	60,000 at most?	
1885	874,507	20 per cent
1890	963,976	15 per cent
1895	731,487	10 per cent
1905	893,099	8 per cent
1911	949,236	7 per cent

Source: Florian Tennstedt, *Geschichte der Selbstverwaltung in der Krankenversicherung von der Mitte des 19. Jahrhunderts bis zur Gründung der Bundesrepublik Deutschland. Soziale Selbstverwaltung,* vol. 2 (Bonn, 1977), p. 27, for 1880. Subsequent figures from *Statistik des Deutschen Reichs,* NF, vols. 24, 59, 90, 177 and 258. The total insured population used to calculate the percentage for 1885 has been drawn from QS,E, Table I.2, which provides a retrospectively corrected figure.

There was this difference between the introduction of accident insurance and the expansion of sickness insurance. The former was based on totally new principles and institutions; the latter used existing institutions, accommodating itself to existing interests. For that reason it did not meet the same degree of opposition in the *Reichstag* and could be passed already in 1883. In its tolerance of voluntary funds it reflected the preferences of Lohmann, who was its real progenitor, rather than of Bismarck, whom illness had removed from the scene at the crucial time. Bismarck was to repudiate the parentage of the law, saying that it had been foisted on him like an infant slipped into the bed of a woman in labour. In particular he felt that it had made too many concessions to voluntarism.[22]

(C) VOLUNTARY FUNDS

The effect of the Law on the voluntary funds was certainly remarkable. That applies not only to those connected with the Liberal trade unions who had still dominated the scene in 1876, but even to Socialist ones who had rapidly come to the fore since then. It would seem at first sight that they were competing with the other funds on very unequal terms, since they had no claim on employers' contributions. But that proved no

---

[22] Tennstedt and Winter, 'Jeder Tag', p. 685, quoting Albert Schäffle, *Aus meinem Leben* (Berlin, 1904), vol. 2, p. 183.

disadvantage in practice. On the contrary, in the years immediately after the introduction of the scheme, membership of voluntary funds increased at a remarkable rate.

There were several reasons for this growth.

1. Unlike compulsory funds voluntary funds were selective and could therefore eliminate bad risks. Since trade union organisation tended to be among the higher paid and more securely employed workers, they were able to provide better benefits.

2. It should be added that by the mid-1880s trade unions largely escaped the consequences of the Anti-Socialist Law of 1878, and particularly their sickness funds which had to be organisationally separate from the union itself. At least for a minority of active and independent workers control over their own fund without reference to employers had its own attraction.

3. Voluntary funds paid out a higher element in cash. In contrast to factory funds, where doctors had been employed both to control entitlement to benefit and to provide medical treatment, voluntary funds had no tradition of medical treatment. Acute cases could go to hospitals, but what members really wanted was cash.

4. Far from discouraging membership of these funds, many employers of artisans actually encouraged it. Some went so far as to dismiss anyone who belonged to funds that required an employer's contribution. Unlike factory employers, they had not been required to contribute to compulsory funds prior to 1883 and did not take kindly to the novelty.[23]

By 1888 Lohmann had become convinced that sickness insurance would never have been accepted in 1883 if its consequences had been anticipated.[24] But no action was taken until 1892. In that year an amending law obliged all voluntary funds to provide medical treatment. They also found themselves increasingly hampered by the authorities, and after the Anti-Socialist Law had lapsed in 1890 their own sickness funds were no longer crucial to Socialist activists. After 1891 the number of voluntary funds began to decline, as did their membership. Politically committed workers transferred to local funds, in whose administration they soon acquired an influential voice. As contributors of two-thirds of the funds the workers had the right to elect a proportionate number of members to the executive. It had originally been difficult to obtain enough nominations from workers, but by the mid-1890s the Socialists had realised the opportunities that this constitutional arrangement gave. Numerous local

---

[23] Tennstedt, *Selbstverwaltung*, pp. 32–3. [24] *Ibid.*, p. 40.

funds began to fall under their control. Trade union activists, who had been black-listed by employers, could now be appointed to administrative posts in the local funds, where they acquired useful training in public administration.[25]

In 1884, when the leader of the Centre party had complained that the local funds as established under the Sickness Insurance Law would provide the Socialists with new means of organisation, Bismarck had replied that 'the insurance system must be lubricated with a drop of democratic oil if it is to run properly', adding that 'here as elsewhere we have to make things palatable'.[26] The authors of the *Reichsversicherungsordnung* (RVO) of 1911, the codification and reform of the insurance laws, thought that lubrication had been overdone. The RVO required the chairman of the executive to be acceptable to a majority of representatives of the employers as well as of the workers, and it replaced the authority of the general assembly by a council elected by proportional representation.[27]

(D) LOCAL FUNDS

The local funds were the most dynamic element of the system. Relative to other categories of funds the growth of their membership was remarkable.

This dynamism is also evident in the invention of the so-called general local fund which was an amalgamation of the various local funds that had originally been established for a single trade. In 1883 the desire to rely on local knowledge for the control of malingering and a preference for funds limited to a single trade had caused a multiplication of small and financially precarious funds. A general local fund retained separate sections for each trade but operated under a single administration. This reduced overheads and made it possible to introduce a range of optional benefits. The pioneers of the general local fund were the big cities of Saxony – Leipzig, Chemnitz and Dresden – but they were quickly followed by cities in other regions. The great increase in the average

[25] Tennstedt, 'Sozialgeschichte der Sozialversicherung', p. 390; Tennstedt, *Selbstverwaltung*, pp. 47–60. For examples of Socialist chairmen of local funds see *ibid.*, pp. 57–8, but there appear to be no figures on this subject.

[26] H. Rubner (ed.), *Adolph Wagner. Briefe, Dokumente, Augenzeugenberichte, 1851–1917* (Berlin, 1978), p. 225, using the translation in Ritter, *Social welfare*, p. 56 for the original vivid German metaphor of the pepper in the sausage.

[27] Tennstedt, *Selbstverwaltung*, pp. 60–1; Dawson, *Social insurance*, p. 73.

Table 8.2. *Membership of German sickness funds*

Type of fund	1885	1895	1905	1911
Parish	587,000	1,223,000	1,435,000	1,602,000
Local	1,535,000	3,288,000	5,470,000	7,075,000
Factory	1,261,000	1,929,000	2,877,000	3,401,000
Building-trade	12,000	15,000	20,000	11,000
Guild	25,000	103,000	245,000	319,000
Voluntary (registered)	731,000	672,000	856,000	914,000
Voluntary (unregistered)	144,000	60,000	37,000	35,000
Totals	4,294,000	7,289,000	10,940,000	13,357,000
As percentage of population	10	16	20	21

Source: Statistik des Deutschen Reichs NF vols. 24, 90, 177 and 258.

Table 8.3. *Average membership per type of fund*

Type of fund	1885	1895	1905	1911
Parish	84	160	190	214
Local	416	775	1,195	1,523
Factory	230	291	369	432
Building-trade	146	299	600	449
Guild	111	214	377	393
Voluntary (registered)	405	488	635	765
Voluntary (unregistered)	303	231	230	272
All types	229	352	493	598

Source: As for Table 8.2.

membership of local funds, recorded in Table 8.3, is mainly due to this innovation.[28]

In 1911 the RVO restructured the range of funds, acknowledging the importance of the general local fund and giving it the central place in the system. Single-trade local funds were to survive only if they had at least 250 members, if they did not threaten the viability of the general local fund in the area and offered benefits equivalent to those provided by it. The RVO also abolished building-trade funds, guild funds and parish funds. The last had always been anomalous. In its place it created rural

---

[28] *Begründung*, pp. 142–3; Dawson, *Social insurance*, pp. 75–9, for a description of the Leipzig general local fund.

Table 8.4. *Numbers of German sickness funds before and after*
the RVO (1911)

Type of fund	1885	1895	1905	1911	1920	1925
Parish	7,025	8,449	8,333	8,198	–	–
Local	3,693	4,475	4,740	4,748	2,545	2,176
Factory	5,473	6,770	7,774	7,921	4,740	4,279
Building-trade	83	102	44	41	–	–
Guild	224	545	710	845	–	–
Voluntary (registered)	1,805	1,388	1,364	1,227 }	48	42
Voluntary (unregistered)	474	263	163	129 }		
Rural	–	–	–	–	511	437
All types	18,776	21,992	23,127	23,109	8,681	7,670

Source: Statistik des Deutschen Reichs NF vols. 24, 90, 177, 258, 303 and 338. It should be
noted that the voluntary funds had been marginalised by the reforms of the RVO.

funds (*Landkassen*) designed to insure domestic labourers, agricultural
and forestry workers, out-workers and any other categories that the
Bundesrat might decide. These funds would operate over a larger territory than the parish. That would usually be the area administered by a
new authority, the district insurance office. These new supervisory
authorities were each to be responsible for the area of a general local
fund or of a rural fund.

In all this reorganisation the general local fund held pride of place. No
rural fund could be established alongside it unless it had at least 250
members, and even then the state legislature, with whom authority over
rural funds was vested, could decide not to do so.[29]

Not all the effect of this reorganisation can be shown in Table 8.4, since
the available statistics do not distinguish between the single-trade local
funds that still survived and the general local funds that had now become
the principal type.

(E) FEDERATIONS

Regional federations of local funds were originally no more intended than
general local funds. They speeded up the dissemination of ideas and
administrative practices. Smaller local funds were largely sustained by
these organisations that provided facilities on a regional basis. The next

---

[29] With some additional details Dawson, *Social insurance*, pp. 34–8.

step occurred in 1894 with the establishment of a Central Association of Local Sickness Funds for the whole Empire. Lohmann's faith in the dynamism of a system that allowed variety and respected existing structures, rather than insisting on neat and tidy bureaucratic central control, was therefore largely justified. The benefits showed in low administrative costs. Members abandoned their earlier preference for the lowest possible contributions, and acknowledged the attraction of optional benefits. These included convalescent homes, outpatient clinics, TB sanatoria in conjunction with invalidity insurance, health education, dental treatment and spectacles. Medical treatment of dependants in this period was, however, still beyond the means of all but the larger general funds.

The significance of the central association was not confined to facilitating the exchange of ideas and the introduction of best practices. After the turn of the century it increasingly represented the interests of the local funds in the politics of social reform. By the time of the debates over the RVO it was one of several nationwide associations, each representing one of the vested interests in insurance and jostling for the attention of *Reichstag* and government.[30]

Like accident insurance, so sickness insurance witnessed a gradual expansion of the population covered by it. Transport and communication workers were included in 1885, agricultural and forestry workers at the discretion of local authorities in 1886, and white-collar workers earning up to 2,000 M p.a. (£100) in 1892. But the greatest expansion occurred as part of the RVO of 1911 with the inclusion of all agricultural and forestry workers, of domestic servants and of white-collar workers up to an annual income of 2,500 M. The effect in terms of population percentages and in comparison with England and Wales can be seen in Table 9.3 below.

[30] Tennstedt, 'Sozialgeschichte der Sozialversicherung', pp. 390–4.

9

Cash benefits, contributions and coverage in the friendly society era

So much for the two systems, the voluntary and the compulsory, and for the political circumstances from which they arose. What can be said about their outcomes? This chapter will look at the Anglo-German comparison in terms of outcomes in the period prior to the establishment of British National Insurance. Chapter 14 will do the same for the period immediately after the introduction of British National Insurance.

(A) BENEFITS

Let us begin with benefits, of which there were three principal kinds in both countries: sick pay, medical treatment and death grant.[1] Medical treatment consisted of the service of a doctor and the provision of the necessary drugs and medical appliances. At this stage we shall deal only with the cash benefits, deferring the politics and the level of provision of medical benefits until later.

(i) Sick pay

In the case of Germany we have detailed information on the minimum payment. In 1876 the law set a minimum level of half a labourer's customary local average daily wage for men and one-third for women, of which up to two-thirds could take the form of medical treatment and drugs.[2] Half a labourer's wage, less the special costs resulting from sickness, cannot have amounted to much above poor relief standards. Under the new set of priorities governing the legislation in 1883, that was no longer regarded as adequate.

---

[1] See David Neave, 'Friendly societies in Great Britain', in Marcel van der Linden (ed.), *Social security mutualism* (Berne, 1996), pp. 55–6, for other benefits sometimes provided by Friendly Societies.

[2] *Gesetz über die eingeschriebenen Hülfskassen vom 7. April 1876*, para. 11. See also Paul Honigman, 'Zur Arbeiterkrankenversicherungsfrage', *Jahrbücher für Nationalökonomie und Statistik*, NF 6 (1883), 113.

The cost of medical treatment and drugs was added to the basic 50 per cent. The customary local average daily wage was to be separately ascertained for women and youths, and the 50 per cent rule applied to them also.

The explanatory memorandum of the 1883 Law revealed some embarrassment over the fact that the minimum benefit had in the past been tied to the customary local average daily wage of mere labourers. That seemed doubly inappropriate when benefit under the accident insurance was to be calculated as a percentage of the claimant's actual wages while contributions by employers were to be based on their actual wage bill. The memorandum pointed out that sickness insurance contributions were paid by the individual; to tie contribution and benefit to the actual wages received by each particular member would have required constant calculations and adjustment. The customary local average daily rate, calculated once a year for all, was defended as a necessary administrative convenience. But except for parish funds, whose members were drawn from a diversity of occupations, and voluntary funds, whose members might well be drawn from numerous localities, the 50 per cent was now to be based on the average daily wage of the particular class of workers for which the fund had been established. For factory funds and building-trade funds, where the relevant information would have been available to the fund administrators, it could be based on the actual wages of the individual concerned. These regulations all point to a desire to move away from a mere subsistence standard and to make the 50 per cent rule more appropriate to the circumstances of different trades and industries. Since the funds would normally have included both skilled and unskilled in the particular trade, the new requirement should not be regarded as a concession to the more highly paid skilled workers. Concessions to wage differentials among the individual members of a fund were confined to factory and building-trade funds. Even they were merely permitted, not required.[3]

That is a point that needs to be made, for it runs counter to the impression that German sickness insurance, like invalidity and old age insurance later, provided higher benefits in exchange for higher contributions by the better off, being 'intended to appeal primarily to the strong, not to the weak, among the German working class'.[4] That does not describe the kind of differentials that had to be taken into account after

---

[3] *Begründung* of the 1883 Bill, pp. 145–6, supplemented by Florian Tennstedt, 'Die Errichtung von Krankenkassen in deutschen Städten nach dem Gesetz betr. die Krankenversicherung der Arbeiter vom 15. Juni 1883', ZSR, 29 (1983), 297–338, in particular pp. 312–13.

[4] E. P. Hennock, *British social reform and German precedents: the case of social insurance 1880–1914* (Oxford, 1987), pp. 184 and 185. For invalidity and old age pensions levels, see chapter 10 below.

1883. Those were differentials between trades, not among wage levels within a trade. It should also be noted that after 1883 the legal minimum was nearly always the amount actually paid in practice.[5]

In England there was no minimum laid down by law until the National Insurance Act 1911. There is no comprehensive information on what was actually paid. But from what we know of benefits and wages in various societies it can be calculated that, for the lower paid, benefits as a proportion of wages were probably not much different in the two systems. For higher paid workers they would often have been more in Germany.

How long did contributors qualify for this level of sick pay? Most friendly societies and trade unions paid for at least six months from the first day of sickness, and thereafter usually paid at a reduced level for the next six months. In the affiliated orders, however, top rates were often paid for a whole year before being reduced to half the amount for the next six months. In cases of prolonged illness or disability the benefit was paid at a lower level for a further limited period, but it was not unusual for it to be continued indefinitely.[6]

In this matter societies in England were far more generous than in Germany. This is shown in Table 9.1. Furthermore German funds paid only from the fourth day of illness.

Thus, in 1872, 63 per cent of funds paid for three months at the most, 25 per cent paid for a maximum of six months. In 1883 the law required a minimum of thirteen weeks, and, in 1891, 80 per cent of all funds also treated that as the maximum period. A further 13 per cent extended the period of payment to a maximum of twenty-six weeks at either full or reduced rates.

---

[5] In 1891, 87 per cent of all local, factory, guild and building workers' funds paid no more than half the wage. The figure in 1911 was 87.5 per cent. Nine per cent in 1891 and 10 per cent in 1911 paid between half and two-thirds of wages. Calculated from *Statistik der Krankenversicherung der Arbeiter im Jahre 1891*, Table A8, *Statistik des Deutschen Reichs*, NF 65 (Berlin, 1893); *Statistik der Krankenversicherung...* *1911*, p. 9*, *Statistik des Deutschen Reichs*, NF 258 (1912). This source gives no figures for the voluntary funds.

[6] Information for these two paragraphs is drawn from Labour Department, Board of Trade, 'Analysis of the rules of trade unions relating to unemployed, sick and accident benefits and expenditure on such benefits by each union', pp. 22–3. 1908 Confidential Print, LSE, Beveridge Collection B.XVII; *Royal Commission on the Poor Laws*, Minutes of Evidence, vol. V, BPP 1909 Cd.4888 XLI; vol. VII, BPP 1910 Cd.5035, XLVII. Also J. C. Riley, *Sick, not dead*, pp. 132 and 276–7; Wilkinson, *Mutual thrift*, pp. 228–9; Gosden, *Friendly societies*, p. 80; Neave, *Mutual aid*, p. 72; Jones, 'Did friendly societies matter?, pp. 342–3; O'Neill, 'Self-help in Nottinghamshire', p. 58; Gosden, *Self-help*, p. 54; E. L. Daniell, *Report on friendly societies in Wales etc.*, Fourth Report Royal Commission on Friendly and Benefit Building Societies, Appendix XVI, BPP 1874 C.961-I, XXIII.

Table 9.1. *German sickness funds, period (in weeks) for which sickness benefit could be paid, percentage of all funds*

	13 or less	14–26		27–52		over 52	
	Full per cent	Full per cent	Reduced per cent	Full per cent	Reduced per cent	Full per cent	Reduced per cent
1872[a]	63	25	–	10	–	2	–
1891[b]	80	10	3	3	4	0.03	0.37
1911	–	96	–	2.2	1.5	–	0.06

Notes:
[a] This line refers to Prussian sickness funds. The total for 1872 excludes 729 funds in which the length of entitlement differed among the members according to some unspecified criterion. There is no reference to reduced benefit in 1872.
[b] The figures for 1891 and 1911 include the free funds.
Source: Hülfskassen, Table 7.II, p. 173; *Statistik der Krankenversicherung . . . 1891*, Table A7, *Statistik des Deutschen Reichs*, NF 65 (Berlin, 1893); *Statistik der Krankenversicherung . . . 1911*, Table 6, p. 76, *Statistik des Deutschen Reichs*, NF 258 (1912).

These figures are surprisingly restrictive. Even when invalidity pensions for the long-term sick were introduced in 1889, they were not paid for the first year of illness. That left the long-term sick with a gap that could be as long as thirty-nine weeks, during which they were left without support. In 1899 this was reduced to thirteen weeks, but it was not fully eliminated until 1904.[7]

To sum up, as a percentage of income the level of benefit in German sickness insurance was usually somewhat higher for the better paid. On the other hand, friendly societies continued to pay benefit for longer. This picture is modified after 1899 by the provision of German invalidity pensions. These ensured a more acceptable future for the chronically sick over the long term, but until 1904 they left a serious gap in coverage at a time when resources would have been already badly eroded.[8]

[7] On that occasion the minimum period for sickness benefit was raised to twenty-six weeks. F. Kleeis, *Die Geschichte der sozialen Versicherung in Deutschland* (Reprint of 1926 publication, Berlin and Bonn, 1981), p. 110; R. van der Borght, 'Die Reform der deutschen Invaliditäts- und Altersversicherung', *Jahrbücher für Nationalökonomie und Statistik*, 3rd Ser. 18 (1899), 374.
[8] Medical treatment, as distinct from cash benefit, is dealt with in chapter 13 below, and under 'Discretionary benefits' in chapter 14 below.

(ii) Death grants

All friendly societies paid a lump sum on the death of a member or that of his wife. This could vary, but £10 and £7 were the most common amounts. It was intended to meet the cost of a decent funeral.[9] On such occasions the fact that friendly societies provided social bonds and not just impersonal insurance contracts was at its most conspicuous. All members were expected to attend the funeral and were fined if they failed to do so. In a world in which someone's standing was judged by the funeral attendance this was a not inconsiderable 'benefit' of membership.

In the 1870s German funds also usually paid a death grant for the member himself and in many cases for his spouse and dependent children as well. Members of artisan funds were accompanied to the grave by a delegation of fellow members; that does not seem to have been customary in factory or local funds to judge by the regulations selected for publication in the 1876 survey. At that date 74 per cent of funds providing funeral benefit either met the actual funeral costs or provided a maximum of 15 Thaler (£2.26).[10]

After 1883 parish funds, which included many of the lowest paid, were not required to pay death grants and in practice hardly ever did. In other funds the death grant was not less than twenty times the average local daily wage used to calculate benefit, and it could be increased up to a maximum of forty times. There were grants of two-thirds that amount on the death of the spouse, of half on the death of a child. The amounts increased over time as wages rose and the regulations were more liberally interpreted. By 1913 the average death grant actually paid, however, was still below £5 compared with the £7–10 customary in England.[11] It is unlikely that this difference can be accounted for by differences in the basic cost of a funeral. A modest funeral in 1914 cost between 140 and 320 M, or £7–16.[12]

---

[9] By 1870 the cost of an adult funeral would have been £5.9sh, and left a good margin for hospitality. Simon Cordery, *British friendly societies, 1750–1914* (Basingstoke, 2003), p. 119.
[10] *Hülfskassen*, Table A1, pp. 14–15, Table A5, p. 142, Anlagen III, pp. 269–308.
[11] *Statistik des Deutschen Reichs*, NF vol. 277, p. 10*.
[12] Information provided in response to an internet appeal by Simone Ameskamp, Georgetown University, but unfortunately without source references.

(B) CONTRIBUTIONS

As significant as the benefits were the contributions by which they were financed. In Germany, for factory workers since 1876 and for all insured workers since 1883, one-third of the cost came from employers unless a worker belonged to a voluntary fund. Until 1911, when the British National Insurance Act copied this provision, the employers' contribution constituted the most important difference between the two systems. But more important still was the fact that German contributions like German benefits were levied as a percentage of wages. Contributions to friendly societies, and subsequently to approved societies under the National Insurance Act, were levied as a fixed sum. With rising wages this German arrangement built an escalator into the income that sickness funds had at their disposal. In the long run this was of enormous importance for their finances and for their capacity to expand their range of benefits. In the period under review it led to greatly increased income and expenditure for quite a modest increase in percentage of wages levied. Since that percentage varied greatly among the numerous funds, an average percentage figure is all that can be provided. In 1885 that was just under 2 per cent of wages; in 1913 it had risen to 2.44 per cent, an increasing proportion of a rising working-class income.[13] What this did to increase income and expenditure well above membership is shown in Table 9.2.

Table 9.2. *Index of growth of German sickness insurance, 1885–1913*

	1885	1900	1913
Membership	100	218	312
Days of sickness	100	252	455
Expenditure	100	326	821
Income	100	300	750

Source: Tennstedt, 'Sozialgeschichte der Sozialversicherung', p. 389.

With weekly contributions of 6d to 1s and possibly another 1d to medical institutes for the treatment of dependants, contributions of Friendly Society members would have been 2.5 to 3 per cent of wages, assuming that the lower contributions applied to those earning 20s a week

[13] Tennstedt, 'Sozialgeschichte der Sozialversicherung', p. 389, also for the subsequent table.

Table 9.3. *Insurance contributors as a percentage of population of working age, summary figures*

	1872	1891	1911	1913	1914
England and Wales	12.5	21.9	22.0	48.5	–
UK	–	–	–	46.7	–
Prussia	9.5	21.6	–	–	–
German Empire	–	23.7	36.1	–	41.8

Source: The figures are taken from the statistical Appendix to this chapter.

and the higher ones to those earning 35s.[14] That would have been somewhat higher than in Germany, but then there were generally no contributions from employers.

(C) COVERAGE

It is possible to compare insurance contributors as a percentage of the population of working age, here taken to be 15–65, both before 1883 and after.

Detailed calculations together with the evidence on which they are based can be found in the statistical Appendix to this chapter. The results are presented in Table 9.3. That includes contributions after the introduction of British National Insurance. What the table does not show is the extent to which dependants were also covered. That is too complex a matter for tabular analysis and is discussed in chapter 14 below. Nor has it been possible to divide contributors by gender. For that the returns used for friendly society membership are uninformative or unreliable. What can be said is that women were under-represented among friendly society members. The emphasis on sociability excluded them from the vast majority of societies. Separate societies for women did exist but were few, and numbers fell with the decline of wage-earning by married women.[15]

These figures need to be treated with caution. As far as I am aware the Prussian figures for 1872 are complete; and where an estimate was used it was a maximum. The English figures are not complete. They relate only to

---

[14] Of the eight working-class budgets that recorded insurance payments in B. S. Rowntree, *Poverty: a study of town life* (London, 1901), ch. 8, it was 2.5 per cent of wages in five and 3.5 per cent in three.

[15] Cordery, *British friendly societies*, pp. 24–5, 70 and 109.

'Friendly Societies making returns to the Registrar', and even of those over 14 per cent failed to return membership figures. It should be borne in mind that the willingness of friendly societies to register was not great. The number of unregistered societies was estimated in the Report of the Royal Commission as one-third of the total.[16]

The under-registration of trade unions providing sickness benefit was also substantial. The unions did not want to submit quinquennial valuations in the form required, which would have obliged them to distinguish between benefit funds and fighting funds. The more important unions did not register. It has been possible to do no more than to include the membership of three of the more substantial of these from other sources.[17]

The figures for Prussia are therefore much more complete than those for England and Wales. It is this that makes the difference between those totals so significant. That such cautious figures, which take no account of the notorious under-registration of the relevant English voluntary institutions, should produce a percentage well above that for Prussia clearly indicates the greater development of participation in insurance contributions against sickness in England and Wales. Rather than speculate on how much greater the percentage in that country really was, it is more profitable to focus on two conclusions: first, that the extent of provision was substantially greater in England and Wales than in Prussia; and, secondly, that the conditions that allowed the voluntary impulse to flourish there placed enormous obstacles in the way of any authority that wished to monitor the process.

How can we explain the greater participation in England and Wales? The Prussian legislation was at this stage restricted to the manufacturing population. English friendly societies, unfettered by legislation of this sort, recruited much more widely. By the 1870s they had penetrated the rural counties of England and Wales, where they recruited not only artisans and craftsmen, but rural labourers too.[18] In this process the affiliated orders

[16] *Fourth Report, Royal Commission on Friendly Societies* (1874), § 871. It is impossible to know how many of these would have covered sickness.

[17] See Table 9.4, note c. Generally, E. W. Brabrook, 'On friendly societies and similar institutions', Jl. Stat. Soc., 33 (1875), 193–4. There is therefore no danger that the final total is significantly affected by double-counting of trade unionists who were also members of friendly societies.

[18] In addition to the evidence in Gosden, *Friendly societies*, p. 43, there is convincing evidence of this in local studies drawn from numerous areas of rural England and Wales. Neave, *Mutual aid*, pp. 52–4; D. Jones, 'Did friendly societies matter? A study of friendly society membership in Glamorgan, 1794–1910', *Welsh History Review*, 12 (1984–5), 337–8; J. O'Neill, 'Self-help in Nottinghamshire: the Woodborough Male Friendly Society, 1826–1954', Trans. Thoroton Soc., 90 (1986), 60.

and the normal range of individual societies were supplemented by the so-called county societies, which were subsidised and largely controlled by the landed classes.[19]

Artisans in rural areas were in practice excluded from the operation of the Prussian law. For local authorities the adoption of compulsion was optional over much of the time. Even when the district authorities overrode their discretion, this was still done on a selective basis. In many areas the manufacturing population was not large enough to make it easy to establish viable artisan provident funds.[20] Compulsion imposes its own limitation; it was confined to where it could be enforced. It is impossible to say how much the numerical difference owed to these practicalities, or how much to the deliberate exclusion of the non-industrial population from the scope of the law.

The Law of 1883 immediately doubled the number of contributors. In 1885 its provisions were extended to transport and communication workers, and in 1886 at the discretion of local authorities to agricultural and forestry. How these results compare with the growth of the English friendly society movement is shown for 1891, taking advantage of the population figures from the census enumeration of 1891 and 1890 respectively. For comparison with England percentages are given for the German Empire but also for Prussia. The Prussian figures are mainly for the purpose of comparison with 1872.

The German figures for 1891 present only one problem. Members of voluntary centralised funds (*Freie Hilfskassen*) were counted as being located where the central office was situated. That may account for the surprising fact that the percentages for Prussia are below those for the Empire as a whole.[21]

The situation in England and Wales was altogether different. Societies were still under no compulsion to register. The Chief Registrar estimated the

---

[19] Baernreither, *English associations*, pp. 185–7.

[20] For artisans and factory workers who escaped the legislation even in as large a town as Breslau see Paul Honigmann, 'Zur Arbeiterkrankenversicherungsfrage', pp. 104–5 and 123.

[21] We have figures for the membership of these centralised voluntary funds for 1886 together with the location of their central offices. The total membership of those with central office outside Prussia was 241,077. Calculated from Rudolf Knaack and Wolfgang Schröder, 'Gewerkschaftliche Zentralverbände, Freie Hilfskassen und die Arbeiterpresse unter dem Sozialistengesetz', *Jahrbuch für Geschichte* (Berlin, 1981), vol. 22, Table A II. Adding all these to the Prussian figure would produce a total of 4,072,778 and a percentage of 22.9 compared with 23.7 for the Empire as a whole. However, we know that the membership figures were lower in 1886 than in 1891, and that they grew by 12.6 per cent between 1887 and 1889 (Knaack and Schröder, 'Gewerkschaftliche', p. 387). On that basis, if we were to make the wild assumption that the proportion of members belonging to funds with central offices located outside Prussia was the same in 1889 as in 1886 it would be possible to calculate a maximum membership of 271,453. That would produce a maximum total for Prussia of 4,103,154 and a percentage of 23.1. Whereas in 1891 the Prussian percentage was certainly not above that for the *Reich*, the two percentages may not have been so far apart.

shortfall in 1892 at about 3 million members.[22] It is impossible to say how many of these were insured against sickness, but many undoubtedly were.

The problem is to decide how to take these missing figures into account for the purpose of comparison.[23] It would take no more than 12 per cent of those estimated 3 million to have been in societies that insured against sickness for the English percentage to exceed that for the German Empire. That is such a modest addition as to suggest that the actual percentage for England and Wales was still considerably higher than that for Germany. The advantage of the German Empire seven years after the passing of the law is to be found not in the percentage of contributors to population but in the full statistical coverage that compulsion made possible.

After 1891 the percentage of the German insurance contributors to population continued to rise, as further occupational groups were brought within the ambit of the law. By 1911 on the eve of compulsory health insurance in Britain and of further legislation in Germany the situation had changed massively in Germany's favour. The figures for England and Wales are no less problematic than those for 1891 and 1874. But in view of the massive difference between them and those for the German Empire, it seems on this occasion not worth considering how to take missing figures into account. Such adjustments as might be made would not significantly alter the comparison.

---

[22] *Royal Commisssion on Labour*, Minutes of Evidence, Q.1331, BPP 1893–4 C.7063-I, XXXIX.

[23] I have decided not to use the well-informed contemporary estimates in J. Frome Wilkinson, *Mutual thrift* (London, 1891), pp. 153–92. They are figures for the UK and provide no basis for identifying those for England and Wales. Those estimates do actually produce percentages of population that resemble mine for England and Wales based on official sources only. That is surprising since the friendly society movement in Ireland was distinctly less vigorous.

    With so much uncertainty about the figures, it is not to be expected that experts will adopt the same procedures for reaching their conclusions. Since these calculations were made David Neave has published an estimate of the male membership of friendly societies in Britain in 1891 of 4.5 million. This estimate is not based on any actual figures recorded but on the Chief Registrar's notional figure of membership of unregistered societies. He rightly regards this as too high. By reducing it by half and assuming that female membership can be disregarded, he has calculated that 'over fifty per cent of men over the age of nineteen probably belonged to a friendly society'. My own calculations based on his figures produces 45 per cent, which looks very different from my own 21.9 per cent. There are several reasons for this. I have confined myself throughout to England and Wales, not to Britain. I have as far as possible avoided constructing notional figures, preferring to reproduce those actually recorded after sifting them for irrelevant categories, and to discuss the problems resulting from under-recording separately in the text. For purposes of comparison with Prussia/Germany, where working women were included in the compulsory membership of the sickness funds, I have presented membership in England and Wales as a proportion of general population. Furthermore I have taken the working population as being aged 15–65, which is closer to realities than taking those over nineteen. If my total were calculated as a percentage of only the *male* population aged 15–65, it would be 45.6 per cent. On that basis Neaves's would be 46 per cent. Neave, 'Friendly societies', pp. 49–50.

The passing of the National Insurance Act almost simultaneously with that of the German Imperial Insurance Consolidation Law (RVO) once more created an entirely new situation. For the first time it is possible to compare the number of contributors produced by compulsory legislation in both countries. The British legislation mobilised a significantly larger proportion of the population than in Germany.[24] Since the information is now also easily available for the United Kingdom as a whole, I have included it.

(D) SUMMARY

To sum up. These three chapters have dealt with the relation between sickness insurance and the role of the State. In Prussia and subsequently in the German Empire insurance was compulsory for specified categories of the population. In England and Wales a Chief Registrar attempted rather unsuccessfully to monitor the action of a multitude of voluntary bodies. Yet in the 1870s voluntary insurance under the social and cultural conditions of England had penetrated the population more thoroughly than locally selective compulsion had done in Prussia. By the early 1890s, after compulsion had been introduced across the Empire, the voluntary system still penetrated English society at least as thoroughly. But once nationwide compulsion had been in place long enough to generate political confidence in its operation, its expansion accelerated and produced results well above anything achieved by voluntary means. The advantage of bureaucratically administered compulsion lay in procedures that, politically acceptable, could be progressively imposed on additional sections of the population.

The advantage enjoyed by voluntary associations lay in their flexibility. They could adapt to meet changing needs and penetrate social strata still unsuited to the more cumbersome political and administrative process of compulsion. Yet despite signs of continuing flexibility, between 1891 and 1911 their growth in England and Wales was slight. This suggests that voluntary provision had lost much of its dynamism.[25]

---

[24] This is contrary to the impression given in W. H. Dawson, *Social insurance in Germany 1883–1911* (London, 1912), pp. 30–1, which provided the basis for the misleading statement on this matter in Hennock, *British social reform*, pp. 182 and 196 n. 34.

[25] Because these figures measure change over two decades, they do not in themselves confirm or deny the suggestion made by Paul Johnson that the first decade of the twentieth century saw an actual fall in the proportion of friendly society members. But he reached his conclusion by ignoring the rising membership of deposit friendly societies. That does not appear to be justified. The inclusion of their members in his figures shows a slight rise in penetration by societies providing sick pay even in that decade. Paul Johnson, *Saving and spending: the working-class economy in Britain 1870–1939* (Oxford, 1985), pp. 55–7, 68–70 and Tables 3.2 and 3.3.

Table 9.3 has dealt with the numerical consequences of the introduction of the British national health insurance. Before fully dealing with that legislation, we should first look at invalidity and old age insurance, the third branch of German workers' insurance to be established in the 1880s.

APPENDIX: INSURANCE CONTRIBUTORS AS PERCENTAGE
OF POPULATION OF WORKING AGE

Table 9.4. *Insurance contributors as percentage of population of working age, England and Wales, 1872*

Members of all friendly societies making returns	1,857,896[a]
Less membership of burial societies	−450,903[b]
Plus members of trade unions with sickness benefit	+273,637[c]
Total relevant membership	1,680,630
Population aged 15–65 (1871)	13,435,400[d]
Percentage of population	12.5 per cent

Notes:

[a] *Royal Commission on Friendly Societies, Fourth Report*, Appendix I, p. 21.

[b] These figures are for 1873, drawn from a special return not available for 1872. *Return of the Number of Registered Burial Societies*, p. 4, BPP 1875 (34) XLII, 339.

[c] Registration for trade unions was introduced in 1872 for the first time. I am therefore using the figures for 1874, by which time the new system was more or less in place. Registrar of Friendly Societies, *Report for 1874* pp. 39–48, BPP 1875 (408) LXXI, 97. I am assuming that all registered trade unions at that date, with the exception of the coal mining unions, provided sickness benefit for their members, and I have removed 88,114, which is the membership of the coal mining unions, from the total provided in the 1874 return. By giving the names and membership figures for each of the 129 registered unions the return makes such an operation possible. Moreover a comparison of that list with George Howell's list of the eleven principal trade unions paying sickness benefit reveals that five of these were unregistered. It has been possible to obtain membership totals for 1874 for three of them and add them to the figures of the registered unions. George Howell, *Trade unionism, new and old* (London, 1891), p. 102; J. B. Jefferys, *The story of the engineers 1800–1945* (London, 1946), Appendix I; H. J. Fyrth and H. Collins, *The foundry workers: a trade union history* (Manchester, 1959), p. 41; R. W. Postgate, *The builders' history* (London, 1923), Appendix II.

[d] B. R. Mitchell and P. Deane, *Abstract of British historical statistics* (Cambridge, 1962), p. 12.

Table 9.5. *Insurance contributors as percentage of population of working age, Prussia, 1872*

Membership of:	
1. State-supervised provident funds for industrial workers offering sickness benefit, 1872	768,977[a]
2. Mining funds (*Knappschaftskassen*), 1873	255,408[b]
3. Railway funds, including salaried staff, ?1873	76,681[c]
4. Guild funds (*Innungskrankenkassen*), 1870	77,825
5. Funds for other self-employed industrial workers, 1870	223,092[d]
6. Workers' provident funds not under state supervision, 1873	50,000[e]
Total	1,251,983
Population aged 15–65 (1871)	15,414,668[f]
Percentage of population	**9.5** per cent

Notes:

[a] *Hülfskassen*, Table I, p. 14. Funds that were restricted to the payment of funeral benefits were identified as such in the table and have been excluded.

[b] *Die Einrichtungen zum Besten der Arbeiter auf den Bergwerken Preussens*, in Auftrag des Ministers für Handel, Gewerbe und öffentlichen Arbeiten, vol. I (Berlin, 1875), Appendix, Table X.

[c] *Hülfskassen, 1876, Teil B. Die bei den Preussischen Staats- und Privatbahnen bestehenden Unterstützungskassen für Lohnarbeiter*. The text provides no guidance to the exact date when this information was compiled.

[d] For these figures and those under item 4, I have used a return of 1870. 'Protokoll der preussisch-österreichischen Konferenz, 18 November 1872', QS,I.5, No. 75, p. 200. These categories of the self-employed would have been included among members of friendly societies.

[e] This is a maximum estimate. Frevert, *Krankheit*, p. 177, quoting *Motive zum Kassengesetzentwurf*, SBRT, vol. 3, 1876, p. 48.

[f] Census of 1871, *Preussische Statistik*, vol. 30.

Table 9.6. *Insurance contributors as percentage of population of working age, England and Wales, 1891*

Members of registered friendly societies	3,861,519[a]
Less estimated membership of societies not insuring against sickness	−526,036[b]
Plus members of trade unions insuring against sickness	+479,201[c]
Total relevant membership	3,814,684
Population aged 15–64	17,457,800[d]
Percentage of population	**21.9 per cent**

Notes:
[a] Chief Registrar of Friendly Societies, *Report for 1891*, p. 45, Table XVI, BPP 1892, C.137-I, LXXIII.
[b] For this period there is no parallel to the 1873 *Return of Burial Societies*. There is, however, for 1892 a list of all societes by name, from which it has been possible to identify burial societies, widows and orphans annuity societies and a few other societies whose titles make it clear that they were not involved in sickness insurance. The name of the society cannot by itself provide an absolutely reliable way of identifying societies that should not be included in this statistical table, but there is no better method available. The figure of 526,036 may therefore be on the low side. *Report of Chief Registrar of Friendly Societies for 1892*, Parts D(1) and D(2), BPP 1893–4 (513) and (513-I) LXXXIV, 447 and 591. The failure to exclude societies not insuring against sickness makes the figures given (for the UK as a whole) in C. G. Hanson, 'Welfare before the welfare state', in R. M. Hartwell *et al.*, *The long debate on poverty* (London, 1972), p. 121, wildly unrealistic, as he himself admits on pp. 124–5.
[c] Calculated from *Report on trade unions for 1891*, BPP 1893–4 C.6990 CII, 85, Tables IV and I.
[d] Mitchell and Deane, *British historical statistics*, p. 12.

Table 9.7. *Insurance contributors as percentage of population of working age, Prussia and German Empire, 1891*

	Prussia	Empire
Membership of sickness funds of all kinds, including miners' funds	3,831,701[a]	6,993,550[b]
Population aged 15–65 (1890)	17,769,051[c]	29,535,000[d]
Percentage of population	**21.6 per cent**	**23.7 per cent**

Notes:
[a] *Statistik der Krankenversicherung der Arbeiter im Jahre 1891*, p. X, n. 1 and p. 16, Table A1, *Statistik des Deutschen Reichs*, NF vol. 65 (1893).
[b] QS,E, Tables I.1 and I.2.
[c] Census 1890, *Preussische Statistik*, vol. 121/1 (1893), calculated from Table II, pp. 50ff.
[d] G. Hohorst *et al.*, *Sozialgeschichtliches Arbeitsbuch II* (2nd edn, Munich, 1975), p. 23.

Table 9.8. *Insurance contributors as percentage of population of working age, England and Wales, 1911*

Membership of affiliated orders	2,402,101[a]
Membership of ordinary friendly societies insuring against sickness	1,962,438[b]
Membership of trade unions insuring against sickness, 1908	728,593[c]
Total relevant membership	5,093,132
Population aged 15–65	23,141,100[d]
Percentage of population	22.0 per cent

Notes:
[a] *Report of Chief Registrar of Friendly Societies for 1911*, Part A, Appendix N, Table I(c), pp. 118–19, BPP 1912–13 (123-I) LXXI.
[b] *Ibid.*, Table III Summary, p. 156.
[c] *Seventeenth Report of the Labour Correspondent of the Board of Trade for 1908–10*, pp. xxxiv–xxxv, BPP 1912–13 Cd.6109 XLVII, 655. These figures for 1908 are the nearest to 1911 available. An unpublished survey of the same year also from the Labour Department of the Board of Trade gives a total of 732,677. Labour Department, Board of Trade, 'Analysis of the rules of trade unions relating to unemployed, sick and accident benefits and expenditure on such benefits by each union', 1908 Confidential Print, LSE, Beveridge Collection B.XVII. I am grateful to Noel Whiteside for drawing my attention to this source. There is no explanation for the small discrepancy, and since it makes no difference to the percentage, I have preferred to cite the published figure.
[d] Mitchell and Deane, *British historical statistics*, p. 12.

Table 9.9. *Insurance contributors as percentage of population of working age, German Empire, 1911*

Membership of sickness funds of all kinds, including miners' funds	14,256,941[a]
Population aged 15–64	39,521,000[b]
Percentage of population	36.1 per cent

Notes:
[a] QS,E, Tables I.1 and I.2.
[b] Hohorst, *Sozialgeschichtliches Arbeitsbuch II*, p. 23.

Table 9.10. *Insurance contributors as percentage of population of working age, England and Wales, and the UK, 1913*

	England and Wales	UK
Members of national health insurance approved societies	11,212,197	13,427,865[a]
Population aged 15–65 (1911)	23,141,100	28,756,200[b]
Percentage of population	48.5 per cent	46.7 per cent

Notes:
[a] *Report for 1913–14 on the administration of national health insurance*, pp. 498, 528, 550 and 564, BPP 1914 Cd.7496 LXXXII. The report for the following year was not published separately, but in a very abbreviated form as part of the 1914–17 period. Hence the use of the figures for 1913 despite the fact that the first figures under the German RVO are for 1914.
[b] Mitchell and Deane, *British historical statistics*, pp. 12–14.

Table 9.11. *Insurance contributors as percentage of population of working age, German Empire, 1914*

Membership of sickness funds of all kinds, including miners' funds	16,525,667[a]
Population aged 15–65 (1911)	39,520,000[b]
Percentage of population	41.8 per cent

Notes:
[a] QS,E, Tables I.1, I.2.
[b] Hohorst, *Sozialgeschichtliches Arbeitsbuch II*, p. 23.

10

German invalidity and old age insurance

(A) THE LAW OF 1889 AND ITS BACKGROUND

Accident insurance was introduced at a time of public concern over the human cost of industrial production and was designed to block off other less acceptable policies in response to that problem. Sickness insurance, although only recently reformed, had to be placed on a more universal basis to provide the immediate services needed by the victims of accidents. Once that point had been accepted, Lohmann used the opportunity for further reform of the defective system established in 1876. But what reasons were there for establishing invalidity and old age insurance in the later 1880s?

There was really only one reason, and that was provided by a series of decisions that Bismarck had taken around 1880. These were taken essentially on his own. The case for invalidity and old age pension funds had attracted much attention in the early 1870s, but it raised such problems that in 1875 it was decided to confine the forthcoming legislation to sickness funds. These funds would be able to pay burial grants, but invalidity and old age as well as support of widows and orphans were excluded from the permitted objects. With that decision, official interest in the subject ceased. In 1878, 1879 and 1880, as was mentioned before, Stumm, the coal and steel magnate, proposed in the *Reichstag* that compulsory insurance against invalidity and old age, which existed for miners through the *Knappschaften*, be extended to other industrial workers. For someone like Stumm, who employed steelworkers as well as miners, that seemed a reasonable idea, not least because steel works had once been under a similar regime. He had already raised the matter in 1869 during the debates on the GewO. Despite a cool reception from the government spokesman, a committee of the *Reichstag* supported the proposal, at least for factory workers. It was forwarded to the federated states and to the Prussian district administrations for their views. Among the states only Saxony supported the idea, and only two of the many Prussian district governors. Meanwhile

Lohmann had launched his proposal for a reform of the law of employers' liability as an alternative policy for the protection of workers' safety. He reported on the replies to Stumm's proposal in 1880 and drew a thoroughly negative conclusion. When Bismarck embarked on accident insurance it looked as if the idea of compulsory invalidity and old age insurance had been well and truly shelved.[1]

That was not the case. While working on the details of accident insurance, Bismarck was also considering provision for old age. What he had in mind were pensions provided or heavily subsidised from public funds and not necessarily limited to industrial workers. In December 1880 he put the idea to the king of Bavaria, who had expressed strong opposition to international socialism, and he commended it as a way to undermine socialist influence among workers. In the same month the *Begründung*, the memorandum in support of the Accident Insurance Bill, stated that the concentration on accident insurance did not rule out, but merely postponed, the bigger issue. Bismarck confided to Lohmann at the time that he was contemplating the use of taxes on luxuries to produce a massive increase in the revenues of the *Reich*. That would make it possible to provide the propertyless with assured pensions and would lead to conservative attitudes among the great mass of them. Bismarck's ideas on this matter were most fully expressed in an interview with a sympathetic journalist in January 1881. They were presented as a policy to reconcile the workers to the State, which should be generous to those in poverty. They were linked to an increase in the tax base of the *Reich* by means of a tobacco monopoly. In August 1881 he told the Prussian cabinet of his intention to introduce the basis of a law on old age provision in the next *Reichstag*, so as to help to launch a linked proposal for an imperial tobacco monopoly.[2]

It was in this form that Professor Adolph Wagner was instructed to make the case for a tobacco monopoly, linking it to the financing of accident and comprehensive old age insurance for workers. But as the disastrous election results in the autumn of 1881 were to demonstrate, neither policy was popular enough to make an increase in indirect taxation on such a popular form of consumption acceptable. In hindsight we know that the

---

[1] Florian Tennstedt, 'Vorläufer der gesetzlichen Rentenversicherung', in Stefan Fisch and Ulrike Haerendel (eds.), *Geschichte und Gegenwart der Rentenversicherung in Deutschland* (Berlin, 2000), pp. 40–5.

[2] QS,I.1, pp. 597–600 and 630; QS,I.2, pp. 402–3 and 428–30; QS,I.6, pp. 445–7. F. Tennstedt, 'Vorgeschichte und Entstehung der Kaiserlichen Botschaft', ZSR, 27 (1981), 684–5. See in general Tennstedt, 'Vorläufer', pp. 46–8.

inadequate tax base, which Bismarck regarded as one of the greatest problems of the *Reich*, would not be rectified along these lines. But Bismarck did not, and he clung to his plans in defiance of every setback. The Imperial Message that he wrote for William I announced his determination to continue with accident insurance and sickness insurance. It added that 'those who become unable to earn a living through old age or invalidity also have a well-founded claim on the community for a higher measure of care from the state than they have so far received'. That statement was once more linked to plans for indirect taxation with explicit reference to a tobacco monopoly and additional duty on spirits. In view of the hostility of the political parties, he hinted that this might be achievable through the development of corporate forms of representation. Tennstedt writes of Bismarck's mood at this time as one of crisis.[3]

In the end, apart from workers' contributions through the participation of their sickness funds, accident insurance was financed by contributions from employers. That was made acceptable in the short run by the abandonment of actuarial methods in favour of pay-as-you-go. But the prominence that had been given to provision for old age and invalidity in the Imperial Message of 1881 had created a new political fact. That was reinforced in April 1883 when the prospect of this legislation during the session of 1884 was held out to the *Reichstag* as an inducement for a quick dispatch of the Accident Insurance Bill and the budget.[4] Thereafter no more was heard on the subject until March 1887 when Heinrich Boetticher, the Secretary of State for the Interior, announced that he hoped to be in a position to present the *Reichstag* in the next session with a draft law on provision against old age and invalidity.

A document setting out the principles (*Grundzüge*) of an old age and invalidity insurance law was submitted in confidence on 6 July 1887 to the governments of the states and to the Prussian ministers, including Bismarck, for their comments.[5] Some aspects of this legislation demand particular attention.

[3] Florian Tennstedt, 'Vorgeschichte', p. 710. Text of Imperial Message on p. 733. For financial reform as an element in the origins of social insurance, see also Ritter, *Social welfare*, pp. 49–54.

[4] Imperial Message in SBRT, 5.LP II, Session 1882/3, vol. 3, p. 1956. For context see Tennstedt, 'Vorgeschichte', pp. 701–2.

[5] Hans Rothfels, *Theodor Lohmann und die Kampfjahre der staatlichen Sozialpolitik (1871–1905)* (Berlin, 1927), p. 81; Ulrike Haerendel, *Die Anfänge der gesetzlichen Rentenversicherung in Deutschland* (Speyer, 2001), pp. 45–9; more fully in QS,II.6.

(i) The contributory principle

The document took the contributory principle so much for granted that it made no effort to justify it. Like sickness and accident insurance, old age and invalidity insurance was to be compulsory, as the matter was put in the accompanying memorandum. And the fact that the right to a pension was dependent on the payment of contributions was not mentioned in the *Grundzüge* themselves until well into the document.[6]

In early September 1887 Bismarck made it clear that he was fundamentally opposed to the insurance principle in this matter. In a statement, circulated among the Prussian ministers, he reminded the authors of the document that his own proposals in 1880–1 had been for a measure financed by the *Reich* out of taxation and were based on the expectation of additional revenue from a tobacco monopoly. He strongly repudiated any suggestion that it was inappropriate to burden the taxpayers in general for the benefit of particular classes of the population: provisions against old age and invalidity were required on grounds of the national interest. He met the anticipated objection that the *Reich* at present lacked the means to undertake anything so costly with the suggestion that legislation should be introduced gradually. A beginning should be made with the cities and industrial districts, where the need was greatest.[7] That would not have been impossible, for the rejection of the contributory system removed the reason for including as large a wage-earning population as possible.[8]

As expected, Boetticher at the Ministry of the Interior objected to his suggestions on the ground of cost, which he calculated for the full scheme on a yearly average as 156 million marks, roughly one-fifth of the total expenditure of the *Reich* at the time. Such a sum, he expected, would be unacceptable to the individual states but could be raised through contributions. 'So let us wait', minuted Bismarck on the first point, adding later that there was no need to abandon the project; it was possible to undertake it gradually. On the second point he minuted that 'the totality of Germans

---

[6] 'Grundzüge zur Alters- und Invalidenversicherung mit Denkschrift', 6 July 1887, QS,II.6, No. 37.
[7] 'Votum Bismarcks für das preussische Staatsministerium', 11 September 1887, QS,II.6, No. 43. Bismarck regarded it as a notorious fact that poor relief was inadequate only in the cities. He had a distinctly rosy view of rural poor relief, and must have been unaware of the damning report on the inadequacy of the small rural poor law authorities that had just been published by the *Deutsche Verein*: F. von Reitzenstein (ed.), *Die ländliche Armenpflege und ihre Reform* (Freiburg, 1887).
[8] See p. 188 below.

can do it more easily still', adding that 'the means have to be raised somehow in any case'.[9]

The view in the ministry was that Bismarck's negative attitude made 'the organic development of the social insurance legislation' impossible.[10] It is remarkable how isolated Bismarck was in objecting to the contributory principle. Others were pushing for a more gradual approach, but none for his reason. But then it was rather late for such fundamental objections! Had he stated his objections in mid-June, when he first learnt the nature of the proposals, and insisted that they be taken into account in the proposed document, things might have been different. But at that stage he seems not to have formulated the alternative proposal that he proposed in September. Otherwise he would surely not have agreed to the circulation of the *Grundzüge* in that form. But he was deeply preoccupied with the 1887 crisis in the Balkans and the danger of an Austrian–Russian conflict and could presumably spare no attention for details of domestic legislation.[11] In 1882, when he had reconstructed accident insurance from the fiasco of the previous year, he had boasted that foreign policy had been 'so set up as to run by itself' and no longer gave him any sleepless nights.[12] Now things were different. There was certainly no enthusiasm for the initiative among the other states. However, by the time that the proposals were discussed in September, none of them raised objections to the contributory principle. So Bismarck acquiesced, but with a marked lack of enthusiasm.[13] He made only two speeches during the extensive *Reichstag* debates.[14]

The draft law, published on 17 November 1887 and widely circulated, was based on the contributory principle, the State providing one-third of the contributions. The date of publication deliberately coincided with the sixth anniversary of the Imperial Message of 1881, to which

---

[9] Haerendel, *Anfänge*, p. 54. Details in Boetticher to Bismarck, 13 October 1887 with Bismarck's marginalia. QS,II.6, No. 48.

[10] Vogel, *Bismarcks Arbeiterversicherung*, p. 169. The phrase was code for the application of the contributory principle as in accident and sickness insurance.

[11] He was briefed on the proposals on 30 June and agreed to their circulation. The *Grundzüge* together with a fuller version of the memorandum were circulated on 6 July 1887. QS,II.6, No. 37 and n. 2.

[12] L. Gall, *Bismarck, the white revolutionary* (London, 1986), vol. 2, p. 155.

[13] Haerendel, *Anfänge*, pp. 46, 49 and 50–1. In January 1888, after discussion in the Prussian *Volkswirtschaftsrat* Bosse commented in his diary on Bismarck's coolness towards the project. Vogel, *Bismarcks Arbeiterversicherung*, p. 161.

[14] He spoke on 29 March 1889 in order to contradict the widespread impression that he was not interested in the Law, and at the crucial third reading on 18 May 1889 in order to appeal for the support of all conservative elements.

frequent but highly selective reference was made in justification of the measure.[15]

What we are observing was the making of a myth. The claim that the measure was legitimised by the wishes that the aged and venerated Emperor had expressed six years earlier was doubly untrue. The wishes had not been those of the distinctly reluctant Emperor but of Bismarck, and the latter well knew that the measure did not represent his intentions at all. So who created the myth? The answer would appear to lie within the Ministry of the Interior's economic section, which was responsible for social policy.

Its head, Robert Bosse, the author of the *Grundzüge* of 1887, had been committed to the idea of a 'double strategy', balancing the repression of Socialists with social reform capable of appealing to the workers in general, ever since he had been secretary to the Deputy Chancellor, Stollberg-Wernigerode, whom he had converted to his views. It was Bosse who had drafted the memorandum in 1878 which had proposed the policy, but which had failed to obtain Bismarck's support and led to Stollberg-Wernigerode's withdrawal from politics. In 1881 Bosse was appointed to head the newly established economic division of the *Reich* ministry, where Boetticher was his immediate superior and Lohmann one of his subordinates. It was Lohmann who had written the memorandum that had first commended accident insurance in terms of the double strategy; he had known Bosse and been familiar with his views for some time. Bosse soon had every opportunity to promote the idea in person, for it was he who drafted the Imperial Message of November 1881 for Bismarck's consideration.[16]

The failure of Bismarck's plans for a tobacco monopoly to give the Empire a secure source of finance seems to have bothered him less than his master. But he realised that, unless the insurance programme was expanded by the pensions for old age and invalidity, to which the Imperial Message had referred, it would not make the hoped-for impact on the working class that was essential to the success of the double strategy. He expected that impact to depend more on the numbers affected than on the source of the money.

---

[15] The use of the *Berufsgenossenschaften* as the basis of the insurance, that was to become so contentious, was justified by a reference to the wording of the Imperial Message: 'Grundzüge mit Denkschrift', QS,II.6, No. 51. For another example see p. 191 below.

[16] F. Tennstedt, '"Bismarcks Arbeiterversicherung" zwischen Absicherung der Arbeiterexistenz und Abwehr der Arbeiterbewegung', in H. Matthöfer *et al.* (eds.), *Bismarck und die Soziale Frage im 19. Jahrhundert* (Friedrichsruh, 2001), pp. 83–5; more fully in F. Tennstedt, 'Glaubensgewissheit und Revolutionsfurcht. Zum sozialpolitischem Wirken Robert Bosses', ZSR, 49 (2003), 831–46. Bismarck's rejection of much of Bosse's draft but retention of the basic idea of the double strategy is documented in QS,II.1. Nos. 3–8.

If the long-term vision had been Bosse's, he had no problem in commending it to Boetticher, his chief and a close friend. Between them they
piloted the measure to its altogether unexpected end. With it triumphed
also the myth that grounded the insurance legislation of the 1880s in the
double strategy and legitimised it by the wishes of the Emperor, as
expressed in his 'Social Message' of November 1881.

(ii) Scope

If the scheme was to be one of compulsory contributory insurance, to
whom should it apply? On the two previous occasions, insurance legislation had been limited to industrial workers and a few other specified
occupations. Only gradually was the insured population extended. On
this occasion it was proposed to include all wage earners straightaway and
all salary earners up to a limit of 2,000 M per annum. The significant
difference was the inclusion of agricultural and forestry workers. Unlike
accident or sickness insurance, entitlement to invalidity or old age pensions
was to depend on contributions paid over the greater part of the recipient's
working life. This consideration pointed to the need to include as large a
range of workers as possible. Labour mobility was such that pensioners
might have been working in many occupations or localities while they built
up their entitlement. Those who left an insurable occupation would be
allowed to go on contributing on a voluntary basis, but otherwise voluntary
insurance was to be kept to a minimum.

Since an employer's contribution was indispensable to the finances of the
pension, those not working for a wage or salary, i.e. home workers and
other small so-called independent producers, were to be excluded.

(iii) Carriers of the insurance

Who was to carry the insurance? That would be a matter of dispute. The
government proposed the *Berufsgenossenschaften*, which were responsible
for accident insurance, but the committee of the *Bundesrat* that examined
the proposals preferred an insurance based on the states. In the case of the
largest states it should be based on the Prussian provinces and their
Bavarian counterparts. In the case of the smallest states various combina-
tions to produce viable units were suggested. Prussia could have rejected
this proposal in the *Bundesrat* with the help of some of its small client
states. But Bismarck decided that he did not care enough about the issue
to antagonise the medium-sized states which supported this Bavarian

initiative. He agreed to both proposals being placed before the *Reichstag*. His desire to boost the *Berufsgenossenschaften* had greatly waned since 1881–4. They no longer formed part of any wider constitutional plans, and the administrative arguments for using an existing institution that appealed to his advisers did not matter enough to him. He regarded the legislation in any case as seriously flawed.[17]

If he thought that the anti-particularist forces in the *Reichstag* would spring to the defence of the *Berufsgenossenschaften*, he was to be disappointed. Not only because particularism had supporters there too, but also because any proposal to enhance the importance of *Berufsgenossenschaften* was now unacceptable to the influential Central Association of German Industrialists (CDI), in which heavy industry had the major voice. It regarded the more broadly based Federation of German *Berufsgenossenschaften*, founded in 1887, as a potential rival for the ear of government, and threw its influence against anything that would add to its importance.[18] The result was the acceptance of state-based insurance and the marginalisation of the *Berufsgenossenschaften*.

This decision gave to the third branch of social insurance a bureaucratic character, quite unlike that of the other two. These had in their different ways been organised on an occupational basis and administered by largely self-governing bodies, the *Berufsgenossenschaften* and the sickness fund. The State was kept at arm's length. Invalidity and old age insurance would be organised on a territorial basis and administered by pension boards.[19] These were controlled by civil servants and subordinated to a ministry of the relevant state, which relied on the local state authorities for contact with the insured in the first instance. Their appeal tribunals did, however, represent both sides of industry equally and were so much more impartial than those organised by the *Berufsgenossenschaften* for accident insurance on formally the same basis, that they were to replace them in 1900.

---

[17] During the height of the dispute within the committee of the *Bundesrat* Bismarck had asked the Bavarian representative whether the state governments, especially Bavaria, still saw any value in putting the draft law to the *Reichstag*. When the latter said 'Yes, since the matter had now been started', Bismarck replied: 'In that case well and good, we shall carry on. Personally I take no more interest in the whole insurance matter.' Hugo Graf von Lerchenfeld-Koefering, *Erinnerungen und Denkwürdigkeiten 1843–1929* (Berlin, 1935), pp. 297f.

[18] The best commentary on the role of the CDI is H.-P. Ullmann, 'Industrielle Interessen und die Entstehung der deutschen Sozialversicherung 1880–1889', HZ, 229 (1979), 574–610, of which there is a useful English version, 'German industry and Bismarck's social security system', in W. J. Mommsen (ed.), *The emergence of the welfare state in Britain and Germany 1850–1950* (London, 1981), pp. 133–49.

[19] Strictly speaking the German term *Landesversicherungsanstalt* (LVA) means territorial insurance institution, but I shall follow Dawson in calling it pension board.

This unforeseen replacement of an occupational basis by a territorial one ruled out any possibility of adjusting the level of contributions to the differential risks experienced by various occupations, a practice that had been regarded as essential for the other forms of insurance, and taken for granted in the original proposals.[20] It was a fundamental change of principle that has been practically ignored in the historical literature.

The *Berufsgenossenschaften* continued to administer accident insurance and still do, but the refusal to add to their powers condemned a form of corporate organisation to relative insignificance that had at one stage seemed to have great potential. Bismarck's plans to use them as an integral part of the constitution had been blocked already by the *Reichstag* and the Prussian legislature. Now the hostility of the CDI proved fatal to their further development as units of administration. In the early 1880s it had looked as if these self-regulating corporations with compulsory membership and an independent existence in law, strongly reminiscent of the guilds, represented a revival of old principles. For sixty years bodies based on status had been abolished or downgraded in favour of associations based on contract, i.e. on relationships deliberately entered into.[21] Exactly because it was a voluntary association, the CDI was far from representative of German industry. It represented the minority able to exercise the influence of wealth and power. But it came to be regarded in government circles as *the* representative of the interests of German industry, and was consulted accordingly. It was an example of what Abelshauser has described as 'societal corporatism' whose established position was able to thwart the 'state corporatism' which Bismarck had envisaged.[22]

From the administrative point of view both of the proposals placed before the *Reichstag* were open to objections. But a single comprehensive *Reich* insurance had been rejected in 1881 and was still politically unacceptable. It could not even be proposed when the law was amended ten years later.[23] The fragmented structure that resulted included some pension

---

[20] Compare 'Die Motive zur Alters- und Invalidenversicherung der Arbeiter' of November 1887 in *Schmollers Jahrbuch*, NF 12 (1888), 313, with the subsequent discussion of the pros and cons of this principle in view of the fact that the decision between *Berufsgenossenschaften* and territorial insurance boards had not yet been taken, in the 'Gesetzentwurf of 22 Nov. 1888 betr. die Alters- und Invaliditätsversicherung. Begründung', p. 55. *Aktenstücke*, No. 10, SBRT, 7.LP IV, Session 1888/9, vol. 4.

[21] For these concepts see Sir Henry Maine, *Ancient law* (1861), p. 170. For Lohmann's disapproval of the *Berufsgenossenschaften* on these grounds see p. 99 above.

[22] Werner Abelshauser, 'The first post-liberal nation: stages in the development of modern corporatism in Germany', *Europ. His. Quarterly*, 14 (1984), 285–318, for this period pp. 288–96.

[23] G. von Witzleben, 'Die Vorschläge zur Reform der Invaliditäts- und Altersversicherung', *Schmollers Jahrbuch*, 23 (1899), 341.

boards which were financially much weaker than others. That created such serious problems that within seven years the government had to return to the *Reichstag* with proposals for an amendment to the Law. The resulting Law of 1899 will be considered later.

(iv) The object of insurance

What was to be insured against? The answer is both old age and invalidity, but primarily invalidity. That was so obvious that, on the second reading, the *Reichstag* decided to call it a law for insurance against invalidity and old age, reversing the order in which the two terms had originally been placed. Indeed, Boetticher had confessed that there had been some doubt at first whether to provide old age pensions at all. 'Anyone still capable of work at the advanced age of seventy', he had said, 'should thank God for this rare gift and could hardly demand a pension.' Since, however, the Imperial Message had explicitly mentioned old age in 1881, it had given them their 'marching orders', to which they should adhere.[24]

The relative unimportance of old age pensions became only gradually apparent from the figures of expenditure. Those aged seventy or over could claim their old age pension at once, whereas entitlement to an invalidity pension took longer to build up. But by 1897 the total number of invalidity pensions exceeded that of old age pensions and by the following year the amount paid out for invalidity exceeded that for old age. By 1900 it was more than double and the discrepancy increased rapidly with every year[25] (see Figure 10.1). The old age pension was, in the words of one historian, no more than a decorative addition.[26] It was also worth significantly less since, unlike the invalidity pension, it was intended for those still fully able to work. It required no proof of invalidity, and could be replaced by the invalidity pension at a higher rate.

Will this explanation finally establish the fact in British minds that German pensions were not a trick to make workers pay for something that few of them would ever enjoy? From a chancellor of the exchequer in 1908 to journalists in the twenty-first century British commentators have

---

[24] Preussischer Volkswirtschaftsrat, 2. Sitzung des permanenten Ausschusses, Session 1887, S.17f, quoted in Florian Tennstedt, 'Vorgeschichte', p. 702. See Haerendel, *Anfänge*, pp. 101–3, for the debate in the *Reichstag*.

[25] QS,E, Table III.2, p. 153.

[26] Hans Günter Hockerts, 'Sicherung im Alter. Kontinuität und Wandel der gesetzlichen Rentenversicherung 1889–1979', in Werner Conze and M. Rainer Lepsius (eds.), *Sozialgeschichte der Bundesrepublik Deutschland. Beiträge zum Kontinuitätsproblem* (Stuttgart, 1983), p. 299.

Million marks

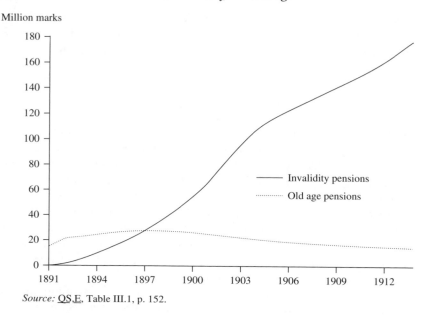

Source: QS,E, Table III.1, p. 152.

Figure 10.1. Expenditure on German old age and invalidity pensions, 1891–1914.

often failed to appreciate that German state pensions, unlike British ones, were linked to invalidity, and to a qualifying age only for those who attained it while still in good health. The fact that average expectation of life at age twenty was then only slightly over sixty is therefore irrelevant. In practice 52 per cent of the 1.1 million invalidity pensions awarded between 1901 and 1909 went to applicants under sixty, and 72 per cent to those under sixty-five.[27]

Traditionally not old age but invalidity had been the object of concern. Compulsory insurance of miners or railwaymen had been for invalidity, i.e. loss of income through inability to work.[28] Not that the new law took the benefits for miners or railwaymen as its model. These were regarded as far

---

[27] Hennock, *British social reform*, pp. 131–4, for 1908; Hamish McRae, *The Independent*, 15 February 2001, p. 4. Figures calculated from Lars Kaschke and Monika Sniegs, *Kommentierte Statistiken zur Sozialversicherung in Deutschland von ihren Anfängen bis in die Gegenwart*, Abt.I, vol. 1 (Skt Katharinen, 2001), Table C7; QS,E, p. 153; Peter Flora *et al.* (eds.), *State, economy and society*, vol. 2, p. 101.

[28] Christoph Conrad, *Vom Greis zum Rentner. Der Strukturwandel des Alters in Deutschland zwischen 1830 und 1930* (Göttingen, 1994), pp. 204–5.

too generous for all workers. The benefits were designed anew and then redesigned in complex debates by the *Bundesrat* and the *Reichstag*.

Originally entitlement to an invalidity pension had required total incapacity to work, measured by inability to earn an amount equal to the basic invalidity pension. That was regarded as too absolute and was replaced by the concept of two-thirds incapacity. When it proved difficult to find a formula to measure this, a compromise was struck between incapacity measured by inability to earn one-third of the applicant's previous wages and inability to earn one-third of the normal wages of ordinary labourers in the locality. The German invalidity pension, unlike the British disability benefit under the 1911 National Insurance Act, was no retirement pension in the sense that recipients were expected to retire from employment.[29]

Pensions could also be paid for temporary incapacity, provided that it lasted at least one year. It should be recalled that support from sickness insurance ended after a mere thirteen weeks.

(v) Pension levels

The amount of the pension was a central issue of debate. The government proposals had originally envisaged a minimum basic pension level for all, augmented for invalidity pensions after fifteen years of contributions by 4 M for each additional year. That meant a basic annual invalidity pension of 120 M, rising to a maximum of 250 M. The old age pension level did not qualify for any augmentation and was set at 60 M (£3), half the basic minimum for invalidity. That was such a derisory sum that the *Bundesrat* raised it to 120 M p.a., equal to the minimum level of the invalidity pension.

In the public debate after the publication of the *Grundzüge* the concept of a basic pension level for all, kept low enough for the requisite contributions to be affordable by even the lowest paid, proved highly controversial. There were those who approved, most prominently Lujo Brentano, the Liberal advocate of social reform. He described the low and uniform pension level and other features of the proposals as no more than a reform of poor relief. He praised the government for replacing poor relief from local taxation by compulsory savings on the part of workers and their employers, which as a Liberal he much preferred. By paying for poor relief,

---

[29] In that respect disability benefit differed also from British old age pensions, whether means-tested as in 1908 or not as after 1925. For the debate in the 1940s over a retirement condition see A. Land, R. Lowe and N. Whiteside, *The development of the welfare state 1939–1951* (London, 1992), p. 30.

workers acquired a right to a pension, a right which they had been denied under the poor law. The pensions would also put an end to the power of employers over the lives of their workers exercised through works-based invalidity funds. All that was now needed, he wrote, was to give workers security of employment without which they would be unable to pay their contributions on a regular basis.[30]

Far from welcoming this support from a long-standing critic, the government was embarrassed by his description of its proposal as merely a reform of the poor law, not least because there was much truth in it. But the proposal became altogether indefensible when it was pointed out that the usual level of poor relief for a single man was 150 M in Berlin, while it was already 156 M in Elberfeld, 36 M higher than the proposed pension level. If contributory pensions were to be acceptable to workers with higher earnings, their pension levels would have to be raised. Yet with labourers' wages in rural areas less than half the rate for skilled men in the industrial areas, it was impossible to raise the level generally without making contributions too burdensome for the low-paid.[31] Such disparity of earnings, and of local prices within the population for whom the legislation was intended, rendered the original proposal inappropriate. The government cast around for ways to accommodate its proposal to objections based on the differences in the local cost of living and proposed to differentiate the pension level by localities. They were divided into five groups, based on the normal wages of local labourers, a piece of information already available as part of the administration of sickness insurance benefits.[32] It was in this form that the law went to the *Reichstag*, only to be thoroughly mauled.

No one believed that the wages of labourers, as returned by the local police authorities, bore any resemblance to reality: they were the product of the worst kind of bureaucratic make-believe. The government proposal lacked credibility. In addition, it was attacked by those who had never accepted the principle of a modest pension level for all. They wanted pensions to be geared to the standard of living of the individual contributor with contributions differentiated accordingly. Even the supporters of a low pension for all, who were mainly to be found among agricultural employers of the eastern

---

[30] Lujo Brentano, 'Die beabsichtigte Alters- und Invaliden-Versicherung für Arbeiter und ihre Bedeutung', *Jahrbücher für Nationalökonomie und Statistik*, NF 16 (1887), 1–46. For Brentano and the place of this article in the development of his thought see James J. Sheehan, *The career of Lujo Brentano: a study of liberalism and social reform in Imperial Germany* (Chicago, 1966).

[31] *Gesetzentwurf betr. die Alters- und Invaliditätsversicherung. Begründung*, p. 55, for references to wages of 80pf to 1 M, and 2.25 M, respectively. *Aktenstücke*, No. 10, SBRT, 7.LP IV, Session 1888/9, vol. 4.

[32] Haerendel, *Anfänge*, pp. 72–5.

provinces, disliked the government's second thoughts and insisted on a return to a uniform pension level modified only by length of contribution. They were apparently impervious to the argument that price differentials made this impossible to sell to the delegates from the western areas.

The government protested that pensions based on the individual earnings of each person were impossible to administer. Caught between two fires, it finally capitulated to the demand for some differentiation by earnings. An elaborate compromise formula was produced for four wage groups based on the average earnings of the category of workers to which the applicant belonged for the purposes of calculating sickness benefits.[33] This was neither simple nor just and was replaced by a different formula in 1899. However, it signalled the definite rejection of the original policy of a modest pension for all, and the acceptance of the principle that pensions should reflect the economic differences within the insured population. The demand for this had come mainly from the members of the Liberal and Centre parties. As one of the former put it: 'workers do not consist of one large undifferentiated mass; the differences within the working class need to be taken into account.'[34]

At the same time that it accepted differentiation by income, the government dropped its proposal for lower pensions and contributions for women. Since their lower earnings would place them in any case in one of the lower pension classes, additional differentiation by gender seemed unnecessary.

The full differentiation of pension levels was modified by a state subsidy for every pensioner. Originally envisaged as one-third of the total contribution, it was finally set at 50 M p.a. per pension. That came at first to more than one-third and gradually declined as reserves accumulated.

Table 10.1. *Old age and invalidity insurance:*
state subsidy as a percentage of total pension
payments

1891	39.5	1907	33.6
1892	40.4	1908	33.1
1895	40.5	1910	32.0
1900	39.1	1914	31.1
1905	34.6		

Source: Calculated from QS,E, p. 152.

[33] Haerendel, *Anfänge*, pp. 117–18 and 152–3. [34] Quoted in Haerendel, *Anfänge*, p. 116.

In practice the state subsidy paid for the so-called 'transitional provisions', which permitted those over forty to qualify for an invalidity pension after only five years of contributions. These older workers presented a high risk which their accumulated contributions did not cover. Yet their early inclusion in the scheme was a political necessity. But for the subsidy their claims would have had to be paid out of the contributions of younger workers. The subsidy also covered the cost of periods of military service and long-term illness, during which no contributions were levied. When one remembers how impossible it had been to provide any subsidy for accident insurance, it is remarkable that this time the protests in the *Reichstag* were limited to a minority, largely of Liberals, and that there was no need to link it to new forms of taxation. This acceptance was not due to the considerations just mentioned; the function of the subsidy in mitigating inter-generational conflict was never mentioned in the *Begründung* of the law. Its principal justification was the 'support of the total economic and social order'. The argument so prominent in the early 1880s that insurance would reduce the burden on public poor relief cropped up once more, but in view of Brentano's comments now played a distinctly secondary role.[35]

The state subsidy and a further 60 M from individual contributions provided a common basis of 110 M per pension before differentiation set in.[36] This 60 M was actually a subsidy to the lower paid from the contributions paid by those with higher income. In its final version the scheme therefore compelled the higher paid to provide themselves with bigger pensions, but it also included an element of cross-subsidy within the insured population that had not originally been envisaged.

(vi) Finance and administration

The state subsidy was financed by means of pay-as-you-go, but the contributions from workers and employers were intended to build up a reserve fund to cover liabilities for a limited period ahead.[37] As with sickness insurance, the payment of contributions was the responsibility of employers, who deducted

---

[35] *Begründung*, p. 58.

[36] Haerendel, *Anfänge*, pp. 119–20, shows how this differentiation affected contributions and pension levels. Since the method was changed within ten years, comparative figures for England and Germany are based on the law of 1899. See Table 14.1 below.

[37] The original intention had been to cover all known liabilities in full, but the decision to go for differential pensions would have increased costs to such an extent that this compromise solution was chosen instead. Such disregard of actuarial methods was, as usual, at the expense of later cohorts of contributors. We now know, however, as they did not, that any reserves built up by 1914 disappeared in any case in the war-time and post-war inflation. Rückert, *Entstehung*, p. 15.

workers' contributions from their wages. In this case it was important to keep a detailed record over many years. That was to be done by issuing every worker with a book to be kept by his employer, into which the latter stuck insurance stamps to the value of each weekly contribution. Unfortunately such a book, while providing a long-term record of contributions, would also have provided employers with information on the employment record of all their workers. That would have created a major grievance, not least among active trade unionists, and it was amended in favour of insurance cards that provided a record for only one year. These cards had to be stored in vast quantities in warehouses specially designated for the purpose and greatly added to the cost and complexity of the system. The administration of this 'stamp-licking law' (*Klebegesetz*), as it was called, caused much resentment among employers who were required to do it at their own expense.[38]

(vii) Conclusion

The law passed the *Reichstag* by a mere majority of twenty. The many issues of principle raised by it cut right across the parties of the *Kartell* – the two Conservative parties and the National Liberals – on whose support the government normally relied. Thirty-seven members of these parties voted in opposition. So uncertain and so crucial was the attitude of the Conservatives that both Bismarck and the young Emperor made special appeals to their loyalty, but even this left some of those on the agrarian wing unmoved.[39] In view of these defections from the *Kartell*, the divisions within the Centre party acquired great significance. It was the refusal of thirteen of its members to follow the party recommendation to vote against the law that ensured its success.

It was a very different law from the one that the government had originally placed before the *Reichstag*, not just in details but in fundamentals. The government had intended to provide everyone covered by the law with roughly similar pensions, of which two-thirds were to be paid out of wages by employers and workers combined. That had ruled out any but the lowest contributions, in view of the need to include low-paid agricultural labourers from all parts of the country. The state subsidy would have done something to increase the pensions level, but since it was spread evenly over the insured population and strictly limited, it could not have prevented the

---

[38] Haerendel, *Anfänge*, pp. 129–30.
[39] Jens Flemming, 'Sozialpolitik, landwirtschaftliche Interessen und Mobilisierungsversuche', in Fisch and Haerendel, *Geschichte und Gegenwart*, pp. 71–92, figures on p. 73. It is impossible to tell which of these appeals was more effective. Rückert, *Entstehung*, p. 19.

pensions from being very low. That was the decisive fact. For someone completely unable to work and with no other means, the sum provided would have been scarcely if at all more adequate than poor relief.

Invalidity and old age between them had in 1885 accounted for 38 per cent of successful applicants for poor relief, or 27 per cent when dependants were included. The proposals could therefore be expected to relieve the poor law authorities and the local taxpayer significantly.[40] Brentano's description of the proposals as no more than a reform of poor relief, but an excellent one from the point of view of the ratepayers, was perceptive, even though strongly repudiated by the government. He had correctly identified many of the assumptions that underlay government thinking. Bosse, the author of the draft law, had also been the man who had pointed out to Bismarck in 1881 the implications of the memorandum on poor law reform produced in his department.[41] But the discovery that in the most prosperous areas the proposed pension would not even equal the customary level of poor relief destroyed the original proposal, and the implausible basis for the differentiation by localities gave the advocates of a very different approach their opportunity.

What was it that the *Reichstag* passed instead? First and foremost, it was a rejection of uniformity, geared to the meagre savings that the low-paid could afford, a rejection of what one *Reichstag* member had called the barest kind of levelling down (*kahle Gleichmacherei*).[42] As part of its embarrassed defence of the original proposal, the *Begründung* had recommended additional voluntary contributions to private or charitable funds, but no one believed that the better-paid workers would be willing to make substantial additional voluntary savings. To obtain a more appropriate income when they were no longer fit to work, they would have to be compelled to save and their employers to contribute.[43]

The shocked reaction of commentators inside and outside the *Reichstag* to the proposed uniformity of benefit irrespective of income level owed much to expectations created by the previous insurance laws. The *Begründung* warded off any suggestion that the new invalidity pensions should in any way be compared with the accident pensions which were based on two-thirds of previous income. But even sickness benefit and

---

[40] Figures from RAS 1885, *Einleitung*, Table 9, p. 40*.
[41] See p. 38 above.   [42] Haerendel, *Anfänge*, p. 116.
[43] *Begründung*, p. 53. Lip-service continued to be paid to the idea of making such provisions for supplementary pensions out of voluntary savings, but with no significant result in practice. Kleeis, *Geschichte*, pp. 144, 145 and 207.

contributions were, wherever possible, related to the average wages earned in the occupation for which the funds had been established.

Sickness insurance furnished more than a precedent; it furnished the administrative device that made the differentiation of invalidity and old age pensions possible. For all contributors were allocated to one of four wage groups according to the average earnings of the members of the sickness fund to which they belonged. Sickness benefit and contribution were calculated as a proportion of that average income and rose smoothly with increasing wages; invalidity and old age pensions and contributions consisted of the specific amount laid down for each wage group and rose in steps from the lower group to the higher one. Nevertheless the basis of the differentiation was the average wage level of the particular sickness fund. It therefore reflected the wage differential between different occupations in different localities, but no more than sickness insurance did it actually reflect the wage differential between skilled and unskilled workers within that occupation and locality. The *Reichstag* amendments certainly introduced significant differentials compared with the government proposals based on what low-paid agricultural labourers could afford. Groups of industrial workers and other better paid groups were greatly affected by the change. But we should be cautious before interpreting them as a strategy to appeal to the skilled rather than the unskilled members of the industrial working class.[44] The government proposal had been so blatantly unsuited to the widely accepted object of social insurance, to appeal to the working class with benefits channelled through the *Reich*, that it was rejected in favour of something more appropriate. Further than that it would be difficult to go.

These changes derive a special significance from the long-term development of the German pension system. Since the 1880s this has been increasingly characterised by differentiation of contributions and benefits according to income. That differentiation was given its fullest expression in the Pension Law of 1957, which provided pensions that carefully reproduced the population's income distribution during the course of the working life. Although somewhat modified in 1972 and later, this is the principle on which pensions in the Federal Republic of Germany have been based. Since the development of comparative studies of welfare provisions in the 1960s, the difference between this and the basis on which British pensions are provided has been generally recognised in the literature. Our investigation

---

[44] Haerendel points out that the better-paid members of a sickness fund might easily find themselves allocated to a wages group that failed to reflect their own actual earnings. She could well have added that on the same ground the lower-paid members of such a fund might be burdened with higher contributions than would have been justified by their actual earnings. Haerendel, *Anfänge*, pp. 117–18.

suggests that the origin of what social scientists (as usual more interested in inventing labels than in historical accuracy) have called the Bismarckian tradition, is located in Lohmann's remodelling of sickness insurance benefits in 1883. It owes little to the priorities of Bismarck's government and even less to those of Bismarck himself.

(B) THE AMENDMENT OF 1899

The law came into force in 1891. By 1896 the government began to propose major changes in its provisions. After initial opposition, the new Invalidity Law was completed in 1899.

This sense of urgency came from the disparity in the resources available to the various pension boards compared to their liabilities. The law laid down that their reserves should be calculated after ten years and higher or lower contributions introduced where that proved necessary. That was something that the government wished to avoid, particularly since the problem was so great that it would have required an increase of 250 per cent to contributions in East Prussia. Rural provinces with a preponderance of the insured in the two lower wage groups were seriously in deficit, whereas large surpluses were building up in the industrial provinces. The system had included a certain amount of cross-subsidy between wage groups in favour of the lower-paid, but once it had been decided not to use *Berufsgenossenschaften* as the basis of insurance, no further attention had been paid to the occupational composition of the insured population in the territorial units responsible for insurance.

For accident and for sickness insurance premiums were adjusted by each *Berufsgenossenschaft* and sickness fund whenever required. But a revaluation of premiums after ten years by what were to all intents and purposes state institutions was bound to have political repercussions. That prospect persuaded the government to drop any thoughts of requiring rates of contributions to be differentiated by occupation. It opted instead for greater national solidarity in the financing of the system. In future, contributions would be paid into a common fund to cover the majority of the liabilities and into territorial funds only for matters that were at the discretion of local pension boards. That left the administration of insurance in the hands of the territorial boards and satisfied particularist demands, while establishing greater national solidarity in matters of finance.[45]

---

[45] R. van der Borght, 'Die Reform der deutschen Invaliditäts- und Altersversicherung', *Jahrbücher für Nationalökonomie und Statistik*, 3rd ser. 18 (1899), 387–94.

While national solidarity was strengthened in territorial terms, the opposite occurred in respect of income. The Law of 1899 took income differentiation several steps further than in 1889. It established a fifth wage group for those earning over 1,150 M. It also removed the subsidy that the higher income groups had originally contributed to the pension levels of the lowest two groups. The relation of contribution to pension was henceforth identical in each, i.e. each wage group derived the full benefit from its own contributions. That was done by replacing the common basis of 60 M for invalidity pensions by one rising from 60 M for group I to 100 M for group V. The additional annual entitlements were somewhat reduced. For groups II–V this meant a significant increase in the pension obtainable once the minimum period of contributions had been satisfied, but also required a reduction of the benefit obtained from a long period of contribution and therefore of the penalty consequent on early invalidity. The old age pension was similarly differentiated by calculating the basic element on a scale ranging from 60 M for group I to 180 M for group V.[46]

To merge the three branches of insurance into a single system was dismissed as too difficult, as it has been at regular intervals ever since. But it had to be admitted that the existing gap of nine months between the expiry of entitlement to sickness insurance and the start of an invalidity pension was a scandal. By awarding pensions for temporary incapacity after twenty-six weeks, the gap was reduced, but it was not to be closed until 1904 when entitlement to sick pay was extended from thirteen to twenty-six weeks.[47]

An attempt to provide invalidity and old age insurance with its own local administrative infrastructure for dealing with applications foundered on the cost involved, but the operation of the local state administration was made slightly less bureaucratic by the involvement of workers' and employers' representatives.[48]

The most unsatisfactory aspect of the original law had been the elaborate formula used to identify invalidity. This was now made simpler and more generous by defining invalidity as the inability 'to earn less than one-third of the amount usually earned by physical and mentally healthy persons of the same kind with similar training in the same locality'. That still required them to seek work in occupations other than that which they had previously exercised (in contrast to the rules applying to miners for instance), but it left room for more discretion in its application to individual cases.

---

[46] The qualifying period was also reduced from 235 to 200 weeks. Borght, *Reform*, pp. 375–7; *Entwurf eines Invalidenversicherungsgesetzes. Aktenstücke Nr. 93*, SBRT, 1899, pp. 663–5.
[47] Borght, *Reform*, pp. 373–5.   [48] *Ibid.*, pp. 383–7.

The immediate repercussions of this change will be examined below. The new formula would have almost exclusively benefited higher-paid workers. Those earning a low wage to begin with, whose impairment was only partial so that they were able to find work suited to their reduced state of health, would most likely be earning at least one-third of what they had earned before. To qualify for a pension they would have had to be to all intents and purposes incapable of work. But highly paid workers, who had to find work suited to a reduced state of health, e.g. less exacting or part-time work, might well be earning only one-third or less of their previous wage and would therefore qualify for a pension.[49] In its greater consideration for the situation of the better-paid this change in the qualification for a pension chimed in with the establishment of a fifth wage group that would increase the amount that they could expect.

Throughout the 1890s the local authorities responsible for dealing with applications in the first instance had on the whole been remarkably liberal. They rejected applicants who had not paid the required number of contributions, and it took a while before the regulations were widely understood. But in their assessment of invalidity they rarely queried the certificate issued by the doctor of the applicant's own choice, and applicants soon learnt to seek out doctors known to be sympathetic.[50] Between 1893 and 1899 the percentage of pensions awarded in this way without the need for appeal procedures ranged from 76 to 82 per cent, which was remarkably high in view of the problems created by the complex regulations on minimum contributions.[51]

This liberality owed much to the attitude of the Imperial Insurance Office (RVA). The inadequate statistics on which to base actuarial calculations had led the authorities to build large safety margins into the figures on which the 1889 legislation had been based. When it became apparent that the number of invalidity pensions was well below expectations, the RVA actually encouraged the territorial insurance boards to be generous in their procedures.

When the new law came into effect in 1900, the award of pensions increased at such a rate that the central authorities at *Reich* level became alarmed and for the first time queried the appropriateness of the procedures. At the instigation of the Ministry of the Interior, the RVA sent officials to check on the procedures adopted, and between 1901 and 1911

[49] Florian Tennstedt, *Berufsunfähigkeit im Sozialrecht* (Frankfurt a.M., 1972), pp. 30–1.
[50] Lars Kaschke, 'Nichts als "Bettelgelder"? Wert und Wertschätzung der Alters-und Invalidenrenten im Kaiserreich', HZ, 270 (2000), 366–7.
[51] Kaschke and Sniegs, *Kommentierte Statistiken*, Table B.15.

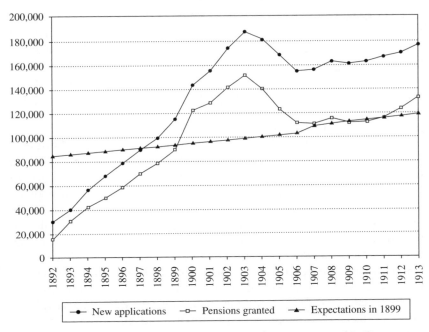

Figure 10.2. Applications for invalidity pensions and pensions granted in Germany, 1892–1913.

they covered every district under its supervision. The insurance boards in the southern states, which were not under the supervision of the RVA, were also encouraged to tighten up procedures.

One reason for the sharp increase was the generous interpretation of the new definition of invalidity. Yet even after it had been brought home to the local authorities that the law still required applicants to seek work in occupations other than their previous one, the figures continued to rise steeply. Stricter control over the evidence submitted in medical certificates, even to the extent of occasional mass inspections by doctors from outside, and the introduction of more detailed questionnaires, finally achieved the desired reduction.[52] By 1904 the increase in new pensions had been sharply reversed until it reached the expected levels calculated in 1899. There it remained until 1911. See Figure 10.2.[53]

[52] *Ibid.*, pp. 20 and 25–7.
[53] *Ibid.* Figure B1. It is not possible to assess the significance of the slight rise recorded after 1911, which was soon overtaken by the outbreak of war.

These generalisations hide significant differences in the working of what was a highly decentralised system. Pensions granted as a percentage of applications were higher in the southern states than in Prussia throughout the whole period, whereas Prussia showed marked differences between its western and its eastern provinces. It was the rural eastern provinces that were sharply out of line. There the proportion of applications among the insured population was much in excess of the rest of the country, as was the proportion of those refused.

In these areas the administration of the system by the state authorities at local level was complicated by the large Polish- or Lithuanian-speaking population and the hostile attitude shown by the authorities as part of Prussia's policy of Polish assimilation. The high number of inappropriate applications reflected a lack of interest on the part of the authorities in providing the necessary information and in particular an unwillingness to provide it in Polish. The discrepancy was explained, however, by saying that Slavs lacked a work-ethic. In actual fact, the proportion of applicants among the insured population was lower in the districts with Slav majorities than in those with German majorities. But their anti-Slav attitude led the local state officials to treat these applications unsympathetically. Most of the evidence that has convinced historians until recently of the unsatisfactory nature of the invalidity insurance system in general comes from these areas in the East.[54]

The cash value of the pensions themselves is best left until a comparison can be drawn with those that would become available in Britain.[55]

(C) WIDOWS AND ORPHANS

The most serious flaw in the legislation of 1889 and 1899 was the failure to make provision for widows. That matter was regularly treated as marginal, but it was not. In the first decade of the twentieth century the average life expectancy of German women aged fifty exceeded that of men by close on two years. Even if men habitually married women of the same age as themselves, which they did not, there would have been a large number of widows not provided for when the pensions of their husbands lapsed on their death. That number would have been greater still but for the higher

---

[54] *Ibid.*, pp. 27–9 and Tables provided there. See also Kaschke, 'Nichts als "Bettelgelder"?', pp. 374–82. The work of Kaschke and of Kaschke and Sniegs with its analysis of regional differences marks a revision of the older literature.

[55] See chapter 14 below.

death-rates among older widows and divorcees compared with their married contemporaries. In Prussia that difference amounted to 8 per cent among those in their sixties; but among those over seventy it had risen to 31 per cent.[56] The consequences were starkly displayed in the figures of public poor relief in 1885, which were freely available during the discussions of the legislation of 1889. These recorded 273,939 widows and their dependants on poor relief. Next to illness, that was the second highest single cause of pauperism recorded in the 1885 statistics.[57] In 1914, two years after pensions finally became available, those who qualified for widows' or orphans' pensions, despite the restrictive conditions imposed on widows, amounted to 40,462. That provides a remarkable measure of the need that had been left unmet. It is impossible to believe that of the 10,222 widows included in that figure more than a tiny proportion would have been taken care of by the philanthropic institutions to which the authors of the law of 1889 had been content to consign them.[58]

There would have been no need for a special decision to include widows' and orphans' pensions, had the legislation followed Bismarck's preference for financing pensions from taxation. It was the reliance on contributions from those in receipt of wages that created the problem of the dependants of deceased wage-earners in the first place. It is very telling that a government, which had refused to consider Bismarck's proposal to postpone the introduction of the complete pensions programme until more resources became available from taxation, was content to postpone pensions for dependants on the grounds of inadequate resources when they were clearly an integral part of a full programme. What this contrast tells us is of course the low priority given to the needs of women. If it was the purpose of the legislation to strengthen the loyalty of workers, the loyalty of women, who had no vote nor any military training, counted for little in these calculations.

The problem of the indigent widow had actually been made worse by a decision in 1889 to allow women workers to withdraw their accumulated contributions on marriage. That turned into a dowry what would have

---

[56] Flora *et al.*, *State, economy and society*, vol. 2, p. 101; Friedrich Prinzing, 'Die sociale Lage der Witwe in Deutschland', *Zeitschrift für Socialwissenschaft*, 3 (1900), 199–205, quoted in Wolfgang Dreher, *Die Entstehung der Arbeiterwitwenversicherung in Deutschland* (Berlin, 1978), p. 39.

[57] RAS 1885, Table 9, p. 40*. The table does not distinguish between male and female recipients of poor relief, but it can be assumed that those whose pauperism was due to the death of the breadwinner were female. The few dependent males in that situation would have fallen into the other categories cited in the table. The figure excludes those whose husbands had died of accidents, i.e. the sort of widows who after 1885 would have had a claim to an accident insurance pension.

[58] *Begründung*, p. 49. The figures are from AN.RVA, 15 February 1915, p. 299.

been an inadequate accumulation for a pension, and ruled out any policy of making it the basis of enhanced pension rights. The sole concession towards a widows' pension made in 1889 was to reimburse the contributions of any worker who had died without ever qualifying for a pension. That arrangement still left the employer's contributions at the disposal of the pension boards.[59]

The government's promise of action in the future was ignored in 1899.[60] Despite demands repeatedly voiced in the *Reichstag*, it would have continued to be ignored but for an initiative taken by the Centre party in 1902. Previously party initiatives in the *Reichstag* had modified government proposals, but the initiative for new social legislation had always been the government's. Now we find the German government for the first time being successfully pressured to initiate a social policy, something with which historians of Great Britain had been familiar well before.

The Centre party obtained the inclusion of a clause in the Tariff Law of 1902 which required the yield of certain customs duties to be accumulated to facilitate the introduction of widows' and orphans' pensions. Of these duties the most important were those on cereals, in so far as the yield exceeded the average for 1898–1903 and did not result from population growth. The new tariff was introduced in response to the demands of a vocal lobby of agriculturalists. Duties were markedly higher than before and the expected effect on food prices was unpopular with working-class voters in the industrial areas. Any protests by the SPD could be ignored, but not those by the Centre party.[61]

The Centre party drew its strength from the agrarian interests in Bavaria and the Rhineland as well as from the Catholic working-class. It could not afford to lose its agrarian voters to the Conservative parties, any more than it could afford to lose its industrial voters to the SPD. Yet there was a

---

[59] That concession was to be withdrawn in 1911. The easy acceptance of the government's proposed exclusion of widows' and orphans' pensions in 1888–9 by the *Bundesrat* was not mirrored in the *Reichstag*. For the demands voiced there and their gradual but nevertheless futile reduction to the needs of orphans see Marlene Ellerkamp, 'Die Frage der Witwen und Waisen', in Fisch und Haerendel (eds.), *Geschichte und Gegenwart der Rentenversicherung*, pp. 189–208. See also Barbara Fait, 'Arbeiterfrauen und -familien im System sozialer Sicherheit. Zur geschlechterpolitischen Dimension der "Bismarckschen Arbeiterversicherung"', *Jahrbuch für Wirtschaftsgeschichte*, 1 (1997), 171–205, esp. 180–6.

[60] There was one exception. In contrast to other occupations invalidity and old age pensions for sailors became the responsibility of the relevant *Berufsgenossenschaft*. This was authorised to provide widows' pensions, and did so from the beginning of 1907.

[61] This paragraph and the following pages are based on Dreher, *Entstehung*; K. E. Born, *Staat und Sozialpolitik seit Bismarcks Sturz* (Wiesbaden, 1957); and *Begründung der Reichsversicherungsordnung*, SBRT, vol. 274, 12.LP II, Session 1909/10, Anlagen zu Nr. 340.

distinct possibility of this. With elections due in mid-1903, the SPD and the more extreme agrarians were using delaying tactics to ensure that the issue was still unresolved by then. In that case it would have become a major election issue. The Centre party therefore hoped to make the tariff more acceptable to its working-class supporters by linking it to its long-standing demand for widows' and orphans' pensions. By November 1901 it had committed itself to this line.

The government wished to see the issue settled before the elections and could see the attraction of the party's proposal. Arthur von Posadowsky, the Secretary of State for the Interior, was accustomed to co-operate with the Centre party over social policy. It was he who helped to draft the wording of the crucial amendment (*Lex Trimborn*) and persuaded Chancellor Bülow to accept it as the necessary price for the despatch of the Tariff Law.

The amendment should be understood as a modification of the Franckenstein clause attached to the original Tariff Law in 1878, which had also been the work of the Centre party. That had required all tariff revenue in excess of 130 million marks to be passed by the *Reich* to the individual states. This prevented the *Reich* from obtaining the financial independence that Bismarck had desired and continued to make it dependent on the individual states represented in the *Bundesrat*, to whom it had to apply for all additional finance. The immediate effect of the measure was to make the states the nett beneficiaries of the revenue collected by the *Reich*. But to rely on the customs as a major source of revenue had its disadvantages. Since their yield fluctuated widely with the trade cycle, it made long-term financial policy difficult. In any case, by 1899 the necessary expenditure by the *Reich* had grown to the point where it once more required additional revenue from the states, the so-called *Matrikularbeiträge*. They thus received with one hand and gave with the other, while complicating their budgets in the process. It made the states more reluctant than ever to agree to further expenditure by the *Reich*.

The *Bundesrat* naturally regarded the Centre party proposals with less favour than had the *Reich* government. There were those who argued that, to maintain the constitutional object of the Franckenstein clause in changed fiscal circumstances, it made sense to allocate income from the customs yield to the *Reich* for specific requirements. But these were not much represented in the Upper House. The states were faced with the immediate prospect of losing a revenue of 50 million marks a year, and of having to make further contributions in the long run. Only the firm hold of the Centre party over the *Reichstag* persuaded them to accept the deal. That laid down a deadline for the introduction of widows' and orphans' pensions by 1910.

In retrospect this achievement was less impressive than it seemed at the time. The resources set aside were neither adequate, nor, on account of the fluctuating nature of the income, were they suitable. Instead of the expected 45 million marks per year, a mere 43 million had been accumulated over the first four years. The government calculated that the fund established by the 1902 Tariff Law would be used up after five years, yet Bavaria and the medium-sized states were strictly opposed to any increase in their contributions to the *Reich* to cover the subsequent costs. This dispute held up progress for close on two years. Nothing would have happened had it not been for the legal obligations to use the accumulated fund for widows' and orphans' pensions, an obligation that not even the *Bundesrat* could abrogate. In January 1910 the *Reich* government finally gave in. It agreed to fund the inevitable expenditure after the first five years from the regular *Reich* budget, i.e. without any call on additional contributions. How this was to be done was left to future governments to resolve. In view of this uncertainty, the new pensions were no more than what was required to meet the letter of the law, and no amendments to increase them were considered. Even then the government failed to meet its commitment; the new provisions came into force only at the beginning of 1912.

This so-called survivor insurance was administered alongside invalidity and old age pensions. The same wage groups applied, as did the waiting period and the principle of a basic pension with an addition according to the number of contributions. Contributions paid before 1912 counted towards entitlement to the basic element of the widow's pension, and, if not enough of these had been paid, they were 'imputed' on the scale of wage group I. Accretion could be claimed only on contributions paid after the beginning of 1912.[62] Total contributions were increased by just on 25 per cent and the government took the opportunity to shift some items of expenditure from the state subsidy to the accumulated contributions. It also increased the element of national solidarity first introduced in 1899.[63]

What the scheme provided was not a widows' pension at all. It was merely a pension for disabled widows unable to earn one-third of the usual amount, according to the formula used to define invalidity. All other widows were assumed to be able to support themselves, even if they had children under fifteen. In that case they received orphans' pensions on their behalf but nothing towards their own support. None of this had any relation to social reality, for it could not be assumed that working wives would be able to continue with their previous job. At most 25 per cent were

[62] See Dawson, *Social insurance*, pp. 142–55, for the details.   [63] *Begründung der RVO*, pp. 379–81.

engaged in wage labour, and far fewer than that would have earned enough to sustain a household when widowed. The data are unreliable, but even after making all possible allowances, at least 70 per cent of widows would have had to take up wage labour anew.[64]

Those who met this highly restricted entitlement received pensions of one-fifth of the invalidity pensions to which their deceased husband would have been entitled, plus 50 M from the state. Orphans' pensions were set at one-twentieth for the first child (with progressively reduced rates for subsequent children) together with a state subsidy of 25 M. These widows' pensions were expected to make no more than a partial contribution to the support of the household. Those claimed immediately after the law had come into effect would have ranged according to wage groups from 1.31 M to 1.54 M per week or 1s.4d to 1s.6½d. After forty years of contributions they were expected to yield weekly pensions ranging from 1.66 M to 2.90 M or 1s.8d to 2s.11d. The period of forty years somewhat exceeded the average period of contributions that could have been expected at the time.[65]

What has to be borne in mind by all differentiated German pensions is that the concept of an average pension has little value. It is the range that must be examined. But in this case even more striking is the generally low level throughout. Poor relief of 4.55 M per week for a widow was fairly normal; these derisory pensions would generally have had to be supplemented by poor relief or charity.[66] See Table 10.2.

A widow entitled to an invalidity pension on account of her own contributions could not receive both pensions together. In such a case she received a lump sum equivalent to a year's widow's pension as compensation for the uselessly accumulated contributions of her deceased husband. There were similar lump-sum arrangements in compensation for a forfeited entitlement to orphans' pensions.

This remarkable story calls for some final comments. It is hard to regard this law as an aspect of social policy at all, if social policy includes some consideration of need. It was a form of gesture politics designed to get the government off the hook that had been fashioned for it in 1902. It was an aspect of this gesture for the government to declare the introduction of widows' and orphans' insurance as an extraordinary advance into an area into which no other country had ventured. Such a comparison ignored all support of widows in other countries that was financed in other ways.

---

[64] Dreher, *Entstehung*, pp. 71–6.   [65] *Begründung der RVO*, p. 378, gives this as 37.5 years.
[66] Dreher, *Entstehung*, p. 160, n. 192.

Table 10.2. *Value of widows' and orphans' pensions, weekly pension in marks*

Years of contributions	Widows' pension	Orphans' pension according to number of children under 15	
		1	3
Wage Group I			
10	1.40	0.70	1.73
30	1.57	0.78	1.85
40	1.66	0.83	1.90
Wage Group II			
10	1.55	0.77	1.83
30	1.89	0.95	2.07
40	2.07	1.04	2.18
Wage Group III			
10	1.78	0.83	1.90
30	2.12	1.06	2.26
40	2.35	1.78	2.37
Wage Group IV			
10	1.78	0.89	1.98
30	2.35	1.18	2.37
40	2.64	1.32	2.56
Wage Group V			
10	1.88	0.95	2.07
30	2.58	1.30	2.53
40	2.90	1.47	2.76

Source: Calculated from table in *Begründung der RVO*, p. 370, SBRT, vol. 274, Anlagen zu Nr. 340.

In view of this outcome the achievement of the Centre party in 1902 should be regarded in only a limited sense as a triumph for a new kind of political initiative, one that emanated from the parties rather than the government. Nevertheless, the achievement was real. But for the events of 1902 there would have been no widows' and orphans' pensions at all before the outbreak of the war.

The minimal provisions made in 1911 are understandable in view of the financial constraints imposed by the individual states. Yet by 1917, when the fund accumulated under the Tariff Law had been exhausted, the world had changed so drastically that the worries expressed in 1911 were irrelevant. The war had produced numerous widows to be provided for, and inflation had made a nonsense of all financial calculations. Few of the pensions were ever paid on the basis of the calculations of 1911. We can regard this legislation as evidence for the intentions and the financial constraints accepted in the pre-war period. It has no bearing on much else.

But it tells us much about priorities in the early twentieth century. There cannot be a stronger argument for the introduction of women's suffrage than the priorities revealed in the shaping of the insurance legislation, be it the willingness to postpone any consideration of widows or the nature of the provision that was finally made.

Before the end of 1911 German invalidity and old age insurance was rounded off by separate insurance for white-collar workers. By then Great Britain had introduced its own National Insurance Act. For ease of comparison it is better to wait until we understand the Act's characteristics and the political processes by which it came about before we deal with German white-collar insurance. Leaving until later those aspects of German provision for sickness, invalidity and old age, that are best presented in comparison with British parallels, we shall now turn to social policy in Britain. We shall start, not as in the case of Germany, with provisions for sickness, but with those for old age.

British old age pensions

(A) THE CONTEXT: POOR LAW AND LABOUR MARKET

The nature and origin of the British Old Age Pensions Act of 1908, which are the subject of this chapter, have already been examined several times in an exclusively British context.[1] Here the subject must be treated differently. The differences between the form that public provision for the elderly took in Britain and Germany require explanation. That shifts the focus of attention.

In Germany, as we saw in chapter 10, the issue of pensions for the elderly was raised in 1880–1 in connection with that of compensation for industrial accidents. Its inclusion in the Imperial Message of November 1881, together with accident pensions, was part of Bismarck's attempt to obtain support for a substantial new source of revenue for the Empire by presenting it as the necessary means for the provision of pensions. Despite the failure of this strategy and the consequent remodelling of the proposals for accident insurance on a quite different financial basis, old age and invalidity insurance was presented by the government as the social policy of the Imperial Message. This more than any other consideration accounts for the presence of old age and invalidity insurance on the political agenda of the later 1880s.

There was no connection between British legislation on industrial injury and the policy on old age pensions. That derived its impetus from different considerations, as did the introduction of national health insurance in 1911.

---

[1] B. B. Gilbert, *The evolution of national insurance in Great Britain* (London, 1966), ch. 4; E. P. Hennock, *British social reform and German precedents* (Oxford, 1987), chs. 7–9; John Macnicol, *The politics of retirement in Britain 1878–1948* (Cambridge, 1998), Part I; Pat Thane, 'Contributory vs non-contributory old age pensions, 1878–1908', in Pat Thane (ed.), *Origins of British social policy* (London, 1978), pp. 84–106; Pat Thane, *Old age in English history* (Oxford, 2000).

There are two further differences to note between the German legislation on invalidity and old age insurance and the British Old Age Pensions Act. One was a difference in object; the other a difference in method.

In Germany the principal object was to provide pensions in the event of invalidity, i.e. the physical or mental condition that precluded people from earning a living. In Britain the object was to provide old age pensions at a fixed qualifying age.

In Germany pensions were financed mainly through compulsory contributory insurance. In Britain they were financed by the State from general taxation. It will be necessary to explain each of these differences in turn.

Providing income-support when invalidity sets in, as was done in Germany, took account of the fact that need arose at different ages for different people. Invalidity rather than old age as such dominated discussions of need in Germany at that time. Pensions at a set age were considered only if financed from endowment insurance policies when a predetermined age was an actuarial requirement or if an employer wished to be able to impose compulsory retirement as part of a general personnel policy.[2]

It is surprising how little interest there was in Britain in invalidity as a qualification for a public pension, particularly since this was the qualification that those trade unions that provided superannuation benefits accepted for their members. But trade unions, like friendly societies, relied on their own medical officers, whose certificate they accepted.[3] The only nationwide medical service in England was that of the distrusted and despised Poor Law. For reasons to be explained the Poor Law was not an acceptable provider of services when pensions for the elderly became a political issue.

It was in fact the Poor Law that provided the context for the origins of old age pensions in Britain. To understand how this arose one should bear in mind that until the 1870s the English Poor Law, at least in the rural areas on which historical research has focused on account of the more complete survival of records, had normally provided regular out-relief for the elderly poor. That was designed to supplement other resources, whether from occasional earnings, charity or the support of their family and friends. The object of poor relief was no more than bare subsistence, but since even the income of younger rural labourers with dependent children hardly rose much higher, their position compared not unreasonably with the general

---

[2] Christoph Conrad, *Vom Greis zum Rentner. Der Strukturwandel des Alters in Deutschland zwischen 1830 und 1930* (Göttingen, 1994), ch. 6. For the exceptions see *ibid.*, pp. 213 and 237.
[3] Kazuto Fukasama, 'Voluntary provision for old age by trade unions in Britain before the coming of the welfare state' (unpublished PhD thesis, University of London, 1996); W. Beveridge, 'The age for pensions: the experience of trade unions', *Morning Post*, 4 June 1908.

standard of living in such impoverished rural communities. Less is known about non-rural communities. Those that have been studied show a lower proportion of elderly paupers to population and smaller payments to individuals, but the principle that the Poor Law made up the shortfall from other kinds of support so as to provide a subsistence living would have been much the same. It was unusual for the elderly to be sent to the workhouse if they were still able to manage with the help of family. The deterrent use of the workhouse instead of out-relief had been recommended in 1834 only for the able-bodied, not for the aged and infirm.[4] We need to bear in mind, however, that we know about relatively few communities and that there was no uniformity across the country.[5]

From around 1870 the Local Government Board, the central Poor Law authority, launched a deliberate attack on the practice of out-relief for the aged and infirm. Although its recommendations lacked the force of law, there is evidence that this resulted in the systematic reduction of out-relief for the elderly. Relief was increasingly refused except on condition that the applicant enter the workhouse. The deterrent use of the workhouse that had been common for the younger 'able-bodied' category of applicants in the past was now extended to the so-called 'aged and infirm'. Systematic pressure was also put on the family to support the elderly by strictly enforcing the legal duty of sons and unmarried daughters to support their parents and even by asking for financial contributions from family members who had no legal obligation to do so.[6] In consequence working men found themselves faced with demands to support their elderly kin at a time when they were already burdened with dependent children.

If James Riley's contention is true that, as the survival rate of workers increased, so did the time they spent being ill, one might have expected an increase in aged and infirm paupers on out-relief. The same might have been expected from the changes in the labour market, which will be discussed below.[7] Yet the number of the aged and infirm in receipt of

---

[4] Sidney Webb and Beatrice Webb, *English poor law policy* (London, 1910), pp. 51–2.

[5] See Thomson, 'Provision for the elderly', as modified by Thane, *Old age*, chs. 8 and 9.

[6] David Thomson, 'I am not my father's keeper: families and the elderly in nineteenth century England', *Law and History Review*, 2 (1984), 265–86; David Thomson, 'The decline of social welfare: falling state support for the elderly since early Victorian times', *Ageing and Society*, 4 (1985), 451–82; but particularly Thomson, 'Provisions for the elderly in England, 1830–1908' (unpublished PhD thesis, University of Cambridge, 1980). English law did not interpret the principle of family obligation as widely as was the case in German law.

[7] J. C. Riley, *Sick not dead: the health of British working men during the mortality decline* (Baltimore and London, 1997). It is hard to know from the evidence provided whether the changes in sickness benefit claims among friendly society members, on which Riley bases his argument, are entirely or only partly accounted for by changes in the labour market. See Macnicol, *Politics of retirement*, pp. 125–31.

out-relief fell, as did the proportion of outdoor paupers to the population aged sixty-five and over. Not all of this would have been the result of the new relief policy, however, for the final quarter of the nineteenth century also saw improvements in working-class living standards, due especially to the fall in the price of essential foodstuffs.[8]

According to Pat Thane, Charles Booth identified forty-one Poor Law Unions in 1894 in which the reduction in out-relief to the elderly over the period 1871–93 was greatly in excess of the national figure. She states that these unions, where the crusade against out-relief appears to have made the biggest impact, were mostly large urban ones, including Liverpool, Manchester, Salford, Birmingham and twenty-four in London. Those were the places in which it was easiest to organise protest movements, and they would be the strongholds of the National Committee of Organised Labour for Old Age Pensions (1899), the pressure group that agitated for pensions financed from general taxation. If there is indeed such clear evidence of the impact of the crusade in the major Poor Law Unions, it would supplement the evidence from national statistics.[9]

This attack on the expectations of the poor to be supported in old age from the poor rates provides the principal context of the British movement for old age pensions from the State. It was probably exacerbated by changes in the labour market that militated against employment of the elderly. The decline in their income, as they moved to easier work on account of failing health and strength and ended up performing no more than the occasional casual job, was nothing new. John Macnicol has suggested that from the 1880s onwards, this process was getting worse. 'Older workers were steadily shaken out of a labour force that was becoming more technology-intensive and segmented into increasingly specialised divisions of labour', a process reinforced, he adds, by the growth of joint-stock companies and generally more impersonal labour relations.

Although Macnicol sees the aged caught in the pincers of these changes in the labour market and the stricter administration of the Poor Law, two trends which made their poverty 'more of a topic of public discussion', his study is explicitly 'built upon the contention that the shift in the mode

[8] Thane, *Old age*, p. 172. The text of that page is marred by the omission of words and at least one table. It needs to be supplemented by figures from Karel Williams, *From pauperism to poverty* (London, 1981), pp. 204–5.

[9] Thane, *Old age*, pp. 174–5. I am unable to find these figures in Charles Booth, *The aged poor in England and Wales* (London, 1894). Her footnotes do not support the claim, and repeated inquiries have produced no additional information.

of production to a "late-industrial" economy was the prime causal agent altering the status of older people'.[10]

Had he paid attention to the changing age-structure of the labour force, he might have been less dogmatic, for there were other reasons why the elderly were finding it more difficult to hold on to their jobs. Each census from 1881 to 1911 saw an increase in the number of males aged 15–19 in the population, the vast majority of whom would have entered the work-force.[11] They created formidable competition for older workers, whether by displacing them from their accustomed jobs, or by making it more difficult to find new and less exacting work once they were displaced. The survey by Charles Booth, with which Macnicol supports his case, provides a great deal of evidence for the competition of the young.[12]

The contentious Poor Law policy towards the elderly lent a special significance to a set of figures collected in 1890, which for the first time broke up the category of the aged and infirm and concentrated on age alone. It gave figures for the recipients of poor relief on 1 January over the age of sixty divided into quinquennial age groups. In 1892 this was followed by further figures based on a whole year's count of those over sixty-five years of age. When these were correlated with the census of 1891 it became possible to calculate the proportion of elderly paupers to population. The percentage of those aged sixty-five and over who were on poor relief, when compared to those aged sixteen to sixty-four, was about 30 per cent to just under 4 per cent.[13] That underlined the importance of the 'aged deserving poor', those who had kept themselves from being dependent on poor relief until advancing age and infirmity forced them into dependence on the Poor Law.

In the light of this information, the recent policy of systematic deterrence appeared both unjust and futile. Since it showed that after the age of sixty dependence on the Poor Law increased for each quinquennial age

---

[10] Macnicol, *Politics of retirement*, pp. 22, 29 and 25.

[11] B. R. Mitchell and Phyllis Deane, *Abstract of British historical statistics* (Cambridge, 1962), pp. 12 and 13, gives a total of 471,000.

[12] Charles Booth, *The aged poor in England and Wales* (London, 1894), pp. 188–9, 218–19, 278 and 311. This survey is his main source of evidence. He accepts that the occupation tables of the census offer no reliable evidence for his thesis, and the same is surely true of the self-serving opinions that he quotes from a range of advocates of old age pensions.

[13] *Return . . . of the number of persons . . . in receipt of indoor relief and of outdoor relief aged over 60 returned in quinquennial groups on 1 August 1890* (Burt's Return), BPP 1890–1 (36) LXVIII, 563; *Return . . . of the number of persons . . . over 65 years and upwards . . . in receipt of indoor relief and outdoor relief on 1 January 1892 and at any time during the 12 months ended Lady Day 1892* (Ritchie's Return), BPP 1892 Session 1 (265) LXVIII. The figure of 3 per cent excluded vagrants and the insane. See also Booth, *Aged poor*, p. 40.

group, it also pointed to the obvious conclusion that the moment of pauperisation was not the same for all. It might have lent support to an argument for invalidity pensions, but that did not happen.

What did happen was that the debate over the way to treat the aged deserving poor led to two kinds of reform proposals, both of which involved the abandonment of the deterrent Poor Law in favour of income-support without stigma. Some thought that the Poor Law Guardians should distinguish within the traditional classification of the aged and infirm a new category of 'deserving aged paupers'. These should be given out-relief on easy terms or, if in need of institutional care, be treated in ways more appropriate to inmates of an almshouse. That was the recommendation of the Royal Commission on the Aged Poor in 1895 and it found expression in circulars by the Local Government Board between 1895 and 1900.[14] These circulars left the Guardians with a great deal of discretion. They could decide whether to follow the recommendations of the central authority, and to what extent. They could decide whom to classify as deserving and when to grant the new status.

The proposals for old age pensions separate from the administration of the Poor Law were based on a rejection of this discretion. Its advocates, whether favouring contributory pensions with a State subsidy or pensions entirely tax-financed, found discretion exercised by the Guardians and their relieving officers totally unacceptable. They looked for a qualification that would automatically trigger entitlement and found it in numerical age, which was variously set at sixty or sixty-five. The level depended on the reformers' view of how much money the taxpayers could be expected to provide.

There were exceptions, but these merely serve to underline how unacceptable proposals were that depended on the discretion of the Poor Law authorities. One such exception was Charles Booth, the advocate of tax-financed old age pensions for all, a vastly expensive proposal from the point of view of the taxpayer. In order to mitigate its cost, he proposed a very high qualifying age of seventy, tempered by discretionary payments at a lower rate after the age of sixty if required. The power of discretion was to rest with the Poor Law Guardians, and that alone ensured that nothing more was heard of the matter. Even those who strongly supported his proposals for universal tax-financed pensions much preferred to demand a low qualifying age. The National Committee of Organised Labour chose sixty-five, as Booth himself had originally done, the Labour Party

[14] Webb and Webb, *English poor law policy*, pp. 231–40.

chose sixty. The Trades Union Congress did suggest that those becoming incapacitated should receive their pension earlier than the general qualifying age of sixty. But since they had nothing to say on the vexed question of who was to make the decision, the suggestion was ignored.[15]

The Liberal Government was well aware that 'one of the primary objects for which the pension was proposed was to take away the discretionary and inquisitorial powers exercised by the outdoor relief committee of boards of guardians', as Asquith, the Prime Minister, was to put it in the House of Commons.[16] When it was finally persuaded to plan for old age pensions legislation, it originally proposed a qualifying age of sixty-five, following what had emerged as the official political consensus. The experience of many workers would have justified a lower age, but that was never regarded as politically realistic. But if the object was to save the deserving aged poor from the stigma of the Poor Law, a qualifying age of seventy was impossible to justify on the basis of the known statistics. When at the last moment the cabinet realised that the money that the Treasury had set aside for pensions was inadequate, and decided to raise the proposed qualifying age to seventy, it essentially undermined the rationale behind its own policy. There was never an attempt to justify this clause of the bill. The Prime Minister made it clear that the bill should be regarded as a first step and that more satisfactory provision would be made once the money was available.

Because that pledge could not be honoured without greater expenditure from taxation than he was prepared to contemplate, Lloyd George, the newly appointed Chancellor of the Exchequer, set off in the direction of imitating Germany. Two aspects of the German scheme appealed to him from the beginning. One was the prospect of abandoning the principle of tax-financed pensions, on which the Act of 1908 had been based, and raising the money for future expenditure largely from the work-force and their employers through compulsory weekly contributions. The other was the fact that in Germany pensions below the age of seventy were provided on a discretionary basis in the form of invalidity pension. It was chiefly to find out about contributory invalidity pensions that he visited Germany in August 1908.[17] The result was the introduction of National Health Insurance in 1911, which provided what was called disablement benefit for those under seventy years of age. That was coupled with insurance against short-term illness and the nationwide establishment of panels of

---

[15] Charles Booth, *Old age pensions and the aged poor* (London, 1899), p. 50; Francis H. Stead, *How old age pensions began to be* (London, n.d. [1909]), pp. 65, 150, 175 and 82.
[16] 4 *Hansard* 190 (24 June 1908), 1742. [17] Hennock, *British social reform*, pp. 130–51.

doctors, who were entitled to certify sickness and disability in the insured population and provide free medical treatment. This legislation moved public provision for the sick and the disabled in Britain, and that included the elderly disabled under the age of seventy, significantly closer to what had existed in Germany since 1889.

(B) CONTRIBUTORY VERSUS NON-CONTRIBUTORY PENSIONS

British advocates of old age pensions were united in regarding the Poor Law as totally unsuited to deal with the needs of decent old people. They were, however, deeply divided between advocates of contributory and of non-contributory pensions. British historians have paid much attention to this division, although for reasons that have usually had little to do with any desire to make Anglo-German comparisons.[18]

It should be emphasised that this was not a division between those willing to adopt German precedents and those who were not. Both parties were equally determined to have nothing to do with German compulsory contributory insurance, one side because it was compulsory, the other because it was contributory – both of them, however, for the same under-lying reason. They knew that legislation on old age pensions would have to be achieved by the mobilisation of public opinion. In contrast to the top-down process that had produced the German legislation, it would need to commend itself to the electorate.

To understand why it was able to do that brings us back to the figures for old age pauperism of 1890 and 1892 and to the numerical importance of the aged deserving paupers which they revealed. The clients of the Poor Law were not, as had been assumed, a marginal group with no capacity to organise themselves politically. The figures revealed that a significant proportion of working-class voters, men whose way of life was far removed from that of the habitual clients of the relieving officer, were not merely exposed to the unprecedented demands of the Poor Law Guardians on their resources in support of their parents at the very time that they were bringing up their children; they were themselves living under the threat of ultimate degradation. These men were capable of organising and delivering

---

[18] Thane, 'Contributory vs non-contributory old age pensions'. Hennock, *British social reform*, is primarily concerned with the impact of the German insurance precedent on British policy-making and only incidentally and occasionally with Anglo-German comparison.

political support and could be mobilised in favour of a pensions policy designed to save people like them from the pauper taint.

The first major politician to understand this was Joseph Chamberlain. His proposals for state subsidies to underwrite savings schemes for old age pensions, including those to be organised by working-class thrift societies, was part of his bid for the vote of the organised working class, i.e. that section of the working class organised in friendly societies, trade unions and similar institutions. It was Chamberlain's political persistence that thrust the issue of old age pensions into prominence and kept it there from 1891 to 1898, by which time the momentum was taken up by others.[19]

Unlike Canon Blackley, an earlier advocate of pensions, whose proposals had included sickness benefit and roused the opposition of the friendly societies, Chamberlain did not make the mistake of challenging one of the country's great vested interests. He concentrated exclusively on provision against old age, which was an area in which friendly societies found it difficult to operate. He made it clear that, unlike Blackley's or that of the Germans, his pension proposals involved no compulsion but relied for their attractiveness on a State subsidy. In fact he was offering the larger friendly societies the benefit of financial support from the State.

He failed, however, to overcome their distrust of the control over their institutions that was likely to follow such a partnership with the State. Since working-class thrift institutions were valued first and foremost for the independence from patronising superior authority that they offered, this went to the heart of the matter. Actuarial experts were already telling the friendly society movement that most of the societies were actuarially unsound. It was hard to believe that the State would not insist on its own notion of soundness before subsidising their work.[20] The attitudes to old age pensions among friendly societies in the 1890s varied widely. There was no solid front of opposition.[21] But there was none of the strong political pressure, without which subsidised pensions were a lost cause. In the absence of such pressure Chamberlain's scheme was destroyed by

---

[19] J. L. Garvin, *The life of Joseph Chamberlain* (London, 1933–4), vols. 2 and 3.

[20] In 1898 and 1899 friendly societies and trade unions were asked whether they would be willing to accept State control and supervision within the context of a subsidised scheme similar to Chamberlain's. Those who bothered to reply overwhelmingly refused. *Report of the Committee on old age pensions*, pp. 8–9, Appendix X, BPP 1898 C.8911 XLV; *Report of the Select Committee on the aged deserving poor*, p. viii, Appendix I, BPP 1899 (296) VIII. See also the resolution of the TUC in 1893 quoted in Thane, *Old age*, p. 199.

[21] Thane, 'Contributory vs non-contributory old age pensions', pp. 92–5.

opposition to increased taxation on the part of the Treasury ministers in the Cabinet.[22]

By 1899 that political pressure was mobilised by the National Committee of Organised Labour for Old Age Pensions, but not in support of Chamberlain. The National Committee united philanthropists and church leaders with the leaders of organised labour in support of Charles Booth's proposal for tax-provided pensions for all.[23]

At first sight the rapport between Charles Booth and the leaders of organised labour seems surprising. Booth had made his proposals to remove the elderly from the Poor Law because he believed in deterrence for the able-bodied but recognised that deterrence for the aged merely exhausted their savings before they qualified for the relief that was ultimately inevitable. His proposals were intended to encourage thrift and to preserve a deterrent Poor Law. He plumped for universal pensions because any means test would discourage savings and because he could imagine no court of inquiry that could be trusted to identify the undeserving.

The completeness and logical consistency of Booth's scheme would meet everybody's needs, at a price. The price was that pensions would go to numerous people who did not need them. To Booth this was not a major objection. He was interested in finding answers to the problem of poverty in a relatively wealthy society, and his was the only pension proposal that was comprehensive enough to provide such an answer. In particular it took into account the fact, highlighted by his own surveys of London poverty, that the casually employed and the elderly widows made up a very high proportion of the poor.[24]

As has frequently been pointed out both at the time and since, contributory pensions of the type that Chamberlain advocated would not have gone to those whose needs were greatest, including the casually employed and most women. They were therefore seriously defective as an answer to the problem of old age poverty. But unlike Booth, Chamberlain was no academic systematiser. As on the occasion of the first Workmen's Compensation Act in 1897, he was interested in launching a new political momentum, not a perfect scheme.[25]

[22] For details on Blackley and Chamberlain, see Hennock, *British social reform*, pp. 109–21. For the cabinet's rejection in November 1899 of all old age pensions schemes and its refusal to go beyond more generous Poor Law treatment of the aged deserving poor, see Thane, *Old age*, p. 210.

[23] For the NCOL see Stead, *Old age pensions*; and National Committee of Organized Labour, *Ten years' work for old age pensions 1899–1909* (London, 1909).

[24] Charles Booth, *Pauperism, a picture and endowment of old age, an argument* (London, 1892), pp. 157, 238 and 167; Booth, *Old age pensions and the aged poor*, pp. 27–8, 50, 32 and 29.

[25] Hennock, *British social reform*, p. 77.

The trade union leaders who set up the National Committee were quick to recognise that Booth's proposals 'would not invite any governmental interference with trade unions or supervision of them'. They added that 'all contributory schemes were held to be incomplete and unsatisfactory. They would not, it was maintained, cover the most necessitous cases, and they would take away the independence of trade unions.' This formula describes the basis on which the labour leaders and Booth were able to co-operate.[26] The pension was to be a bonus added unconditionally to whatever income a citizen had from other sources, 'affording the means of additional comforts', as the Amalgamated Society of Engineers put it when describing the relation of the proposed State pension to the superannuation benefit enjoyed by their own members.[27] In other words there was to be no means test nor any subsidies to existing institutions.

It was this that made Booth's proposal attractive to organised labour. They paid little if any attention to Booth's other views on Poor Law matters but were happy to join him in his rejection of State subsidies to contributory pension schemes. That these could be dismissed as inappropriate for the needs of women was a useful point to make, particularly in public debate, but its significance can be overstated. Organised labour at the time did not usually give much priority to the needs of poor women. State subsidies to voluntary contributory schemes failed to appeal to the representatives of organised labour primarily on other grounds that went to the heart of their interests as they saw them.

Thus in 1899 when the Select Committee on the Aged Deserving Poor tried to obtain the views of trade unions and friendly societies on two schemes for State subsidies to voluntary savings schemes, the Executive of the Amalgamated Society of Engineers simplified the questions to what it obviously regarded as the essentials and put the following alternatives to their members:

1. Are you in favour of State subsidy and interference with trade unions by the State as proposed by Sir James Rankin and the Hon. Lionel Holland?
2. Are you in favour of State pensions to all deserving persons, leaving the independence of the trade unions intact as at present?

It is these objections to which Thane pays too little attention, as she does to the crucial influence of organised labour on the decisions made by government, when she claims that 'awareness of the particular problem of women

---

[26] Stead, *Old age pensions*, p. 28.
[27] *The Amalgamated Engineers' Journal*, November 1898, p. 3, quoted in Fukasawa, 'Voluntary provision for old age', p. 99.

had a profound influence in shaping the discourse about pensions and the problems of the aged poor *and the subsequent legislation*'.[28]

The trouble with Booth's proposals for universal pensions was their cost. His critics estimated this at £26 million, which was just over one-sixth of the total central government revenue in 1899. Booth's own figure varied from £17 million to £20 million. 'Proposals which could never have been recommended by a government to Parliament', was how the Chancellor of the Exchequer described them in 1899.[29] Nothing but an over-sanguine belief in the possibility of transforming electoral politics can explain the willingness of the leaders of organised labour, including the fledgling Labour Party, to commit themselves to such proposals. Indeed they went even further than Booth by demanding a pensions age of sixty.

The National Committee became a remarkably effective pressure group. By 1901 the support of the Trades Union Congress and the Co-operative Movement had been won; by 1904 that of the Labour Party. The National Conference of Friendly Societies was less easy to convert, but in 1902 they declared themselves in favour of non-contributory pensions, not on a universal basis but for the poor if thrifty and deserving, in other words for their own members when in need.

In the 1906 general election the work of the National Committee and its supporters helped to return a substantial body of MPs, both Liberals and Labour, who were pledged to old age pensions. The skilful deployment of that back-bench pressure in the House of Commons against the government induced Asquith, then Chancellor of the Exchequer, to commit the government in April 1907 to a Pensions Bill in the following session and to set £4.5 million aside for the purpose.[30]

In this way a reluctant government was forced to find some means to extricate itself from the pressure generated in the Commons and backed up by appeals to public opinion. By then it was generally accepted that the aged deserving poor could not be left to the good-will of the Guardians.[31] Their pensions would have to be administered in some other way.

---

[28] *The Amalgamated Engineers' Journal*, January 1899, pp. 3–4, quoted in Fukasawa, 'Voluntary provision', pp. 100–2; Thane, *Old age*, p. 209 (emphasis added).

[29] Sir Michael Hicks-Beach, 'Aged poor', Cabinet memorandum, 20 November 1899, PRO, CAB 37/51/89.

[30] Stead, *Old age pensions*; Hennock, *British social reform*, pp. 123–30.

[31] This was only accepted slowly. The Select Committee on the aged deserving poor in 1899, which recommended that the local Pensions Authority should be independent of the Board of Guardians, was still insisting that Guardians provide a majority of its members. See the Select Committee report (note 20 above), p. xii. The complete break occurred in 1903. See *Special Report, Select Committee on the aged pensioners' bill*, p. iv, BPP 1903 (276) V, 393.

Ministers also knew that in order to take the wind out of the National Committee's sails pensions would have to be non-contributory. Much of the rest depended on calculations of financial expediency. The money immediately available was under £7 million. That led to a harsh means test, and caused the qualifying age to be set at seventy not at sixty-five as everybody had assumed. Other qualifications for receiving the pension were British nationality, residence in the UK, not having been sentenced to prison without the option of a fine, not having been guilty in the opinion of the pension authority of 'habitual failure to work according to his [*sic*] ability, opportunity, or need, for his own maintenance and that of his legal relatives', and not having been in receipt of Poor Law relief after 1 January 1908. These last three clauses underline the fact that in 1908 the British pension policy was still only intended for the deserving.[32]

That object could not be achieved: first, because failure to work proved to be an unenforceable ground for withholding a pension and, secondly, because the decision to raise the qualifying age to seventy forced many of the deserving back on to the Poor Law. By withholding a pension from anyone in receipt of poor relief after 1 January 1908 the Act ensured that many of them would never qualify for the pension at all. This Poor Law disqualification was so much at odds with the alleged object of government policy that Parliament insisted on its removal by 1911. Only then was the vast body (95 per cent) of those over seventy on out-relief able to opt out of the Poor Law and receive old age pensions instead.

The Act of 1908 therefore failed to meet its proclaimed objective of saving the deserving elderly poor from the Poor Law. Only when regarded as a mere legislative gesture by a government ducking out from under pressure does the Act make sense. Its inadequacy was frankly admitted, excused on financial grounds and accompanied by a pledge that provisions would be improved when more money became available.

(C) CONCLUSION

This chapter has attempted to explain the reasons for the differences between the provisions enacted in Germany in 1889 and in Britain in 1908. Whereas in the 1880s German pensions policy was part of a government

---

[32] The government proposal had been for a means test of £26 per annum. This was changed in Parliament to a sliding scale. The full pension of 5 shillings per week was limited to those whose annual income was £21 or less, reducing to nil for those with an annual income above £31.10s. See Macnicol, *Politics of retirement*, pp. 156–62, for the various qualifications and the problems caused by them.

agenda, British old age pensions were the response to a broadly based revulsion against the Poor Law treatment of the aged deserving poor. This was articulated by pressure-group politics in which organised labour played, if not a sufficient, at least a necessary role. It was therefore able to give expression to its priorities. Although the legislation fell far short of its demands, these priorities helped to set the parameters.

In any comparison of pensions policy in England and Germany up to and including 1908, the differences are at first sight immense and the similarities small. The political context was different, as was the timing, and the actual provisions were shaped accordingly. German pension policy was initiated from above so as to enhance the role of the recently established Empire in the provision of benefits to the population and particularly to the industrial working-class. British pension policy was initiated from below and was the expression of popular grievances over the working of the Poor Law.

In Germany there was nothing like the British determination to provide an income-support that would be a full substitute for poor relief and remove their recipients from all contact with the Poor Law authorities. The German pensions did not always give the pensioner from a low-paid occupation an income adequate for subsistence and were supplemented by public poor relief, if necessary. At this formative stage in Britain the two forms of support were alternatives; in Germany they were not.[33] There is no comprehensive information on the number of German pensioners who had to augment their invalidity pension from public poor relief. A figure between 8 and 12 per cent, and significantly higher for Berlin, has been suggested.[34] Although German insurance developed a vast statistical apparatus, no one thought this information worth collecting on a regular basis. That speaks volumes for the difference between the policy preoccupations in the two countries. The Act of 1908 is thus best understood as Poor Law reform; the pensions were means tested and limited to the very poor. Poor Law reform was a minor consideration in Germany by comparison.

Yet first impressions can mislead. Once we look beyond the German measure that was actually enacted to consider that which Bismarck himself had originally desired, some interesting similarities emerge. Bismarck had

---

[33] The British ruling in this matter was abrogated in 1919 in the face of the decline in the value of the pension. B. B. Gilbert, *British social policy 1914–1939* (London, 1970), p. 239. Hence intention was one thing, outcome another.

[34] See p. 63 above.

also proposed tax-financed pensions and had met objections to the burden on taxpayers by suggesting a strictly limited piece of legislation that was to be regarded as a first step. The limitations that he had envisaged were not the same as those that appealed to Asquith and Lloyd George. He certainly never contemplated a means test; that would have run counter to all his objectives. Nor had he any desire to limit the pension to the deserving. His policy was not driven by moral but political considerations.

In Germany it had, however, become possible to contemplate an alternative source of finance to general taxation. The attraction of compulsory contributory insurance meant that Bismarck's objections could be brushed aside. British policy-makers were also to discover this attraction but only in the course of the struggle over the bill.

12

National health insurance for Britain

(A) SOCIAL SECURITY ASPECTS

This chapter is the counterpart not only to chapter 2, which dealt with insurance against sickness in Germany, but also to chapter 4, since it includes the treatment of invalidity, or disablement as it was called in Britain. It is because British national health insurance derived its original impetus from the need to deal with business left unfinished by the Old Age Pensions Act, and in particular from a commitment to lowering the pension age, that it can only now be dealt with here. As in the previous chapter we shall be comparing a German measure that dates from the 1880s with a British one introduced a generation later.

The British government's lack of interest in compulsory insurance against old age right up to 1908 has already been explained. This accounts for its ignorance of the details of the German schemes. Civil servants had not considered it necessary to brief ministers on a matter that was regarded as irrelevant to British circumstances. That applied to Asquith, who had been responsible for the drafting of the Old Age Pensions Bill, and at first also to Lloyd George, newly appointed as Chancellor of the Exchequer and entrusted with the passage of the bill through the House of Commons.[1] Not until the debate on the second reading was his attention drawn to the fact that German pensions for the under-seventies were targeted exclusively on those suffering from invalidity. He did not have to work out for himself the relevance of this fact to a government under pressure to lower the *general* pensions age; his informant spelt it out for him.[2]

---

[1] E. P. Hennock, *British social reform and German precedents: the case of social insurance 1880–1914* (Oxford, 1987), pp. 128–41 and 146.
[2] For the role of Harold Cox, Liberal MP for Preston, and the details of Lloyd George's subsequent interest in German insurance see Hennock, *British social reform*, pp. 143–51, 163–4 and 169–70. This

It was his interest in compulsory contributions as a source of finance and in invalidity pensions for the under-seventies as a way of limiting the commitment of the State that led him to inquire personally of the German insurance system during a visit to Germany in August 1908. There his attention was also drawn to sickness insurance. 'I never realised before on what a gigantic scale the German pension system is conducted', he announced on his return. 'Old age pensions form but a comparatively small part of the system. Does the German worker fall ill? State insurance comes to his aid. Is he permanently invalided from work? Again he gets a regular grant whether he has reached the pension age or not.'[3]

By introducing compulsory contributory insurance and confining pensions for the under-seventies to cases of infirmity, Lloyd George departed from the strategy of his predecessor. Between 1906 and 1908 the government had first yielded reluctantly to irresistible pressure from inside and outside Parliament and then attempted to limit its scope so as to fit in with what the Treasury was willing to provide. Now it took its own initiative and proposed a policy for which there was scarcely any demand among its supporters and which was met with great suspicion. That brought it closer to what had happened in Germany under Bismarck in the early 1880s, both in substance and in tactics. Like Bismarck, Lloyd George initiated a radical change of policy in the face of objections from those whose consent he needed. He was to liken it to the progress of an ambulance driver over a twisting and rutted road.[4]

Like German accident insurance, and indeed like German invalidity and old age insurance, British health insurance, as it was to be called, emerged from the political process in a form that differed fundamentally from the original proposal.[5] In Germany change had been in response to party issues such as *Reich* versus the states, public subsidies, and differentiation of benefit. Vested interests, whether commercial insurance or industry, had been relatively ineffective. The British scheme was shaped and reshaped in response to three institutions, which considered themselves closely affected by the proposals: the friendly societies, the commercial insurance industry

---

evidence, of which he was unaware, makes Bentley Gilbert's treatment of the role of the German precedent in the origins of national health insurance defective in information and emphasis. B. B. Gilbert, *David Lloyd George, a political life* (London, 1987), esp. p. 343.

[3] *The Daily News*, 27 August 1908, quoted in Hennock, *British social reform*, pp. 149–51.

[4] In a speech in Birmingham on 10 June 1911. H. N. Bunbury (ed.), *Lloyd George's ambulance wagon* (Bath, 1970), p. 177.

[5] It was originally called invalidity insurance on the German model, but, drawing on the analogy of life insurance, it was decided at an early stage that health insurance sounded more positive. Bunbury, *Lloyd George's ambulance wagon*, pp. 129 and 132.

and the medical profession.[6] Of these the friendly societies were the first in the field.

Any British government intending to provide sickness benefit coupled with infirmity pensions entered the territory already occupied by friendly societies. So far no government had dared to do so. All such proposals had met the political objections or at least the non-cooperation of a body of organised labour more numerous than any other. Lloyd George's first task was to reassure them that their interests would not be endangered and to obtain their co-operation. There were, however, a great variety of bodies that were called friendly societies. On the one hand, there were the great affiliated orders with their nationwide organisations and permanent funds. On the other, there were small local dividing clubs, which returned their accumulated funds annually to their members only to begin anew in the following year. Between these extremes were any number of bodies, registered and unregistered under the terms of the Friendly Societies Acts. Beyond the members of the most ephemeral of these there were those who did not belong to any organisation of mutual help for times of sickness and had nowhere to look in times of infirmity except to Poor Law or charity. A government that wished to co-operate with the friendly society movement had to distinguish between societies that were suited to its purpose and those that were not. That left a portion of the working-class population for whom no appropriate provision existed and for whom it had to be provided.

Fortunately for Lloyd George the large and politically significant societies had come to regret their non-cooperation over old age pensions. That attitude had deprived them of influence in government circles and worked to the disadvantage of their members when the qualifications for pension were decided. Their plea that friendly society benefit be disregarded in the means test that determined entitlement to a pension had been ignored. They were therefore not inclined to reject Lloyd George's advances out of hand. Co-operation with the government had its possible attractions.

The first version of Lloyd George's proposals was drawn up in December 1908 after consultation with the leaders of the affiliated orders and with their interests in mind. Insurance against sickness and infirmity was to be compulsory for all manual workers who were not already subscribing to an approved friendly society. They were to be obliged to join such a society and would receive a weekly payment in the event of short-term sickness or

---

[6] This chapter draws heavily on B. B. Gilbert, *The evolution of national insurance in Great Britain: the origins of the welfare state* (London, 1966).

long-term infirmity. In the event of death their widows and dependent orphans would receive a pension. There was to be provision for medical treatment, a maternity grant for the wives of insured men and a 'sanatorium benefit'. Contributions would be withheld from wages by employers, who would themselves contribute an equal amount. There would be a State subsidy, probably as a proportion of benefits rather than of contributions. At five shillings a week these benefits would be substantially less than could be expected by normal friendly society members paying the customary level of contributions. These normally received twice that amount for the crucial sickness benefit. They were not to have their contributions withheld from wages but would pay directly to the society, receiving the employer's contribution for the purpose. The permanent friendly societies that met the criteria for becoming approved societies under the scheme were thus to administer a statutory scheme designed to pose no threat to their ability to recruit their own members at a higher level of contributions and benefits.[7]

It should be noted that no provision was contemplated for funeral benefit, the most common of all benefits provided by voluntary mutual help societies, even by many who did not cover any other contingency. That omission was designed to avoid competing with commercial insurance, particularly with the so-called industrial insurance companies (and the similar industrial insurance collecting societies) with their door-to-door collectors, who specialised in the provision of money for funeral expenses but had no connection with sickness insurance.

Widows' and orphans' pensions did, however, form part of Lloyd George's plans at this stage. They were perhaps the most original of the proposals. Friendly societies did not normally make provisions of this sort. He had learnt of the intention to provide them in Germany and referred to them for the first time on his return from his German visit. From then on they regularly featured as one of the intended benefits.[8]

The government announced its intention to introduce compulsory health and unemployment insurance in the Budget speech of 29 April 1909, but these matters were overshadowed by the details of the Budget itself. The most controversial proposals were those for a supertax on the rich and for a valuation of all land. The latter was interpreted as preparation for a subsequent taxation of land values, i.e. a capital gains tax targeted on land.

---

[7] *Report of the Actuaries*, 21 March 1910, in Library of Political and Economic Science, London School of Economics, Braithwaite Papers, Part II.4. See also Gilbert, *Evolution*, pp. 295–9.
[8] They were absent from Lloyd George's speech on the second reading of the Old Age Pensions Bill in June 1908, which listed the further 'problems with which it is the business of the State to deal', but they figured in his speech in Swansea in October 1908.

These aspects of the Budget sparked off a conflict with the Conservative party and ultimately with the House of Lords that dominated politics and led to two general elections, in January and December 1910. Although the government actuaries reported in March 1910 on the details of the insurance plans submitted to them, no further action could be taken at the time.

It was at this point, during the summer of 1910, that the industrial insurance companies, alerted to the contents of the government proposals, decided to object to the introduction of widows' and orphans' pensions. They argued that any payment on the death of the wage-earner would reduce the incentive to insure separately against the costs of a funeral, and would therefore threaten their business. In their collectors, who called weekly for the premiums and who received substantial commissions on the business, these companies and the similar collecting friendly societies possessed a body that could be easily mobilised in the defence of their vested interest. With an election due in December, Lloyd George was in no position to resist their demands unless he formed an alliance with the Opposition in support of his plans.[9] The failure of his attempt at a cross-party coalition led to the scrapping of the proposals for widows' and orphans' pensions, but not before the industrial insurance industry, thoroughly alarmed at Lloyd George's prevarications, had extracted pledges from the election candidates to oppose any measure of State insurance that was likely to prejudice the interests of industrial life assurance.[10]

Widows' and orphans' pensions would have been costly. They had accounted for roughly half the government contribution envisaged. The freeing of these resources made it possible to increase sickness benefit from 5s to 10s a week, a more adequate level of support, but one that removed the main advantage that ordinary friendly society members would have enjoyed over those in the State scheme. Instead of 'underpinning the existing voluntary agencies by a comprehensive system – necessarily at a lower level – of state action', which was how Churchill had described the insurance strategy in December 1908, what now emerged was a competing State programme of insurance for all. The friendly societies were induced to accept this change by a government promise to underwrite the liabilities arising from their older members, whose claims were likely to be in excess of the contributions on their behalf. This surprising act of State generosity

---

[9] On this matter see also below.
[10] They claimed to have obtained pledges from 490 out of the 670 MPs elected. Gilbert, *Evolution*, p. 336. For a detailed description of the conflict with industrial insurance at this stage see *ibid.*, pp. 318–43.

removed at one stroke the fear that inadequate reserves might lead to bankruptcy that had dogged the friendly society movement for decades. It left the societies free to use what were now surplus reserves for the benefit of their members.[11]

That was not the end of the concessions that the industrial insurance industry were able to obtain. Although they had expressed no interest in sickness insurance in the past, their distrust of the future direction of the new developments had caused them to insist on their right in principle to take part in the administration of the proposed insurance. After the publication of the bill they decided that friendly society recruitment among their clients insured for funeral benefits might constitute a threat to their business. They decided to enter the field themselves by creating subsidiaries that could operate as an approved society under their control.

Such a development was something originally never considered by the authors of national health insurance. With some exceptions drawn from Germany their proposals had been modelled on the practice of friendly societies and were intended to enable these to extend their membership beyond the existing limits. If industrial insurance companies were going to compete with friendly societies in this field, they would need to insist on conditions appropriate to their own structures. In practice, that meant two things. Unlike friendly societies, they were not geared to providing medical treatment, nor did their form of government satisfy the conditions for approved societies as specified in the bill. They were not self-governing institutions elected by their contributors and operating through local committees, as friendly societies were. Like other commercial companies they were run from a central office by directors responsible to shareholders.

They set out to change the bill in alliance with the British Medical Association (BMA), who had their own reservations about the government proposals. Lloyd George had originally assumed that friendly societies would be responsible for providing medical treatment as they had done before. But by the time that the bill was published he had been persuaded of the merits of transferring the provision of medical care to local health committees of the counties and county boroughs. Since he was well aware that this would be strongly opposed by friendly societies, the bill merely contained a clause that gave approved societies the option of transferring

---

[11] Gilbert, *Evolution*, pp. 340–1; W. S. Churchill to H. H. Asquith, 29 December 1908, quoted in Hennock, *British social reform*, p. 169. Churchill and Lloyd George were in close consultation over their insurance plans at this time.

medical treatment to local health committees if they so wished. That was not an option that would have appealed to the friendly societies since they relied on their club doctor to keep down unwarranted claims.

It was this system of club doctors that formed a long-standing grievance of the medical profession. It excluded all local doctors from treating friendly society members but for the one appointed to the post. It placed the man appointed under the control of the local committee, where complaints against his conduct could be heard. It also left his remuneration, based on so much per member, to a market over-stocked with impoverished doctors only too willing to undercut their rivals.[12]

The alliance of industrial insurance companies and BMA was able to obtain a double concession. To the great relief of doctors the provision of medical treatment through local health committees was made mandatory, and approved societies were no longer required to have elected local committees. One obstacle to the entry of industrial assurance into the scheme was thus removed. However, as long as members of approved societies were entitled to elect their officers, the proposed subsidiaries of the companies were in danger of falling under the control of the collectors, for these were in an excellent position to direct their clients how to vote. By the time Parliament reassembled after the summer recess, the directors of the industrial insurance companies were safe from this threat. They had obtained all the necessary concessions from the government to be able to operate much as they had always done. The prospect of an administrative structure based on self-governing societies on the friendly society model had receded. The latter would be faced with the competition of commercial insurance companies, and in the long run these were the more effective.

This was a far-reaching transformation of the original bill, as far-reaching as the introduction of *Berufsgenossenschaften* into the original proposals for German accident insurance or of graduated pensions into the original proposals for German invalidity and old age insurance. It has been ascribed, both then and since, primarily to the pledges obtained from MPs during the previous general election and to the power that these gave over the government.[13] But it was also due to Lloyd George's appreciation of the services that the companies could provide. To administer a compulsory scheme through voluntary associations, each of which was free to reject

---

[12] For details of the long-standing friction between the societies and the British Medical Association see David G. Green, *Working class patients and the medical establishment* (Aldershot, 1985). See also p. 245 below for more information.

[13] Gilbert, *Evolution*, pp. 356–87, for details of this complex reconstruction of the bill and its politics.

those whom it did not wish to admit, as was proposed, was ultimately impossible. There was bound to be a residue of contributors whom no society wished to have and for whom other arrangements would have to be made. No one knew how many there would be, but Lloyd George had decided to make only minimal provision for them and to rely on the societies to keep that residue small. This minimal provision was not in fact insurance nor was it subsidised by the State. It was no more than a deposit account with the Post Office. The scheme would probably have been politically acceptable only if the number of such deposit contributors was insignificant. It was a gamble whether the societies would compete for new members, especially since many of these would be women whose health record differed from that of men who dominated most of the societies. It was a gamble that Lloyd George had decided to take. Yet friendly societies were traditional bodies known for their cautious attitude to the admission of members. Many had no tradition of admitting women, who constituted a disproportionate number of those still to be recruited. The revision of the proposals originally put to them, which to all intents and purposes abolished the distinction between ordinary society members and members of the State scheme, would have done nothing to make them eager to accept doubtful risks. These could affect the society's finances to the detriment of established members. The industrial assurance industry, whose collectors were in touch with the very people who had to be recruited, must have seemed well worth bringing into the scheme.

(B) COMPARISON

The hiving-off of medical treatment makes it possible to conclude the examination of British health insurance as a measure of social security with a structural comparison with Germany, before returning to the issues raised by the medical side of the scheme. The separation of the two aspects and their allocation to different institutions was certainly one respect in which British health insurance differed from its German counterpart. The implications will be explored in the next chapter. But there were at least five others.

1. In Britain support for invalidity, or disablement benefit as it was finally called, was part of the same scheme as support for short-term illness. Those unable to work passed seamlessly from one category of support to the other. In its final version the British Act provided sickness benefit of 10s a week for men and 7s.6d for women for twenty-six weeks. Thereafter they received disablement benefit of 5s a week for as long as necessary. Both

benefits were paid by the same approved society, as they had been paid by friendly societies in the days of voluntary insurance.

That was not the case in Germany. There invalidity pensions were the responsibility of the territorial pension boards established under the Invalidity and Old Age Insurance Law of 1889. Sickness benefit was the responsibility of the sickness funds under the Sickness Insurance Law of 1883 and its subsequent amendments. Far from passing seamlessly from one category of support to the other, those whose entitlement to sickness benefit had expired qualified for invalidity pensions only after enduring several weeks without any support at all: thirty-six weeks under the Law of 1889 and still thirteen weeks under that of 1899. There was no justification for this other than the reluctance of vested interests to assume additional burdens. Not until 1904 was the gap finally closed. But the different institutions with their different procedures for establishing entitlement remained, repeatedly resisting efforts to merge the three insurance schemes into one.

2. Bismarck decided at an early stage that commercial insurance should play no part in his plans. It was one of his basic principles, to which he clung throughout the tortuous process of compromise on many other things. Lloyd George had originally also not intended the commercial insurance industry to have any role in his original plans. He had excluded any death grant from the state benefits, and then reluctantly expunged widows' and orphans' pensions at its behest, but had still been unable to exclude the industry from the scheme.

Any explanation for this contrast can be only tentative. Did Britain offer private enterprise, and the insurance industry in particular, a more favourable ideological climate than Germany? The history of workmen's compensation provides grounds for such a view. In 1897 there had been no intention to prescribe any form of insurance whatever. At that stage the state was not in the business of establishing 'approved societies', and the field was left open for any measure that those employers affected by the law chose to take. This resulted in a growing business for accident insurance companies.

But in 1911 the situation was different. The old ideological rejection of compulsion and prescription was much weakened. The issue was now no longer whether to prescribe means of dealing with sickness and disablement through approved societies. The issue was which societies to approve and under what conditions. Lloyd George had originally assumed that the success of his scheme required him to conciliate the political power of friendly societies. Although some of his advisers were committed to supporting the friendly society movement on ideological grounds, Lloyd George himself carried little ideological baggage of that kind. When he realised that the political power and astuteness of commercial assurance exceeded that of friendly societies, he adjusted his scheme accordingly. What happened in Britain was an assertion not of ideology but of parliamentary power.

For a comparison with Germany, one has to go back to the beginning of the political initiative of the 1880s, to the establishment of accident insurance. That was the moment when the situation was still fluid and fundamental decisions were made. The details required for such a comparison are in chapter 8 above. They lead to two conclusions. Bismarck's opposition to the inclusion of insurance companies was ideological in a way that Lloyd George's was not; it went beyond his personal dislike of commercial insurance. It was linked to the problem of finding the necessary financial resources, but had also acquired a constitutional dimension in Bismarck's mind.

None of that would have ensured Bismarck's victory. He came near to being faced with the choice between a reluctant compromise and the failure of his bill. In view of the financial implications of a compromise, failure would have been the more likely outcome. In the end he got his way because the private insurance companies were politically weaker than they were to be in Britain in 1911.

The strength of the British industrial assurance companies came from their particular form of doing business. This provided them with a large body of collectors, who had a vested interest in the premiums they collected on the doorstep and who were successfully mobilised to obtain pledges from candidates of both parties in the general election of December 1910. The companies were therefore able to put pressure on the governing party and did not hesitate to do so. The German insurance companies, who wished to participate in accident insurance, did not have this direct access to the voters. They relied on their links with the three Liberal parties but were apparently unable to influence the remaining parties in the *Reichstag*. They were only as strong as the Liberal parties, and these did not control the balance in the *Reichstag* on their own. The masterly game of political chess, to use Lohmann's words, that Bismarck played to isolate them involved significant concessions to the Centre party but left the Liberals and their championship of the insurance companies without support. The German insurance companies lost because the German Liberals on their own were weak and the Centre party had other priorities.[14]

---

[14] QS,II.2/1, No. 184 for the quotation from Lohmann and his bitter condemnation of the measure.

3. The participation of commercial insurance in the British scheme had a number of important consequences. The separate administration of medical benefit was one of them. But undoubtedly the gravest consequence was the exclusion of any provision for widows and orphans. Widows and orphans were considered one of the categories of the deserving poor for whom the stigma of the Poor Law was altogether inappropriate. There was no inclination in Britain, and least of all on the part of Lloyd George, who had been himself an orphan, to justify their exclusion as of merely marginal importance, as had been done in Germany. His memorandum in favour of a coalition government, written soon after the insurance companies had objected to the inclusion of widows' and orphans' pensions in an insurance bill, contains a long passage on the impossibility of introducing such pensions without the co-operation of the opposition party. The young widow is described as the most urgent and pitiful case of all those in undeserved poverty.[15]

As long as the insurance industry could threaten the government with a switch to the opposition, it was impossible to lift widows and orphans out of the Poor Law. But in the 1920s, with the Labour party hostile to contributory insurance and toying with tax-financed benefits paid by a capital levy, the insurance companies became vulnerable to Conservative government plans for pensions reform. By the Widows', Orphans' and Old Age Contributory Pensions Act of 1925 they were obliged to accept the provision of widows' and orphans' pensions, their own exclusion from the administration of the scheme, and to watch their financial surpluses being raided to help pay for it. Like the German scheme the Act of 1925 provided orphans' pensions, but it was if anything less solicitous of the widow under the age of sixty-five than its German counterpart.[16]

4. 'In Germany the system is much more bureaucratic in its management and does not nearly to the same extent adopt the system of self-government.' This boast stood on the first page of the memorandum in support of the Bill. Subsequently the section on 'approved societies' stated that 'no Society will be approved ... unless its constitution provides for absolute control of its affairs by its members'.[17] Historians of national

---

[15] Sir Charles Petrie, *The life and letters of the Rt Hon. Sir Austen Chamberlain* (London, 1939), vol. I, Appendix I, pp. 384 and 385. For the context of this memorandum see G. R. Searle, *The quest for national efficiency* (Oxford, 1971), pp. 77–98.

[16] Bentley Gilbert, *British social policy 1914–1939* (London, 1970), pp. 235–51. The difference in the treatment of the widow was due to the more generous interpretation of invalidity in Germany than that of disablement in Britain. See chapter 14 below.

[17] National Insurance Bill, *Memorandum explanatory of the Bill as passed by the House of Commons*, pp. 1 and 8, BPP 1911 Cd.5995 LXXIII, 69.

health insurance have paid a great deal of attention to the degree of self-government among the approved societies. Attention has focused on two developments in particular.

One is the admission of subsidiaries of industrial assurance companies as approved societies. Unlike traditional friendly societies these had no local management committees. Their directors were accountable instead to annual general meetings of their members held in London. Under such circumstances attendance was small and control a mere formality.[18]

Even the control over these subsidiaries by their directors was heavily circumscribed. As in the case of all approved societies, action was tightly controlled by central government, at first by the National Insurance Commissioners and after 1919 by the Ministry of Health. Members' contributions were paid through the purchase of stamps issued by the General Post Office. The money was then paid from there into the government coffers and only passed on to the societies on receipt of audited accounts every six months. That made it easy to withhold sums for any expenditure that did not strictly conform to regulations. Every five years the Government Actuary used these accounts to predict future profitability. He decided how much could be used to fund additional benefits, how much was to be held in contingency funds and how much was to be invested. All this required a uniform system of book-keeping. It indirectly led to increased centralisation of the affiliated orders of friendly societies, fearful of any loss of income through unauthorised expenditure. The damage that the regulation of national health insurance did to local discretion and local autonomy among friendly societies contributed to the dwindling interest by local members in the management of society affairs. The result was a travesty of Lloyd George's original vision of extending mutuality, independence and self-government, particularly since the expansion of health insurance membership was overwhelmingly the achievement of the industrial insurance companies, where none of these qualities were found.[19]

How did German insurance compare in these respects? The ease with which the British Treasury could withhold income from approved societies until their six-monthly accounts had been examined was made possible by the use of stamps purchased at the Post Office for the payment of

---

[18] This is the emphasis of Braithwaite in Bunbury, *Lloyd George's ambulance wagon*, as well as of Gilbert in his *Evolution of national insurance*.

[19] Noel Whiteside, 'Accounting and accountability: an historical case study of a private–public partnership', in R. A. W. Rhodes (ed.), *Transforming British government*, vol. 2, *Changing roles and relationships* (London, 2000), pp. 167–81.

contributions. That idea had been copied from German invalidity and old age insurance but did not apply to contributions to insurance against sickness. Sickness insurance funds, with the exception of those for the building trade and perhaps some guild funds, were local in their membership. There was usually no problem for employers in paying their contributions and those of their workers directly. For those workers who belonged to the centralised voluntary funds employers neither paid nor deducted contributions from wages. Stamps purchased from the Post Office were designed to solve the problem created for invalidity insurance by the mobility of workers over their working life. In consequence sickness insurance funds experienced no waiting period and no conditionality in the flow of their income.

Until 1911 they were not even under the supervision of any State authority, but of their local government authority. In Prussia these were entitled to examine the accounts and had to do so at least once a year. They could ensure that the law was adhered to and in extreme cases of non-compliance could dissolve the fund and take over its powers.[20] In 1911 the RVO placed sickness funds under State authority by establishing district and provincial offices. But until 1924, when regulations were tightened or at least made more explicit, their powers of supervision were the same as had previously been exercised by local government.[21] The State did not intrude on the detailed administration of benefit by what were considered to be self-governing bodies.

The explanation is surely that they had fewer long-term responsibilities. Even in 1911 all but a small number of factory funds paid benefit for no more than twenty-six weeks (see Table 29.1 above). They were obliged to adjust the level of contributions, when this was needed to balance their books. It was the responsibility of approved societies for the unlimited length of disablement benefit that goes far to explain the detailed monitoring of long-term solvency by central government in Britain. The relevant comparison here is with invalidity insurance, administered in highly bureaucratic ways by the territorial pension boards, which in their turn were under the central control of the Imperial Insurance Office (RVA). That this could lead to drastic central intervention when long-term

[20] E. von Woedtke, *Das Reichsgesetz, betr. die Krankenversicherung der Arbeiter* (11th enlarged edition by G. Euken-Addenhauser, Berlin, 1905), pp. 165–70, 223–4 and 408–10. We may assume that in other states arrangements were not significantly different.

[21] Gugel and G. Schmid, *Kommentar zur Reichsversicherungsordnung* (Berlin, 1912), vol. 1, pp. 88–94; K. Lippmann, *Die Reichsversicherungsordnung in der Fassung der Bekanntmachung vom 15. Dezember 1924* (Berlin and Leipzig, 1925), p. 144.

solvency was perceived to be at risk is demonstrated by the action of the RVA in the first decade of the century.[22]

Another difference between German sickness insurance and both German invalidity insurance and British health insurance may also be relevant. The former received no state subsidy; the latter did. Such a privilege notoriously brought restrictions in its turn.

5. The most significant difference between the two countries was the assessment of the level of benefits and contributions. In Germany graduated benefits were tied to graduated contributions, differentiated according to income levels. The burden on German workers was therefore roughly proportionate to their ability to pay, while benefits for the well-paid were considerably greater than those for the lower-paid. In Britain there were uniform levels of benefit and contributions, differentiating only between men and women.[23] Lloyd George explained this to the Commons by saying that he had decided in favour of a uniform flat-rate scale as the simplest means of providing benefits large enough to keep contributors' families from want.[24] The issue aroused no comment in the Commons at the time: there seems to have been no interest in differentiation by income. Interest in German precedents in the course of the introduction of British national insurance was highly selective, as such interest tends to be.

What the German precedent had to offer Lloyd George was first and foremost a way to complete the provision of old age pensions. By failing to provide pensions for those under the age of seventy, the Act of 1908 had not adequately dealt with the claims of the deserving aged poor for support free from the stigma of the Poor Law. The government had been left with a promise to reduce the age limit as soon as possible. In this predicament, what interested Lloyd George were two aspects of the provisions made in Germany. One was the possibility offered by invalidity insurance of limiting non-stigmatising income support under the age of seventy to those who were unable to work. The other was the use of compulsory contributory insurance to contain the cost of this reform to the State. That could and did have implications for other reforms for which the case also rested on the inappropriateness of the Poor Law.

---

[22] See chapter 10, including Figure 10.2, above.

[23] The only exception was designed to include those with exceptionally low wages. They were to pay less than the standard rate of contribution while still being entitled to the standard benefits. The employer of low-wage labour was obliged to make up the balance of the contribution; in extreme cases the State added 1d per week (clauses 3–7). This was differentiation of a sort, but by protecting the flat-rate level of benefits its effect was to achieve the opposite of what was done in Germany.

[24] 5 *Hansard* 25 (4 May 1911), 616.

British national insurance was an aspect of the politics of poverty and was judged by what it did to protect the families of the poor from want. Its impetus came from the conjunction of two wider considerations. One was a concern to protect the human resources of the nation at a time of international rivalry, both economic and military. The other was the need to reassure the citizen-voter that he would not be allowed to fall into the non-citizen class of paupers for reasons over which he had no control. It was not the maintenance of comfort but the prevention of want that was at stake.

Up to 1876 compulsory sickness insurance, first in Prussia and then in Germany, had been as much about providing a substitute for poor relief as it was to be in Britain. Even in 1888, when plans for compulsory invalidity and old age insurance were drawn up, they proposed no more than a flat-rate benefit geared to the contributions that the lower-paid could be expected to afford. But an important change had already taken place in the early 1880s. Sickness insurance, now linked to accident insurance, had become a means to commend the newly created *Reich* to industrial workers by enhancing its role in meeting their needs. In the light of this new priority it was remodelled to reflect, as far as was thought administratively feasible, the ability of wage earners to pay for benefits suited to their economic position. The draft of the original old age and invalidity insurance bill was remodelled in 1889 at the insistence of the parties in the *Reichstag* according to the same priorities.

National health insurance, although also extensively remodelled at the behest of politically powerful groups, underwent no such transformation. It remained part of the reform of the Poor Law. Within those limits compulsory insurance was grudgingly accepted, but the widespread belief in the merits of voluntary provision had not been fundamentally challenged. 'Regimentation and regulation', the terms in which German insurance had once been rejected altogether, still had the same pejorative meaning as before.[25] All influential elements believed that, once dire need had been met, British workers should be left to make their own provision free from government control. The fact that public money played a decisive role in the provision of the necessary minimum was bound to be a constraint on the operation of the approved societies within the scheme, be it commercial companies, friendly societies or trade unions, even if the full extent of that constraint would be revealed only after the passing of the Act. None of these bodies wanted this kind of compulsion to

[25] For these concepts, see Hennock, *British social reform*, pp. 171–2.

be extended, nor did any other elements in society with influence in Parliament.

That is an important difference between the two countries. German policy-makers repeatedly expressed their belief that in the absence of compulsion workers would not make the savings to ensure their needs.[26] That conviction fuelled the process of increasing differentiation of pensions that was to reach its climax in the Pension Law of 1957.[27] The opposite belief held sway in Britain. It was justified in the case of some and not of others. It can be argued that it has led in the long run to the shortcomings of the British pension system, which are now generally recognised. It is not difficult to understand why the belief was hardly challenged in 1911. Why it was still unchallenged in the 1940s is another question, and one beyond the scope of this study.

---

[26] E.g. QS,I.5, pp. 203–4, for 1872; *Begründung* of the Sickness Insurance Law of 1883, SBRT, 5. Legislaturperiode II. Session 1882–3, vol. 5 *Anlagen*, p. 141; *Begründung* of the draft legislation for old age and invalidity insurance, 22 November 1888, SBRT, 7. Legislaturperiode IV, Session 1888/9, vol. 4 *Anlagen*, and vol. 1, p. 49.

[27] For the reform of 1957, see H. G. Hockerts, 'German post-war social policies against the background of the Beveridge Plan', in W. J. Mommsen (ed.), *The emergence of the welfare state in Britain and Germany* (London, 1981), pp. 315–39, esp. pp. 328–31.

13

National health insurance: medical aspects

(A) THE DOCTORS

By the time that the National Insurance Bill had passed through the Commons in November 1911, the industrial insurance companies had obtained their objective. Not the British Medical Association (BMA), however. The doctors had escaped from under the thumb of the friendly societies in August when the provision of medical treatment had been placed with local health committees, or local insurance committees as they were ultimately to be called in the Act. Instead of doctors being appointed by friendly societies as their own club doctor, as in the past, a panel was established of all local doctors willing to provide medical treatment to the insured. From it the insured could select the doctor with whom he or she wished to be registered. That meant free choice of doctors and it had serious implications for the finances of approved societies by encouraging doctors to be lenient in the issue of sickness certificates.

Major questions remained outstanding, of which the most important were discipline, limitation on those who could claim to be treated and level of payment.

On the local health committees, where they met together with representatives of the local authority and the National Insurance Commissioners, doctors were to be in a minority. Three-fifths of the committee were to consist of representatives of the insured. What the BMA wanted was for doctors to be under the exclusive control of fellow-doctors in all matters of medical conduct and discipline. It obtained this by the establishment of medical committees alongside but not under the control of the local health committees.

By providing insurance to those who would otherwise not have been able to afford the cost of medical treatment, the Act promised to increase the income of the medical profession. But in so far as it was to include those who would normally have been able to pay their doctors as private patients, it was perceived as a threat to medical incomes. The BMA objected to the choice of £160 per annum as the ceiling for compulsory insurance and even more to the inclusion on a voluntary basis of some persons earning more than that amount. But their demand for an income limit of £2 per week was brushed aside. Only on the issue of voluntary contributors did they win a concession. These were to receive their benefit entirely in cash and were expected to make their own arrangements with a doctor.

The panel system promised to make it impossible for fees to be as low as they had often been when friendly societies had taken advantage of the weak position of individual doctors in the labour market. Lloyd George had from the first held out the prospect of improvement and financial provision had been made for a 6s capitation fee, of which the cost of drugs and medical appliances would have been about 1s. The BMA had demanded 8s.6d, excluding the cost of medicine and appliances, and called upon its members not to take service under the insurance committees unless all its demands were met. It reckoned that they would have to be met by January 1913, when the insured population qualified for medical treatment.

The decisive conflict between the government and the medical profession did not therefore take place until 1912. It was fought in an atmosphere of great bitterness. The turning point came with the publication of an investigation into the average income of general practitioners per patient. This turned out to be no more than 4s.5d per annum for all patients, whether private or insured, and demonstrated the weakness of the claim for 8s.6d. When the BMA stuck to its demand, the profession split. The split was largely between the well-paid consultants, who provided the leadership of the BMA, and the lowly general practitioners who realised that they were being asked to refuse a substantial increase in their income. The BMA thereby lost the sympathy of the public and put Lloyd George in a strong position, which he exploited with his usual political skill. The government increased the money for medical treatment by another 2s.6d per head, which made the offer practically irresistible to those whose co-operation mattered. But it had a stick to accompany this carrot. The Act permitted insurance committees to make alternative arrangements for medical treatment, where appropriate, and the Chancellor made it clear that he was willing to contemplate a full-time salaried service if necessary. With rumours rife of impoverished Scottish doctors being recruited to work in English towns, the resistance of the general practitioners collapsed and the BMA leadership was left isolated and embarrassed. The story is complicated by a change in the leadership. The general secretary's acceptance of a place on the National Insurance Commission, while the demands of the BMA were still unmet, threw the leadership of the BMA into the hands of hard-liners unable to recognise the moment to accept a favourable settlement. Nevertheless, although apparently defeated, their intransigence added a substantial sum to medical incomes.[1]

While the BMA was organising its boycott of national insurance, a similar conflict was taking place in Germany over the provisions of the RVO of 1911. This legislation was more than a mere codification of previous insurance laws. It extended the coverage of sickness insurance to all workers in agriculture and forestry as well as to domestic servants. It also raised the income limit for non-manual workers from 2,000 to 2,500 M p.a. That added over 2 million to the insured population and increased the discontent of doctors with their position in the insurance scheme.[2]

It is a remarkable fact that the German medical profession had not been consulted at all in 1883 over the making of the Sickness Insurance Law. The sickness funds were given the duty to provide medical treatment and were left, as in the past, to make any arrangements with doctors that seemed appropriate.[3] German statutory insurance therefore placed doctors in a similar position to that in which they found themselves in England and Wales under voluntary insurance provided by friendly societies.

In England and Wales friendly societies, including the individual lodges of the affiliated orders, generally appointed a single doctor to treat their members, and if necessary made special arrangement for those living further afield. These were part-time appointments and doctors were paid on a capitation basis, irrespective of the actual amount of treatment required for any individual member. Alternatively, several societies in a locality combined to establish medical institutes in rented premises. These employed one or more doctors, usually on a full-time basis, supplied drugs and generally also gave treatment to the wives and children of members. Finally, from around the turn of the twentieth century it was not unknown

---

[1] For details of the conflict see B. B. Gilbert, *The evolution of national insurance in Great Britain: the origins of the welfare state* (London, 1966), pp. 401–16; and with a fuller use of the medical press, Ingo Tamm, *Ärzte und gesetzliche Krankenversicherung in Deutschland und England 1880–1914* (Berlin, 1998).

[2] Compulsory insurance of agricultural and forestry workers had previously been at the discretion of local authorities. For figures of total coverage see Tables 9.9 and 9.12 above.

[3] Claudia Huerkamp, *Der Aufstieg der Ärzte im 19. Jahrhundert. Vom gelehrten Stand zum professionellen Experten: Das Beispiel Preussens* (Göttingen, 1985), p. 278. For an abbreviated version in English of this, the most important book on the history of the profession in the nineteenth century, see Huerkamp, 'The making of the medical profession, 1800–1914: Prussian doctors in the nineteenth century', in G. Cocks and K. H. Jarausch (eds.), *German professions, 1800–1950* (New York and Oxford, 1990), pp. 66–84.

for societies to appoint a limited number of doctors to a panel, from which their members could choose. What these various methods had in common were that the number of appointments was strictly limited and that the terms of service, including the remuneration, were laid down by the societies or by the joint management committee of the institute, to whom the doctors were held accountable.[4]

The situation in Germany was fairly similar. It was customary for sickness insurance funds to appoint a single doctor or, if larger, to subdivide their area into districts, appointing a single doctor to each. Unlike England and Wales, where payment on a capitation basis was normal, payment could be either per insured member or per treatment given. A sample survey in 1886 revealed that 40 per cent of funds paid per treatment, but the 60 per cent who paid on a capitation basis tended to be the larger ones.[5]

Although payment on a capitation basis was not unknown in public appointments such as that of Poor Law doctors, it caused growing resentment among insurance doctors as workers became more accustomed to visiting their doctor and thereby depressed the value of the fee per treatment. Their subordination to the workers, who increasingly came to dominate the executive of the local funds, was resented by German doctors even more than British ones, for all German doctors were university educated and considered themselves part of the prestigious *Bildungsbürgertum*, the university-educated middle class. That status was probably not important in Britain until much later in the twentieth century. Compared with their ideal of an independent practice, work for insurance funds brought German doctors loss of independence and of status.

The supply of qualified doctors was also basically similar to the position in England, although with minor differences. One difference lay in the fact that since the 1850s all newly qualified German doctors had to have completed a course of university study in both medicine and surgery. In Britain the qualification required under the Medical Act of 1858 for inclusion on the Medical Register could be acquired by apprenticeship or by study. Study could be in one of several medical schools across the country or in universities, which ranged from Oxford and Cambridge via Scotland to Ireland and operated to very different standards. There were twenty licensing bodies and sixty-one qualifications from medical

---

[4] David G. Green, *Working-class patients and the medical establishment: self-help in Britain from the mid-nineteenth century to 1948* (Aldershot, 1985), pp. 12–14 and 21–7.

[5] Huerkamp, *Aufstieg*, p. 200.

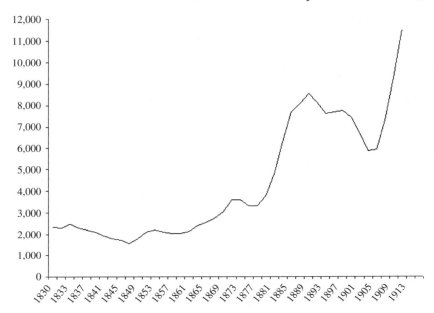

Source: Huerkamp, *Aufstieg,* pp. 62–3.

Figure 13.1. Medical students at German universities, in the winter semester, 1830–1911.

corporations and universities in the UK, all of which provided qualifications accepted for registration. Until 1886 these qualifications could be
either in medicine or surgery.[6] The requirements for the British profession
were thus lower and more diverse, and the status of medical practitioners
less uniform.

Despite these differences there was the basic similarity that the position
of the medical practitioner was much desired, and in neither country was much
effort made to stem the flood of new recruits to the profession. In Germany
the number of medical students rose gradually after 1860 and then very
steeply from 1880 to 1890 before declining and then rising anew after 1905
(see Figure 13.1). From 1876 to 1909 the number of doctors rose by 122.6 per
cent and the ratio per 10,000 inhabitants by 50 per cent. Figures of doctors
on the Medical Register in Britain do not lend themselves to comparison
since they were affected by the indiscriminate admission of established
practitioners immediately after the Medical Act of 1858. Accordingly the

---

[6] Anne Digby, *The evolution of British general practice 1850–1948* (Oxford, 1999), p. 51.

increase from 1861 to 1901 was a mere 14.6 per cent. The lower qualifications required throughout most of this period must go some way to explain the big difference in the number of doctors per 10,000 of population, which at the beginning of the twentieth century was 6.4 in Britain and 4.9 in Germany.[7] Whether one takes the increase in the number of doctors in Germany or the high ratio of doctors to population in Britain, it is clear that in both countries doctors competed with each other in a market that after the mid-1880s was highly favourable to the purchasers of medical services. In both countries the 1890s and early 1900s were a period of heightened grievances on the part of the medical profession. Despite all efforts, the medical profession in England and Wales, organised since the 1850s in the BMA, found it impossible to maintain a common front in their demands for increased fees.[8] The same problem beset the local German medical societies, organised on a national basis since 1873 in the *Deutscher Ärztevereinsbund* (ÄVB), the German League of Medical Societies.

Caught in an unfavourable market situation, British doctors had at this stage nothing to hope for from the State. Their attempts to persuade the General Medical Council to support them in their fight against canvassing and advertising did not touch their conflict with the friendly societies and medical institutes.[9] Among German doctors expectations were different. They had enjoyed a special relationship to the State before 1869. They had been protected from unqualified competition, had relied on an official scale of fees with maxima and minima for every form of treatment, were obliged by law to attend to anyone in urgent need irrespective of ability to pay and could be disciplined by having their licence to practise removed by State authority.[10] That was certainly not the position to which they wished to return, but they tried to obtain the establishment of corporate bodies (*Ärztekammern*) from the State with powers of discipline over all its members. They obtained representative bodies of this kind in a number of states, and finally in 1887 also in Prussia. But these bodies had hardly any teeth, and it was not until 1900, with the establishment of disciplinary tribunals in Prussia, that it became possible to punish gross breaches of professional conduct with serious fines. The threat of these tribunals was used to harass those who repudiated professional solidarity, but these

---

[7] German figures from Statistisches Bundesamt (ed.), *Bevölkerung und Wirtschaft 1872–1972* (Stuttgart and Mainz, 1972), p. 124; British figures from Charles Webster, *The health services since the war* (London, 1996), vol. 2, p. 827.
[8] Green, *Working-class patients*, pp. 27–30.
[9] *Ibid.*, pp. 45–6.   [10] Huerkamp, *Aufstieg*, pp. 242–3 and 255.

threats only rarely led to successful prosecutions. For the effective enforcement of solidarity in the face of the insurance funds, these bodies proved largely useless.[11]

At first, doctors had been mainly preoccupied with increasing their remuneration. The willingness of newly qualified doctors to undercut their more established colleagues in the competition for appointments caused a rethinking of tactics. In the 1890s there was increasing support for the suggestion that patients should have a free choice of doctors in the locality. By providing everyone with a place at the feeding trough, this would meet the needs of the new recruits to the profession and have the additional advantage of appealing to the large majority of the insured. In fact, free choice of doctors had originally been a working-class demand, directed in particular against the close relationship between employer and doctor in factory-based funds. In many localities medical societies were established committed to the introduction of free choice of doctors. Their aim was to negotiate collectively on behalf of their members. Any doctor who accepted the terms negotiated would have the right to practise among insurance fund members. To the extent that they were successful, as they occasionally were, this would lead to a significant change in power relations. The medical society would be in a position to insist on higher rates of pay per patient or per treatment, and this in turn could be expected to persuade those doctors already holding an appointment to drop their initial opposition.

For insurance funds, free choice of doctors had the disadvantage that doctors, eager to attract as many patients as possible, would no longer be reliable defenders of the financial interests of the funds. Free choice of doctors would require other forms of control over doctors in the exercise of their discretion. The vast majority of funds were strongly opposed to the demand.[12]

In this they had the support of the authorities at *Reich* and state level, anxious to protect the financial viability of the insurance funds. In the struggle between the doctors and the funds they were firmly on the side of the latter. As Boetticher, the Secretary of State of the Interior, put it in 1885, 'when all is said and done the sickness insurance law was not meant to be in the interest of doctors but of needy workers'. The Sicknes Insurance Law of

---

[11] *Ibid.*, pp. 254–73. In Baden such powers had existed since 1883. Hamburg and Saxony granted them in 1894 and 1896 respectively, and Prussia's example was followed by Lübeck in 1903 and Bavaria in 1910.

[12] Huerkamp, *Aufstieg*, pp. 224–40, more fully in Tamm, *Ärzte*, pp. 173–88.

1892 specifically affirmed the right of insurance funds to determine that medical treatment should be given only by doctors specifically appointed for the purpose. There was nothing new in that except the perceived need to spell out what had previously been taken for granted. In 1895 the Prussian Minister of Trade confirmed the decision of the Berlin municipal authority to veto a collective contract between eighteen insurance funds and the local medical society, insisting that every fund enter into an individual contract with every doctor in its employ. The annual conference of the ÄVB had demanded the statutory introduction of free choice of doctors since 1899. When the Sickness Insurance Amendment Law of 1903 was under consideration, however, the government declared the moment not ripe for any statutory regulation of doctors' employment, and it carried the *Reichstag* with it. In such matters the doctors found little support from the parties, who were at best ambivalent.[13]

The events of 1903 issued a decisive rebuff to the tactics of the ÄVB, which had relied on resolutions and petitions to influence the public and the legislature. They threw power into the hands of those who advocated militant confrontation of their employers, the insurance funds. The Leipzig League, also known as the Hartmann League after its founder and leading personality, originated in 1900 after a series of local strikes had been broken by the importation of doctors from outside the locality. It aimed at national organisation, the creation of a large strike fund and the systematic use of trade union methods. But it was the events of 1903 that turned it into a serious player. Its membership increased within six months from 8 per cent to 35 per cent of all civilian doctors. Its funds remained separate, but in all other respects it now received recognition as a section of the ÄVB. It used the influential journal, the *Ärztliche Vereinsblatt*, to publish blacklists of insurance funds in dispute with their local doctors and set out to ensure local medical solidarity by means of organisation and recruitment. Those refusing to join had their names published and were put under pressure. In 1904 it called a strike of all local doctors in Leipzig, which was the seat of the largest general local fund. It won a spectacular victory that established the right to collective bargaining, the introduction of free choice from a panel of 375 doctors and an increase in fees. This success was quickly followed up in Cologne.[14]

What distinguished the situation in Germany from similar disputes with friendly societies in England at the time was the decisive role that

---

[13] Huerkamp, *Aufstieg*, pp. 278–9; Tamm, *Ärzte*, pp. 197–215.
[14] Huerkamp, *Aufstieg*, pp. 279–93.

intervention by the local authority could play. The Sickness Insurance Law laid on the local authority an obligation to ensure the provision of medical treatment, and once it became clear that the Leipzig general local fund was unable to recruit a sufficient number of doctors from outside to provide an adequate service, the municipal authority stepped in as arbitrator. It was a peculiarly one-sided form of arbitration, since the local authority could enforce its view on the insurance funds but not on the doctors, and this threw power into the hands of the latter.

By 1909 membership of the Hartmann League had risen to 74.3 per cent; by 1911 to 76.6 per cent of all civilian doctors.[15] As numbers increased, it became easier to enforce measures against black-legs when the local society was in a dispute without having to resort to strike action that damaged patients and troubled the conscience of the profession. The Hartmann League claimed victory in 921 out of 1022 conflicts between 1900 and 1911. The number of places with free choice of doctors greatly increased, especially in the larger towns, although exact numbers are not available. To protect the financial interest of insurance funds medical inspectors were sometimes appointed to check on the work of doctors.[16]

When in 1909 the government issued the first draft of the RVO, which would greatly enlarge the insured population, it confronted a different and more militant organisation than in 1903. Yet it refused to yield to the demand for the statutory introduction of free choice of doctors and adopted a position of neutrality on contracts between doctors and insurance funds. In the event of disagreement between them it proposed conciliation and, if necessary, compulsory arbitration. These proposals were acceptable to neither party, who regarded themselves as victims of a compulsion to which no other parties in a wage dispute had to submit. Supported by the ÄVB, the Hartmann League threatened strike action unless this discriminatory legislation was withdrawn.

A second draft did withdraw the obligation to submit to arbitration, to accept the decision of the arbitrators and the various means by which that decision was to be enforced. It also removed what it considered a justified grievance and required all patients to be given a choice between at least two doctors. But in the event of a doctors' strike, the provincial supervisory authority (*Oberversicherungsamt*) could authorise the payment of increased sick pay instead of the statutory medical treatment and could do so on

---

[15] Huerkamp, *Aufstieg*, Table on p. 283. The degree of organisation, however, varied greatly by regions: *ibid.*, p. 287.

[16] *Ibid.*, pp. 294–301.

the authority of certificates by persons other than registered doctors. Alternatively, it could, in the absence of adequate certification, withhold all benefits in cash or kind, thus setting the doctors at odds with the insured population as a whole. With these provisions the RVO became law in May 1911. The newly insured population would be entitled to medical treatment at the beginning of 1914.

None of this was acceptable to the doctors. The year 1912 thus saw the medical profession in both countries in dispute over the conditions imposed on them by the recent legislation. But while by January 1913 the threatened strike had collapsed in Britain, the crisis of the German insurance system dragged on for another year. An offer of the Ministry of the Interior to act as conciliator was rejected in May, and by September all negotiations between doctors and insurance funds had broken down. The insurance funds protested that by yielding to the demands of the doctors they would be reduced to mere places for the collection of contributions and payment of sick pay.[17] That was of course the position in which British approved societies had been placed already. As the country drifted towards a doctors' general strike, the government intervened once more by calling separate conferences with both sides. On Christmas Day 1913 all parties to the dispute bound themselves for the next ten years to accept what became known as the Berlin Concordat.

Access to insurance practice in Germany was settled by the creation of a local register of all doctors willing to treat the insured. In areas where not all registered doctors were given access, i.e. where there was no free choice of doctors, those admitted were to be chosen by a joint committee drawn from insurance funds and doctors. There was to be at least one doctor to 1,350 of the insured, and to 1,000 if insurance extended to family members. Disagreement over registration or selection would be settled by an equally balanced committee of representatives, chaired by a civil servant. Contracts between insurance funds and individual doctors would be drawn up by a committee composed equally of representatives of the doctors and the funds. That was the most significant of the decisions. It established collective bargaining, with the Hartmann League as one of the recognised parties. Failure to reach agreement was to be followed by arbitration. The decisions of an equally balanced tribunal under an official chairman would be binding and so would its interpretation of existing contracts in cases of dispute. Although the doctors obtained neither the statutory implementation of free choice of doctors nor payment by individual items of

---

[17] Tamm, *Ärzte*, p. 237.

treatment – indeed all existing arrangements were to remain in force for the moment – this machinery of collective bargaining placed the Hartmann League in a position to achieve these points gradually where a strong demand for them existed.[18]

The Berlin Concordat and the final details of the British settlement as incorporated in the National Insurance Amendment Act of 1913 provide the basis for a comparison of the place of doctors in the insurance system of the two countries.

The statutory introduction of free choice of doctors, which had been sought in vain by German doctors since before 1903 and not even obtained in the Berlin Concordat, was obtained by British doctors within three months of the launching of the National Health Insurance Bill in 1911. It was obtained as part of a development that had no German parallel, namely the removal of the provision of medical treatment from the approved societies, placing it in the hands of public authorities in the form of local insurance committees and at national level in the form of Insurance Commissioners responsible to Parliament. After the decision to alter the draft bill in this way the doctors dealt directly with the Chancellor of the Exchequer. The British government made the decisions on how medical treatment was to be provided, which the German government refused to make.

Instead of dealing directly with the doctors, the German government proceeded to create a complex machinery of collective bargaining between insurance funds and doctors, both represented by national federations. It backed this by recourse to conciliation procedures and binding arbitration.

The threat of a strike gave the doctors a massive increase in the level of remuneration in both countries. In Britain the increase, to 8s.6d per patient from an average level of 4s.6d, was around 88 per cent; in Germany it was around 50 per cent.[19] But this was achieved within a very different context. In Germany it was achieved within the semi-permanent framework of collective bargaining, whereas the British medical profession obtained no such framework. Its pay increase was a concession made by the government under the particular political circumstances of 1912. Here is the other

---

[18] Rolf Neuhaus, *Arbeitskämpfe, Ärztestreiks, Sozialreformer. Sozialpolitische Konfliktregelung 1900 bis 1914* (Berlin, 1986), pp. 351–6. This provides a detailed narrative of the conflict, as does Tamm, *Ärzte*. In English see A. Labisch, 'From traditional individualism to collective professionalism: the state, compulsory health insurance, and the panel doctor question in Germany, 1883–1931', in M. Berg and G. Cocks (eds.), *Medicine and modernity: public health and medical care in nineteenth- and twentieth-century Germany* (Cambridge, 1997), pp. 35–54.

[19] Tamm, *Ärzte*, p. 141.

structural difference between the two systems. In Britain the State was a major source of finance and its willingness to pay was the crucial determinant in any financial concessions made to the doctors. In Germany the State did not contribute to the cost of sickness insurance at all and its fixed contribution to invalidity insurance had no implications for the conflict over medical treatment.

These are the important differences. Two other differences are secondary. First, demands for a limit on those entitled to claim insurance-based medical treatment were partly successful in Britain and not at all in Germany. Secondly, in Germany, where payment by individual items of treatment was fairly common, the demand to make it universal failed. In Britain, where it had originally been excluded altogether in favour of capitation payment, the doctors gained a slight concession in that local insurance committees were to be free to introduce it in exceptional circumstances.[20]

Such minor matters should not distract us from the big picture. It is a picture dominated in Britain by the State, which controlled the system largely because it paid for a significant proportion of it and on which expectations were focused. It is a picture of corporate bodies and professional associations in Germany organised on local, regional and national levels and engaged in collective bargaining, with the State reluctant to intervene financially and legislatively. Although chaired by a nominee of the Minister, the Central Committee to oversee the implementation of the Berlin Concordat was not a government body but a committee of the insurance funds and the doctors that were party to the agreement.

These differences were structural and not easily dismantled in the inter-war years. In Britain the level of doctors' pay rested on a special government subsidy extracted in 1912 by the threat of strike action. The government desire to rescind that subsidy in the economic era of the early 1920s was thwarted only by the threat of another strike in 1923. That gained the doctors an impartial inquiry into their salary claims, whose findings were binding on the government and obliged it to continue to find extra money to support doctors' remuneration. In 1931 and 1934, however, the doctors were helpless in the face of government economic cuts.[21] The approved

---

[20] Gilbert, *Evolution*, p. 403. This happened in Manchester and Salford in the 1920s. See N. R. Eder, *National health insurance and the medical profession in Britain, 1913–39* (London, 1982), ch. 6.

[21] For details see B. B. Gilbert, *British social policy 1914–1939* (London, 1970), pp. 271–84 and 296; A. Digby and N. Bosanquet, 'Doctors and patients in an era of national health insurance and private practice, 1913–1938', Econ. HR, 2nd ser. 41 (1988), 75–6.

societies were dominated by the Treasury throughout.[22] In Nazi Germany on the other hand government hostility to the insurance funds with their socialist past led to a strengthening of the doctors in the process of collective bargaining.[23]

In national health insurance the provision of medical treatment was never under the control of the approved societies, as it had been under that of the friendly societies before 1911 and as it remained under that of the German insurance funds both before the conflict of 1911–13 and after. The determination of the level and distribution of expenditure on medical treatment was made in Britain by the State and in Germany by the insurance funds, a distinction that is now attracting much attention. It does not date from the establishment of the National Health Service but goes right back to the origins of national health insurance in 1911.

In subsequent years the contrast became even greater. By 1924 expenditure by German insurance funds on medical treatment exceeded that on cash benefits, and thereafter the ratio tipped increasingly in favour of medical expenditure. In 1970 all employers were obliged to pay their workforce in periods of sickness and the process that converted German insurance funds exclusively into providers of medical treatment was complete.[24] Well before then the National Insurance Act of 1946 had deprived British approved societies of their role in the provision of sick pay, abolishing them altogether and vesting their social security functions in the State. The abolition of these mutual non-profit-making providers of insurance ensured that the decision made in mid-legislation in the summer of 1911, when approved societies were stripped of their control over the provision of medical treatment, cannot now be reversed. With their abolition, the alternative providers of medical treatment to the State are insurance companies, and principally ones with shareholders' interests to consider. It is in those terms that the reform of the National Health Service is now being debated in Britain. Appeals to emulate Germany and other countries with systems of mutual non-profit-making providers too often overlook this crucial difference.

[22] N. Whiteside, 'Regulating markets: the real costs of poly-centric administration under the National Health Insurance scheme, 1912–46', *Public Administration*, 75 (1997), 464–85.

[23] Florian Tennstedt, 'Sozialgeschichte der Sozialversicherung', in Maria Blohmke *et al.* (eds.), *Handbuch der Sozialmedizin* (Stuttgart, 1976), vol. 3, pp. 407–8.

[24] *Ibid.*, pp. 403 and 421.

(B) TUBERCULOSIS OF THE LUNGS

One aspect of national health insurance that owed its existence entirely to imitation of Germany was the funding of institutional care for pulmonary tuberculosis (TB) from the insurance contributions. This had been a feature of German invalidity insurance since the 1890s and attracted the attention of Lloyd George in 1908. Unlike many aspects of the Act of 1911, it had no precedent in the practice of friendly societies.

Such imitations can never be exact. It is worth drawing attention in advance to two differences. German invalidity insurance did not limit institutional care to sufferers from pulmonary TB; that was merely the most prominent of its provision for a number of diseases. They included lupus, which was a tubercular disease, but also alcoholism and sexually transmitted diseases.[25] The provision was at the discretion of the pension boards and was justified in terms of financial prudence. By contrast the similar provision made under the National Insurance Act was in practice confined to pulmonary TB. Nor was it at the discretion of approved societies or local insurance committees. It was a duty laid on them by the Insurance Commissioners, who were responsible for the administration of the Act in each of the component countries of the UK. The provision was not on grounds of financial prudence but of public health. Nor were these the only significant differences, as we shall see. In this, as in other cases of imitation, the transfer from one country to another was to prove highly problematic.

German invalidity insurance developed a particular interest in TB because it was a lingering disease which affected the relatively young and left them incapacitated for several years before they died. Thus, from 1896 to 1899, 21 per cent of all male recipients of invalidity pensions from industry and mining were victims of TB, and 17 per cent from transport and commerce, but in the age group 25–29 the respective figures were 58 per cent and 51 per cent.[26] Medical treatment under sickness insurance

---

[25] In 1912 those suffering from TB of the lungs or larynx constituted 53 per cent of the total patients supported by the pension boards and accounted for 63 per cent of their total expenditure on curative treatment. AN. RVA, 1913, 1. Beiheft, Tables 1 and 2.

[26] The percentage from agriculture was markedly lower. L. Teleky, 'Die Tuberkulose', in A. Gottstein *et al.* (eds.), *Handbuch der Sozialen Hygiene und Gesundheitsfürsorge* (Berlin, 1926), vol. III, pp. 115–402, here p. 121. Important among recent studies is Flurin Condrau, *Lungenheilanstalt und Patientenschicksal. Sozialgeschichte der Tuberkulose in Deutschland und England im späten 19. und frühen 20. Jahrhundert* (Göttingen, 2000), one of the few examples of a monograph comparing Germany and Britain. For a regional study see Sylvelyn Hähner-Rombach, *Sozialgeschichte der Tuberkulose. Vom Kaiserreich bis zum Ende des Zweiten Weltkriegs unter besonderer Berücksichtigung Wüerttembergs* (Stuttgart, 2000).

was about temporary sickness and was intended to restore the insured to work in the statutory thirteen weeks. Even when that period was extended to twenty-six weeks in 1904, it was still inappropriate for a chronic disease such as TB. On the other hand, invalidity pension boards had not been intended to provide anything other than financial support. Because of the gap between the expiry of sickness insurance benefit and the beginning of invalidity pensions the Act of 1889 had, however, permitted pension boards to provide medical treatment for anyone no longer entitled to treatment under sickness insurance whose illness was likely to entitle them to an invalidity pension. In 1891 Hermann Gebhard, director of the pension board for the Hansa Towns, arranged with the sickness insurance funds that the pension board would take over the treatment of TB even in its early stages and continue it for suitable cases on the expiry of the thirteen weeks. There would be no savings for the sickness funds, which would provide financial support for the dependants of the patient up to the amount of their statutory liabilities. The idea was to prevent the insured from becoming long-term invalids. This intervention strained the letter of the law, but received the support of the Imperial Insurance Office. It encouraged other boards to follow suit and in the amending Act of 1899 placed the practice on a legal footing.[27]

The assumption was that TB could be cured by sanatorium treatment or at least that the patient would be able to return to some form of work. The pension boards were following in the wake of a sanatorium movement for the treatment of pulmonary TB that looked back to the pioneering work of Hermann Brehmer, the founder of the first private TB sanatorium in 1854, and more particularly to that of Peter Dettweiler, whose sanatorium at Falkenstein in Taunus dated from 1876, in a mountain location not far from Frankfurt. From the later 1880s those private sanatoria for wealthy patients inspired a philanthropic movement to bring the benefits of the sanatorium to the working class. The initiative came from doctors in local medical societies and from municipalities. On the prompting of its company doctor, the chemical firm BASF also established a sanatorium of its own.

Robert Koch's discovery of the TB bacillus in 1882 had little effect on this sanatorium movement. Dettweiler's sanatorium doctors aimed to increase the body's resistance to the disease by carefully supervised treatment. They merely incorporated the new discovery into their way of thinking, distinguishing between soil (the constitution) and seed (the

[27] Florian Tennstedt, 'Sozialgeschichte der Sozialversicherung', in Maria Blohmke *et al.* (eds.), *Handbuch der Sozialmedizin* (Stuttgart, 1976), vol. 3, pp. 453–4; AN.RVA, 1913, 1. Beiheft, pp. 15–42.

bacillus) and emphasising the role of the former in resisting the spread of the bacillus. Koch's short-lived claim to have found a cure for TB by inoculation with tuberculin was announced in 1890, just as the movement for people's sanatoria was getting under way, but delayed its launch only briefly. Indeed, the realisation that his claim was baseless helped the dissemination of sanatorium treatment. The first 'people's sanatorium' was opened in 1892, once again in Falkenstein near Frankfurt. It was soon followed by others no longer exclusively in mountain regions. The fees were paid by municipal hospitals and soon by sickness funds and pension boards.[28]

By 1895 these local initiatives were sufficiently extensive to justify the launch of a national co-ordinating body, the German Central Committee for the Establishment of Sanatoria for Sufferers from Pulmonary Disease. It was a prestigious body under the patronage of the Empress, with the Chancellor of the day as honorary president.[29] By 1899 there were around thirty-three people's sanatoria. By 1908 the number had risen to ninety-nine, with a total of 10,500 beds.[30]

The pension boards contributed to this development in three ways. They sent patients and paid for their treatment and maintenance, they contributed towards the capital cost of sanatoria and they raised the capital to start sanatoria of their own.[31] They did this by drawing on the reserves which they were obliged to accumulate. The Invalidity Insurance Law of 1899 permitted them to use up to half their funds for purposes that exclusively or predominantly benefited the insured population.[32]

The legislation was based on the assumption that the success rate of the sanatorium treatment would justify the expenditure from the insurance funds. Gebhard had originally argued the case for the intervention of pension boards from estimates of relative costs, but, although the costs in Württemberg regularly exceeded any savings from pensions, the pension board took no notice of cost/benefit calculations.[33] Nor did the Imperial

[28] I. Langerbeins, *Lungenheilanstalten in Deutschland 1854–1945* (Cologne, 1979), pp. 24–40; Condrau, *Lungenheilanstalt*, pp. 119–23.

[29] Condrau, *Lungenheilanstalt*, pp. 104–11.   [30] Langerbeins, *Lungenheilanstalten*, p. 59.

[31] Condrau, *Lungenheilanstalt*, pp. 87–8; Adelheid Gräfin zu Castell Rüdenhausen, 'Zur Erhaltung und Mehrung der Volkskraft', in I. Behnken (ed.), *Stadtgesellschaft und Kindheit im Prozess der Zivilisation* (Opladen, 1990), p. 29. The pension board for Württemberg, having originally contributed towards the capital cost of a sanatorium, found that this gave it too little control. It subsequently bought it. Hähner-Rombach, *Sozialgeschichte*, pp. 174–9 and 189–90.

[32] Tennstedt, 'Sozialgeschichte der Sozialversicherung', p. 454.

[33] Hähner-Rombach, *Sozialgeschichte*, pp. 164–5 and 197.

Insurance Office put pressure on them to do so.[34] It accepted the forecast that after thirteen weeks of treatment an increasing proportion of patients, as many as 92 per cent by 1914, would be able to return to work for at least another five years. In retrospect, the evidence gave a very different picture. Of the 1908 cohort 66 per cent were not drawing a pension one year later; after five years it was 48 per cent.[35]

Those results would probably not have justified the expenditure, but sanatoria were generally recommended in terms that by-passed these awkward facts. The pension board accepted the views of the sanatorium doctors, who naturally presented their work in the best light. Sanatoria selected patients in the early stages of the disease, on the ground that these were most likely to benefit from a treatment designed to build up their constitution through rest in the open air, a good diet and confidence-building regimes. Success was measured in terms of weight-gain or general well-being. There was no rival treatment that held out any better prospects for individual patients, and it was the temporary restoration of individual patients that constituted the aim of the sanatoria.[36]

From the point of view of public health this concentration on the mildest cases was quite marginal, and after the turn of the century criticism to this effect became more common. Public health reformers of the bacteriological school wished first and foremost to prevent the spread of infection from acute cases. But their proposals for compulsory notification of the disease and of patients' changes of address, together with compulsory isolation of acute cases, were rejected by the Prussian legislature in 1905.[37] Hope was placed instead on educating patients during their temporary stay in the sanatorium in a hygienic life-style designed to prevent the spread of infection. That meant a campaign against such proletarian habits as spitting. The lasting infectiousness of dried sputum was one of the messages constantly reiterated for the education of the tubercular, and patients were

[34] During the debates on the RVO in 1911 it transpired, however, that the RVA had expressed concern that the rising trend of expenditure on medical treatment was exceeding the permitted measure. In response to this the legislation released the pension boards from the requirement to obtain a saving on the cost of pensions. A proposal that expenditure in excess of 7 per cent of total contributions could be vetoed by the RVA ran into objections from the pension boards. The RVA was therefore merely given an undefined right to raise objections. In Berlin and the port cities expenditure was at this time running at 25 per cent of total contributions. SBRT, 12.LP, vol. 267, 180. Sitzung, 20 May 1911, p. 6958.

[35] Condrau, *Lungenheilanstalt*, p. 148. These were still surprisingly good results, but admission to sanatoria was often intended to prevent further deterioration; it did not always indicate entitlement to an invalidity pension at that stage. Teleky, 'Tuberkulose', p. 243.

[36] Langerbeins *Lungenheilanstalten*, p. 41. [37] Condrau, *Lungenheilanstalt*, pp. 82–3 and 143–5.

taught to use spittoons and portable bottles. Far less attention was paid to cross-infection from droplets during sneezing, coughing and even ordinary breathing. It was easier to label TB as the disease of the working class, spread through its unhygienic habits, than to accept the uncomfortable fact that infection was spread among all classes in ways that were impossible to prevent.[38]

That social insurance made sanatorium treatment, once the privilege of the well-to-do, available to the working class was a matter of great pride and overrode any doubts that were occasionally expressed about the appropriateness of the treatment. The workers themselves, whose money it was and who had a voice in the running of the pension boards, if a distinctly subordinate one, appreciated the prospect of thirteen weeks of rest and good food, as long as the needs of dependants were met, as they mostly were under the Law of 1899. Until the 1920s, when work-regimes were introduced from Britain, German sanatoria considered strict rest in the open air as the most important means of recuperation.[39]

In 1906 the Central Committee dropped the exclusive reference to sanatoria from its title and described itself as 'for the Fight against Tuberculosis'. After 1908 no new sanatoria were built. National coverage seems to have been achieved. The number of beds in existing sanatoria continued to increase up to 1914, but attention increasingly focused on providing care through dispensaries. These were centres for diagnosis and advice that used women as volunteer home visitors. In deference to the financial interests of doctors and unlike their French prototypes they provided no treatment.

The necessary finance for dispensaries, as previously for sanatoria, was raised by the Central Committee and the local societies under its aegis. There the new rich rubbed shoulders with the nobility, the health experts and those in high political office. They were rewarded for their generosity with honorific titles. Control lay in the hands of ministers, in particular of Friedrich Althoff, the Prussian minister for education and medical affairs, who might be described as the grey eminence behind the TB campaign. Althoff used these voluntary bodies to circumvent the opposition of the Prussian finance minister and the Prussian legislature to anything that required additional taxation. The German movement for the establishment of dispensaries had originated in 1899 in Halle. It benefited from Althoff's appointment of its originator to a key post at Berlin's leading hospital with instructions to launch a philanthropic movement for

---

[38] *Ibid.*, pp. 151–8.   [39] *Ibid.*, pp. 129–31; Teleky, 'Tuberkulose', pp. 131–4.

dispensaries in the poorer quarters of the city. The Central Committee received some State funds on an *ad hoc* basis, but the whole movement got under way without the need to challenge the political objections to regular subsidies to the municipalities. Like Prussia, Württemberg also made no State contributions towards the establishment of dispensaries before 1922. By 1914 there were close on 2,000 dispensaries located in practically every city and in many other districts across the Empire.[40]

All this was part of an international movement and had its parallels in other countries. 1898 saw the founding of the 'National Association for the Prevention of Consumption and other forms of Tuberculosis' in Britain in imitation of the German Central Committee of 1895, and of similar bodies in Pennsylvania (1892) and France (1891). The Association appealed for funds to establish sanatoria and to educate TB sufferers in a hygienic life-style.[41] By the later 1890s TB sanatoria were being opened in Britain in direct imitation of the German ones. Some were for middle-class patients not rich enough to go abroad; others for the working class and the poor. The latter were either philanthropic foundations or established by Poor Law authorities and both kinds relied heavily on patients paid for from the rates.[42]

The international anti-TB movement spawned congresses, where Germany took a prominent part. One held in Paris in 1905 actually voted in favour of compulsory invalidity insurance to combat the disease. The British delegates reported strongly in favour of the German sanatorium movement, and the Local Government Board thereupon commissioned a report, which turned out to be a paean of praise for the work of the German pension boards.[43] This was published in 1908 and was but one of several publications and conference resolutions around this time that

---

[40] In addition to 1,145 dispensaries, this includes 604 similar places in Baden, 154 under the pension board of Thuringia and 87 in Bavaria. Teleky, 'Tuberkulose', Table 108 and generally pp. 263–318. On the politics, see P. Weindling, 'Hygienepolitik als sozialintegrative Strategie im späten Kaiserreich', in A. Labisch and R. Spree (eds.), *Medizinische Deutungsmacht im sozialen Wandel des 19. und frühen 20. Jahrhunderts* (Bonn, 1989), pp. 37–55; Castell Rüdenhausen, 'Volksgesundheit', pp. 26–42. On Württemberg, Hähner-Rombach, *Sozialgeschichte*, p. 87. Additional information on finance in Condrau, *Lungenheilanstalt*, pp. 104–11.

[41] Condrau, *Lungenheilanstalt*, pp. 103–18 for a detailed comparison of the British and German organisations. On the National Association see also Linda Bryder, *Below the magic mountain: a social history of tuberculosis in twentieth century Britain* (Oxford, 1988), passim. Its third proclaimed objective was to stamp out TB in cattle.

[42] Bryder, *Below the magic mountain*, pp. 22–9, corrected in the light of Michael Worboys, 'The sanatorium treatment for consumption in Britain', in J. V. Pickstone (ed.), *Medical innovations in historical perspective* (London, 1992), pp. 47–67.

[43] H. Timbrell Bulstrode MD, *Report on sanatoria for consumption and certain other aspects of the tuberculosis question*, in *Supplement to Local Government Board, 35th Annual Report of the Medical Officer for 1905–6*, BPP 1908 Cd.3657 XXVII, 1.

attested to an interest in TB. Yet Lloyd George's inclusion of a sanatorium benefit in the National Insurance Bill owed little to this, except for the welcome it received when the Bill was published in May 1911.

The starting point for the British sanatorium benefit was Lloyd George's visit to Germany to look at German invalidity insurance as a possible solution to the problems of the under-seventies, left untouched by the Old Age Pensions Act. He was impressed by what he was told there about the contribution of invalidity insurance to the provision of TB sanatoria. It chimed in with his own preoccupation with a disease from which his father had died. The outcome was a proposal to set aside 1s.3d a year per insured person from the insurance fund for the sanatorium treatment of TB, to contribute a capital sum of £1.5 million towards the building of sanatoria and 1d per insured person for research. The proposal was based on a widespread though certainly not a universal belief among doctors at the time that tuberculosis was curable, but it ignored the many doubts about the effectiveness of sanatorium treatment. In fact, the growth of sanatoria in Britain was beginning to level off and the government initiative gave it renewed impetus.[44]

This unexpected initiative was at first welcomed by all parties but soon ran into objections. The provision of sanatoria would tie up much capital when it was far from certain that they provided the best form of treatment then or in the future. Moreover, treatment under an insurance scheme limited to a part of the population only seemed an inappropriate response to a disease that was by far the most important cause of death in the population as a whole. From the opposition benches Austen Chamberlain proposed at one stage to remove the sanatorium benefit altogether from the bill on the grounds that 'what you are proposing in this case is to carry out a health campaign for stamping out a particular disease at the expense of the Insurance Fund. That health campaign ought to be conducted, but . . . it ought to be dealt with by a separate measure and out of different resources.' Joseph Rowntree, the philanthropist and Liberal MP, added, 'We want a system whereby this treatment . . . shall easily be extended, not to one class of the community but to all classes.' Others objected to the privileging of one disease, however widespread.[45]

Lloyd George's response was to move towards greater inclusiveness in so far as that was possible within the limits of insurance. As finally passed, the

---

[44] 5 *Hansard* 25 (4 May 1911) 625 for Lloyd George on curability; also Bryder, *Below the magic mountain*, pp. 38–9. Worboys, 'Sanatorium treatment', pp. 61–5, for the contemporary controversy.
[45] 5 *Hansard* 28 (12 July 1911) 382–456.

Act authorised insurance committees to provide treatment for insured persons 'suffering from tuberculosis or any other such disease'.[46] They could do so 'in sanatoria and other institutions' as well as 'otherwise', i.e. at home.[47] At the discretion of the local insurance committee treatment could be extended to the dependants of the insured. This was the only instance where the Act permitted the inclusion of dependants in the medical benefit, or indeed provided specialist institutional treatment. 'We have practically engaged ourselves to a real national campaign against consumption', was Lloyd George's gloss on this concession.[48]

Once the Act was passed it became the task of a departmental committee to turn this deliberate vagueness into a policy. Its chairman was Waldorf Astor, an MP connected with the National Association for the Prevention of Tuberculosis. The committee took the trend towards greater inclusiveness well beyond the limit of an insurance scheme, for it laid down the principle that treatment should be available for the whole community. It placed administrative responsibility with county councils and county boroughs, while leaving them free to delegate some aspects to the lower tier of local authorities.[49]

The government accepted these recommendations. In addition to the money already made available to the insurance committees, it provided local authorities with a sum of money approximately equal to half the estimated cost of treating non-insured persons, including the dependants of the insured. It also provided capital grants for the necessary institutions over and above the £1.5 million already envisaged in the National Insurance Act. By 1913 what had begun as part of an insurance scheme for workers earning less than £160 p.a. had become a comprehensive policy to combat TB across the nation. Notification of TB cases by medical practitioners had been introduced on a voluntary basis in an increasing number of local authorities since 1899 and it became compulsory after 1903 in certain authorities and institutions. Now it was extended to the whole country.

---

[46] This extension of the scope of the Bill was a mere gesture designed to meet the objections that had been made. In practice the provision for treatment, as distinct from research, was confined to the treatment of pulmonary TB. Gilbert, *Evolution*, p. 394. See also the terms of reference of the Departmental Committee on Tuberculosis referred to below.

[47] 'The result of the wording of the Act itself is that the expression "sanatorium benefit" is not used in the restricted sense of a course of treatment carried out in an institution called a sanatorium.' Departmental Committee on Tuberculosis. *Interim Report*, p. 9, BPP 1912–3 Cd.6164 LXVIII.

[48] 5 *Hansard* 29 (4 August 1911) 735–6; National Insurance Act 1911, sections 16 and 17. In Germany insurance funds had discretion to extend all forms of medical treatment to dependants.

[49] Departmental Committee on Tuberculosis, *Interim Report, Final Report*, vols. I and II, BPP 1912–3 Cd.6164, Cd.6641, Cd.6654 XLVIII.

That was ten years earlier than in Prussia, although Württemberg had introduced a fairly extensive requirement in 1910. The complexity of legislation on compulsory notification makes detailed comparison difficult. In any case the information provided was considered unreliable everywhere.[50]

All local authorities were to provide dispensaries headed by a tuberculosis officer and staffed by nurses. They were to act as diagnostic centres and direct patients to the most suitable form of treatment. Treatment could be in sanatoria but could also be at home or in 'shelters'. Secondly, local authorities were to arrange for the provision of sanatoria, using whatever facilities already existed and adding to them as needed. Thirdly, there were to be voluntary care committees to support the work of the dispensaries. Far from privileging sanatoria, the proposals placed the dispensary at the heart of the system in line with up-to-date ideas.[51]

The acceptance of the committee's recommendations meant that in future existing sanatoria could rely on a steady income, as local authorities rented a greater part of their accommodation. New sanatoria and extensions to hospitals were also opened across the country.

The figures in Table 13.1 show the remarkable increase in the provision of beds for sanatorium treatment of TB resulting from the acceptance of the recommendations of the Astor Committee. The great disparity compared with Germany that had existed on the eve of the National Insurance Act was more than made up by 1920.

In contrast to Germany, this ample supply of sanatorium beds was not restricted to patients in an early stage of the illness. Many acute cases were, however, still cared for in Poor Law institutions.[52] The same was even more true of Germany.

In 1911 dispensaries had existed in England and Wales only in some pioneering places. Their number had been greatly increased by 1920. Yet contrary to what one might have expected from the emphasis that the Astor Committee had laid on their provision, their number still compared badly with those in Germany, where a considerable increase had also occurred. See Table 13.2.

The significance of the sanatorium benefit in the 1911 National Insurance Act lies therefore mainly in the development to which it gave

---

[50] Bryder, *Below the magic mountain*, pp. 40–3, 73 and 103–4; Condrau, *Lungenheilanstalt*, pp. 84–5; Hähner-Rombach, *Sozialgeschichte*, pp. 88 and 240–3.

[51] *Interim and final reports. Departmental committee on Tuberculosis.*

[52] Bryder, *Below the magic mountain*, p. 79.

Table 13.1. *Beds for tuberculosis treatment, excluding Poor Law institutions*

		Beds	Population per bed
1911	Germany	14,079	4,603
1911	England and Wales	2,769[a]	13,050
1919	Germany	16,769	3,751[b]
1920[c]	England and Wales	15,781	2,360[d]

Notes:

[a] Worboys argues convincingly that the official figure for England in 1911 of 5,500 beds, which could be made available to insurance patients receiving the planned sanatorium benefit, included beds in isolation hospitals and in proposed temporary accommodation, and that there was also some double counting: p. 59.

[b] Based on population prior to loss of territories under the Treaty of Versailles.

[c] The figures relate to March 1920 and are therefore not significantly later than for Germany 1919.

[d] Based on civilian population only. If based on total population, it would be 2,379. The difference, when compared with Germany is not significant.

Source: Langerbeins, *Lungenheilsanstalten*, p. 106; Worboys, 'Sanatorium treatment', Appendix.

Table 13.2. *Tuberculosis dispensaries*

1912	Germany	1,250
1911	England and Wales	64
1919	Germany	3,048
1920	England and Wales	398

Source: Teleky, 'Tuberkulose', pp. 266–7; Bryder, *Below the magic mountain*, p. 34; First Annual Report, Chief Medical Officer, *Ministry of Health 1919–20*, BPP 1920 Cmd.978 XVII, 577.

rise outside national insurance. By the anomalies that it created, it served to pump-prime provisions for the treatment of TB on a national basis. By 1921 the sanatorium benefit was so anomalous that it was altogether removed from national insurance. County councils and county borough councils assumed full responsibility for the prevention and treatment of TB.[53]

In the previous year the Medical Research Committee, which had owed its existence to the 1d per head from the insurance fund, had also severed all connection with insurance. It was thereafter financed directly by the Exchequer and renamed the Medical Research Council under its own

[53] *Ibid.*, pp. 70–1.

charter. In 1911 the Insurance Commissioners, who then controlled the disposal of the money, had already obtained a legal ruling that research did not have to be exclusively on TB. Between 1918 and 1947 neither the Medical Research Council nor its predecessor undertook any major epidemiological study into the disease. Important as the 1911 Act had been in initiating significant State support for medical research, here too it served to pump-prime more comprehensive developments.[54]

It should be added that in neither country did the introduction of sanatorium treatment, or indeed of any other therapy prior to BCG inoculation after World War II, lead to any sudden drop in the steady long-term decline of death rates from tuberculosis.[55]

These parallel histories prompt two reflections. Although Lloyd George had begun by largely copying German invalidity insurance, while adding some provision for research, it had not been possible to return to the frame of mind that had prompted German policy in the 1890s. TB was no longer regarded merely as a threat to the finances of workers' insurance. It was also considered a threat to the health and efficiency of the nation. German pension boards had been permitted to spend their funds on the treatment of TB. The British legislation was not permissive; the Act made a statutory allocation of funds specifically for the purpose. In other words, British policy was *dirigiste* in a way that German policy had not been and still was not in 1914.

Nor did the implications of the new perspective on TB end there. Sanatoria for those in the early stages of the disease would need to be supplemented by other measures and institutions. For that purpose neither the finance nor the administrative structures of national insurance were comprehensive enough, and comprehensiveness of nationwide coverage had become the issue. Provision against TB therefore became the responsibility of the comprehensive network of public health authorities, whose remit was the nation as a whole. Here is the second important difference. In Britain that responsibility was a statutory obligation imposed on county and county borough councils and subsidised from central government funds. There was no statutory obligation or regular State finance in Germany. With the help of official encouragement, provision was left to voluntary action or municipal discretion.[56] In these matters Britain was the

---

[54] A. L. Thomson, *Half a century of medical research*, vol. 1, *Origins and policy of the Medical Research Council (UK)* (London, 1973), pp. 1–54; Bryder, *Below the magic mountain*, p. 98.

[55] Condrau, *Lungenheilanstalt*, pp. 40–6.

[56] In 1913 local authorities provided just over half the German dispensaries. Teleky, 'Tuberkulose', p. 267.

land of obligatory public provision and State finance; Germany the one that relied on discretionary or voluntary action.

This was not the only occasion on which a serious public health problem was financed by German invalidity insurance. The willingness of the German pension boards to provide medical treatment for long-term illnesses had never been entirely limited to TB. It was to include the provision of advice centres (*Beratungsstellen*) for sexually transmitted diseases, similar to TB dispensaries. The original initiative in 1913 was once again taken by the pension board for the Hansa Towns. With the encouragement of the Imperial Insurance Office this example was followed during the war by most others. They provided soldiers with advice and supervised their treatment. What had originally been intended only for the military became available almost at once to the whole insured population and their families, and after the war to the population as a whole. Treatment was obligatory and provided by registered doctors. The cost was met by the insurance funds. Once again the British response to the problem was to treat it as an issue of public health along the accepted lines. The Public Health (VD) Regulation of 1916 made it the duty of all county and county borough councils to provide free treatment centres for sexually transmitted diseases and a free diagnostic service. These were in effect based on the local hospital. Of the cost 75 per cent was met by the Treasury and 25 per cent from local rates.[57]

We are therefore dealing with a more general difference between the two countries. Germany repeatedly relied on its social insurance system for provision to deal with what in Britain were regarded as matters of public health. The distinction between a public health matter that affected the whole population and insurance-based medical treatment, which was a fundamental principle of British policy, was never accepted as such in Germany.

---

[57] For Germany L. Sauerteig, *Krankheit, Sexualität, Gesellschaft: Geschlechtskrankheiten und Gesundheitspolitik in Deutschland im 19. und frühen 20. Jahrhundert* (Stuttgart, 1999), pp. 166–86 and 449–50, with a brief reference to Britain. For England see David Evans, 'Tackling the "hideous scourge": the creation of VD treatment centres in early twentieth century Britain', *Social History of Medicine*, 5 (1992), 413–33. The chapter on syphilis in Peter Baldwin, *Contagion and the state in Europe, 1830–1930*, is primarily concerned with the choice between compulsory and voluntary treatment.

14

Contributions and benefits in the national insurance era

It is time to turn from comparison of the benefit systems as they existed by 1911, including British non-contributory old age pensions, to a comparison of contributions and benefits provided.

(A) CONTRIBUTIONS

Little time need be spent on the contributions. In Britain they were 4d a week for men and 3d a week for women, to which the employer added 3d a week and the State added two-ninths of the total joint contribution for men and one-quarter for women. The only exception was that the contribution of those whose wages were below 2s.6d a day was reduced and that of their employer proportionately increased. In contrast to this relative uniformity the German contributions consisted of a percentage of wages, which could vary between insurance funds. That makes comparison of the level of contributions difficult.

There is a further problem. British contributions to health insurance covered sickness and disablement, whereas in Germany sickness and invalidity required separate contributions, each levied as a percentage of wages but calculated in different ways. For invalidity pensions, contributions were divided equally between workers and employers with a uniform State subsidy; for sickness insurance, workers paid two-thirds of the contributions and the State paid none.

It is therefore not surprising that German contributions were much higher than those for British health insurance. For German sickness insurance alone, contributions in 1913 represented on average 2.44 per cent of wages. For the British contribution of 4d a week to have represented the same percentage of wages, the wage would have had to be as low as 13s.8d a week. That is well below even the 15s that the poorest rural labourer

Plate 14.1. A German insurance stamp issued on 1 January 1891 under the Invalidity and Old Age Insurance Law of 1889. Note the name of the territorial pension board and the number of the wage group. Source: *Die Beitragsmarken der deutschen gesetzlichen Rentenversicherung* (Frankfurt, 1974), p. 13.

Plate 14.2. A British national health insurance stamp issued on 1 January 1912 under Part 1 of the National Insurance Act 1911. Contributions towards German sickness insurance were not paid by means of stamps. The idea was copied from German pensions insurance. Source: *National Archive*, PIN10/18 and 10/11.

Plate 14.3. A British national unemployment insurance stamp issued on 1 January 1912 under Part 2 of the National Insurance Act 1911. Source: *National Archive*, PIN10/18 and 10/11.

Plate 14.4. A British national health and pensions insurance stamp issued on 1 January 1926 under the Widows, Orphans and Old Age Contributory Pensions Act 1925. This is the first stamp which, like the German stamp, was for pension entitlement. Source: *National Archive*, PIN10/18 and 10/11.

might have earned, not to mention the 20s that would have characterised extreme poverty in urban England. And the German figure was an average not an extreme.

That conclusion is little modified by yet another difference between the two systems. German contributions covered a death grant. In Britain this would have cost on average a further 2d a week in premiums for separate burial insurance.

(B) BENEFITS

Comparison is complicated by the fact that in Germany invalidity and old age pensions had been available since 1891, so that by 1908 a total of 1,476 million marks had been paid out. In that year there were over one million German pensioners.[1]

None of the British benefits were available before 1909. No comparison of the number of pensions or of the sums spent is therefore possible before that date and it makes no sense before 1911, when Britain at last had a workable old age pensions system shorn of the pauper disqualification in the original Act. Disablement benefit under the National Insurance Act of 1911 became available only in 1913.

That leaves little time before war-time inflation eroded the real value of the sums paid out. They had to be supplemented in a variety of ways sooner or later, but usually later. The whole subject became entangled with provisions for those disabled or widowed in the war. Germany's post-war inflation was so severe that by 1923 invalidity insurance had totally broken down and had to be reconstructed when the currency crisis was over. It is therefore difficult to find any basis on which to compare the way in which the systems actually affected the population of the two countries. It is possible to compare intentions but not achievements.

With this proviso in mind, let us look at the benefits. I shall use the exchange rate of 1s = 1 M, as was used by W. H. Dawson from whom most of these figures are drawn.[2]

---

[1] According to the official statistics the exact figure of pensioners in receipt of invalidity pensions and of the very similar *Krankenrenten* (pensions paid to those still incapable of work after exhausting their twenty-six weeks' entitlement to sickness insurance benefit) was 1,118,749. The 1,476 million marks is the total paid out in pensions since 1891 as calculated to the nearest million. The figures are calculated from QS,E, pp. 152–3.

[2] The calculations in E. H. Phelps Brown and Margaret H. Browne, *A century of pay* (London, 1968), Table 2, are based on an exchange rate of £1 = 20.45 M. That rate would slightly reduce the value of the German benefits in Table 14.1.

Sickness benefits under the German legislation has been described in chapter 9. There comparisons were drawn with those provided by friendly societies under voluntary insurance. We are now in a position to draw comparisons between the compulsory insurance systems of the two countries.

(i) Sick pay

Since 1904, this was paid in Germany for twenty-six weeks. That was the same period as under the British Act. It followed the German rule, previously quite unknown to friendly societies, that nothing was paid for the first three days. Any comparison of levels of sick pay, however, encounters the difference between the amounts paid in Germany on a graduated scale according to the rate of wages and the uniform amounts paid in Britain irrespective of wage levels. The British scales distinguished merely between men and women, a distinction that did not need to be spelt out in the German case but was built into the system by the lower wages that women generally earned.

In Britain sick pay was 10s a week for men and 7s.6d for women.[3] In Germany sick pay by the local and the factory funds, which between them insured the vast majority of workers (see Table 8.2 above), could vary from 6s to 15s a week. In 1910 the average actually paid by all funds was 7s.6d a week and 9s a week by factory funds, which paid the most. Before 1911, the general level of payment was therefore below the British scale, while the highest-paid German workers obtained somewhat more.[4]

(ii) Death grant

Among the statutory benefits provided by British national health insurance there was no parallel to the death grant that formed part of German benefits.[5] The reason for this has already been explained. The cost of funerals had always been voluntarily insured in England to a far greater

---

[3] This difference reflected a difference in workers' contributions between 4d a week for men and 3d a week for women.

[4] W. H. Dawson, *Social insurance in Germany 1883–1911* (London, 1912), pp. 52 and 54. Those receiving more than the British level of 10s paid a weekly contribution of between 6¾d and 8½d, compared with the 4d paid in Britain. To this 4d was added 3d a week from the employer and a State contribution of two-ninths of the total benefit. In Germany employers paid only half the amount paid by workers and there was no State contribution at all. This explains the higher level of the workers' contribution.

[5] See pp. 230–1 above for details.

extent than any other contingency and continued on that basis. From around 1914 the number of burial insurance policies in force exceeded the total population of the country. This in itself tells us little about the number of the insured, but evidence for 1920 suggests that this kind of insurance was practically universal among the working class. On average 2d would have to be added for this item to the 4d per week that British workers paid for their compulsory insurance.[6]

(iii) Maternity benefit

Both countries provided maternity benefit, but on such different principles as to make comparison of rates of benefit hardly appropriate. The German maternity grant was paid at the same rates as sick pay for six weeks after child-birth, but only to insured women workers.[7] The British grant of 30s, equal to that received in Germany by those earning 18s a week, was paid to the wives of all insured workers.[8]

(iv) Medical attendance and medicine

These were provided under both schemes. In Germany this might be in hospitals, in which case sick pay for dependants was paid at only half the normal rate. Except for tuberculosis, no hospital treatment was provided under the British Act. The voluntary hospitals mostly continued to take patients without payment, as did all Poor Law infirmaries.[9]

(v) Discretionary benefits

In both countries insurance funds were permitted to provide a range of these, if they could afford them. In Germany the most important was the extension of medical treatment to family dependants of the insured. Only the best local funds could afford this before 1914, and there is no comprehensive information on the extent to which this happened. The large

---

[6] Paul Johnson, *Saving and spending: the working-class economy in Britain 1870–1939* (Oxford, 1985), pp. 22–5, provides a detailed survey of the evidence.

[7] This was connected to the prohibition of the employment of women after child-birth under the GewO. See chapter 6 above.

[8] Dawson, *Social insurance*, pp. 49–52.

[9] The best introduction to British hospital provision is still Brian Abel-Smith, *The hospitals 1800–1948* (London, 1964), complemented by Robert Pinker, *English hospital statistics 1861–1938* (London, 1966).

Leipzig general local fund, established in 1886, provided it from the start in return for additional contributions. In Silesia 40 per cent of all insured members were obtaining it in 1896; in the Cologne administrative district 25 per cent in 1904.[10] By 1930, when it became obligatory, it had already been almost universally available.[11]

British friendly society members had for a long time made arrangements for their dependants in return for additional contributions, mostly through medical institutes. But with the short-lived exception of treatment for TB, it was not an option available under the National Insurance Act.

Medical institutes, like friendly societies, could become approved societies in national health insurance, although that was a grudging concession and limited to the ones already in existence in 1911. They continued to provide services for the dependants of those who were now statutorily insured and to charge a regular subscription additional to the national health insurance contribution. But they were marginalised within the statutory scheme and found it hard to recruit additional members. That in turn made it difficult to expand their treatment of dependants. The steady increase in the provision for dependants up to 1911 was followed by stagnation in the era of national health insurance. In 1913 the total of 'uninsured' members of medical institutes was 138,600; in 1929 it was 142,000.[12] In 1913 it would probably not have compared badly with the total of dependants provided with treatment by German insurance funds. In 1929, when the coverage in Germany was almost total, the contrast was huge.

What had happened? In Germany, where provision for dependants had been an option for the funds under statutory insurance and contributions were a percentage of wages, the rising wages of workers since 1914 were translated into rising contributions to their insurance funds. With treatment for dependants as the most popular of the optional benefits, it became increasingly available. In Britain, where medical treatment was financed by the Treasury, the commitment to economy by successive governments in the 1920s never allowed the extension of treatment to dependants to be seriously considered.

[10] Claudia Huerkamp, *Der Aufstieg der Ärzte im 19. Jahrhundert* (Göttingen, 1985), pp. 204–5.

[11] Florian Tennstedt, 'Sozialgeschichte der Sozialversicherung', in Maria Blohmke *et al.* (eds.), *Handbuch der Sozialmedizin* (Stuttgart, 1976), vol. 3, p. 401.

[12] Figures from the returns of the Registrar of Friendly Societies quoted in David G. Green, *Working-class patients and the medical establishment: self-help in Britain from the mid-nineteenth century to 1948* (Aldershot, 1985), p. 168. For the medical institutes and the discrimination they experienced under national health insurance, see *ibid.*, pp. 151–74.

In 1926 the Royal Commission on National Health Insurance claimed that the cost of medical benefit would be more than doubled by the inclusion of dependants and added that such large expenditure could not be contemplated in present circumstances. But irrespective of financial considerations, they opposed such an addition to health insurance on grounds of policy. 'We consider', they wrote, 'that medical provision for dependants should form an integral part of any scheme of general health services, administered by the Local Authorities .... Medical service for dependants is too large a problem to be considered apart from medical services for the whole working-class and, perhaps, middle-class popula-tion.' In support of their view they quoted the evidence of the National Conference of Friendly Societies. This had pointed out that merely to extend medical benefit to dependants of insured persons would still leave at least 1.5 million unprovided for.[13]

Between 1911 and 1913 recognition of the inappropriateness of restricting treatment for TB merely to the insured population had led the government to accept a scheme administered by the local authorities for everyone.[14] Now that the political climate had changed, the best was made to serve as the enemy of the good. Until the introduction of the National Health Service in 1948 dependants of British workers had to rely overwhelmingly on the out-patients' departments of voluntary hospitals, dispensaries, doctors' clubs, the public medical service and other forms of charity or providence.[15] Those approved societies that could afford to give additional benefits opted for glasses or dental care.

(vi) Invalidity and old age

For cash benefits available after the expiration of sickness benefit, three points have been selected to calculate German invalidity pension levels. Following Dawson's example, the first is for a period of 500 weeks of contributions (roughly ten years), while the third is for what was at the time officially described as an average period of working capacity, i.e. 1,763 weeks or roughly thirty-four years. That period could not have been reached by anyone before war and inflation transformed the scene. I have

---

[13] *Report, Royal Commission on National Health Insurance*, pp. 161–5, BPP 1926 Cmd.2596, XIV, 311.
[14] See chapter 13, section (b) above.
[15] This is no doubt a defective list. It should, however, dispel any impression that might have been created in that the medical institutes were the only form of provision. For some of the alternatives see the brief survey in Political and Economic Planning, *The British health services* (London, 1937), pp. 149–54.

Table 14.1. *Pension levels per week*

		British	German		
			Minimum	Maximum	Difference as percentage of minimum
Old age pension		5s	2s.1d	4s.5d	108 per cent
Disablement or	c.10 years	5s	2s.5d	4s	68 per cent
invalidity pension	c.24 years	5s	2s.10d	5s.8d	102 per cent
after	c.34 years	5s	3s.2d	7s	122 per cent

Note:
The German figures were originally given in annual sums. Percentage differences were first calculated and weekly figures then rounded up or down to the nearest penny.
Source: calculated from Dawson, Social insurance, pp. 143–5.

also inserted a mid-way stage of 1,200 weeks or roughly twenty-four years, which is the longest period of contributions that would have been possible by 1914.[16] The figures are the same for men and women, but in practice women would have been towards the lower end of the scale.[17]

To inquire into the income available to a married couple, although more realistic, would take us even further into the realm of conjecture. Only for the British old age pension is it possible to state a figure (10s), and even that was progressively reduced for those earning between £21 and £31.10s. For German old age pensions the figure depended on whether the wife had been a contributor in her own right. For invalidity pensions or disablement benefit the couple received a double sum only if the wife had been a contributor in her own right and both husband and wife were suffering from loss of earning capacity.

The British statistician A. L. Bowley estimated in 1914 that an old age pensioner spending nothing that was not essential for mere physical health would have required 4s.7d a week plus rent.[18] This provides a standard against which to measure the figures shown in Table 14.1. It demonstrates

---

[16] Since the calculations are based on the rules in force in 1912, which did not take effect until 1900, the figures slightly overstate the maximum pension levels and therefore the difference between minimum and maximum.

[17] This table takes no account of widows' and orphans' pensions for which there was no British equivalent at the time. The German figures are given in Table 10.2 above.

[18] Calculated from A. L. Bowley and A. R. Burnett-Hurst, *Livelihood and poverty* (London, 1915), pp. 80–2. They estimated a pensioner's food requirement as 60 per cent of those of a working adult. That is not far off the 65 per cent of the energy intake of very active men aged 35–65, which is

that even the British pension did not cover subsistence except in someone else's house. In both countries the pension was regarded as supplementary to other resources and was recommended on the ground that it would make the pensioner more acceptable as a lodger than he or she would otherwise have been.

When comparing these figures differences in the cost of living should also be taken into account. According to a survey of 1908 on the cost of living in British and German towns an English manual worker trying to maintain his standard of living in Germany would spend one-fifth more on rent, fuel and food than in England.[19] If these figures are relevant and reliable, the purchasing power of the British pension or benefit of 5s would have been about 6s when compared with that of German town dwellers, i.e. those at the upper end of the scale. There are no comparable estimates for rural districts, where the lower wage-bands were more likely to have been found.

It is also possible to calculate average pensions as a ratio of average earnings, as Christoph Conrad has done for a selection of years including 1913.[20] Unfortunately the calculation of an average pension entirely disregards the variation in entitlement to German invalidity pensions, which is an essential feature of the system. Nevertheless, they are of interest in that they show a higher ratio of pensions to average earnings in Britain than in Germany, by 21 to 17.6. This demonstrates that the higher British pensions did not merely reflect higher British wages. They reflected deliberate differences in social policy.

None of the figures in Table 14.1 can be taken as a basis of comparison without considering the differences in the qualifications required. Two differences are crucial.

The British old age pension was dependent on a means test. The full pension of 5s was restricted to those earning no more than £21 per

---

recommended by modern nutritionists for men aged 65–75 leading a sedentary life. Department of Health and Social Security, *Recommended intakes of nutrients for the United Kingdom*, Reports on Public Health and Medical Subjects, No. 120 (London 1969), Table I, p. 4. This sophisticated modern source has been used only to check how realistic Bowley had been in reducing the food cost for active adults to those for pensioners. In view of his state of knowledge on nutrition and our ignorance of the contemporary cost of buying food containing the correct amount of vitamins, I have concentrated on calorie intake.

[19] Board of Trade, *Cost of living of the working classes: German towns*, BPP 1908 Cd.4032 CVIII, 1, pp. li–lii.

[20] Christoph Conrad, 'The emergence of modern retirement: Germany in an international comparison (1850–1960)', *Population: An English Selection*, 3 (1991), 171–99, Table 3. These figures are based on an exchange rate of £1 = 20.45 M, as calculated by Phelps Brown. See note 1919 above. Conrad altogether fails to mention the existence of disablement benefit, the British version of invalidity pensions, but since this was at the same rate as old age pensions, his figures are not affected.

annum, and those earning above £31.10s received nothing at all. The German old age pension could be received by anyone, aged seventy, irrespective of their means who had paid the necessary 1,200 weekly contributions. Not until 1925 was there an old age pension entitlement in Britain without a means test, based as in Germany on compulsory insurance contributions.[21]

Secondly, British disablement benefit was only for those 'incapable of work'. There was no pension for the partly incapacitated, as in Germany. This was also an important difference. Those who did receive a pension obtained, however, significantly more than all but the highest-paid long-serving workers in Germany.

These two considerations seriously qualify the impression given in Table 14.1, which applies in Britain to a far more restricted group than in Germany. It would therefore have been useful to compare the numbers of recipients of disablement benefit with those of invalidity pensioners, as a proportion of population. That has proved impossible. The German figures are available on an annual basis, but I am unable to find the British total for any year between the wars. The relevant figures would have been compiled by each of the numerous approved societies, but no government agency appears to have collected them at national level or, at least, to have published them. Government and parliament were interested in the financial soundness of the societies and collected totals of expenditure, including that on disablement. There was apparently no national interest served in knowing how many recipients of its modest amount there were in Britain. How different from the present! Now that incapacity benefit is less inadequate and paid from general taxation, the national total of recipients is not just recorded, it is closely scrutinised.

---

[21] Under the Widows', Orphans' and Old Age Contributory Pensions Act 1925. See B. B. Gilbert, *British social policy 1914–1939* (London, 1970), pp. 235–54. It was to be paid at the age of sixty-five. The age of entitlement had already been reduced in Germany to sixty-five in 1916. F. Kleeis, *Die Geschichte der sozialen Versicherung in Deutschland* (reprint of 1928 edition, Berlin and Bonn, 1981), p. 231.

15

White-collar insurance

There is one further aspect of the insurance of the German Empire to be considered. That is the special insurance for white-collar workers introduced late in 1911, later than the RVO which had included widows' and orphans' insurance.[1] There is nothing in British social policy like it. With a few exceptions, which applied equally in Germany, British national insurance covered everyone 'under contract of service' and set an income ceiling of £160 a year. It made no distinction between wage- and salary-earners or between manual and other workers.

The separate white-collar insurance in Germany (*Angestelltenversicherung*) was for workers earning up to 5,000 M or £250 a year in a number of specified non-manual occupations and provided more generous pensions than those available to manual workers.[2] White-collar workers qualified for an old age pension at sixty-five, not seventy. Manual workers qualified for invalidity pensions if their earning capacity was reduced by two thirds, white-collar workers if theirs was reduced by one-half. In assessing reduction in earning capacity manual workers were expected to take any job across the entire labour market. White-collar workers were not expected to take up manual work, and the range of work they were in practice expected to take was further restricted by the regulations of the Imperial Insurance Office. Widows of manual workers were entitled to pensions only if their own earning capacity was reduced by two-thirds. Widows of white-collar workers were not required to prove invalidity. Being a widow was in itself

---

[1] Barbara Bichler, *Die Formierung der Angestelltenbewegung im Kaiserreich und die Entstehung des Angestelltenversicherungsgesetzes von 1911* (Frankfurt a.M., 1997), provides the fullest modern treatment and largely subsumes and corrects the important contemporary study, Emil Lederer, *Die Pensionsversicherung der Privatangestellten* (Tübingen, 1911).

[2] The German contrast *Arbeiter* and *Angestellte* will be translated as manual workers and white-collar workers. The terms wage-earners and salary-earners, as used by Dawson, *Social insurance*, ch. X, would have been an acceptable alternative. Neither of these descriptions is entirely correct, but then *Angestellte* was itself an imprecise term. See p. 289 below; and J. Kocka, *Die Angestellten in der deutschen Geschichte 1850–1980* (Göttingen, 1981), ch. 4, for details.

enough. Pensions for orphans were paid until the age of eighteen, those for manual workers until fifteen. A more generous allocation of money for medical care was intended to ensure a higher quality of institutional provision.[3]

That indicates that one of the objects of the separate insurance system was to provide white-collar workers with benefits specifically suited to their status. There was no financial injustice involved. The liberal benefits were paid for by higher contributions on the part of white-collar workers and their employers. Unlike invalidity and old age insurance, the separate white-collar insurance received no subsidy from the State.

In a pensions system in which the better off had always enjoyed higher benefits, this differentiation took the principle one step further and thereby one step further away from that which governed policy in Britain.

Britain provided neither separate nor superior benefits for white-collar workers. It raised the income limit for compulsory insurance to £250 in 1919 in recognition of the general rise in money wages and then not again until the 1940s.[4] The object of national insurance continued to be the provision of a minimum standard, to be topped up in other ways by those who wished to enjoy a standard of living more suited to their status.

If German white-collar insurance differed from national insurance in Britain, it also marked a significant break with previous German policy. The income ceiling of 2,000 M per annum for compulsory insurance on the part of certain categories of non-manual workers as laid down in 1889 was not raised in 1899 nor in the RVO of 1911. The categories to whom it applied were widened only slightly in the interests of equity.[5] Participation in State insurance on a voluntary basis was possible in both countries. One object of this voluntary insurance was to extend the range of the compulsory scheme laterally to members of certain other occupational groups, provided that their income was below the ceiling for the compulsorily insured. Another was to accommodate, on a very restricted basis, those who had once been regular members of the compulsory scheme but whose

[3] Peter A. Köhler and Hans F. Zacher (eds.), *The evolution of social insurance 1881–1981: studies in Germany, France, Great Britain, Austria and Switzerland* (London, 1982), p. 41; Michael Prinz, 'Die Arbeiterbewegung und das Modell der Angestelltenversicherung', in Klaus Tennfelde (ed.), *Arbeiter im 20. Jahrhundert* (Stuttgart, 1991), pp. 438–9. On the qualification for invalidity, see also F. Tennstedt, *Berufsunfähigkeit im Sozialrecht* (Frankfurt a.M., 1972), pp. 30–1 and 61–70.

[4] Gilbert, *British social policy 1914–1939*, pp. 265–6.

[5] Unlike British national insurance, the German legislation on invalidity and old age insurance made a distinction between manual workers and others. It applied to all manual workers irrespective of the level of their income, but to specific categories of non-manual workers only if their income was below the specified ceiling.

income had risen above the permitted level. These objects were accepted in both countries and provision was made accordingly. In 1899 the Germans went further. They permitted anyone earning between 2,000 and 3,000 M per annum to take out voluntary insurance and obliged their employers to make at least a basic contribution.[6] That introduced a new principle for which there was no British parallel. It was the beginning of a process of yielding to the desire of better paid groups to participate in contributory insurance, a process that led the government to accept entirely separate arrangements for white-collar insurance in November 1911.

The word 'accept' is the key to this innovation. It signalled not only a difference of principle from the past, but also a novelty in the political process. German workers' insurance had been handed down from above. Its terms had been proposed by the imperial government and modified in the *Bundesrat* by the individual state governments and in the *Reichstag* by the parties. These had been the areas of political conflict. The demand for white-collar insurance came from an extra-parliamentary movement, which persuaded the parties to fall into line. The role of the imperial government was largely reactive, and the *Bundesrat* followed its lead.[7] It was also reluctant. It has sometimes been suggested that separate insurance with its own elections for representatives was designed by a Machiavellian government to insulate white-collar workers from the influence that social democrats had gained over the election of representatives in existing social insurance.[8] The creation of an institutionally separate insurance was, however, not of its own choosing. It resulted from pressure by the *Reichstag* that it was unable to resist. The argument that it would contain the influence of the social democrats originated from the movement itself and was adopted by politicians in the *Reichstag*.

It is therefore the creation and effectiveness of the movement that requires explanation. A historical literature, largely produced or inspired by Jürgen Kocka in the 1980s, places this in the context of a changing employment structure, as division of labour spread from industrial production to clerical and technical work. That process led to an increase in the proportion in the labour force of the occupations that were to be

---

[6] This voluntary insurance could be in any wage group of the worker's choice, but the employer was not obliged to contribute an amount above that appropriate for the second wage group.

[7] Bichler, *Formierung*, pp. 127 n. 1 and 201–4.

[8] This is the view expressed both in Tennstedt, *Berufsunfähigkeit*, p. 60, and Gerhard A. Ritter, *Social welfare in Germany and Britain* (Leamington Spa, 1986), p. 192, and influenced the treatment of the subject in Peter Hennock, 'Public provision for old age: Britain and Germany 1880–1914', AfS, 30 (1990), 99–100.

singled out in 1911 for separate insurance. It also increasingly produced internal differentiation within these occupations. Kocka has described the self-image of this group as modelled on that of State and other public officials. These served it as a reference group in a country in which the public service was more numerous and more prestigious than in Britain.

This literature includes a comparison with the USA and to a lesser extent with Britain and France. While primarily concerned to explain the susceptibility of white-collar workers to right-wing politics in the period leading up to 1933, it also pays attention to the formation of the white-collar movement prior to 1911.[9] Since division of labour had its parallels in Britain and the USA, comparison has focused on the significance of German public officials as a reference group. The term *Privatbeamte*, i.e. official in the private sector of the economy, was widely used in the early stages of the white-collar movement.[10] The German *Beamte* enjoyed security of tenure and guaranteed pension rights, and the use of the term served therefore to justify the demand for similar privileges for white-collar workers in the private sector. In 1904 it formed the basis of the detailed claims on which the movement campaigned for the next three years.

The white-collar movement also increasingly compared itself to another reference group. Drawing on an idea of Gustav Schmoller, the prominent social scientist, its members were portrayed as the new *Mittelstand*. Unlike the old *Mittelstand* of independent craftsmen, peasants and retailers they were dependent on employment, but like them were conscious of a distinction between themselves and the proletariat. This, it was suggested, made them an important middle group that prevented society from a dangerous polarisation between two warring classes. Since it was an accepted political strategy to shore up the old *Mittelstand* by special concessions, the spokesmen of the movement were staking out a claim to special treatment on similar grounds.[11]

When government calculations of the costs of claims for pensions based on those provided in the public service showed that these could never be afforded, even by compelling employers to bear one-third of the cost, the movement reduced its aspirations. Less was heard of the *Beamten*, who, it

[9] J. Kocka, *White collar workers in America 1890–1940* (London, 1980); Kocka, *Die Angestellten*; J. Kocka (ed.), *Angestellte im europäischen Vergleich* (Göttingen, 1981); J. Kocka, 'Capitalism and bureaucracy in German industrialization before 1914', Econ. HR, 2nd ser. 34 (1981), 453–68; and his earliest treatment of the theme, J. Kocka, *Unternehmungsverwaltung und Angestelltenschaft am Beispiel Siemens, 1847–1914* (Stuttgart, 1969).

[10] For the origin of this term see Kocka, *Die Angestellten*, pp. 12–89.

[11] Kocka, *Die Angestellten*, ch. 4; Bichler, *Formierung*, pp. 86–93.

was now suggested, had provided the wrong model; more was heard of white-collar workers as the new *Mittelstand*.[12]

Clerks in Britain, the so-called black-coated workers whose dress code emphasised their difference from manual workers, were as status-conscious as their German counterparts. It has therefore been suggested that the crucial difference lay in the fact that the German working class was considered a threat to the established order and that this provided German white-collar workers with a powerful political appeal.[13]

That last point may indeed have contributed to the support of a wider political constituency for its demands, but it fails to explain why there was such a movement in the first place. No one has so far explained why there was a political demand for separate white-collar insurance superior to that established for manual workers in Germany and not in Britain. What has so far been overlooked is the fact that such a movement would have been altogether inappropriate in Britain.

By creating a further wage group to cater for the highest paid, the Invalidity Insurance Law of 1899 confirmed that the principle of differentiating contributions and benefits according to income levels, originally imposed by the *Reichstag* on a reluctant government, had become generally accepted.

The British principle of a uniform level of contributions and benefits at a minimum level never invited a comparable process. Aspirations for benefits suited to status were channelled into private insurance, to be purchased additionally by the individual or provided on a joint contributory basis by employers.[14] In any case prior to 1925 British national insurance gave no entitlement to a pension except on the grounds of disablement under far more restrictive conditions than in Germany. Not some slight difference in status-consciousness, but the large difference in the insurance systems provides the principal explanation.

Not that the needs of white-collar workers with earnings above the limit for compulsory insurance were ignored by the larger German employers, particularly banks and merchant houses. But when the commercial crisis of

---

[12] Bichler, *Formierung*, pp. 135–6 and 138.

[13] See the brief comparison between Britain and Germany in Kocka, *White collar workers in America*, pp. 268–71. For British clerks in this period see Gregory Anderson, *Victorian clerks* (Manchester, 1976); and David Lockwood, *The black-coated worker* (London, 1958), ch. I.

[14] There was a marked growth in British investment in life policies at the lower end of the market both before and after 1911. The main suppliers were the Prudential and the Refuge Assurance Companies, but other life offices also entered the field. Barry Supple, *The Royal Exchange Assurance* (Cambridge, 1970), pp. 223 and 435–6. For the growth of company pensions, see Leslie Hannah, *Inventing retirement: The development of occupational pensions in Britain* (Cambridge, 1986), ch. 2.

1900/1 produced a wave of bankruptcies, it brought home to employees how unprotected these funds actually were and boosted demands for appropriate compulsory insurance underwritten by the State. The coincidental publication in May 1901 of a compulsory insurance bill for white-collar workers in the Austrian legislature drew attention to the possibility of such a project. In many ways the Austrian political situation was different for there was no workers' insurance for old age and invalidity at the time. But the Austrian proposal provided an attractive model. That the Austrian initiative owed much to a movement that emphasised the status of *Privatbeamten* was considered highly relevant. The Austrian law was not passed until 1906 and in a different form from the original proposals. Its provisions were highly controversial and were soon amended.[15] That matters little. It was the example set in the initial stages that had been important.[16]

By 1903 two agitations for white-collar insurance for old age, invalidity and dependants' pensions – one initiated in Hanover, the other in Aachen – had coalesced to form a Principal Committee (*Hauptausschuss*).[17] Supported by many occupational organisations and with local branches across the country, this body approached the *Reich* Ministry of the Interior responsible for social policy. At the Ministry's suggestion, it undertook a statistical survey on which to base detailed proposals. It also intervened actively in the *Reichstag* elections of 1903, demanding declarations of support from candidates and urging the members of its affiliated organisations to vote only for those who had pledged themselves to the cause. Favourable references to special insurance for white-collar workers began to be included in the programmes of the National Liberal, Conservative and Centre parties. By the end of the year the movement had become a significant political fact.[18]

That is where a comparison with the politics of social policy reform in Britain is illuminating. Historians of British politics are familiar with the nationwide pressure group, operating through Parliament and pushing a reluctant government towards measures it would not otherwise have undertaken. The politics of British old age pensions and the role played

---

[15] Gustav Otruba, 'Privat-, Handlungsgehilfen- und Angestelltenorganisationen. Ihr Beitrag zur Entstehung des österreichischen Angestelltenpensionsversicherungsgesetzes 1906 (unter besonderer Berücksichtigung der Diskussion über den Angestelltenbegriff)', in Kocka (ed.), *Angestellte im europäischen Vergleich*, pp. 240–56.

[16] Bichler, *Formierung*, pp. 60–2.

[17] Referred to as 'the main committee' in Ritter, *Social welfare*, p. 92.

[18] Bichler, *Formierung*, pp. 62–85, 112–14 and 118.

therein by the National Committee of Organised Labour (NCOL) provide a good example. The tactics of single-purpose pressure groups had been gradually elaborated over seven decades of British politics.[19]

To anyone familiar with that process the conduct of the Principal Committee shows some striking similarities. Of these the insistence on election candidates pledging themselves to the movement's programme is the most important. It gave it the foothold in the *Reichstag* that was to be a condition of ultimate success. Its renewed intervention in the elections of 1907 was to galvanise the non-socialist parties into convincing a procrastinating government to address the issue. That is reminiscent of the role of the NCOL in the British election of 1906.

A government memorandum, which was published in July 1908, was described as merely a clarification of the issues involved. But after more than two years of internal debate it became the basis of a draft law. The memorandum, the work of experts in the *Reich* Ministry of the Interior, rejected both main proposals then being canvassed: the creation of a separate insurance fund and the extension of the existing insurance to accommodate the demands of white-collar workers.

The main obstacle to the creation of a separate insurance fund lay in the numerous white-collar workers already insured under the existing scheme. They amounted to 68.29 per cent of all men and 93.57 per cent of all women covered by the Principal Committee's survey in 1903.[20] To transfer them all to a separate new fund, it was suggested, would seriously weaken the existing insurance financially and require impossibly complicated calculations. These contributors would lose their state subsidy, since the government was not prepared to subsidise the more generous arrangements that white-collar workers were demanding. Indeed many supporters of the movement had never really believed in the likelihood of a separate fund. They knew that it was becoming increasingly difficult to distinguish between manual and white-collar workers among those with an income of under 2,000 M. They were prepared, if necessary, to settle for an extension of the existing scheme that would raise the income limit for compulsory insurance and add higher wage groups with more adequate benefits and easier qualifications.

---

[19] Patricia Hollis (ed.), *Pressure from without in early Victorian England* (London, 1974); D. A. Hamer, *The politics of electoral pressure* (Brighton, 1977); F. H. Stead, *How old age pensions began to be* (London, n.d.[1909]).

[20] Of the men 58.12 per cent were compulsorily and 10.17 per cent voluntarily insured. Of the women the respective figures were 92.44 and 1.13. Bichler, *Formierung*, p. 133.

Such an extension was, however, also ruled out by the government memorandum. The easier qualifications for invalidity pensions, so its authors argued, would have to be extended to all existing contributors and would double the contributions, while the addition of new contributors would increase the state subsidy to an amount quite unacceptable to the federated states. They also thought it unlikely that the pensions for dependants in the form that was then envisaged would have satisfied the white-collar contributors. The memorandum therefore suggested a separate additional insurance fund confined to white-collar workers, that would provide higher benefits and easier qualifications for invalidity and dependants' pensions. This proposal would cause white-collar workers with an income below 2,000 M to be doubly insured, both as members of the old insurance and as members of the additional insurance fund alongside the better paid members of their occupation. They would have the right to vote for representatives to both insurance funds.[21]

A change of government left these proposals in limbo. It was not until the end of 1909 that the new government under Bethmann Hollweg with Delbrück at the Ministry of the Interior finally rejected all ideas of extending invalidity and old age insurance as part of the RVO. Not until February 1910 did Delbrück promise to produce a draft law for separate additional insurance for white-collar workers. The date of the announcement is significant, for the government had been pinned down in a *Reichstag* debate on the budget by the concerted tactics of the non-socialist parties. Behind these moves lay the Principal Committee which had been thrown into disarray for much of 1909 by the governmental silence and was now once more determined to make itself felt.[22]

The promised draft legislation was published in January 1910 but did not come before the *Bundesrat* until March. It proposed a separate additional insurance fund along the lines of the earlier memorandum, as had been accepted by the Principal Committee and the parties, but made further adjustments to the finances.

Yet, as the government explained to the *Bundesrat*, these proposals were only *pro forma*. Far from regarding them as desirable, it was confident that they would prove unacceptable. It was producing a draft law, as the *Reichstag* had insisted, but expected it to be contested by the employers who had consistently opposed this additional burden. That would put the onus on the *Reichstag* to square the conflicting interests which, in its anxiety to placate the white-collar movement, it had chosen to ignore. The need to

[21] Bichler, *Formierung*, pp. 138–41 and 152–3.   [22] *Ibid.*, pp. 171–81.

deal with prior business, not least the complex codification and reform of the insurance laws, would leave it no time to settle these contentious matters before its dissolution and the elections of 1912. They would then be decided under the new conditions established by the elections. On that understanding the *Bundesrat* agreed to the draft law.[23]

Long before October 1911, when they were at last able to consider the draft law, the parties in the *Reichstag* had been watching its slow progress with mounting anxiety. The elections of 1907 had seen a remarkable mobilisation of the white-collar vote, a development which had benefited the anti-socialist parties. If by the next elections there was still no legislation to meet the white-collar demands, there was every reason to fear a revulsion. Those who had always doubted whether a separate insurance was politically feasible and were willing to settle for an extension of the present insurance might well vote for the SPD, the one party that had consistently advocated such a policy.

These fears were not as fanciful as they might seem in retrospect. The Principal Committee had been unable to maintain its unity in the face of the government tactics. In the autumn of 1908 ten of its fifty-seven occupational associations had broken away to found a body committed to extension. Other associations shared this preference and had remained loyal only for tactical reasons. A quarter of the total membership of the movement belonged to occupational associations with a preference for the extension of the present insurance system.[24] These occupational bodies were no part of the socialist trade union movement. But their demand for additional wage groups to provide benefits appropriate to their status within a single insurance for manual and white-collar workers was not significantly different from the position of the socialist trade union movement. This was demanding an extension of insurance to the whole employed population and explicitly expressed its sympathy for the position of the white-collar workers.[25] Associations committed to separate insurance made up less than half the constituent associations of the total movement.[26] The secession was led by associations of technical workers but included many others.[27]

By 1911 the non-socialist parties felt threatened by a potential revolt of white-collar voters, precisely because class antagonism was an issue for only a part of those to whom they needed to appeal. For the rest, the reformist stance that the socialist trade union movement had adopted in this matter

---

[23] *Ibid.*, pp. 183 and 204.   [24] *Ibid.*, pp. 139–41, 144–5 and 161–4.   [25] *Ibid.*, pp. 146–7.
[26] See *ibid.*, table on p. 141.   [27] *Ibid.*, pp. 160–1.

made voting for the SPD far from inconceivable. The voting system with its provisions for a second ballot provided an easy way to switch.[28]

The principal parties were therefore determined to complete their business in time, and they confounded the government's expectations. The law was passed on 11 December 1911, less than two months after the *Reichstag* received the draft. This was achieved by drastically curtailing debate in the full session, by accepting the basic proposals and by keeping objections to a minimum. Since all the principal parties agreed on the importance of completing business in time, they were reluctant to raise major issues. Many matters of detail were settled in private conclave between representatives of the parties and of the *Bundesrat*, since clauses that might be vetoed in the second chamber had to be avoided. That put the government in a strong position over matters of substance but totally frustrated their tactical intentions.

The main victims of this haste were the employers' organisations, whose strong objections to the cost of the insurance were disregarded as 'lacking all objective justification'.[29] Their other concern was for the future of insurance funds that they had already established for their employees. Here they obtained concessions when their objections were shared by the insurance industry.[30]

Of the three principal employers' organisations, only the relatively small League of Industrialists (*Bund der Industriellen*) finally accepted the new law in principle with some minor reservations. The spokesmen for the master-craftsmen and the normally influential voice of heavy industry, the CDI, entirely rejected the legitimacy of what the latter dubbed 'an election present to white-collar workers at the expense of their employers'. A leading member of the CDI condemned the political process behind the legislation in round terms.

This is a legislative measure based neither on destitution nor on regard for the maintenance of the nation's strength. It is merely an aspect of so-called social policy, i.e of consideration for the wishes of those voters to whom it is desired to show consideration. If it becomes the custom in Germany that, whenever any particular group of the population wishes to be maintained in greater comfort, the government makes a law to satisfy their wishes, it will not be long before we are in a socialist state.[31]

---

[28] *Reichstag* elections were decided by a majority of those voting. For that reason close on half of all election contests from 1893 to 1914 required a second ballot. Brett Fairbairn, *Democracy in the undemocratic state: the German Reichstag elections of 1898 and 1903* (Toronto, 1997), pp. 16–17.

[29] Bichler, *Formierung*, p. 215, generally pp. 210–14.

[30] *Ibid.*, pp. 206–9, 217–18 and 222–30. [31] *Ibid.*, pp. 190–3 and 245.

This resentment goes far to explain the receptiveness for Ludwig Bernhard's biting criticism in his *Unerwünschte Folgen der deutschen Sozialpolitik* (1912) and the wave of hostility to social policy to which it gave rise.

It is remarkable that the CDI should have been so ineffective. These masters of organised representation were on this occasion defeated by the tactically superior Principal Committee. The latter's ability to speak on behalf of what would otherwise have been a miscellany of occupational bodies each with a slightly different message had been crucial from the beginning. Just how crucial is shown by the failure of comparable demands in 1904 for insurance appropriate to self-employed craftsmen. That made no headway in the *Reichstag*, because deputies were bewildered by contradictory positions on the issue taken by the various occupational associations.[32] Not until 1938 did self-employed craftsmen obtain their own compulsory invalidity, old age and dependants' insurance.[33]

It was the demands of the Principal Committee to which the parties paid attention and which ultimately formed the basis of the government bill. Once the government had signalled its rejection of any further extension of existing insurance and published its proposals for a separate additional insurance fund, the break-away elements returned to the fold and reinforced the Committee's authority in the final deliberations. Meanwhile, the internal disagreements within the white-collar movement had served an important function. They had alerted the non-socialist parties to the fact that the support of the movement could not be assumed unless they delivered the required legislation. That had in turn fuelled their persistence. If in the words of the historian of the process, 'it was the legislature that drove the development forward', it was the Principal Committee that drove the legislature.[34] As early as 1904, one observer had commented, 'if one wants to know how to achieve advances in social legislation, one should take the endeavours of the white-collar workers for the introduction of a state insurance for pensions as one's model'.[35] That view was no less appropriate in 1912.

Naturally the Committee did not get all that it wished. No extra-parliamentary pressure group ever does. It had to accept the recognition of existing insurance funds as alternative funds, but only on the most stringent terms. Contributions were also lower than it had demanded and benefits were accordingly lower too.[36]

---

[32] *Ibid.*, p. 232 and n. 9.   [33] Köhler and Zacher (eds.), *Evolution of social insurance*, p. 54.
[34] Bichler, *Formierung*, p. 121.
[35] *Sozialpolitische Rundschau*, 6 July 1904, quoted in Bichler, *Formierung*, p. 99.
[36] Bichler, *Formierung*, pp. 142, 188 and 228.

Important as was the organisation with its branch structure, its public meetings, its sophisticated use of the press and its spokesmen in the *Reichstag*, the movement's ability to relate its programme to widely accepted norms was at least as crucial. The projection of the white-collar workers as *Privatbeamte*, and subsequently as the 'new *Mittelstand*', with the claims to special treatment that this implied, was an essential contribution to its success. It may be compared to the concept of the deserving poor that had propelled the British campaign for old age pensions.

These terms were more useful for persuasion than for the purpose of legal definition.[37] Even the term *Angestellte* lacked the necessary clarity. The Law could provide merely a list of occupations to which it applied, and even that included terms that were vague and disputed. There was nothing that they all had in common and that distinguished them from others, whether judged by objective indicators or of subjective perception.[38]

Much of the necessary demarcation and consolidation occurred in the process of administration and through an amendment of 1924. Yet the importance of the Law of 1911 was such that the separate treatment of manual workers and white-collar workers became a feature of much subsequent German legislation. The Law defined what became an increasingly important status category.[39] It represented a major innovation in legal and political terms.

The promised benefits could not be delivered. By the time that the ten years' qualifying period had expired, the accumulated capital reserves had been destroyed by inflation. The pensioners' only benefit was the *gehobene Fürsorge*, the higher level of support from public assistance that distinguished them from those who had made no effort to provide for their needs. However, the belief in social insurance was so deep rooted that by 1924 the ruined structures had been restored. The concept of a separate insurance for non-manual workers was actually reinforced by the havoc that inflation had caused. With the destruction of past accumulated claims, it was possible to do in 1922 what had seemed too complex in 1911, to abolish double membership of the insurance funds. Thereafter an insurance contributor belonged either to the manual workers' or the white-collar workers' insurance, each with its own set of entitlements. This reinforced a simple bi-polar sense of status.[40]

---

[37] *Ibid.*, p. 43.
[38] See Toni Pierenkämper, *Arbeitsmarkt und Angestellte im Deutschen Kaiserreich 1880–1914* (Stuttgart, 1987), for the most systematic analysis of the former.
[39] Kocka, *Die Angestellten*, pp. 140–1; Ritter, *Social welfare*, pp. 95–6, for a survey of this subsequent legislation.
[40] Ludwig Preller, *Sozialpolitik in der Weimarer Republik*, pp. 283–6 and 325–6; Kleeis, *Geschichte*, pp. 237–41 and 280–2.

We need to return to the initial point of comparison. There is nothing in British social policy to compare with German white-collar insurance, whether in the enhanced provision made or in the compulsory inclusion of those earning up to 5,000 M a year. The qualifications for invalidity pensions were far more generous even under the ordinary insurance in Germany than for disablement benefit in Britain. This difference was further accentuated by the provision now made for white-collar workers.

To sum up. The years between 1889 and the RVO of 1911 saw a progressive differentiation of contributions and benefits among the insured. Ever greater consideration was given to adjusting benefits to the needs of the better paid. This paved the way for the aspirations of the white-collar movement. The coincidence of the commercial bankruptcies of 1900–1 with the publication of a draft law for white-collar insurance in Austria produced greater awareness of the advantages of State-sponsored insurance over private or occupational pension arrangements. The former would ensure contributions from employers and provide a guarantee for the security of the fund. The conjunction of all these elements created an interest in compulsory insurance among those above the 2,000 M limit and led to the founding of the white-collar movement. Much against the government's will, this achieved the establishment of a separate insurance, thereby giving further expression to the principle of differentiation. This affected the amount of the pension as usual, but now for the first time explicitly also the qualifications required.[41]

The white-collar insurance law built on the progressive differentiation that had characterised invalidity and old age insurance since the *Reichstag* had transformed the original government draft in the summer of 1889.[42] It became a precedent for the establishment of insurance for self-employed craftsmen in 1938 and provided the administrative framework for that extension of compulsory insurance to yet another economic group.[43] These developments were far from being 'social solidarity', in Peter Baldwin's sense. On the contrary, they were highly divisive. But they represented moves towards universalism such as were quite unknown in Britain before the 1940s.[44]

---

[41] For an earlier implicit differentiation see p. 202 above.

[42] For sickness insurance the 2,000 M income level had been breached earlier that year, when the RVO raised the ceiling for non-manual workers to 2,500. M. That had done something to compensate for the substantial rise in average earnings since 1883. No such justification exists for raising the ceiling to 5,000. M. Köhler and Zacher (eds.), *Evolution of social insurance*, p. 38.

[43] *Ibid.*, p. 54. See Peter Baldwin, *The politics of social solidarity: class bases of the European welfare state 1875–1975* (Cambridge, 1990), pp. 268–75, for its subsequent history.

[44] Baldwin, *Politics of social solidarity* (Cambridge, 1990).

PART IV

Unemployment

A study that has been dominated by German preoccupation with compulsory insurance and its subsequent adoption in Great Britain must necessarily include the introduction of compulsory insurance against unemployment under the National Insurance Act of 1911.

The principles of that policy, in so far as they parallel those of national health insurance, are already familiar. They include the conscription of one of the great institutions of working-class mutual help for the basis of a national policy, relying on compulsion and subsidy to extend the partial cover already achieved on a voluntary basis in independence of the State. Once again the object of national insurance was to organise those not previously included. Just as the friendly societies found that discretion in the treatment of their members had to be sacrificed to accountability to obtain public funding, so the trade unions were to find the same. There are also striking similarities in the political process that had propelled the two problems to the top of the policy agenda.

But no Anglo-German comparison is possible. Just as there was no separate national white-collar insurance in pre-war Britain, so there was no national unemployment insurance in Imperial Germany. That is not to say that there was no unemployment insurance policy in Germany at the time. But it was not a national one. It was on a municipal basis and limited to a few towns only. Why there was such a policy at all and why in these towns only, requires explanation.

As always, it is important to place the subject in its proper context. In this case unemployment insurance was part of a wider preoccupation with unemployment. That had produced other initiatives before it led to insurance, in particular public relief works for the unemployed and the establishment of labour registries by philanthropic or municipal bodies. In England as in Germany unemployment insurance policy can be understood only in conjunction with these. For both countries the best starting point is the history of public relief works.

16

Unemployment policies in Britain

We begin with Britain or, in so far as the Poor Law was involved, with England. In the early nineteenth century work had been extensively subsidised from the poor rates so as to give employment to labourers who would otherwise have been unemployed or underemployed.

In regions of tillage local labour was needed for the regular periods of peak demand and had therefore been supported at other times in the year. The various means to do this with the help of the parish rates were all strongly condemned in 1833 when the Royal Commission on the Poor Laws examined what was known as the Speenhamland System. Under the New Poor Law of 1834, employment dependent on wage subsidies was to be abolished. The able-bodied were intended to be relieved only in the workhouse. The aim was to allow wages to find their market level which, quite erroneously as it turned out, was expected to rise once farmers could no longer subsidise their wage bill from the rates.[1]

In industrial districts the labour market had its own fluctuations, especially where a single industry was dominant. Here the priority for the employers, who had dominated the vestries and were to dominate the Boards of Guardians, was to retain the local skilled and semi-skilled labour in times of bad trade. To refuse relief except in the workhouse would have put an impossible strain on workhouse accommodation and no such policy was ever introduced. The attempt to reduce out-relief led in the course of the 1840s to harsh labour tests, such as stone-breaking, oakum-picking or wood-chopping, as a condition for the receipt of relief.[2] These policies were in practice subverted both in agriculture and in industry, but in the new mental climate the use of the rates to create employment found no wide acceptance.

[1] See chapter 1 above and the literature cited there.
[2] S. Webb and B. Webb, *English poor law policy* (London, 1910), pp. 22–31 and 90–1 for the process which was consolidated in the Outdoor Relief Regulation Order of 1852.

These dominant assumptions were briefly shaken when the American Civil War interrupted the supply of cotton for the Lancashire textile industry. The severity of the 'cotton famine' of 1861–5 was well beyond the capacity of traditional soup kitchen charity to relieve. It threw skilled men on the parish who were far removed in character from the dependent class. That administered a shock to socially approved self-respect and revealed the limitations of the conventional labour test. It led to a crisis of social policy and resulted in the Public Works (Manufacturing Districts) Act of 1863. Local rating authorities were authorised to recruit the unemployed for works of public utility, paid from the rates supplemented by charity and backed by Treasury loans.[3]

The policy lapsed once the crisis was past. Those displaced by cyclical unemployment or any other kind of exceptional distress depended once again on out-relief under the conditions of the Poor Law. But the experience of 1863–6 was not forgotten. There were to be many proposals for a regular policy of 'useful' public works modelled on the Lancashire experiment, which would not compete with private enterprise but would recruit the unemployed and prevent their deterioration during periods of depression.[4]

These proposals owed their appeal to a concern for the 'respectable' working-class. The failure of the Poor Law to distinguish according to moral status was widely considered the weakness of the existing system. It produced ambitious attempts by charitable bodies, particularly by the Charity Organisation Society founded in 1869, to identify the respectable poor among those in distress and to provide for them in ways that would keep them away from the Poor Law. It was a policy that received the approval of the central Poor Law authority, which recommended co-operation between local Boards of Guardians and local charities wherever possible, But only in exceptional areas were charitable resources up to the challenge.[5]

Until the cyclical downturn of 1885–6 the pressure of events was lacking to translate proposals for municipal public relief works separate from the Poor Law into practice. Then demands were increasingly heard for public works schemes modelled on the Lancashire precedent. Demonstrations of

---

[3] W. O. Henderson, *The Lancashire cotton famine 1861–1865* (Manchester, 1934).
[4] José Harris, *Unemployment and politics: a study in English social policy 1886–1914* (Oxford, 1972), p. 3, n. 2.
[5] C. L. Mowat, *The Charity Organisation Society 1865–1913* (London, 1961); Robert Humphreys, *Sin, organised charity and the poor law in Victorian England* (London, 1995); Michael Rose (ed.), *The poor and the city: the English poor law in its urban context 1834–1914* (Leicester, 1985).

the unemployed in many cities, and those in London in particular, received much attention in the press. When the House of Commons also became restless, the government began to shift its original opposition to any form of State intervention, and in March 1886 Joseph Chamberlain, the President of the Local Government Board, sent a circular to local authorities. He asked them to schedule necessary public works for periods of depression and to co-operate with Poor Law Guardians in providing temporary non-pauperising employment for the deserving unemployed. As Chamberlain explained to the future Mrs Webb, the purpose was to remove the 'danger that public sentiment should go wholly over to the unemployed and render impossible that state of sternness to which you and I equally attach importance. By offering reasonable work at low wages we may secure the power of being very strict with the loafer and the confirmed pauper.'[6]

This circular is conventionally regarded as initiating an important change of policy, but it lacked any powers of compulsion. In practice there were so many problems with these proposals that only a few local authorities were able to put suitable plans in place. With the upturn of the trade cycle concern subsided, until the downturn in 1892–5, followed by exceptionally severe weather, brought another period of distress. Local pressure from demonstrations of the unemployed revived, and so did relief works by local authorities. Yet unemployment levels tended to be highest where rateable value was particularly low, and this produced demands for central government subsidies. The plight of these local authorities was ably voiced by Keir Hardie, the founder of the Independent Labour Party, who had been elected to Parliament in 1892 for West Ham, an area of just that kind.

The experience of 1892–5 demonstrated that relief works were usually inefficient and expensive and often no less demoralising than work in the stone-yard. Few local authorities had either the staff or the funds or the practical facilities to provide work that complied with the conditions for obtaining the necessary loans as laid down by the Local Government Board. Yet it had become almost impossible for them to disclaim responsibility and to rely on the Boards of Guardians, as in the past. Under these circumstances pressure in the Commons and outside produced the appointment in 1895 and again in 1896 of a Select Committee on Distress

---

[6] Peter Fraser, *Joseph Chamberlain: radicalism and empire 1836–1914* (London, 1966), p. 125. See p. 221 above for the same considerations expressed by Charles Booth when advocating old age pensions. The desire for a consistently deterrent Poor Law produced some of the most influential advocates of the provision of benefits for deserving groups on an entirely separate basis.

from Want of Employment, 'the first national inquiry into unemployment and the first official recognition that it might be a fit subject for remedial legislation'.[7]

The recommendations of the two committees were, however, ignored by government, parliament and press. By 1896 unemployment had become a stale subject of little interest in a period of economic boom. Hardie, the most vocal champion of the unemployed, had lost his parliamentary seat in 1895 and the interest of the trade unions was diverted to other matters. Nevertheless 1892–6 was a significant period for proposals, analysis and debate. In practical terms change was limited. A few local authorities introduced relief works and labour registries, while certain voluntary organisations had experimented with paying for relief works rather than soup kitchens.

The next cyclical downturn began in 1902. Once more it was the experience of London that dominated public debate. Reliance on the Guardians to deal with the unemployed by means of the stone-yard was now no longer a serious option. The traditional Lord Mayor's appeal to the charitable public posed a question of the appropriate use of the money. Local relief committees were appointed across London to co-operate with the Guardians and to separate the temporarily out-of-work from ordinary paupers. A Central Unemployed Body experimented with several policy initiatives, not only relief works but also farm colonies to train urban labour for emigration or resettlement on the land, and labour registries to reduce the unemployed surplus to more manageable proportions.

With the Unemployed Workmen Act of 1905 this arrangement in London became a model for national policy. All towns over 50,000 inhabitants were to set up Distress Committees to co-ordinate and rationalise the relations between charity, Poor Law and municipality. The Act was intended to repair the chaos into which the system of tripartite responsibility had fallen.

Even with better co-ordination, relief works required more than charitable funds to underwrite them. That issue was fudged by the government. The original proposal for a rate of one penny in the pound to finance relief works was deleted for fear that it would establish a precedent for public finance on an ever larger scale. The bill authorised the use of the rates for the management expenses of distress committees and some of the other

---

[7] The quotation is from Harris, *Unemployment*, pp. 89–90, to which this and subsequent sections are largely indebted.

provisions, but pointedly excluded public relief works. It was presented as an experiment limited to three years.

This measure, devised by a failing Conservative government in its last year of office, became a millstone round the neck of the incoming Liberal ministers. They had recognised its inadequacy and criticised the rating clause when in opposition. That did not mean, however, that they were prepared to permit payment for relief works out of the rates. They knew that the inadequate resources of many a local authority would produce an irresistible demand for Treasury subsidies. There lay the way to recognising the 'right to work' with its incalculable implications for the normal operation of the labour market, not only in time of temporary depression but in general. The outgoing government, well knowing the muddle into which it had got itself, had appointed a Royal Commission to investigate both the operation of the Poor Law and the relief of distress due to lack of employment. The new government was content to benefit from this classic device for shelving an awkward subject and announced its readiness to await the results of the investigation. Unfortunately, the commissioners were determined to be thorough. The Poor Law was a sprawling, complex subject in desperate need of systematic review.

But was it possible to resist the demands for relief work paid from the rates and the obvious need therefore for Treasury subsidies? As a holding measure Parliament voted a grant of £200,000 for additional administrative expenses in 1906 and again in 1907. That was not what was needed. Almost inevitably the Labour Party, in consultation with the TUC, stepped into the policy vacuum. It demanded that the State take responsibility for the provision of work, or, failing that, of acceptable relief for the registered unemployed. It was to use local agencies if possible, national agencies where necessary. They produced a bill in 1907 and, in the absence of an official Liberal policy, this attracted significant support among Liberal backbenchers. Filling the gaps revealed by the experience of the previous years was the obvious next step to take. When reintroduced in 1908, a year of steeply rising unemployment, it attracted an ominous amount of backbench support and served notice on the government that the time for stalling was over.[8]

But monitoring those on relief work had revealed that very few did actually return to the regular work-force when employment revived. Experience showed that it was impossible to separate the deserving

---

[8] In addition to Harris, *Unemployment*, Kenneth Brown, *Labour and unemployment 1900–1914* (Newton Abbot, 1971).

temporarily unemployed from casual or semi-casual workers. In effect the Labour Party's proposals for a right to employment or honourable relief abandoned the very distinction that had been at the root of the 1905 Act. Their effect on the self-regulating labour market was brushed aside rather than confronted. What had been an attempt to deal with cyclical and temporary unemployment for a limited number might easily become an intervention in the labour market of incalculable dimensions and consequences. Many in authority believed that these developments had to be stopped. But what alternatives would address the legitimate concerns of Liberal backbenchers? Farm colonies had seemed promising in 1905, but they were discredited by 1908.

In this situation William Beveridge, still in his twenties but with several years of experience in the administration of unemployment relief in London, provided an alternative policy under the slogan 'organisation of the labour market'. From 1908 Britain embarked abruptly on a national policy of labour exchanges and unemployment insurance.

Like the realisation of the inappropriateness of public relief works for the temporarily unemployed, the organisation of the labour market through labour exchanges was based on recent experience in London. That is not to say that there were not some non-profit-making exchanges, since at least the 1880s, including municipal ones. Suggestions for a nationwide network were rejected by the Royal Commission on Labour in 1894 and the Board of Trade was also uninterested. When the few municipal labour bureaux that still existed in London at the turn of the century were declared *ultra vires*, i.e. beyond the legal capacity of the municipal authorities to finance, a local Act for London was passed in 1902 to authorise their maintenance from the rates. In 1905 there were ten. There was also a Central Employment Exchange set up by the Lord Mayor's charitable London Unemployment Fund.[9]

In 1906 Beveridge was appointed as the first chairman of an Employment Exchange Committee for London, established at his suggestion by the Central Unemployed Body under the Unemployed Workmen Act. This forced him to elaborate his ideas. He had begun with an interest in casual labour, which had been linked to poverty in East London ever since Charles Booth's London-based investigation into the 'Life and Labour of the People' (1889).[10] Like

---

[9] Harris, *Unemployment*, pp. 199–200 and 279–282.

[10] Charles Booth, *Life and labour of the people*, vol. I, *East London* (London, 1889). See Booth, 'Inaugural address' *Jl Royal Stat. Soc.*, 60 (1892), 521–57, for his subsequent views. On the prevalence of casual labour in East London see also Gareth Steadman Jones, *Outcast London* (Oxford, 1971).

Booth he wished to see casual labourers replaced by a smaller regularly employed work-force and the surplus absorbed elsewhere in the economy.

'The organisation of the labour market' was his phrase to describe the systematic use of labour exchanges by employers and workers but *also* the deliberate use of the exchanges to reduce casual employment. By early 1907 he was advocating the nationwide application of public labour exchanges for a wide range of purposes: decasualisation, monitoring and forestalling depressions and the maintenance of maximum labour mobility generally. His committee took over the few labour exchanges in London and established one in every London borough. To obtain the necessary co-operation of employers and trade unions, he tried hard to distance exchanges from their traditional association with charity and distress and to identify them with the normal process of filling vacancies. He also tried to devise a generally acceptable policy for dealing with vacancies produced by trade disputes. In practice, labour exchanges were slow to win over either employers or organised workers. But their limited success on the ground was less important than the fact that Beveridge was putting forward an alternative policy to that of the Labour Party. Under the sponsorship of Sidney and Beatrice Webb he converted Winston Churchill, the newly appointed President of the Board of Trade. In July 1908 Beveridge joined the staff of the Board of Trade.[11]

Since public relief works were inappropriate for the normal workman, Beveridge argued that the most suitable form of relief was a simple money payment. The mutual insurance of the trade unions did this in the cheapest and most effective way. Both for those whom the trade unions were not able to reach and for their own members, labour exchanges could also be used to test applicants' inability to obtain employment and their qualification for insurance benefit.

When Beveridge discovered an official German survey that had also described labour exchanges as the essential prerequisite for any scheme of unemployment benefit or insurance, he went to see the labour exchanges in Germany.[12] Giving evidence to the Royal Commission on his return, he argued for the establishment of a national system of labour exchanges both

---

[11] Harris, *Unemployment*, pp. 201–7, and her *William Beveridge, a biography* (Oxford, 1977), ch. 6. William Beveridge, *Unemployment: a problem of industry* (London, 1909), provides a systematic exposition of the issues as he saw them at the time.

[12] William Beveridge, *Power and influence* (London, 1953), pp. 61 and 56–8. The report in question was Kaiserliches Statistisches Amt, *Die bestehenden Einrichtungen zur Versicherung gegen die Folgen der Arbeitslosigkeit im Ausland und im Deutschen Reich* (3 vols., Berlin, 1906). The quotation is from the end of volume I.

as the answer to the better organisation of the labour market and as a prerequisite for compulsory unemployment insurance in those trades most susceptible to cyclical unemployment.[13] That was in October 1907 but Beveridge's ideas were well ahead of government policy. As late as July 1908 Churchill was not yet committed to unemployment insurance. He deliberately omitted any reference to it from a memorandum on labour exchanges that he circulated among an inner group of ministers. But by the beginning of 1909, that had changed. Compulsory contributory insurance was now officially proposed both for those suffering from sickness and invalidity and for the deserving unemployed.[14]

In 1911 the National Insurance Act required weekly contributions from manual workers and their employers in shipbuilding, in engineering and ironfounding, and in building and a number of construction trades.[15] Not merely were the chronically irregular occupations excluded from the scope of the insurance, so were occupations, such as mining or textiles, which normally responded to lack of demand by retaining workers but reducing the number of hours worked. Insurance was intended to deal with short-term seasonal or cyclical unemployment on the part of those who were normally regularly employed. Entitlement to benefit was accordingly confined to those who had been employed in each of twenty-six weeks of the preceding five years. It was restricted to one week for every five weeks of contributions and to fifteen weeks in any twelve months. Nor was benefit paid for the first week of unemployment, thereby establishing a clear-cut distinction between being employed and being unemployed. Unemployment caused by a trade dispute did not qualify for benefit.[16] Thus the target group for compulsion was carefully selected and entitlement carefully restricted.

The Act did, however, include all manual workers in the specified occupations, irrespective of their degree of skill or of trade union membership. It thereby greatly increased the number who would enjoy unemployment benefit in those trades most vulnerable to short-term fluctuations. Of

[13] *Royal Commission on the poor laws and relief of distress due to lack of employment*, Minutes of Evidence, QQ.77831–78370a, BPP 1910 Cd.5066, XLVIII.

[14] See Hennock, *British social reform*, chs. 9–11, esp. pp. 163–5 for the evidence that the British government's conversion to compulsory contributory insurance was driven by Lloyd George's problems with old age pensions for those under seventy and that it was he, not Churchill, who initiated the new departure.

[15] For each worker employers paid 2½d, as did the workers themselves, while the State provided one-third of their joint contribution, i.e. 1⅔d.

[16] The conditions are itemised in *National Insurance Bill (Part II: Unemployment): explanatory memorandum*, p. 3, BPP 1911 Cd.5991. Flat-rate benefit was 7s per week.

those covered by the Act in 1913 no more than 20 per cent at most had previously been entitled to trade union out-of-work benefit.[17]

How was unemployment insurance administered? Health insurance relied on friendly societies to administer benefits in their capacity of 'approved societies'. It was left to employers to withhold workers' contributions from wages and to pay these together with their own contributions by purchasing stamps issued at the Post Office. The collection of contributions was relatively straightforward; it was the benefits that required careful judgment of entitlement, and supervision to prevent malingering. Those, for whom the 'approved societies' (and in the end that also meant insurance companies) were unwilling to take responsibility, were in effect excluded from the system and had to make do with a mere savings bank. They were an insignificant proportion of the insured, as had always been intended.

That was not how unemployment insurance operated. Here it was the labour exchanges that normally dealt with claims and the payment of benefits. The reason was not merely the large gap in the voluntary system that had to be filled. It was also a recognition that measures to impel workers to join trade unions would not have been generally acceptable to employers, whereas in the case of friendly societies they largely were. That fact mattered, since employers' contributions were essential. Nevertheless, a striking feature of the scheme is the range of concessions offered to trade unions.

For the payment of contributions the machinery was the same for all, regardless of trade union membership. Employers bought the requisite stamps and stuck them into each worker's insurance book in their keeping. They withheld 2½d from wages, and added an equal amount of their own.[18] That was similar to their duties under health insurance. It was over the administration of benefit that concessions were made. Trade unions that provided their own unemployment benefit were permitted to go on paying this to their members under their own rules as before, and to receive a rebate to the amount of the State benefit for any who qualified for it. Since this rebate was limited to three-quarters of the total payment, the union had an incentive to top up their members' benefit to at least 9s.4d per week. Once a worker had lodged his unemployment book at the labour exchange

[17] *Unemployment insurance: proceedings of the Board of Trade under Part II of the National Insurance Act, 1911*, p. iii, BPP 1913 Cd.6965 XXXVI, 677. That excluded those entitled only to trade union travelling benefit.

[18] The State contributed a further one third of their joint contribution, i.e. 1⅔d.

as proof of entitlement and applied for benefit, his contact would be solely
with the officers of his union branch. The State did not obtrude. It was the
union that paid and made its own arrangements for him to sign on
regularly to prove unemployment. Unions could arrange for this to be
done at the labour exchange, but only if they wished.[19]

Unions were still free to pay voluntary benefit to their members for
whatever period they wished. For this they could receive a State subsidy of
one-sixth of the amount. That subsidy was available to all unions paying
voluntary unemployment benefit, whether their trade was in the compulsory scheme or not. It was intended to encourage voluntary unemployment
insurance across the whole spectrum of organised labour and applied to a
maximum benefit of 12s a week.[20]

In addition to compulsory insurance applicable to certain trades and
subsidised by employers and the State, the Act therefore offered all trade
unions a subsidy towards their voluntary unemployment insurance. That
kind of subsidy was a feature of the Ghent system, familiar in several
European countries including Germany. But there it was local, confined
to certain municipalities. In Britain it was available everywhere.

There was a price to be paid. To qualify for a subsidy, a union had to
make its rules and accounts available to inspection. In practice it would
have to keep its benefit fund separate from other funds. Public subsidies to
unemployment benefit was one thing; subsidies to the unions' fighting
funds quite another. One was politically acceptable; the other not. This
demand for benefit funds to be separate from other union funds represented a major infringement of union autonomy. Unions had always
regarded unemployment benefit as a means of support for their members
in trade disputes, and had framed their rules with that in mind. Yet far
from being spurned, the money was overwhelmingly accepted.[21] The
scrutiny of their accounts, and in the case of section 106 of their rule
books too, necessarily changed the way that unions could spend their
funds. It led to greater central control over branches, to ensure that State
rebates and subsidies were not endangered by breaches of the rules.[22]

---

[19] Section 105 of the Act and administrative arrangements described in *Unemployment insurance:
proceedings of the Board of Trade*, pp. 6–7.

[20] Section 106 of the Act. Unions that qualified under section 105 (see above) could not count their
expenditure twice, i.e in their case this subsidy applied only to expenditure between 9s.4d and 12s.
per week.

[21] *Unemployment insurance: proceedings of the Board of Trade*, pp. 14–15, for the figures.

[22] Noel Whiteside, 'Mutuality and politics: state policy and trade union benefit systems in Britain,
France and Germany in the late nineteenth century' (unpublished paper given at the European Social
Science History Conference, May 1996), pp. 17–18.

Employers were also offered concessions in exchange for their co-operation. To encourage regularity of employment, they were offered a rebate of one-third of their contribution for any worker whom they had employed continuously for twelve months (cl.94). To encourage systematic short-time working in periods of depression the contributions of both employer and worker could be remitted altogether (section 96). To encourage employers to engage their workers solely through a labour exchange, all administrative responsibilities for national insurance could be transferred to the exchange (section 99). On the other hand, employers of casual labour in the insured trades were penalised by having to pay a full week's contribution for every separate period of employment within that week.[23]

British unemployment insurance therefore paid careful attention to the ways in which fluctuations in demand for labour impinged on different industries, and provided a policy for a condition that applied to only some of them. The state of 'unemployment' which the Act addressed was relatively easy to distinguish from the state of 'employment'. That was not the case across the economy as a whole, where the very concept was blurred by short-time working or chronic irregularity. By limiting the Act to these trades and further insisting on a waiting period of a week before entitlement set in, it was possible to disregard the many conceptual problems inherent in the notion of 'unemployment' elsewhere.[24] This focus on the condition of the trade was reinforced by a requirement to keep separate accounts for each group of trades. Benefits and contributions could be adjusted by the Board of Trade according to the state of the particular fund. The Board's power to extend the Act to further trades, far from indicating an intention to extend it indiscriminately across the economy as was to happen after the war, indicated the opposite. The limited scope of the Act was at the time justified by caution, but the caution was prompted not so much by a lack of statistics as by the problems of administration inherent in the policy.[25]

Within these bounds the administrative problems were successfully surmounted. The scheme did not have to deal with any cyclical downturn before 1914. It was easily able to weather the short-lived turmoil in the labour market that followed the outbreak of the war. Thereafter the problems of unemployment and the so-called unemployables disappeared

---

[23] The same applied to the contribution of workers. For employment of two days or less, the contribution was slightly reduced but still represented a penalty.

[24] Noel Whiteside, *Bad times* (London, 1991), ch. 3.

[25] Harris, *Unemployment*, pp. 301–2, 304, 306 and 312.

under the demand for maximum industrial production. But so did the conditions for which it had been designed. Its extension to cover munitions work within any industry or trade in 1916 could still be justified in terms of the original concepts. Attempts to extend it more widely, so as to build up reserves for the uncertain future, fell foul of the refusal of the trade unions to co-operate.[26] However, the end of war-time conditions inaugurated a new era. As it staggered from one expedient to the next the government subverted a policy that had once been carefully designed. In 1920 compulsory unemployment insurance was extended with minor exceptions to the economy as a whole. But the onset of long-term mass unemployment in 1921 turned what had once been an actuarially calculated insurance scheme into a 'dole' given on conditions that were a political compromise between the demands of the unemployed and those of the Treasury. The principle of a flat-rate benefit for all, originally a fundamental principle of British national insurance, was dropped in 1921 in favour of dependants' allowances, on very understandable grounds but at the cost of complicating the relation between the two forms of national insurance, with dire consequences.[27] In short, after the war British unemployment insurance entered a new phase with only superficial resemblance to the previous years.

---

[26] W. R. Garside, *British unemployment 1919–1939: a study in public policy* (Cambridge, 1990), pp. 34–5; Noel Whiteside, 'Welfare legislation and the unions during the First World War', HJ, 23 (1980), 857–74.

[27] Garside, *British unemployment*, passim.

17

Unemployment policies in Germany

(A) MUNICIPAL GOVERNMENT

There has been no need so far to know much about the German municipality. For purposes of poor relief, most municipalities met their responsibilities as local poor law authorities by delegating them to a body which, while legally subordinate, was constituted differently from the mayor, *Magistrat* and directly elected councillors who are the subject of this section.

British historiography on the origins of the welfare state encompasses both central and local government. The changing relations of central to local government form a significant part of the subject, as we saw in the previous chapter.[1] Not so in Germany. There, exclusive emphasis on social insurance has focused attention on central government, chiefly on the *Reich* and occasionally on the federated states represented in the *Bundesrat*. By starting the detailed study in the 1880s, it has been easy to overlook the fact that sickness insurance laws were originally permissive, depending for their adoption on the decision of the local authority.

This chapter on German unemployment policies should serve as a reminder that policy developments were not always initiated by central government but also occurred at municipal level.

How was a German municipality governed? We cannot take account of every variation across the states of the Empire. However, since Prussia was by far the largest state and contained most of the larger cities, we shall not go far wrong if we concentrate at this stage on the principal Prussian models. There were minor differences in the southern parts of Germany and in the parts of Prussia annexed in the 1860s, which are shortly mentioned in Dawson, but 'most German forms of urban government

---

[1] See generally, E. P. Hennock, 'Central/local government relations in England: an outline 1800–1950', *Urban History Yearbook*, 9 (1982), 38–49.

repeat with greater or lesser fidelity the leading features of the Prussian bi-cameral system as in operation in the eastern provinces'.[2]

The government of Prussian towns was in many ways like that of the Prussian state.[3] Policy was not made, as in an English borough, by the elected town council operating through subordinate committees, but by a separate executive body, known as the *Magistrat*. Its members were nominated by the elected town council, as was the head of the executive, the mayor or *Bürgermeister*, but their appointment had to be confirmed by the state authority. The members of the *Magistrat*, most of whom had responsibility for a particular aspect of the administration, fulfilling as it were the function of a minister, were either honorary or salaried.[4] If honorary, they were respected citizens with past service on the town council appointed for six years at a time. If salaried, they were appointed for twelve years at a time. The duties of treasurer, town clerk, director of education and director of public works had to be undertaken by salaried specialists. With the expansion of municipal functions in the 1890s and after, there was a tendency for the number of salaried members to increase and for the *Magistrat* to become progressively professionalised.[5]

In their responsibility for a particular department of administration, these salaried members of the *Magistrat* combined the role of the committee chairmen of an English town council with that of its salaried chief official, except that power rested, not with a committee, but with them.

The mayor (*Bürgermeister*) was always a salaried professional civil servant, nominated by the town council but appointed by the state. The appointment was for twelve years in the first instance, and thereafter usually for life. He was the head of the municipal government. In the eastern provinces of Prussia the members of the *Magistrat* were jointly responsible with him for the conduct of the administration (as in a British cabinet); in the western provinces they were his subordinates (as Secretaries of State were to a Prussian Prime Minister or a German Chancellor). The directly elected town council exercised full control over finance and was

---

[2] W. H. Dawson, *Municipal life and government in Germany* (London, 1914), pp. 85–6.
[3] The parallel is W. H. Dawson's, who provides the best description in English of the functions and constitution of German municipalities in this period: Dawson, *Municipal Life*, pp. 84ff.
[4] I have avoided calling them aldermen, as Dawson did. English aldermen were no different in function from the rest of the council; the only difference was that they were indirectly elected for six years. The members of the *Magistrat* were functionally different from councillors.
[5] Wolfgang Hofmann, 'Aufgaben und Struktur der kommunalen Selbstverwaltung in der Zeit der Hochindustrialisierung', in K. G. A. Jeserich *et al.* (eds.), *Deutsche Verwaltungsgeschichte* (Stuttgart, 1984), vol. 3, pp. 606–20; Wolfgang Krabbe, *Die deutsche Stadt im 19. und 20. Jahrhundert* (Göttingen, 1989), pp. 137–9.

entitled to give or withhold its consent from all policy proposals emanating from the *Magistrat*.

To sum up, a German town was governed by a professional *Bürgermeister* in conjunction with an executive body composed partly of prominent citizens, partly and increasingly of salaried officials. This was chosen by the elected council and acted with its consent and under its financial control. An English borough was governed by an elected town council operating through policy-making committees with the advice of salaried officials.

How were town councillors elected? The municipal franchise was a taxpayers' franchise of a very peculiar kind. The Prussian version was first introduced in 1845 for the Rhineland and extended to the other provinces in 1850.[6] It divided the total electorate into three classes according to the amount of taxes paid by each person. The first class contained as many of the largest taxpayers as accounted for one-third of the total tax revenue between them. The second contained those medium-sized taxpayers who contributed the second third of the revenue. The third class contained all the rest. It was a system that represented wealth, and produced great contrasts between the size of the classes. The tax reforms of 1891, intended to reduce the burden on recipients of small incomes, also reduced their political power in local elections. In the late 1890s the third class in the Rhineland contained more than 90 per cent of the local electorate. In addition to representing wealth, the franchise also made special provisions for the representation of house property. In Saxony the municipal franchise was very similar, but it was significantly less extreme in the southern states, a factor whose significance will be taken into account later.

The objects on which English municipalities could spend the rates were governed by the principle of *ultra vires*, by means of which the courts had sharply restricted municipal discretion.[7] Although German municipalities were also ultimately accountable to the courts, these had developed a generous interpretation of municipal powers, ruling in 1885 that these included 'everything that promotes the well-being of the community and the material interests and mental development of the individual'.[8] Tax reforms, first in Prussia in 1891 and soon followed in the larger states of

---

[6] Helmuth Croon, *Die gesellschaftlichen Auswirkungen des Gemeindewahlrechts in den Gemeinden und Kreisen des Rheinlands und Westfalens im 19. Jahrhundert* (Cologne and Opladen, 1960); Dawson, *Municipal life.*

[7] W. O. Hart, *Hart's introduction to the law of local government and administration* (6th edn, London, 1957), pp. 271–9.

[8] Christian Engeli and Wolfgang Haus (eds.), *Quellen zum modernen Verfassungsrecht in Deutschland* (Stuttgart, 1975), pp. 19–20; Dawson, *Municipal life*, pp. 31–7.

southern Germany, improved their potential revenues. Whereas the revenue of English municipalities was mostly dependent on the taxation of 'real' i.e. immovable property, German municipalities were also free to impose an addition to the state income tax.[9] It was largely this that enabled the bigger German towns to develop the innovative policies around the turn of the century for which they became internationally famous.

(B) PUBLIC RELIEF WORKS AND LABOUR REGISTRIES

The role that the economic downturn of 1885–6 had played in England in heightening awareness of unemployment as a social problem was played in Germany by the downturn of 1892–4. Thus the difference in timing was not great. A conference in Frankfurt in October 1893, attended by 150 representatives of local authorities, trade unions, industry, commerce and academic experts, demonstrated widespread awareness of the problem. It also changed the terms in which unemployment was perceived. By focusing on seasonal and cyclical unemployment, it revealed the inadequacy of traditional charity and the inappropriateness of stigmatising poor relief. It therefore turned attention to work-creation and the placement of the unemployed.[10]

Anselm Faust's treatment of public relief works shows marked similarities to that of José Harris for England and this highlights differences where they occur. Like Harris, he aims to confine himself to municipal policies outside the scope of poor law authorities, and for the same reason, namely the unacceptability of the deterrent and stigmatising features of poor relief. As in England, municipal relief works were limited to the winter months.

The numbers of municipalities that provided public relief works between 1891 and 1913 show peaks in 1894–5, 1901–3 and 1907–9, as does the maximum number employed at any one time. These were the years of economic downturn. But some municipalities provided relief work in the winter even in normal times. A census in 1895 had revealed the large proportion of building workers among the unemployed in a year of good

[9] For England see E.P. Hennock, 'Finance and politics in urban local government in England, 1835–1900', HJ, 6 (1963), 213–25. For Germany, see Heffter, *Deutsche Selbstverwaltung*, pp. 719–20; Wilhelm Gerhoff and Franz Meisel (eds.), *Handbuch der Finanzwissenschaft* (Tübingen, 1929), vol. 3, pp. 50–2.

[10] Anselm Faust, *Arbeitsmarktpolitik im Deutschen Kaiserreich. Arbeitsvermittlung, Arbeitsbeschaffung und Arbeitslosenunterstützung 1890–1918. Vierteljahrschrift für Sozial- und Wirtschaftsgeschichte, Beiheft 79.* (Stuttgart, 1986), pp. 43–4 and 121. A condensation of Faust's work in English can be found in W.J. Mommsen (ed.), *The emergence of the welfare state in Britain and Germany 1850–1950* (London, 1981), pp. 150–63.

trade.[11] Some authorities were apparently willing to provide relief work for the seasonally unemployed, not merely inadvertently in times of general distress but as a matter of policy. The figures suggest that in years of economic downturn more municipalities were persuaded to provide relief works and for a larger total of workers, as other groups added their weight to the demand for action.

The distinction between municipal relief works and poor relief was in practice no easier to make than in England. Although some limited range of unskilled work was provided in the winter months, the considerations that went into the hiring of workers were driven by the priorities of poor relief. Considerations of need took preference to those of efficiency and led for instance to the employment of married men in preference to single ones. Considerations of poor law entitlement led to the exclusion of anyone without a claim on local funds. All this added to the cost, as did the deliberate use of labour-intensive methods when mechanical means were available, but it was justified as a means to reduce the cost of poor relief. Since commercial discipline was less important, deterrence and stricter eligibility criteria were relied upon to keep the numbers down. 'Specially scheduled public works in times of distress are poor relief, though poor relief that partly covers its costs', as one Frankfurt official put it bluntly.[12]

Although public relief works in the winter had become a regular occurrence in some towns, many municipalities wanted to avoid this development. Hence their reluctance to establish the co-ordinating institutions that would have made for efficiency and which were developed in England.[13] The need for the equivalent of the English distress committees was perhaps less obvious where poor relief, although administered separately by its own officials, was rarely the responsibility of an altogether separate elected authority. Charitable involvement was also less important. Faust does not refer to it and gives the impression that the finance was entirely municipal. There is evidence from Barmen in the 1870s that charity did contribute to the cost of relief works, but this appears to have been

---

[11] Table 16 in Faust, *Arbeitsmarktpolitik*, p. 298. Within that cyclical pattern there was a marked rise in total numbers, especially towards the end of the period. That is plausible, but it is hard to know how much of this was due to better reporting by the several sources on which the table relies. For the census of 1895 see Karl Christian Führer, *Arbeitslosigkeit und die Entstehung der Arbeitslosenversicherung in Deutschland 1902–1927* (Berlin, 1990), pp. 13–14. This work devotes 114 pages to the period up to 1914 but concentrates on unemployment insurance. For that reason Faust's work is the more illuminating.

[12] Karl Flesch, quoted in Faust, *Arbeitsmarktpolitik*, p. 120, n. 43. See also *ibid.*, pp. 115–16 and 118.

[13] Faust, *Arbeitsmarktpolitik*, pp. 117 and 121.

exceptional.[14] These two considerations may explain why co-ordination seemed less urgent than in England.

In crisis years municipal expenditure on public relief works could be substantial. The cost had to be met from revenue; state regulations normally precluded the use of loans. In 1908/9 costs were 1.1 per cent of total revenue, and in Düsseldorf as much as 4.6 per cent. These problems could not be solved by appealing to the state or the *Reich* for help. Neither authority was prepared to be involved. They rejected all requests on the ground that poor relief was a local responsibility and advised municipalities to solve their problem by phasing their normal work into the winter months. Municipalities already knew that this was greatly preferable, but their scope for such a course was quite inadequate.[15]

Here lay the greatest difference between the two countries. In England central government had also originally declared these matters to be the province of local authorities and had been content with exhortation. It maintained this stance until 1905. Even then it merely insisted on the establishment of local distress committees, who were left to decide what should be done. But from 1906, demands in Parliament for the State to accept some responsibility for financing public relief works became impossible to ignore. Unwilling to embark on that course of action, the government turned to labour exchanges as its chosen instrument of policy, hoping to reduce the problem of unemployment to bearable proportions. At that point labour exchanges were few in England, whereas they had long been widely diffused in Germany. They had developed there in a very different context.

German labour registries as instruments of social policy were established by a public authority, usually the municipality, or by a voluntary association with the help of a municipal subsidy.[16] They never constituted more than a minority of labour registries. These also included those of trade unions, employers or guilds, but above all private ventures run for profit.[17] The last enjoyed far and away the largest part of the business. They lost some

---

[14] Wolfgang Köllmann, *Sozialgeschichte der Stadt Barmen im 19. Jahrhundert* (Tübingen, 1960), p. 174. See also *ibid.*, p. 172, for 1848–9. F. Reitzenstein, 'Über Beschäftigung arbeitsloser Armer', in *Schriften des Deutschen Vereins für Armenpflege und Wohltätigkeit*, vol. 4 (Leipzig, 1887), pp. 1–17.

[15] Faust, *Arbeitsmarktpolitik*, pp. 118–20 and 122–4.

[16] The German word *Arbeitsnachweis* was not translated as labour exchange until Beveridge did so in October 1907 in the *Morning Post*. Prior to that it was translated as labour registry, as in D. F. Schloss, *Report of the Board of Trade on agencies and methods for dealing with the unemployed in certain foreign countries*, BPP 1905 Cd.2304, LXXIII, 471. I shall use 'labour registry' for the German institution throughout.

[17] Faust lists eight categories of non-profit-making registries. Not all need be discussed here.

of their business share in the course of the years, but in 1912 all the several types of non-profit-making registries are estimated to have accounted still for only about 30 per cent of the total business. After 1869 private registries were free of official control until 1900 when they had to obtain a licence. The terms on which this was issued became stricter in 1910. One of several motives for the official encouragement of public registries was the recognition of the ease with which profit-making registries could abuse their position.[18]

Trade unions regarded measures to find jobs for their members when unemployed as part of a strategy to emancipate workers from the pressure of want and strengthen their bargaining power in the labour market. For the increasing number of unions that gave unemployment benefit, some form of registry of jobs available in the trade was in any case essential. From 1889 registries established by the 'free'. i.e. social democratic, unions increased steadily. But they tended to be small and limited to the skilled occupations in which the trade union movement had taken hold. The non-socialist unions entered the field only in the early 1900s and did so to a lesser extent. In 1904 the Liberal, Christian and free trade unions between them accounted for roughly 11 per cent of places filled by non-profit-making registries, but they lost momentum thereafter. In 1912 their share was just under 10 per cent, at a time when that of public registries was 36.1 per cent and of employer-controlled ones 33.5 per cent.[19]

Like those of the unions, the large regional registries set up by employer federations in the early 1900s were instruments of the class struggle, designed to weaken trade union influence by black-listing and generally discriminating against labour activists. They also served the interest of productivity by improving the selection process of workers. They tended to be in trades with a high demand for skilled labour, particularly where trade unions had taken hold. Large firms in heavy industry were less interested. Their labour force was weakly organised and largely unskilled, while selection of key personnel could be handled in-house.[20]

Most public registries were originally founded by philanthropic bodies. The increase in public and publicly subsidised registries in the 1880s signalled, however, a move away from traditional links with poor relief and charity towards a focus on the normal labour market. In other words what Beveridge was arguing for after 1905 had already occurred in Germany a decade earlier. This was partly due to an interest in monitoring

---

[18] Faust, *Arbeitsmarktpolitik*, pp. 70 and 48–51.
[19] *Ibid.*, pp. 52–4, Tables 7 and 10.   [20] *Ibid.*, pp. 55–56 and 91–101.

and reducing fluctuations in local labour demand. It also represented a new social policy to act as mediators in the conflict between capital and labour. It was a local manifestation of the *Neue Kurs*, Berlepsch's reform programme after Bismarck's fall, and saw the establishment of labour courts (*Gewerbegerichte*) along the lines of Berlepsch's law of 1891. It survived in certain localities long after the *Neue Kurs* had fallen victim to reaction at *Reich* level.[21] The significance of labour courts for labour registries was due to their assessors, who were recruited in equal numbers from employers and workers. They could be drawn upon for the committee of management of the public registries wherever an equal representation of capital and labour (known as the principle of parity) was regarded as important.

Like public relief works, public registries were given a boost by the economic downturn of 1892–4. In 1890 there were only four but at least sixty-nine were established in 1894–6 in Prussia alone. There were 122 new foundations across the *Reich* in the course of the 1890s. By 1904 there were 216 more or less active public registries, compared with the twenty-one recorded in England in 1905.[22]

Public labour registries received various degrees of encouragement and support from the governments of individual states. Prussia and Saxony confined themselves largely to exhortation. Württemberg gave subsidies to municipalities, whereas Baden, being a smaller state, subsidised a more centralised system. Bavaria had established registries in the 1890s under the police authorities but recommended their transfer in 1900 to municipalities and their incorporation into a multi-purpose municipal labour office (*Arbeitsamt*). In Hesse there were registries at the higher level of the *Kreis* instead of the municipal model. Alsace-Lorraine established a regional network. There were measures in many other parts of Germany to extend the reach of public registries across the region.[23]

[21] On Berlepsch's reforms generally see pp. 124–7 above, and p. 127, n. 18 above, for the law of 1891. This had been framed in consultation with Frankfurt where such a court had been in existence since 1886. J. D. Rolling, *Liberals, socialists and city government in imperial Germany: the case of Frankfurt am Main 1900–1918* (Madison, 1979), pp. 351–3. For these courts in their municipal setting see also W. R. Krabbe, 'Die Gründung städtischer Arbeitsschutzanstalten in Deutschland', in W. Conze and U. Engelhardt (eds.), *Arbeiterexistenz im 19. Jahrhundert* (Stuttgart, 1981), pp. 425–45; A. von Saldern, 'Gewerbegerichte im Wilhelminischen Deutschland', in K-H. Manegold (ed.), *Wissenschaft, Wirtschaft und Technik* (Munich, 1969).

[22] Faust, *Arbeitsmarktpolitik* Table 8 for Germany; A. Lowry, *Labour bureaux*, BPP 1906 (86) CII, 363 for England. For the earlier figures see Faust, *Arbeitsmarktpolitik*, Tables 10 and 11.

[23] Faust, *Arbeitsmarktpolitik*, pp. 76–9; W. Breunig, *Soziale Verhältnisse der Arbeiterschaft und der sozialistischen Arbeiterbewegung in Ludwigshafen am Rhein 1869–1919* (Ludwigshafen, 1976), pp. 383–5; Hans Peter Jans, *Sozialpolitik und Wohlfahrtspflege in Ulm 1870–1930* (Stuttgart, 1994), pp. 240–6; R. G. Huber, *Sozialer Wandel und politische Konflikte in einer süd-hessischen Industriestadt. Kommunalpolitik der SPD in Offenbach 1898–1914* (Darmstadt, 1985), pp. 251–2.

The effectiveness of public registries depended, however, less on the intentions of their sponsors than on the willingness of employers and workers to use them. Originally their clients were mainly unskilled labourers but the rise of employer registries gradually convinced trade unions to reconsider their tactics. They had originally viewed public registries with distrust. Now they realised that these might well give them more influence, if they played their hand well in municipal politics. The decisive turning point for the free trade unions, as marked by congress resolutions, came in 1908 but locally there was much variety. By then the Liberal and Christian trade unions had long accepted that participation in public registries was their only possible course of action. Trade unions therefore increasingly turned their attention to public registries organised on the basis of parity of representation and used their local political influence to obtain maximum control.[24]

Some municipalities established registries under their direct administrative control, others kept them at arm's length by means of a committee of management based on parity of representation. The disadvantage of the purely municipal model lay in the unrepresentative nature of the municipal franchise, which generally threw municipal power into the hands of the propertied classes at the expense of the workers.[25] A purely municipal model was therefore irrelevant wherever the views of organised labour had to be taken into account. This explains the increasing adoption of the indirect model. In most towns the balance between the powers of the committee of management and those of the municipal administration, i.e. the mayor and *Magistrat*, became an issue of conflict, since the superior organisation of the free unions made their control of the committee a distinct possibility. The appointment of the director and his staff, the determination of the procedures, especially those for labour disputes, were not matters that municipal authorities were willing or able to surrender. Such issues were also fiercely debated by the Association of German Labour Registries, the forum for all non-profit-making registries, which after 1909 received a subsidy from the *Reich*.[26] The procedure that became widely adopted was to announce the fact of a labour dispute but to publicise the vacancies nevertheless. This was subsequently also done in Britain.[27]

---

[24] Faust, *Arbeitsmarktpolitik*, pp. 80–8.   [25] See the Introduction above.
[26] Cf. the German Central Committee to combat TB, discussed on p. 260 above.
[27] Faust, *Arbeitsmarktpolitik*, pp. 64–8; Harris, *Unemployment and politics*, p. 287.

Employer federations with their own registries were even by the end of this period still hostile to the principle of parity. They objected to public registries as interference in their own affairs, based too often on ignorance, sentimentality and a willingness to make political concessions to the unions. They filled almost as many places in 1912 as did public registries. But the situation differed between branches of industry. Since not all employers belonged to federations, there were always some willing to serve on the management committees of public registries.[28] The principle of parity was more generally accepted in the towns of southern Germany, with their mixed economies, than in the more monolithic industrial regions of Westphalia and the Rhineland.[29]

The more that public registries tried to woo employers, the more suspicious trade unions became in their turn. Ideally they would have preferred to keep the municipality out of these matters and to establish registries by direct agreement with employers.[30] Such arrangements were rarely feasible.[31]

Except for measures to control profit-making registries, no policy commanded a majority in the *Reichstag*. But there was an increasingly vocal lobby in favour of establishing public registries on a national basis, as in Britain. That would prevent them from being used as instruments in the class struggle, but that object was far more contentious than in Britain. Well aware of employer opposition, Delbrück, the Secretary of State for the Interior, went no further than to express the pious hope that the two sides of industry would establish registries by mutual agreement and so make state intervention unnecessary. That would become a fertile idea in post-war Germany, where labour relations had been totally transformed. But it was irrelevant in 1913 and merely a cover for inaction. Such inaction carried implications for unemployment insurance. For in the words of the authoritative report of the Imperial Statistical Office on that issue, 'in every form of unemployment benefit or insurance an adequate system of labour registries is of the first importance'. In that context adequate meant acceptable to both capital and labour.[32]

---

[28] On the complexities of employer politics, see Faust, *Arbeitsmarktpolitik*, pp. 91–9.

[29] *Ibid.*, p. 63.

[30] *Ibid.*, pp. 84–6. Hugo Lindemann, the social democratic expert on municipal affairs, sharply condemned the ambitions of municipal social reformers to mediate in the relations between capital and labour, declaring that workers were adults and did not stand in need of tutelage. *Ibid.*, p. 139.

[31] Mainly in printing, food retailing, leather and wood working. Faust, *Arbeitsmarktpolitik*, Table 14(c), see also *ibid.*, p. 108.

[32] Faust, *Arbeitsmarktpolitik*, pp. 103–7; Kaiserliches Statistisches Amt, *Die bestehenden Einrichtungen zur Versicherung gegen die Folgen der Arbeitslosigkeit im Ausland und im Deutschen Reich* (Berlin, 1906), vol. I, p. 667, as quoted in Beveridge, *Power and influence*, p. 61.

(c) INSURANCE

The rising cost of municipal public relief works and the growing realisation of their unproductiveness made German municipalities receptive to any policies that would encourage workers to save for their needs in times of unemployment.

Provident funds subsidised by employers or the charitable public had long been familiar when Cologne launched a municipal insurance fund against winter unemployment in 1896. The details were drawn from Berne, the Swiss federal capital, where a similar fund had been started in 1893. Membership was voluntary and open to male workers over eighteen with at least two years' residence. A weekly contribution qualified for full unemployment benefit in the winter months for the first twenty days and on a reduced basis thereafter. The scheme's viability depended heavily on contributions from the charitable public but any deficit was met from municipal funds. Anyone able to join a trade union that paid unemployed benefit would have had a less restricted deal. Those who joined did so because they were highly likely to be unemployed in winter. Thus 69 per cent of the membership in 1904–5 belonged to the building trades. The contributions originally covered less than half the outlay. As charitable contributions declined, the municipality raised workers' contributions while at the same time adapting its regulations in a largely futile attempt to appeal to a wider range of workers. The scheme limped on until 1911 when it was reconstructed on the principle of the Ghent system.[33]

It was against this background that attention turned in 1901 to the practice introduced in Ghent, the industrial city in Belgium.[34] What the two programmes had in common was a municipal subsidy to encourage workers to insure against unemployment. In most other respects they were profoundly different. The Ghent system avoided the danger of attracting only the worst risks. It recruited, not individuals, but the trade unions that had recently begun to pay unemployment benefit in increasing numbers

---

[33] Faust, *Arbeitsmarktpolitik*, pp. 139–41. More fully in Kaiserliches Statistisches Amt, *Die bestehenden Einrichtungen*, vol. 1.

[34] For the Ghent system in its German context see the work cited in n. 10 above, as well as Führer, *Arbeitslosigkeit* and Hansjoachim Henning, 'Arbeitslosenversicherung vor 1914: das Genter System und seine Übernahme in Deutschland', in H. Kellenbenz (ed.), *Wirtschaftpolitik und Arbeitsmarkt* (Munich, 1974). In English see Bénédicte Zimmermann, 'Municipal innovations versus national wait-and-see attitudes: unemployment policies in *Kaiserreich* Germany (1871–1918)', in Michèle Dagenais *et al.* (eds.), *Municipal services and employees in the modern city: New historical approaches* (London, 2003); and in particular George Steinmetz, *Regulating the social: the welfare state and local politics in imperial Germany* (Princeton, 1993). There is a description by Beveridge in *Royal Commission on the Poor Laws*, Minutes of Evidence, Appendix XXI (K). BPP 1910 Cd.5068.

Table 17.1. *German trade union unemployment insurance*

	percentage of all unions	percentage of all members
Free, i.e. Social Democratic, unions		
1895	26	22
1900	36	34
1905	64	66
1910	81	83
1914	92	97
Hirsch-Duncker, i.e. Liberal, unions[a]		
1904	81	99.7
1913	70	88
Christian unions		
1904	35	17
1913	68	68

Note:
[a] The Liberal trade unions paid no benefit for seasonal unemployment. Numerically it was the free unions that mattered.
Source: Faust, *Arbeitsmarktpolitik*, Tables 17 and 19, and p. 138.

(see Table 17.1). Unions needed to retain members who had been recruited in periods of good employment and militant action and they saw the provision of benefits as a possible answer to that problem.

The German proposals based on the Ghent precedent added a municipal subsidy to union unemployment benefit. That normally increased benefit by 50 per cent for a defined maximum number of days. To the individual trade union members this offered a sum markedly less inadequate than they received through their union.[35]

There were other advantages in the Ghent precedent and these appealed to the municipal authorities. As in Ghent, they would be able to hand responsibility for the administration of the scheme to the unions, which could identify cases of genuinely involuntary unemployment more effectively than any bureaucratic authority provided that the interests of the two bodies were made to coincide. That was to some extent achieved. Unions were required to pay their members the full amount of the subsidised benefit but could reclaim the subsidy only retrospectively. They also had to

[35] Where the Ghent system was adopted it applied equally to white-collar unions not listed in the table from Faust reproduced as Table 17.1.

separate their unemployment benefit accounts from those of other union funds and make them available to scrutiny.

Even that left much scope for contention over the circumstances under which unemployment could be regarded as genuinely involuntary. Was relevant employment to be limited to places that paid the union rate? Was refusal to accept work where there was an industrial dispute to be regarded as involuntary unemployment? Was dismissal for non-cooperation with management policies to count as involuntary? In practice the Ghent system presupposed agreement over disputed matters such as these. Whatever may have been the case in Belgium, in Germany such agreement was not easy to reach.

That is why in Germany municipal subsidies were limited to places with a public labour registry and a management committee recruited in equal numbers from employers and workers. Nowhere else could acceptable rules be drawn up on such contentious matters. This largely removed hiring and firing from the sphere of the class struggle.

There was a snag in all this. The more the public subsidies were targeted on improving the unemployment benefits of trade unionists, the less appropriate were they as a substitute for public relief works. Relief schemes dealt overwhelmingly with unorganised workers or with workers, like those in the building trades, whose unions did not pay unemployment benefit. It is true that subsidies were usually also available to individual members of a savings scheme but these schemes never caught on. Where the subsidy was proportionate to the original benefit, as it had been in Ghent and was in the majority of German towns that adopted the system, proportionality consistently favoured the better off. In Freiburg 61 per cent of municipal subsidies went in 1912 to the relatively well-paid printers, whose level of organisation and benefit was exceptionally high, and who suffered from seasonal unemployment.[36] Far from targeting the normal clientele of public relief schemes and making such expenditure less necessary, the Ghent system ignored the most vulnerable among the unemployed and channelled public funds to those who were already to some extent provided for.

It is probably more appropriate to regard the adoption of the Ghent system in Germany as designed to give public authorities a role in

---

[36] *Der gegenwärtige Stand der Arbeitslosenfürsorge und Versicherung in Deutschland. Schriften der Deutschen Gesellschaft zur Bekämpfung der Arbeitslosigkeit.* Heft 2 (Berlin, 1913), pp. 41–2. See also *Verhandlungen des Dritten Deutschen Städtetags am 12. Sept. 1911 zu Posen zur Frage der Arbeitslosenversicherung* (Berlin, 1911), p. 13.

moderating local class conflict. It built on public labour registries, just as these depended on the labour courts for the personnel of their management committees. In the absence of these institutions, there could be no support for unemployment insurance.

Yet public labour registries on the basis of parity were a highly contested policy. They were unacceptable to the employer federations, who had no intention of giving up their own registries. That blocked any move towards public registries on a national basis. If their opposition also precluded any consideration of unemployment insurance at *Reich* level, so much the better from their point of view. To the advocates of social policy, unemployment might be a social problem; to many powerful employers it was a factor that weakened the influence of trade unions in the labour market. The less that was known about its dimensions, the less evidence there would be to create a demand for *Reich* unemployment insurance alongside the other branches of insurance.

Even those who regarded unemployment as a social problem with undesirable consequences for the health of the nation and the quality of German labour could be critical of the Ghent system for its irrelevance to the needs of the very poor. In addition dependence on the financial resources of a single locality made it unaffordable except where the employment structure was highly diversified. Even there it exposed the municipal finances to a worrying risk. There were far fewer towns prepared to adopt the system than even the skewed distribution of public labour exchanges would have suggested.

It is remarkable that there were any at all. Between 1907 and 1914 the Ghent system was adopted in eleven towns of more than 50,000 inhabitants and some smaller ones. The first group consisted of Strassburg (Alsace) in 1907, Mühlhausen (Alsace) in 1909, Freiburg (Baden) in 1910, Cologne and Schöneberg (both Prussia) in 1911, Kaiserslautern (Bavaria) in 1912, Stuttgart (Württemberg) in 1912, Offenbach (Hesse) in 1913, Heidelberg and Mannheim (Baden) in 1913 and Frankfurt am Main (Prussia) in 1914. Mannheim had introduced a subsidised savings scheme for individuals in 1911 and the Ghent system in 1913. Frankfurt's unemployment insurance, adopted only four days before the outbreak of war, was shelved for the duration and never came into effect at all.[37]

---

[37] The list is from George Steinmetz, *Regulating the social*, p. 205 and n. 142. Steinmetz examines the various conflicting claims made in the earlier literature. The small towns were Schiltigheim, Bischheim, Illkirch and Grafenstade in the immediate vicinity of Strassburg; Erlangen and Frankenthal in Bavaria; Schwäbisch-Gmünd, Esslingen and Feuerbach near Stuttgart in Württemberg; and Friedrichshaide (bei Ronnenberg) and Eupen in Prussia.

What made the policy possible in these towns when it had been rejected in many others?[38] The employment structure is one factor. Where the local economy was dominated by large employers, particularly those of unskilled or semi-skilled labour, the power conferred on the highest ratepayers by the voting system of almost all the states gave the policy no chance. That was dramatically exemplified in Ludwigshafen where a successful last-minute opposition was mounted by the large chemical firms despite a majority on the town council being in favour.[39] In most similar towns things never got so far. The great industrial concentrations of Saxony and Prussia are missing from the list, as they are largely unrepresented among the location of parity-based public labour registries.

That permitted a more favourable political environment. For the bias towards the south-west was due not only to economic differences but also to the municipal franchise, which deliberately over-represented the higher taxpayers. Of the various states it was Prussia and Saxony whose municipal franchise was most biased in this respect.[40] Matters were less extreme in the south-west with the most egalitarian adult male franchise in the annexed territories of Alsace-Lorraine and in the small state of Hesse. Three of the eleven towns were located there, among them Offenbach and Mühlhausen, which were prior to 1914 the only municipalities of any size to be governed by an SPD majority.

Five further towns, and a significant number of the group of smaller ones, were located in Württemberg, Baden and Bavaria. While declaring unemployment relief to be a municipal matter, these states did not entirely wash their hands of it. They recommended the adoption of the Ghent system although they offered no financial support. In Prussia and the rest of the north even that degree of Platonic support was ruled out. The

---

[38] By 1913 at least thirty-five towns had considered the policy but rejected it, including Augsburg, Danzig, Dresden, Duisburg, Düsseldorf, Essen, Hamburg, Ludwigshafen, Munich, Nürnberg and Berlin. Führer, *Arbeitslosigkeit*, p. 116; Ilse Fischer, *Industrialisierung, sozialer Konflikt und politische Willensbildung in der Stadtgemeinde. Ein Beitrag zur Sozialgeschichte Augsburgs 1840–1914* (Augsburg, 1977), pp. 390–6; *Soziale Praxis* (the weekly publication of the *Gesellschaft für Soziale Reform*), the best source on this subject.

[39] They appealed to the state government. Details in Steinmetz, *Regulating the social*, pp. 208–9, based on Willi Breunig, *Soziale Verhältnisse der Arbeiterschaft und der sozialistischen Arbeiterbewegung in Ludwigshafen am Rhein 1869–1919* (Ludwigshafen, 1976).

[40] See the Introduction above. The Prussian franchise described there did not, however, apply to Frankfurt. When this was annexed in 1867 it received a different municipal constitution from the older Prussian territories. Its municipal electorate was restricted by a modest taxpayers' qualification but not divided into three unequal classes each with a right to elect one-third of the council. It was therefore more egalitarian than that of towns in the older Prussian territories. Heinrich Heffter, *Die Deutsche Selbstverwaltung im 19. Jahrhundert* (Stuttgart, 1950), p. 484.

difference was due to the party-political composition of the respective state legislatures. The details need not concern us.

For the party politics that finally mattered were those of the municipal councils. The adoption of the Ghent system required the authorisation of money, and that could be done only by a majority of the full town council. Party politics are therefore a crucial element in any explanation for the adoption of municipal unemployment insurance.

That is so evident that it is surprising that it has been ignored in almost every German study of the subject. One reason may be the nature of the most obvious sources. The administrative problems of unemployment insurance loomed so large at the time that contemporary surveys focused on administrative details and on regulations through which to minimise the objections of critics.[41] Yet as Führer points out, in the absence of agreement among employers and workers on whether to regard unemployment as a weapon in the class struggle, or of a higher authority able and willing to impose a policy on both sides, these administrative problems were secondary for any explanation of action or inaction.[42]

A further reason lies in the focus of traditional German historiography on outstanding mayors, thereby largely accepting the view, frequently asserted at the time, that party politics were unimportant in municipal affairs. Studies of outstanding mayors are about policy and show little interest in their subject's capacity to navigate the seas of party politics. Yet party politics had become a fact by the early twentieth century, the period during which the Ghent system became an issue.[43]

The few studies that pay any attention to this matter at municipal level are from outside Germany. One significant examination of the policy in English, and up to now an indispensable source for those unable to read German, is by the American sociologist, George Steinmetz. He rightly regards the Ghent system as the outstanding example of a fundamental change in German welfare policy, in that it accepted trade unions as legitimate actors in the regulation of social problems.[44] Unlike Faust, he is not content merely with structural explanations for the pattern of acceptance and rejection. He pays attention to the party-political composition of the councils, but is hampered by a sociologist's disdain for narrative

---

[41] That applies also largely to the reports provided in *Soziale Praxis*, the weekly publication of the *Gesellschaft für Soziale Reform*.

[42] Führer, *Arbeitslosigkeit*, p. 50.

[43] Jan Palmowski, *Urban liberalism in imperial Germany. Frankfurt am Main, 1866–1914* (Oxford, 1999), pp. 1–23, for the historiography of municipalities and party politics.

[44] He labels it proto-corporatism. Steinmetz, *Regulating the social*, pp. 205 and 212–13.

history. He has preferred to construct a model based on regression analysis, into which he fed the number of Social Democratic councillors and of Liberal councillors in the relevant towns among other factors. These 'political variables' led to the conclusion that Liberal council strength related negatively to the introduction of the Ghent system, whereas Social Democrat council strength related positively. But he confesses to being unable to distinguish between different kinds of Liberals and this seriously impairs the value of his conclusion. As he had earlier pointed out, the National Liberals were usually too close to employer opinion to be in favour of the policy but various groups of Left Liberals were sympathetic.[45] Since it was only in municipal politics that Liberalism remained strong enough to play the effective governing role that was denied it at *Reich* or state level, variations of Liberalism deserve more attention than Steinmetz's model can provide. In the *Reichstag* these Left Liberal groups carried little weight, but there were towns, particularly in Greater Berlin and the south-west, where that was not the case.

Steinmetz is on firmer ground with the Social Democrats, and his observation that 'the original impetus behind the Ghent system in all cities seems to have come from either the socialists or the unions', takes us some way but not far enough to understand the outcome.[46]

Only for Frankfurt does any study provide a rounded picture of the political dynamics involved.[47] In his Oxford-based research Palmowski argues strongly for the importance of party in the history of Frankfurt well before the impact of the SPD. He demonstrates that the development of different Liberal parties there, clearly distinctive in policies, aims, religious profile, rhetoric and organisation, dates from the 1860s. These were the National Liberals, who in the absence of a significant Conservative presence rallied all pro-government groups, a small Progressive party (*Freisinn*) and a Democratic party with its roots in the politics of Frankfurt before Prussian annexation. Over the next half-century the Progressives moved from their initial alliance with the National Liberals to a merger with the

---

[45] Steinmetz, *Regulating the social*, pp. 209–11, esp. nn. 185 and 191–2.

[46] Steinmetz, *Regulating the social*, p. 205.

[47] John D. Rolling, *Liberals, socialists and city government in imperial Germany: the case of Frankfurt am Main 1900–1918* (Madison, 1979), and Palmowski, *Urban Liberalism*, based on doctoral theses from the University of Wisconsin and the University of Oxford, respectively. They can be usefully supplemented by Ralf Roth, *Gewerkschaftskartell und Sozialpolitik in Frankfurt am Main. Arbeiterbewegung vor dem ersten Weltkrieg zwischen Restauration und Liberaler Erneuerung* (Frankfurt, 1991), a German study in the tradition of labour movement history; and Hans Killian Weitensteiner, *Karl Flesch – Kommunale Sozialpolitik in Frankfurt am Main* (Frankfurt, 1976), a good example of the historiography of municipal officialdom.

Democrats in 1910. In the early years of the twentieth century there was a firm body of Left Liberals able and willing to accommodate the SPD, preferring municipal control with their support to yielding power to the National Liberals.[48]

The Democrats had in the 1880s begun to take an interest in the inequalities of the formal labour contract and in municipal intervention to increase working-class income, as of right and not merely out of charity. Karl Flesch, the leading mind behind these ideas, was appointed to the *Magistrat* in 1884. After tackling the reform of poor relief he turned to labour issues. Frankfurt was in the forefront of measures to establish conciliation procedures, to introduce and to expand the function of a public labour registry based on parity and to provide non-pauperising public relief works. To these causes we can add measures to raise the income and the rights of municipal workers, to provide them with sub-sidised housing and to require municipal contractors to pay standard wages. These measures were the result of collaboration with the SPD, who generally voiced the views of the trades council (*Gewerkschaftskartell*).[49]

The idea of unemployment insurance had been floated by the Democrats around 1904–6 but had elicited no interest in the socialist camp. In 1908, as a reaction to mounting pressure on trade union benefit funds, the matter was raised by the trades council and quickly thereafter by the SPD in the council chamber. Here was a proposal that the Democrats found more congenial than the extension of public relief works for which the socialists had previously agitated. The council appointed a committee to work with the *Magistrat* on the details of the policy. But unlike previous social reforms, this found no support from the mayor, Franz Adickes, who adopted effective delaying tactics. But on his retirement in 1912 the council appointed a more co-operative successor. Disagreement over administra-tive details were resolved only in July 1914, which is why a policy in which Frankfurt had been something of a pioneer was introduced only on the eve of war.

For no other town are the secondary sources so informative, in so far as they exist at all. But fragmentary evidence for another four towns suggests that the common feature is a conjunction of Left Liberals and SPD in

[48] Palmowski, *Urban liberalism*, pp. 313 and 339, for the summing up and the composition of the city council respectively.

[49] Weitensteiner, *Karl Flesch*; Rolling, *Liberals*; and, with a more nuanced view of relations of the SPD and trade-unions, Roth, *Gewerkschaftskartell*.

control of the elected council, working together with a reformist mayor and *Magistrat*.

Strassburg, the first German town to adopt the Ghent system, had been in the van of social policy since the 1890s, when a public labour registry was established. It was reorganised in 1903 under a vigorous director, an ex-printer turned journalist with good connections in the trade union world. He gained the confidence of organised labour and then the co-operation of the employers. In 1903 Strassburg was also the first town to include a minimum wage clause in municipal contracts. At that time the SPD held over one-third of the council seats. The policy was the work of Rudolf Schwander, a forceful member of the *Magistrat*. In 1905 Schwander was responsible for a revised labour contract for municipal workers that was remarkable for including annual wage increments, family allowances, pension rights, workers' committees and paid holidays.

In 1906 Schwander was elected with the support of the substantial body of SPD members on the council to succeed the retiring mayor. His election was strongly contested by an anti-socialist bloc of Centre and Liberals which the Left Liberals had refused to join. The principal division was over social policy. A mere two months later Strassburg adopted unemployment insurance on the Ghent model. Although the anti-socialists bloc had by 1908 much reduced the SPD presence on the council, Schwander's social policies survived unscathed. That suggests an important role for the Left Liberal *Demokratische Volkspartei*, founded in Alsace in the mid-1890s and active in the municipal politics of Strassburg and Mühlhausen. Its support of Schwander and its co-operation with the SPD minority on the council would appear to have been crucial.[50]

Electoral arrangements between these two parties in the municipal politics of Mühlhausen gave the SPD its foothold in the council and briefly produced an absolute majority for the SPD from 1902 to 1904. It resulted in a spectacular series of social policy measures along the now familiar lines. From 1904 to 1914 the SPD was dependent on Left Liberal support for its measures, which included the adoption of the Ghent system in 1910.[51]

Offenbach was a working-class town whose upper class lived across the river in Frankfurt. It had a large working-class electorate, since in Hesse even quite small taxpayers qualified for the vote. These were favourable

[50] H. D. Soell, 'Die sozialdemokratische Arbeiterbewegung im Reichsland Elsass-Lothringen 1871–1918' (PhD thesis, Heidelberg University, 1963); Alexander Dominicus, *Strassburgs deutsche Bürgermeister. Back und Schwander 1873–1918* (2nd edn, Frankfurt, 1939), the most useful of several studies of Schwander.

[51] Soell, 'Sozialdemokratische Arbeiterbewegung'.

conditions for the SPD; less favourable was the rule that the highest one-third of taxpayers was entitled to elect half the council. For the SPD, control was therefore impossible without support in that section of the electorate. Much depended on relations between the other parties and their willingness to support each other on the second ballot. The hold of the SPD over the town, first obtained in 1900, fluctuated therefore throughout the next decade, but the precarious relations between the other parties did not permit the reversal of the SPD policies. These were 'progressive' measures of a kind found elsewhere, for example better school provision, free school milk, school swimming baths, infant milk depots and the like. To these were added improvements in the condition of municipal workers, as in Strassburg and Frankfurt. In 1907, shortly before losing control of the council once more, the SPD succeeded in nominating a new mayor, a Left Liberal who was receptive to innovations in social policy. They returned to power in 1910, this time in coalition with the Left Liberals, and in 1913 adopted the Ghent system. The case of Offenbach is strongly reminiscent of Frankfurt, except that in this working-class town the SPD was the dominant partner in the alliance with the Left Liberals.[52]

When we turn to the expanding suburbs beyond Berlin, we find Schöneberg under the control of a large-scale developer whose tenants voted as they were told. That state of affairs was ended in 1908 by a new Left Liberal organisation. Its focus was on land reform, including the taxation of rising land values, and on reform of the municipal franchise to remove the privileged status of house-owners. Two years later the death of the mayor gave Left Liberals the opportunity to appoint a congenial successor. They chose Alexander Dominicus, Schwander's right-hand man in Strassburg. That provides the context for the adoption of the Ghent system in what was essentially a dormitory suburb, but where an island of man-ufacture and small industry provided an SPD stronghold. The *Magistrat* soon took on a Left Liberal complexion although not without bitter internal conflict.[53]

These towns suggest a common pattern. Whether it is the only pattern can be determined only through research in local records and the press. This pattern shows a striking resemblance to the relation of Liberals and the Labour Party in Britain at the time. Here, at municipal level, we find

[52] R. G. Huber, *Sozialer Wandel und politische Konflikte in einer süd-hessischen Industriestadt. Kommunalpolitik der SPD in Offenbach 1898–1914* (Darmstadt, 1985).

[53] Christoph Bernhardt, *Bauplatz Gross-Berlin* (Berlin, 1998), pp. 181–99. For Strassburg's record in housing reform see Max Rehm, *Rudolf Schwander und Kurt Blaum, Wegbahner neuzeitlicher Kommunalpolitik aus dem Elsass* (Stuttgart, 1974), pp. 26–7.

the effective reformist Liberalism that was missing from German national politics.

Even towns that embarked on what was widely seen as a step into the unknown often did so experimentally and for a limited period. Many others were convinced that unemployment insurance required compulsion and nationwide risk-sharing. That was the German tradition. The issue came to a head in 1911 at the meeting of the German association of municipal corporations, the *Städtetag*, where Adickes from Frankfurt, speaking on behalf of the executive committee, subjected the Ghent system to detailed and devastating critical analysis.[54] He pointed out the irrelevance of subsidies to trade union unemployment benefit when the vast majority of building workers, who were the most seriously affected by seasonal unemployment, were not included. He argued the case for distinguishing between different occupations and their respective requirements, as was being done in Britain. Only the obvious needs of the building trades should be given immediate attention. The rest should be left for later detailed investigation. Where insurance was required, as in that instance, it had to be compulsory if those in greatest need were not to be ignored. He pointed out that even in Britain, where trade unionism had a far longer and more successful history, no more than 14 per cent of the workers in the trades that were to be insured were unionised.[55] Whether insurance required public subsidy or whether contributions from employers would meet the case, was left an open question. With the acceptance of these proposals and the decision to forward them to the *Bundesrat* for consideration, the *Städtetag* passed the initiative to the *Reich* government. The government took no notice of even so modest an appeal as this, regarding its modesty as merely the thin end of the wedge.

The fact is that the government intended to take no notice unless the *Reichstag* forced it to do so, and there was no sign of that. In 1902 with an impending election at a time of heightened unemployment, there had been just enough agreement among the parties to request the Chancellor to set up a joint commission of representatives from the government and the parties together with independent experts to investigate existing provisions for the unemployed and make proposals for an appropriate extension of *Reich* insurance. The requirement to make proposals was removed by the *Bundesrat*, as was the notion of a joint commission. The Imperial Statistical

---

[54] *Verhandlungen des Dritten Deutschen Städtetags* (Berlin, 1911).
[55] He was quoting from the memorandum in support of the bill as originally introduced. By 1913 it was 20 per cent. See p. 300 above.

Office was merely instructed to undertake an investigation of existing provisions.[56] That proved to be the high-water-mark of agreement between the parties. They were unable to prevent this dilution of their request, nor ever again to mount a majority initiative.

Both Conservative parties and the National Liberals sympathised to varying degrees with the employer organisations' rejection of any form of unemployment insurance. They were unwilling to exert pressure on the government. The Centre party, which had taken the initiative in 1902, was torn between the conflicting views of their rural, employer and trade union supporters. In practice they preferred to work with the Conservatives in support of the Bülow and Bethmann-Hollweg governments. That left the Left Liberals and the SPD. The former had a clear position on unemployment insurance but insignificant numbers of *Reichstag* deputies. The SPD had in 1902 formally committed itself to a *Reich* insurance under the control of all the insured. But the trade unions had already declared for the nationwide adoption of the Ghent system, which would give them sole control of what they regarded as exclusively their business. Since it was unlikely that the party's preferred option would be adopted in the near future, it compromised by regarding the extension of the Ghent system as its short-term goal and a proper *Reich* insurance under the control of all the insured as their long-term one. That was the position which it reaffirmed in 1913. Although it was then the largest party in the *Reichstag*, an SPD initiative supported by only the Left Liberals left the government unimpressed.[57]

It should be remembered that the years 1908 to 1911 had been taken up, first, with codification of the insurance laws including the introduction of insurance for widows and orphans, and then with the controversial introduction of separate white-collar insurance. On that issue the middle-class parties had produced a majority, but their unity was achieved in opposition to the socialists. Under pressure from the white-collar movement and on the eve of an election, they had forced the government into a policy contrary to its own preferences and those of the employer organisations. The politics of white-collar insurance had been expensive for employers and had hardened their opposition to further measures of insurance. After that bruising experience the government did not wish to return so soon

---

[56] This was a thorough work in three parts on provisions both at home and abroad, *Die bestehenden Einrichtungen*, published in two volumes in 1906. Führer, *Arbeitslosigkeit*, pp. 94–5, for the politics of 1902.

[57] Führer, *Arbeitslosigkeit*, pp. 51–69 and 93–109; Faust, *Arbeitsmarktpolitik*, pp. 163–70.

to the subject or to take on the employers yet again. This time there was patently no need.

In the government's view, a pause was needed after 1911 to smooth the ruffled feathers of employers. In January 1914 Delbrück told the *Reichstag* that he regarded social policy measures as now essentially complete.[58]

The small number of German towns that adopted the Ghent system, and the small number of trade unionists that qualified for support should be compared with the provision made under the National Insurance Act for subsidies to British trade unions that paid unemployment benefits to their members. That had proved highly acceptable to trade unions despite the conditions attached to it. The Board of Trade had decided in the autumn of 1908 not to model British unemployment insurance on the Ghent system but to opt for compulsion to be imposed on all workers, unionised and non-unionised, in a specific number of trades.[59] That did not, however, prevent the Ghent system, from exerting influence on British policy. Comparable figures are impossible to obtain, but subsidies on the Ghent model undoubtedly benefited more trade unionists in Britain than ever they did in Germany.[60]

That is not as surprising as it might at first sight appear. There is something odd about the attraction of the Ghent system for reformers in a country as little unionised as Germany, and one in which the dominant form of trade unionism, that of the social democrats, was so contested.[61] German reformers had tried hard to publicise the administrative safeguards designed to ensure that public funds did not support the strike funds of the

---

[58] Karl Erich Born, *Wirtschaft- und Sozialgeschichte des Deutschen Kaiserreichs (1867/71–1914)* (Stuttgart, 1985), p. 146. That does not mean that the government would not have been prepared to yield to pressure on behalf of powerful vested interests in German industry, as it had done for tobacco and potash in 1909 and 1910 respectively. Faust, *Arbeitsmarktpolitik*, pp. 187–90. It means that there was no sign of further painful requirements.

[59] Harris, *Unemployment*, pp. 303–4. Churchill wanted contributions from employers as well as workers and that ruled out any scheme solely limited to trade union members.

[60] By 12 July 1913, 343 unions with an estimated 1,259,846 members had applied to qualify for subsidies under section 106 of the Act. Of these 275 with an estimated 1,104,223 members had been admitted; the rest were still being processed. *Unemployment insurance: proceedings of the Board of Trade under Part II of the National Insurance Act, 1911*, BPP 1913 Cd.6965 XXXVI, 677, p. 15. Whatever the complete figures of trade unionists qualifying in the limited number of German towns, they could not possibly have been of such proportions.

[61] Klaus Saul, 'Repression or integration? The state, trade unions and industrial disputes in imperial Germany', in Wolfgang Mommsen and Hans-Gerhard Husung (eds.), *The development of trade unionism in Great Britain and Germany, 1880–1914* (London, 1985), pp. 339–56, provides a good idea in English of the contradictions and inconsistencies of German labour policy in this period. See Saul's massive book, *Staat, Industrie, Arbeiterbewegung im Kaiserreich. Zur Innen- und Sozialpolitik des Wilhelminischen Deutschland 1903–1914* (Düsseldorf, 1974), for further details.

unions, but they never succeeded in quashing the view that it was proposed to throw millions into the lap of the socialists.[62]

In Ghent half the labour force was unionised and trade unions were widely regarded in a positive light. At all levels of Belgian politics the socialist *parti ouvrier* played a prominent role and worked with other parties. Resistance to the Ghent model in Germany is less surprising than its limited reception.[63] On the other hand, in Britain rejection of the Ghent model was largely on technical grounds. Measures to boost the position of trade unions were widely acceptable, particularly to Liberals.[64]

It is hard to decide which political explanation for the absence of unemployment insurance at *Reich* level before the First World War is the more important: the relative weakness of organised labour in the German political system compared with Britain, or the white-collar factor. For the purpose of comparison with Britain I would choose the former. Obstructive employers and reluctant governments were not unknown in Britain. Unemployment policy provides as good an example of that as any. They were neutralised by the recognition that organised labour through the Labour Party and the influence of trade unions in the Liberal Party could exert pressure that a Liberal government ignored at its peril – pressure to take up the issue, not necessarily pressure to tackle it in the manner that labour would have wished, and pressure to make time for it even in as crowded a programme as in 1909–11. That is not to discount the reasons why white-collar insurance was important in Germany and not in Britain. It is to emphasise that organised labour was effectively integrated as a part of the British political system, whereas in Germany at *Reich* level it was not. At that level the SPD was frozen out most of the time. Most of the time it merely provided the rallying point against which the other parties were able to unite.

Could there have been non-political differences to account for the primacy of unemployment policy in Britain and not in Germany? It is often suggested that, compared with Britain, the German economy in the

---

[62] Adickes in 1911. *Verhandlungen des Dritten Deutschen Städtetags* (Berlin, 1911), p. 15. See also Führer, *Arbeitslosigkeit*, p. 89, for the view of the CDI that this 'would make the employer whet the knife that was turned against him'.

[63] In 1905 of the approximately 132,000 trade unionists in Belgium, around 70 per cent were in socialist or related unions and about 10 per cent in Catholic ones. The Belgian provinces, led by that of Liège, also subsidised trade union benefit funds, as after 1908 did the State. Constance A. Kiehel, *Unemployment insurance in Belgium: a national development of the Ghent and Liège systems* (New York, 1932), pp. 73–101.

[64] E.g. the legal privileges enjoyed by trade unions under the Trade Union Act of 1906 and the acceptance of unions as approved societies under Part 1 of the National Insurance Act 1911.

early years of the twentieth century was enjoying the benefits of its later take-off into industrialisation and for that reason experienced lower levels of unemployment. In other words that it was for economic reasons that unemployment was less of an issue in German politics. Both contemporary perceptions of unemployment and modern sophisticated historical estimates suffer, however, from a lack of reliable information. That is particularly true for contemporaries, whose perceptions are more relevant here. British statistics of unemployment were published regularly since 1888 by the Board of Trade. They were based on the returns of trade unions that provided unemployment benefit to their members and were easily available. Regular figures based on the records of German trade unions were not officially published until 1903.[65] The officially published trade union returns between 1904 and 1913 in both countries show the German totals to be generally lower except in 1913.[66] But the percentage of unemployment in the trade unions that made returns tells us little about actual unemployment in either country, and it tells us less about Germany than Britain. Both sets of figures under-represent the less skilled, who were more liable to unemployment. The far smaller proportion of the labour force that was unionised in Germany under-represented them even more than in Britain. Since before 1913 German building workers, even if unionised, did not receive unemployment benefit the highly seasonal building trades were scarcely represented in the German figures. It is therefore interesting that these exceeded those for Britain in 1913 for the first time.[67]

These regular returns from trade unions with all their shortcomings were not the only source of information on German unemployment. In 1895 the Imperial Statistical Office did something that had no British parallel. It produced comprehensive figures on unemployment for the total German labour force, based on a special set of questions inserted into both the occupational census (*Berufszählung*) and the general census of that year.

---

[65] The interest in unemployment created by the cyclical down-turn of 1892–4 led after 1892 to the publication of trade union figures in the *Sozialpolitisches Zentralblatt*, later *Soziale Praxis*, but little notice was taken at the time. Even now these figures are not used by such historians of the subject as Faust and Führer.

[66] C. H. Feinstein, *National income, expenditure and output of the UK, 1855–1965* (Cambridge, 1972), Table 57; Führer, *Arbeitslosigkeit*, Table I.

[67] The Board of Trade and the German Imperial Statistical Office engaged in a debate over the comparability of their respective unemployment statistics. Whereas not all the British explanations for the difference in the level of the figures could stand scrutiny, there was enough to suggest that the German figures did indeed under-represent the situation compared with the British ones: *The cost of living in German towns*. Appendix IX, *Comparability of British and German statistics of unemployment*, BPP 1908 Cd.4032, CVIII; Kaiserliches Statistisches Amt, *Gebiete und Methoden der amtlichen Arbeiterstatistik* (Berlin, 1913), pp. 71–4.

That made it possible to compare unemployment levels in June and December 1895. They were 1.1 per cent and 3.4 per cent respectively of the total labour force. This exercise said nothing about cyclical unemployment, but it provided information on seasonal unemployment in a good year and identified the occupations that were most at risk. It was never repeated. In 1912, when the *Städtetag* petitioned for an investigation of unemployment in individual industries, this was opposed within the Prussian government on the ground that such investigations only caused unnecessary anxiety.[68] That reasoning brings us sharply back to the consideration of politics. In the final analysis, the difference between the two countries over the need for a national unemployment policy was due, not to the state of the economy, but to their different political priorities.

---

[68] Führer, *Arbeitslosigkeit*, pp. 12–15; Linda A. Heilmann, *Industrial unemployment in Germany 1873–1913* (London, 1991).

Conclusion and epilogue

What do we now know about the connection between the German Poor Law and compulsory insurance? Has our understanding of British social policy been enriched in return by what we have learnt about Germany? Where has an Anglo-German comparative approach led us? These are the questions that should now be addressed.

A study of German social insurance should start not with Bismarck, but with Prussia in the 1840s. That was when the precedents were established which acquired a national dimension in the 1880s. The imposition of compulsory insurance at the discretion of Prussian local authorities was part of the process whereby the state in Prussia broke the hold of guilds over the economy. The emancipation of labour relations from guild control required new policies on poor relief compatible with labour mobility. These in turn created problems for which compulsory insurance under state control was regarded as a solution.

Here is a significant difference between Prussia and England. In Prussia the history of compulsory insurance followed from the decline of the guilds both logically and chronologically. In England the guilds had declined so much earlier that there was no obvious connection with working-class mutual help. What we do find in both countries is a close connection between Poor Law reform and the growth of insurance.

It is a connection based on the desire of those in authority to protect the interests of local taxpayers. In England and Wales protection was primarily through deterrence, designed to give workers the incentive to meet their needs by other means. In Prussia local relief authorities were authorised to protect their finances by reviving structures of mutual obligation familiar from the recent past. Workers' insurance in Prussia drew its precedents from the *Gesellenladen*, the structures of mutual help that had previously been imposed on journeymen by the guilds. English workers' associations of mutual help were established, at least in the eighteenth and early nineteenth centuries, in independence of the masters, if not in actual opposition to them.

331

English friendly societies sprang from the capacity of workers to meet their needs through free association and gradually also to construct institutions beyond the immediate locality. In Prussia the State distrusted any developments of this kind. But it wished workers to meet the needs that authority itself had identified, and drew on a tradition of *dirigism* to compel them to do so under its supervision. That had the additional advantage from its point of view of ensuring that they did not again endanger the established order.

Hence relations with the State contrasted in a number of ways.

1. Compulsion in Prussia; voluntary association in England.
2. Local State supervision in Prussia; in England after 1830 the development of a new and Liberal notion of the appropriate role of the State.
3. Increasingly tighter definition of the benefits to be provided on the one hand, flexibility in response to changing circumstances on the other. The change in 1876 from *Hilfskassen* to *Krankenkassen* is one example of the former; the requirement in 1892 on all funds to provide medical treatment is another.[1]

In 1876 compulsory insurance as it had developed in Prussia was adapted to the conditions of the new Empire, but the 1880s brought further big changes. So far State compulsion had been at the discretion of local authorities. In the 1880s local discretion was replaced by national uniformity. And whereas insurance had previously been intended to reduce the cost of poor relief, its primary objects were now different. They were to deal with the consequences of industrial accidents in the interests of expanding industrial production, to enhance the power of the new *Reich*, and to commend it to the loyalty of the industrial working class.

That had implications for the needs to be met. Having been targeted on support for limited periods of sickness and the cost of funerals, compulsory insurance now also provided support for long-term impairment of earning capacity, through industrial accidents in 1884 and through other forms of invalidity and old age in 1889. The administrative structures designed for these purposes were themselves innovative. By the end of the decade there were three laws and three forms of administration. But in no case was reducing the cost of poor relief the priority any more. Thus compulsory insurance diversified and developed.

By starting in the 1840s the innovations of the 1880s appear in a different light, yet without losing their significance. Compulsory insurance now takes off in different directions, different from before and different from England.

---

[1] See pp. 156 and 161–2 above. See also p. 335 below.

The poor law context, that had originally provided a striking element of similarity, does so no longer. Under the impulse of new priorities poor law considerations become marginal to German insurance policy.

From this point on there are two sets of conclusions to be drawn. The most important is to trace the consequences of this break in the continuity of German priorities, and to contrast these with developments in England, where poor law considerations continued to exert the dominant influence. But before we turn to that matter we should pursue the question that has never been given the sustained attention in German historiography which it deserves. What role did poor law considerations continue to play in the history of German social policy in this period?[2]

The poor law could never be entirely irrelevant to compulsory insurance in Germany. The attraction of insurance benefits depended on being in some measure preferable to poor relief, and their payment was bound to reduce the need for poor relief expenditure, if not in general, at least in these particular cases.

For the recipient the attraction of the insurance pension lay in the fact that it was a right and came in cash. It was not necessarily intended to remove him or her from dependence on the poor law authority, as was the case in England. In a significant number of cases it was too small for that. But it gave the pensioner an improved status in the eyes of the authority and of the community. That he or she had cash to contribute was especially important where poor relief took the form of boarding-out in someone else's home, as it often did in the countryside. And the same consideration made him or her more welcome when taken in by family members, as happened everywhere.[3]

The relief of poor law authorities from what was diagnosed in November 1881 as an excessive burden played no part in the decisions that led to accident insurance, since the relevant decisions had already been made.[4] On the contrary, Bismarck was only too willing to make poor law authorities contribute some of their putative savings to the cost of insurance for lower-paid workers. That would have increased the inequality of the burden placed on individual authorities, which had been one of their great grievances. It was the discovery that this was impossible on technical grounds, since the place of residence and that of employment did not

---

[2] The obverse of this question, the effect of social insurance on the continuing history of poor relief, has been dealt with in chapter 2, section (e), above.

[3] A point eloquently made by Bismarck in the *Reichstag* on 2 April 1881. Bismarck, *Gesammelte Werke* (Berlin, 1935), vol. 12, pp. 236ff, partly quoted in Ritter, *Social welfare*, p. 48.

[4] See pp. 38–9 above.

necessarily coincide, that made him propose to place the burden on the states instead, or even on the *Reich*.[5]

The plans to reform the poor law by imposing some of the financial burden on the states were shelved, but they can be regarded as evidence for the thinking in the Economic Section of the Ministry of the Interior that dealt with social policy. Robert Bosse, its head, had been responsible for these abortive poor law reforms; he was also responsible for pushing ahead with old age and invalidity insurance in 1887 quite independently of Bismarck. Those pensions would have a greater impact on the expenditure of poor law authorities than accident insurance could ever have.[6]

The overt justification for old age and invalidity pensions was always the Imperial Message of November 1881 that Bosse himself had drafted. When Brentano, a complete outsider, welcomed them as really a reform of the poor law, which would shift the burden from local taxpayers to workers and employers and the *Reich*, he was vehemently repudiated. As I have suggested, that might well have been due to the fact that objectively speaking the draft bill certainly lent itself to such an interpretation and bore an interesting resemblance to suggestions that had been made in confidential memoranda of 1881.[7] The problem with this appeal to the Imperial Message is that the proposals failed to fulfil the promise held out on that occasion. The Imperial Message had spoken of a *higher* measure of state support for those suffering from old age and invalidity.[8] Now it was proposed that an important minority should receive *less* than before while paying one-third of the cost themselves! The low level of the proposed pensions was fatal to the proposal in its original form. But it could be argued that, even after the *Reichstag* had taken control of the legislative process, the law in its final form still served the purpose of removing much of the burden of old age and invalidity from the poor law. The discourse was about commending the *Reich* to the loyalty of the workers. Yet if there was ever a quiet intention to address the problem of the excessive financial burden on the poor law, that intention was certainly fulfilled. To that extent one can detect the shadow of that earlier preoccupation with the problems of the poor law in the events of the later 1880s.[9]

---

[5] For the *Reichstag's* rejection of that policy see p. 90 above.
[6] See p. 187 above.   [7] See p. 191 above.
[8] 'Abdruck der Kaiserlichen Botschaft', ZSR, 27 (1881), 730–5, here p. 735.
[9] During the debate on the second reading of the bill Boetticher held out the prospect that, once the majority of those who were now the responsibility of poor relief were dealt with by insurance, it would be easier to reach agreement on the allocation of the burden of the remainder. SBRT 1888/9, vol. 5 (6 April 1889), p. 1340. No poor law reform on those lines was ever undertaken; matters were left as before but the pressure for reform seems to have been dissipated.

With that glance at the issue of the poor law let us return to the principal theme, i.e. the consequences of the new priorities in German insurance policy. The diversification and development that had begun in the 1880s did not end with the law of 1889. Four developments deserve particular attention. The first and most significant was the differentiation of contributions and benefits according to wage levels, which was accentuated with almost every legislative amendment. Significant stages in this process are the sickness insurance law of 1883, the amendment by the *Reichstag* of the original bill for invalidity and old age insurance in July 1889, the invalidity law of 1899, and the white-collar insurance of 1911. That marks the point reached by 1914, but the process was not over. It found its fullest expression in the technically more sophisticated differentiation introduced by the Pensions Law of 1957.[10]

The second development was the provision of long-term medical care by the pension boards.[11] The third was the emphasis on rehabilitation by the *Berufsgenossenschaften* responsible for accident insurance.[12] Finally there was the requirement on the free funds under sickness insurance in 1892 to provide medical treatment in addition to income support, and the beginning of medical treatment for dependants.[13]

The dynamic nature of German social insurance owed much to the importance attached to making it acceptable. In that respect it succeeded. Fifteen years after its nationwide introduction in the face of a sullen population membership had come to be regarded as a good thing, a bonus sought after by those who were still excluded. The attraction for wage and salary earners was that it obliged employers to contribute to the needs. State compulsion not state finance was the attraction. The state subsidy towards invalidity and old age pensions was willingly dispensed with by white-collar workers in 1911, as it had already been by voluntary contributors to invalidity insurance before. That in turn produced a new dynamism from below, taking the process further than governments would have wished and involving them in conflict with employers. But as the case of unemployment insurance demonstrates, not all such demands could be mobilised across the Empire as a whole.[14]

---

[10] See Hockerts, *Sozialpolitische Entscheidungen in Nachkriegsdeutschland. Allierte und deutsche Sozialpolitik 1945 bis 1957* (Stuttgart, 1980), or Hockerts, 'German post-war social policies', in W. J. Mommsen (ed.), *The emergence of the welfare state in Britain and Germany 1850–1950* (London, 1981), pp. 328–31.

[11] See chapter 13, section (b), above.   [12] See p. 114 above.   [13] See pp. 272–3 above.

[14] See also the more ambiguous case of the scheduling of occupational diseases as qualifying for compensation under accident insurance. In that case a majority in the *Reichstag* obtained an amendment of the law but could not force the government to act in the limited time available. See p. 116 above.

It also owed something to self-interest on the part of the insurance bodies, who introduced measures that might reduce expenditure in the long run. These initiatives drew on funds that had to be accumulated as reserves under the invalidity and old age legislation. The existence of these funds seems to have led the civil servants in charge of the pension boards down avenues that could never have been justified on financial grounds.[15]

In contrast to the stultifying effect of Treasury control on British national insurance, the history of German social insurance shows outcomes repeatedly exceeding the intentions of the legislators. A range of institutional developments never envisaged in 1883 did much to justify Lohmann's faith in self-government. The involvement of the SPD after 1892 in the elections for the local sickness insurance funds gave Social Democrats a degree of influence that had certainly not been intended, and contributed towards their identification with the potentialities of that branch of social insurance. The systematic implementation of the optional clause in the Law of 1884, which allowed *Berufsgenossenschaften* to issue safety regulations and appoint inspectors if they thought it in their financial interest, owed much to the enthusiasm with which the senior officials of the newly created Imperial Insurance Office threw themselves into their work. This elevated what had been regarded as a marginal aspect of accident insurance into a significant feature of the system. That had at least been an option within the law, which is more than can be said of the involvement of pension boards in medical treatment. It was the Imperial Insurance Office supporting the original initiative, establishing its legality, and chivvying other pension boards into following suit, that made a major new development possible.

This dynamism was in marked contrast to the British approach to national insurance. The flexibility that had characterised the voluntary associations had originally enabled them to appeal to a larger percentage of the working population than compulsion coupled with local discretion in Germany ever did. Even compulsion by *Reich* legislation brought no clear numerical advantage as long as the new forms of administration were still experimental. But judged by numbers and percentages of the working

---

[15] The 'investment' in sanatoria and other medical institutions was not the only example. By 1914 between 3,000 and 4,000 low-cost dwelling units had been constructed with loans from the pension boards, on which the financial returns compared most unfavourably with what could have been earned from other investments. Florian Tennstedt, 'Sozialgeschichte der Sozialversicherung', in Maria Blohmke *et al.* (eds.), *Handbuch der Sozialmedizin* (Stuttgart, 1976), vol. 3, p. 460. On German housing policy in general, see N. Bullock and J. Reid, *The movement for housing reform in Germany and France 1840–1914* (Cambridge, 1985).

population covered, in the course of the 1890s compulsion and the establishment of nationwide institutions proved to be the more effective formula.

The flexibility that had characterised voluntary associations was still in evidence. That is demonstrated by the growth of new provident societies that were no longer linked to sociability at a time when new commercialised leisure facilities had reduced the attraction of the weekly 'club evening'. For those who did not value the old sociability, centralised societies were able to offer savers a higher return on their money. But the fact remains that once nationwide coverage mattered, voluntarism was not enough, and no amount of belief in progress would make it so.

That national insurance plays a significantly smaller role in Britain than in Germany is well known to students of contemporary welfare states. This book has demonstrated that this difference goes right back to the founding years before 1914. Decisions taken in that period are crucial to the long-term difference between the countries.

I shall make three points about this difference. One deals with the contrast between flat-rate contributions linked to minimal benefits and graduated contributions linked to benefits according to income levels. The second is about the greater reliance on general taxation as an alternative to social insurance. The third contrasts the control exercised in Britain by the state over the provision of medical treatment and the remuneration of doctors with the powers of the German insurance funds.

(A) FLAT-RATE VERSUS GRADUATED CONTRIBUTIONS AND BENEFITS

There are two fundamental questions to be asked about British social policy in 1906–11, of which the first comes in two parts. Why was the Poor Law replaced, first by old age pensions financed from general taxation, and then almost immediately by national insurance for health and unemployment? And why did national insurance retain the emphasis on flat-rate contributions and minimal benefits that had been abandoned in Germany? The first question arises from British development and has been frequently addressed. The second question is posed by the comparative approach and has usually been neglected. The answer to the two parts of the first question is found in chapters 11 and 12. What is the answer to the second?

I would suggest that this difference between Britain and Germany stems from an abiding difference of attitude to compulsory savings. It was one thing for compulsory local taxation that had financed the poor law to be replaced by compulsory savings, if that made it possible to adopt a non-deterrent approach to some deserving groups. That the savings were imposed on the beneficiaries and relieved the taxpayers in an era of rearmament was an additional attraction. It was quite another to regard compulsory saving as an acceptable substitute for the voluntary savings of those able and willing to practise the virtue of thrift. For compulsion prevented thrift from being a virtue. Those who saved because they must could no longer be regarded as mature persons able to look ahead and to forego immediate pleasures in the greater interest of safeguarding future necessities. Minimum savings might have to be imposed on all for the sake of the feckless and improvident – in this period on all below a certain income, in the 1940s on all heads of households – but that did not make them as acceptable as voluntary savings had always been. Compulsion remained decidedly a *pis aller* in British society with its liberal values. The willingness of German policy-makers to accept that workers in general could not be relied upon to make the savings necessary for their future needs unless they were compelled, a point repeatedly made in the 1870s and never again repudiated, had no parallel in Britain in this decisive period, and for only the briefest period since. While these words are being written a British government is once again unwilling to require compulsory savings adequate for an income on retirement, despite the overwhelming evidence that this is the only way to ensure the future well-being of the population.

The years leading up to 1914 witnessed the reluctant abandonment of the belief in voluntary provision in areas outside those few, such as public health and elementary education, where that had already happened. Here was a society rethinking one of its core values. For New Liberals the justification for compulsion was the greater freedom of individual action. Like any Liberal they wished to confine state compulsion to a minimum. But they took seriously the traditional argument that a limited degree of coercion created the conditions for liberty, and applied it to the problem of poverty.[16] Compulsory savings and prescribed benefits, far from being the royal road to the collective satisfaction of human needs, were no more than the necessary stimulant to enable people to take responsibility for themselves in accordance with their individual circumstances, whether through associations of mutual help or commercial insurance.

That certainly happened, as is demonstrated by the increase in insurance policies for small savers between the wars. But at least as significant was the

---

[16] L. T. Hobhouse, *Liberalism* (London, 1911), chs. 6 and 7; M. Freeden, *The New Liberalism* (Oxford, 1978).

increase in occupational pension schemes. The disregard in 1911 of insurance-based pensions apart from those for total disability, and the application of national insurance in 1925 to pensions on the same minimal basis as before, left the field open for employers to make the membership of occupational pension schemes a condition of employment. They did so for their own purposes, partly to retain the loyalty of those who would have been difficult to replace, partly to make it easier to impose compulsory retirement as part of their manpower planning. It is ironic that the government insistence on leaving maximum discretion to individuals to make provisions on a voluntary basis in practice gave employers the discretion to impose occupational pension schemes on a compulsory basis on an ever growing section of the work-force. The retention of the flat-rate contribution and the flat-rate minimal benefit in 1946 created a nation divided into those who could look forward in retirement to an occupational pension geared in some measure to their accustomed standard of living, those who had made some provision for themselves that had survived the ravages of inflation, and a large part of the population who could rely on little but the minimal state pension and were dependent on national assistance, as a more humane poor law was then called.

When the shortcomings of the traditional policy of flat-rate contributions and benefits were finally exposed by Richard Titmuss and his collaborators, and the Labour Party adopted proposals for income-related contributions in 1957, occupational pensions already covered a third or more of the work force. The National Insurance Act of 1959, the Conservative government's response to the Labour challenge, for the first time introduced a state graduated pension scheme. It gave members of occupational pensions schemes the right to contract out, but was so modest that it ensured the extension of occupational pensions schemes, as had been intended. When Labour introduced a more serious state-earnings-related pension scheme (SERPS) in 1975, it was too late for this growth to be reversed. Occupational pensions dominated the field and its members could not be denied the right to contract out of SERPS.[17] By these measures the British work-force was compelled to contribute a proportion of income towards future needs, but most of its members were locked into a system of compulsion devised by their employers rather than the state. The higher benefits were balanced by conditions that effectively tied them to the firm and acted as a brake on labour mobility. For that reason they were unsuited to the conditions that the Thatcher government desired to

---

[17] Leslie Hannah, *Inventing retirement: the development of occupational pensions in Britain* (Cambridge, 1986), pp. 55–64.

bring about, and in 1987 the members of occupational pension schemes were 'set free' to make their own arrangements with commercial insurance, enjoying a state subsidy but losing any contribution from their employer. Liberty had been restored to the individual, and to the employers too. These were not required to contribute to their employees' portable pension policies, but were still free to offer occupational pensions or not, and to decide the terms, provided they met those of the state scheme. They have used that freedom in the early years of the twenty-first century sharply to reduce their financial commitments.

This excursion into the more recent past demonstrates the far-reaching implications of decisions taken in the founding years. It provides an instance of that 'path-dependency' of which students of social policy speak – not an iron law, but a tendency which it takes special circumstance as well as unusual political imagination and courage to overcome.

(B) TAXATION VERSUS INSURANCE

Flat-rate contributions linked to minimal benefits were one way in which compulsory insurance has played a smaller role in British than in German social policy. It was not the only one. Even for purposes for which compulsion was accepted, the commitment to national insurance in Britain has been less than in Germany. There has been a greater commitment to taxation as an alternative.

Compulsory insurance was after all a policy made in Germany and until 1908 was seen in Britain as of little more than academic interest. That was no longer the case in 1911, but even Lloyd George regarded it as merely a temporary expedient. He hoped, as he put it, that at no distant date the State would acknowledge full responsibility for sickness breakdown and unemployment, not through the Poor Law, as it already did, but in a way that was honourable and not degrading, adding that insurance would then be unnecessary.[18] He clearly regarded tax-provided benefits as the normal policy and the one for the future. That was understandable. Tax-provided benefits had been the first method adopted to enable a group of the deserving poor to escape the stigma of the poor law.

The Labour Party was persuaded to vote for the National Insurance Bill at the crucial third reading, but more because the government had

---

[18] Lloyd George to G. R. Hawtrey, 7 March 1911, H. N. Bunbury (ed.), *Lloyd George's ambulance wagon* (London, 1957), pp. 121–2. For this paragraph generally, see Hennock, *British social reform*, pp. 133–52.

promised to introduce payment of MPs in return, than from any wide-spread enthusiasm for what was after all a regressive form of taxation. A few Labour MPs with Snowden and Lansbury as their spokesmen opposed Ramsay MacDonald's support of insurance to the end and argued that the deserving poor had a right to be supported by the general taxpayer.[19]

The plans for the extension of unemployment insurance in the war-time years of full employment fell foul of opposition from organised labour, and in the early 1920s the Labour Party considered a capital levy to finance an extension of pensions. It was only the Pensions Act of 1925, introduced by a Conservative government firmly committed to low taxation, that signalled the end of uncertainty and made national insurance the established British policy.

Tax-provided services had been for decades the way to meet the needs of public health. First financed from local taxation, they were increasingly subsidised by the Treasury, as the yield from local rates proved inadequate. And by the turn of the century public health was no longer limited to the provision of a common sanitary infrastructure. It increasingly required personal health services and there was considerable uncertainty about its future scope.

In the familiar division between poor law policies and public health policies, national insurance belonged firmly on the poor law side of the divide.[20] That was demonstrated when Lloyd George chose to limit medical treatment to restoring the earning capacity of household providers while ignoring the health of their dependants.

It was further demonstrated by the fate of the sanatorium benefit for the treatment of TB, whose rapid subversion by public health considerations is recorded in chapter 13. It was because the medical treatment of dependants was identified in 1926 as a health-of-the-nation issue, which had a claim on the resources of the taxpayer but one that could not be afforded at the time, that the Royal Commission on Health Insurance refused to recommend the extension of national insurance in that direction.[21] In the same spirit but in a different fiscal climate the Beveridge Report in 1942 proposed to take medical treatment out of a universalised national insurance, a proposal

---

[19] D. Marquand, *Ramsay MacDonald* (London, 1977), pp. 138–41.

[20] For an unsuccessful attempt to convert the British public to a consistent public health approach to all poverty issues, see S. Webb and B. Webb, *The prevention of destitution* (London, 1911). Their approach left no place for national health insurance and hardly any for national unemployment insurance.

[21] See p. 274 above.

on which the Labour government acted in 1946 by establishing the National Health Service.[22]

Thus despite the importance ascribed to the legislation of 1911, 1925 and 1946, national insurance has never been considered in Britain as more than one possible strategy for ensuring nationwide provision. The close identification of social insurance with the welfare state, which has led German historians to regard the 1880s as marking the beginning of their welfare state, is not found in British historiography. There its establishment is normally placed in the 1940s, when the tax-provided National Health Service occupied as prominent a place as the extension of national insurance to cover all classes of the population. In studies of the 'origins of the welfare state' a crucial role is assigned to the Edwardian legislation with tax-provided old age pensions (1908) and indeed rate-provided and tax-supported free school meals (1906 and 1914) featuring as prominently as the National Insurance Act of 1911.[23]

This difference between the two countries has its explanation in the particular circumstances of the newly established German Empire, which saw a modest Prussian institution raised to the level of a major national policy. At its establishment the *Reich* had very limited powers of indirect taxation and was largely financed by the individual states. It had been Bismarck's objective almost from the beginning to replace that dependence with an independent revenue. When protective tariffs were introduced in 1878, however, the *Reich* benefited from the increase in customs duties only very little, owing to the Franckenstein amendment that had been imposed in the *Reichstag*. That severely restricted the amount of customs revenue that could be retained; the rest had to be passed to the states.[24] By the early 1880s, when Bismarck took up the problem of compensation for industrial accidents and saw in it the beginnings of a policy whereby the *Reich* would meet the needs of industrial workers, the necessary financial resources had still to be found. As we know, he had intended to rely on indirect taxation on tobacco and on contributions from employers. When the *Reichstag* refused him the former, he reduced the immediate burden on employers by removing the original requirement for a reserve fund. The responsibility of

---

[22] National insurance was originally intended to contribute one-fifth of the cost of the NHS but that was quite unrealistic. By 1957 the proportion was no more than one-seventeenth. A. Land *et al.*, *The development of the welfare state 1939–1951: a guide to documents in the Public Record Office* (London, 1992), p. 26.

[23] See B. B. Gilbert, *The evolution of national insurance: the origins of the welfare state* (London, 1966).

[24] W. Gerloff, *Die Finanz- und Zollpolitik des Deutschen Reiches* (Jena, 1913); J. von Kruedener, 'The Franckenstein paradox in the inter-governmental fiscal relations of Imperial Germany', in P. C. Witt (ed.), *Wealth and taxation in central Europe* (Leamington Spa, 1987), pp. 111–23.

sickness funds for the first thirteen weeks in practice imposed contributions on all grades of workers including the lowest-paid, although that had not been Bismarck's own intention.[25] His officials subsequently regarded contributions from workers and employers as a suitable source of revenue for invalidity and old age pensions, adding only a relatively small proportion from state funds, and since Bismarck had no equally attractive alternative to offer, they got their way. Even they were not to know how ample this revenue would become once the *Reichstag* had finished with the bill, and what potential there would be in graduated contributions effectively applied.

In Britain, where old age pensions and rearmament had already pre-empted the direct taxes from the innovative but politically contentious budget of 1909, while the taxation of articles of consumption was ruled out for the Liberal government, compulsory insurance was attractive at least for the moment, and for any other moment when steep tax increases were ruled out.[26]

Yet, as we have seen, national insurance, despite its name, was inappropriate for services required by the nation as a whole. Not only because in Britain flat-rate contributions severely limited its yield, but also because it excluded all but the regularly employed. Casual workers, and women, for whom regular employment was no more than a brief phase in their life-cycle, could not build up the requisite entitlement in their own right. Under those circumstances the usefulness of national insurance was strictly limited, at least as long as contributions were regarded as qualifying for benefit and not merely as another tax.[27] No wonder that in the 1940s, when progressive direct taxation was buoyant and acceptable, it was considered more appropriate for policies where inclusiveness mattered.

(C) STATE CONTROL OF MEDICAL PROVISION

From the British point of view compulsory insurance is about social security. From the German point of view it is also about medical treatment. Not merely, as has already been pointed out, because pension boards

---

[25] See pp. 90–1 and 97 above.

[26] By 1940 compulsory insurance for some or all of the purposes that Germany had pioneered could be found in fourteen countries of western Europe, sometimes subsidised from taxation, sometimes not. It was, indeed, well suited to any government which wished to provide benefits for the mass of wage earners without levying large amounts of additional direct taxes or further taxing articles of consumption. Jens Alber, *Von Armenhaus zum Wohlfahrtsstaat* (Frankfurt and New York, 1987), Table A2.

[27] That significant change did not occur until the 1950s.

provided treatment for TB and certain other lingering diseases.[28] Nor because *Berufsgenossenschaften* supported rehabilitation clinics. But first and foremost because German sickness funds financed medical treatment for their members, as friendly societies had done and as approved societies under national health insurance never did.[29] That was a matter in which Lloyd George did not follow the example set by existing forms of sickness insurance, whether voluntary in Britain or compulsory in Germany. Not because he had never intended to, but because he was blown off course by forces that had to be accommodated. In consequence, instead of entering into contracts with approved societies, doctors were able to ensure that the level of their remuneration and their conditions of service depended on the state. Approved societies were merely agencies for the distribution of cash to their members.[30] It was the government, and especially the Chancellor of the Exchequer, with whom the British Medical Association had to come to terms.

That contrasts sharply with the way in which the State in Germany kept out of issues of remuneration of doctors and their access to insurance patients. There the medical association dealt with the national associations of the various kinds of sickness funds, who controlled the money and obtained it on an expanding basis from the rising contributions of their members.[31]

That expanding income from graduated contributions is highly relevant. Even had friendly societies been able to retain some of their previous control over doctors, the State would still have had to subsidise the cost of medical treatment. The minimal flat-rate contributions that were being planned could not have paid the cost. If only for that reason, the Chancellor of the Exchequer could not have kept out of bargaining over salary levels between doctors and approved societies. He would have had to pick up the bill. So yet again, adherence to flat-rate contributions is central. The struggle over who controls whom was played out within the financial constraints that follow. For when the government has to subsidise, it is the government that will ultimately be the body that controls.

Thus the State has provided medical treatment in Britain not merely since the introduction of the National Health Service in 1948 but from the inception of national health insurance in 1911. Contributions graduated

---

[28] See chapter 13, section (b), above.   [29] See chapter 13, section (a), above.
[30] They could pay for the cost of glasses and dentures out of any surplus funds.
[31] For all this see chapter 13, section (a), above.

according to income have in some form or other been a feature of German sickness insurance since it turned its back on poor law priorities in 1883.

Between them these elements have produced a fundamental difference of attitude to social insurance. Sometimes it has been due to British distrust of compulsion and its restrictive consequences; sometimes to British preference for taxation and its greater inclusiveness. The outcome is clear: in matters of social insurance British policy has been restrictive and German policy expansive. That pattern was established by 1914 and is still with us today.[32]

---

[32] The most recent example is the provision of long-term nursing care for the elderly through social insurance in Germany. This contrasts with means-tested rate-financed care on a minimal basis from local authorities in England and tax-financed care on a comprehensive basis in Scotland.

Bibliography

MONOGRAPHS AND ARTICLES

'Abdruck der Kaiserlichen Botschaft', *Zeitschrift für Sozialreform*, 27 (1981), 730–5

Abel Smith, Brian, *The hospitals, 1800–1948* (London, 1964)

Abelshauser, Werner, 'The first post-liberal nation: stages in the development of modern corporatism in Germany', *European History Quarterly*, 14 (1984), 285–318

Alber, Jens, *Vom Armenhaus zum Wohlfahrtsstaat* (Frankfurt and New York, 1987)

Andersen, Arne, 'Arbeiterschutz in Deutschland im 19. und frühen 20. Jahrhundert', *Archiv für Sozialgeschichte*, 31 (1991), 65

Anderson, Gregory, *Victorian clerks* (Manchester, 1976)

Anton, Günther K., *Geschichte der preussischen Fabrikgesetzgebung bis zu ihrer Aufnahme durch die Reichsgewerbeordnung* (2nd edn, Berlin-Ost, 1953)

Aretin, K. O. von, *Franckenstein. Eine politische Karriere zwischen Bismarck und Ludwig II* (Stuttgart, 2003)

Aschrott, P. F., *The English poor law system: past and present* (2nd edn, London, 1902)

Ashforth, David, 'The urban poor law', in Derek Fraser (ed.), *The new poor law in the nineteenth century* (London, 1976)

Asmuth, Margaret, *Gewerbliche Unterstützungskassen in Düsseldorf* (Cologne, 1984)

Ayass, Wolfgang, '"Der Übel grösstes". Das Verbot der Nachtarbeit von Arbeiterinnen in Deutschland (1891–1992)', *Zeitschrift für Sozialreform*, 46 (2000), 189–220

'Bismarck und der Arbeiterschutz', *Vierteljahrschrift für Sozial- und Wirtschaftsgeschichte*, 89 (2002), 400–26

Böhmert, C. V., *Das Armenwesen in 77 deutschen Städten und einigen Landarmenverbänden* (Dresden, 1886–8)

Baernreither, J. M., *English associations of working men* (London, 1889)

Baldwin, Peter, *The politics of social solidarity: class bases of the European welfare state 1875–1975* (Cambridge, 1990)

'Can we define a European welfare state model?', in Bent Grieve (ed.), *Comparative welfare systems: the Scandinavian model in a period of change* (London, 1996)

Contagion and the state in Europe 1830–1930 (Cambridge, 1999)

Bartrip, P. W. J., 'British government inspection, 1832–1875: some observations', *Historical Journal*, 25 (1982), 605–25

Workmen's compensation in the twentieth century in Britain (Aldershot, 1987)

'Too little, too late? The Home Office and the Asbestos Industry Regulations 1931', *Medical History*, 42 (1998), 428

The Home Office and the dangerous trades (Amsterdam and New York, 2002)

Bartrip, P. W. J., and Burman, S. B., *The wounded soldiers of industry: industrial compensation policy 1833–1897* (Oxford, 1983)

Bartrip, P. W. J., and Fenn, P. T., 'The administration of safety: the enforcement policy of the early factory inspectorate, 1844–1864', *Public Administration*, 58 (1980), 87–107

'The evolution of the regulatory style in the nineteenth century British factory inspectorate', *Journal of Law and Society*, 10 (1983), 218

'Factory fatalities and regulation in Britain, 1878–1913', *Explorations in Economic History*, 25 (1988), 60–74

Bartrip, P. W. J., and Hartwell, R. M., 'Profit and virtue: economic theory and the regulation of occupational health in nineteenth and twentieth century Britain', in K. Hawkins (ed.), *The human face of law: essays in honour of Donald Harris* (Oxford, 1997)

Bellamy, Christine, *Administering central–local relations 1871–1919: the Local Government Board in its fiscal and cultural context* (Manchester, 1988)

Berger, Giovanna, *Die ehrenamtliche Tätigkeit in der Sozialarbeit. Motive, Tendenzen, Probleme, Dargestellt am Beispiel des Elberfelder Systems* (Frankfurt, Bern and Las Vegas, 1979)

Berlepsch, Hans-Jörg von, *'Neuer Kurs' im Kaiserreich? Die Arbeiterpolitik des Freiherrn von Berlepsch 1890–1896* (Bonn, 1987)

Bernhardt, Christoph, *Bauplatz Gross-Berlin* (Berlin, 1998)

Beveridge, W., 'The age for pensions: the experience of trade unions', *Morning Post*, 4 June 1908

Unemployment: a problem of industry (London, 1909)

Power and influence (London, 1953)

Bichler, Barbara, *Die Formierung der Angestelltenbewegung im Kaiserreich und die Entstehung des Angestelltenversicherungsgesetzes von 1911* (Frankfurt, 1997)

Bismarck, O. von, *Gesammelte Werke* (Berlin, 1935), vol. 12

Blaug, Mark, 'The myth of the old poor law and the making of the new', *Journal of Economic History*, 23 (1963), 151–84

'The poor law re-examined', *Journal of Economic History*, 24 (1964), 244

Bocks, W., *Die badische Fabrikinspektion. Arbeiterschutz, Arbeitsverhältnisse und Arbeiterbewegung in Baden 1879 bis 1914* (Freiburg, 1978)

Boettcher, H., *Fürsorge in Lübeck, vor und nach dem ersten Weltkrieg* (Lübeck, 1988)

Bojanowski, V. von, *Unternehmer und Arbeiter nach englischem Recht* (Stuttgart, 1877)

Booth, Charles, *Life and labour of the people*, vol. I, *East London* (London, 1889)

'Inaugural address', *Journal of the Royal Statistical Society*, 60 (1892), 521–57

Pauperism, a picture and endowment of old age, an argument (London, 1892)

The aged poor in England and Wales (London, 1894)

Old age pensions and the aged poor (London, 1899)

Borght, R. van der, 'Die Reform der deutschen Invaliditäts- und Altersversicherung', *Jahrbücher für Nationalökonomie und Statistik*, 3rd Ser. 18 (1899), 374

Born, K. E., *Staat und Sozialpolitik seit Bismarcks Sturz* (Wiesbaden, 1957)
  Wirtschaft- und Sozialgeschichte des Deutschen Kaiserreichs (1867/71–1914) (Stuttgart, 1985)

Bosanquet, C. B. P., *London: some account of its growth, charitable agencies and wants* (London, 1868)

Bowley, A. L., and Burnett-Hurst, A. R., *Livelihood and poverty* (London, 1915)

Brabrook, E. W., 'On friendly societies and similar institutions', *Journal of the Statistical Society*, 33 (1875), 193–4
  Provident societies and industrial welfare (London, 1898)

Breger, M., 'Der Anteil der deutschen Grossindustriellen an der Konzeptualisierung der Bismarckschen Sozialgesetzgebung', in Lothar Machtan (ed.), *Bismarcks Sozialstaat* (Frankfurt and New York, 1994)

Brentano, Lujo, 'Die beabsichtigte Alters- und Invaliden-Versicherung für Arbeiter und ihre Bedeutung', *Jahrbücher für Nationalökonomie und Statistik*, NF 16 (1887), 1–46

Breuilly, John, *Labour and liberalism in nineteenth-century Europe* (Manchester, 1992)

Breunig, W., *Soziale Verhältnisse der Arbeiterschaft und der sozialistischen Arbeiterbewegung in Ludwigshafen am Rhein 1869–1919* (Ludwigshafen, 1976)

Brown, Kenneth, *Labour and unemployment 1900–1914* (Newton Abbot, 1971)

Brubaker, R., *Citizenship and nationhood in France and Germany* (Cambridge, MA, 1992)

Brundage, Anthony, *The making of the new poor law: the politics of inquiry, enactment and implementation, 1832–1839* (London, 1978)

Bryder, Linda, *Below the magic mountain: a social history of tuberculosis in twentieth century Britain* (Oxford, 1988)

Bullock, N., and Reid, J., *The movement for housing reform in Germany and France 1840–1914* (Cambridge, 1985)

Bunbury, H. N. (ed.), *Lloyd George's ambulance wagon* (Bath, 1970)

Carr, W., *History of Germany 1815–1990* (London, 1991)

Castell Rüdenhausen, Adelheid Gräfin zu, 'Zur Erhaltung und Mehrung der Volkskraft', in I. Behnken (ed.), *Stadtgesellschaft und Kindheit im Prozess der Zivilisation* (Opladen, 1990)

Churchill, R. S. (ed.), *Winston S. Churchill*, vol. II, *Companion*, Part 2 (London, 1967)

Condrau, Flurin, *Lungenheilanstalt und Patientenschicksal: Sozialgeschichte der Tuberkulose in Deutschland und England im späten 19. und frühen 20. Jahrhundert* (Göttingen, 2000)

Conrad, Christoph, 'The emergence of modern retirement: Germany in an international comparison (1850–1960)', *Population: An English Selection*, 3 (1991), 171–99
  Vom Greis zum Rentner. Der Strukturwandel des Alters in Deutschland zwischen 1830 und 1930 (Göttingen, 1994)

Cordery, Simon, *British friendly societies, 1750–1914* (Basingstoke, 2003)

Croon, Helmuth, *Die gesellschaftlichen Auswirkungen des Gemeindewahlrechts in den Gemeinden und Kreisen des Rheinlands und Westfalens im 19. Jahrhundert* (Cologne and Opladen, 1960)

Crowther, M. A., *The workhouse system 1834–1929* (London, 1983)

Dawson, W. H., *Municipal life and government in Germany* (London, 1914)
  Social insurance in Germany 1883–1911: its history, operation, and results, and a comparison with the National Insurance Act 1911 (London, 1912, reprinted Westport, 1979)

Deane, Phyllis, 'New estimates of gross national product for the United Kingdom, 1830–1914', *Review of Income and Wealth*, 14 (1968), 2

Deane, Phyllis, and Cole, W. A., *British economic growth 1688–1959* (Cambridge, 1964)

Der gegenwärtige Stand der Arbeitslosenfürsorge und Versicherung in Deutschland. Schriften der Deutschen Gesellschaft zur Bekämpfung der Arbeitslosigkeit, Heft 2 (Berlin, 1913)

Die Einrichtungen zum Besten der Arbeiter auf den Bergwerken Preussens. Im Auftrag des Ministers für Handel, Gewerbe und öffentlichen Arbeiten (Berlin, 1875)

Die unter staatlicher Aufsicht stehenden gewerblichen Hülfskassen für Arbeitnehmer … im preussischen Staate. Bearbeitet im Auftrage des Ministers für Handel, Gewerbe und öffentliche Arbeiten (Berlin, 1878)

Digby, Anne, 'The labour market and the continuity of social policy after 1834: the case of the eastern counties', *Economic History Review*, 2nd Ser. 28 (1975), 69–83
  The evolution of British general practice 1850–1948 (Oxford, 1999)

Digby, A., and Bosanquet, N., 'Doctors and patients in an era of national health insurance and private practice, 1913–1938', *Economic History Review*, 2nd Ser. 41 (1988), 75–6

Dinsdale, W. A., *History of accident insurance in Great Britain* (London, 1959)

Dominicus, Alexander, *Strassburgs deutsche Bürgermeister. Back und Schwander 1873–1918* (2nd edn, Frankfurt, 1939)

Dreher, Wolfgang, *Die Entstehung der Arbeiterwitwenversicherung in Deutschland* (Berlin, 1978)

Eder, N. R., *National health insurance and the medical profession in Britain, 1913–39* (London, 1982)

Eghigian, Greg, *Making security social: disability, insurance, and the birth of the social entitlement state in Germany* (Ann Arbor, 2000)

Eisenberg, Christiane, *Deutsche und englische Gewerkschaften. Entstehung und Entwicklung bis 1878 im Vergleich* (Göttingen, 1986)

Ellerkamp, Marlene, *Industriearbeit, Krankheit und Geschlecht. Zu den Kosten der Industrialisierung: Bremer Textilarbeiterinnen 1870–1914* (Göttingen, 1991)
  'Die Frage der Witwen und Waisen', in Stefan Fisch and Ulrike Haerendel (eds.), *Geschichte und Gegenwart der Rentenversicherung in Deutschland* (Berlin, 2000)

Emminghaus, C. B. A. (ed.), *Das Armenwesen und die Armengesetzgebung in den europäischen Staaten* (Berlin, 1870), translated and abridged as *Poor relief in different parts of Europe* (London, 1873)

Engeli, Christian, and Haus, Wolfgang (eds.), *Quellen zum modernen Verfassungsrecht in Deutschland* (Stuttgart, 1975)

Erdmann, Gerhard, *Die Entwicklung der deutschen Sozialgesetzgebung* (1st edn, Berlin, 1948)

Die Entwicklung der deutschen Sozialgesetzgebung (2nd edn, Göttingen, 1957)

Esping-Andersen, G., *The three worlds of welfare capitalism* (Cambridge, 1990)

Evans, David, 'Tackling the "hideous scourge": the creation of VD treatment centres in early twentieth century Britain', *Social History of Medicine*, 5 (1992), 413–33

Evans, Eric J. (ed.), *Social policy 1830–1914: individualism, collectivism and the origins of the welfare state* (London, 1978)

Führer, Karl Christian, *Arbeitslosigkeit und die Entstehung der Arbeitslosenversicherung in Deutschland 1902–1927* (Berlin, 1990)

Fairbairn, Brett, *Democracy in the undemocratic state: the German Reichstag elections of 1898 and 1903* (Toronto, 1997)

Fait, Barbara, 'Arbeiterfrauen und -familien im System sozialer Sicherheit. Zur geschlechterpolitischen Dimension der "Bismarckschen Arbeiterversicherung"', *Jahrbuch für Wirtschaftsgeschichte*, 1 (1997), 171–205

Faust, Anselm, *Arbeitsmarktpolitik im Deutschen Kaiserreich. Arbeitsvermittlung, Arbeitsbeschaffung und Arbeitslosenunterstützung 1890–1918. Vierteljahrschrift für Sozial- und Wirtschaftsgeschichte*, Beiheft 79 (Stuttgart, 1986)

Feinstein, C. H., *National income, expenditure and output of the UK, 1855–1965* (Cambridge, 1972)

Finer, S. E., *The life and times of Sir Edwin Chadwick* (London, 1952)

Fischer, Ilse, *Industrialisierung, sozialer Konflikt und politische Willensbildung in der Stadtgemeinde. Ein Beitrag zur Sozialgeschichte Augsburgs 1840–1914* (Augsburg, 1977)

Fischer, W., et al., *Sozialgeschichtliches Arbeitsbuch 1815–1870* (Munich, 1982)

Flemming, Jens, 'Sozialpolitik, landwirtschaftliche Interessen und Mobilisierungsversuche', in Stefan Fisch and Ulrike Haerendel (eds.), *Geschichte und Gegenwart der Rentenversicherung in Deutschland* (Berlin, 2000)

Flora, Peter, and Heidenheimer, Arnold J. (eds.), *The development of welfare states in Europe and America* (New Brunswick, 1981)

Flora, P., et al. (eds.), *State, economy and society in western Europe 1815–1975: a data handbook* (Frankfurt, London and Chicago, 1987)

Fraser, Derek, *The evolution of the British welfare state* (London, 1973)

(ed.), *The new poor law in the nineteenth century* (London, 1976)

'The English poor law and the origins of the British welfare state', in W. J. Mommsen (ed.), *The emergence of the welfare state in Britain and Germany 1850–1950* (London, 1981)

Fraser, Peter, *Joseph Chamberlain: radicalism and empire 1836–1914* (London, 1966)

Freeden, M., *The new liberalism* (Oxford, 1978)

Freund, R., *Armenpflege und Arbeiterversicherung. Schriften des Deutschen Vereins für Armenpflege und Wohltätigkeit*, Heft 21 (Leipzig, 1895)

Frevert, Ute, *Krankheit als politisches Problem 1770–1880* (Göttingen, 1984)

Fukasama, Kazuto, 'Voluntary provision for old age by trade unions in Britain before the coming of the welfare state' (unpublished PhD thesis, University of London, 1996)

Fyrth, H. J., and Collins, H., *The foundry workers: a trade union history* (Manchester, 1959)

Gall, Lothar, *Bismarck, the white revolutionary* (London, 1986)

Garside, W. R., *British unemployment 1919–1939: a study in public policy* (Cambridge, 1990)

Garvin, J. L., *The life of Joseph Chamberlain*, vols. 2 and 3 (London, 1933–4)

Gerloff, W., *Die Finanz- und Zollpolitik des Deutschen Reiches* (Jena, 1913)

Gerloff, Wilhelm, and Meisel, Franz (eds.), *Handbuch der Finanzwissenschaft* (Tübingen, 1929), vol. 3

Gilbert, B. B., *The evolution of national insurance in Great Britain: the origins of the welfare state* (London, 1966)

    British social policy 1914–1939 (London, 1970)

    David Lloyd George, a political life (London, 1987)

Gosden, P. H. J. H., *Friendly societies in England 1815–1875* (London, 1961)

    Self-help: voluntary associations in Great Britain (London, 1973)

Gray, Robert, *The factory question in industrial England, 1830–1860* (Cambridge, 1996)

Green, David G., *Working-class patients and the medical establishment: self-help in Britain from the mid-nineteenth century to 1948* (Aldershot, 1985)

Gugel, and Schmid, G., *Kommentar zur Reichsversicherungsordnung* (Berlin, 1912)

Hähner-Rombach, Sylvelyn, *Sozialgeschichte der Tuberkulose. Vom Kaiserreich bis zum Ende des Zweiten Weltkriegs unter besonderer Berücksichtigung Württembergs* (Stuttgart, 2000)

Haerendel, Ulrike, *Die Anfänge der gesetzlichen Rentenversicherung in Deutschland* (Speyer, 2001)

Hamer, D. A., *The politics of electoral pressure: a study in the history of Victorian reform agitations* (Brighton, 1977)

Hanes, D. G., *The first British Workmen's Compensation Act 1897* (New Haven, 1968)

Hannah, Leslie, *Inventing retirement: the development of occupational pensions in Britain* (Cambridge, 1986)

Hanson, C. G., 'Welfare before the welfare state', in R. M. Hartwell *et al.*, *The long debate on poverty* (London, 1972)

Harling, P., 'The power of persuasion: central authority, local bureaucracy and the new poor law', *English Historical Review*, 107 (1992), 30

Harris, José, *Unemployment and politics: a study in English social policy 1886–1914* (Oxford, 1972)

    William Beveridge, a biography (Oxford, 1977)

Harrison, Barbara, *Not only the 'dangerous trades': women's work and health in Britain, 1880–1914* (London, 1996)

Hart, W. O., *Hart's introduction to the law of local government and administration* (6th edn, London, 1957)

Heffter, Heinrich, *Die Deutsche Selbstverwaltung im 19. Jahrhundert* (Stuttgart, 1950)

Heilmann, Linda A., *Industrial unemployment in Germany 1873–1913* (London, 1991)

Henderson, W. O., *The Lancashire cotton famine 1861–1865* (Manchester, 1934)

Henning, Hansjoachim, 'Arbeitslosenversicherung vor 1914: das Genter System und seine Übernahme in Deutschland', in H. Kellenbenz (ed.), *Wirtschaftspolitik und Arbeitsmarkt* (Munich, 1974)

Hennock, E. P., 'Finance and politics in urban local government in England, 1835–1900', *Historical Journal*, 6 (1963), 213–25

  Fit and proper persons: ideal and reality in nineteenth-century urban government (London, 1973)

  'Central/local government relations in England: an outline 1800–1950', *Urban History Yearbook*, 9 (1982), 38–49

  'The creation of an urban local government system in England and Wales', in H. Naunin (ed.), *Städteordnungen des 19. Jahrhunderts* (Bohlau, Cologne and Vienna, 1984)

  British social reform and German precedent: the case of social insurance 1880–1914 (Oxford, 1987)

  'Public provision for old age: Britain and Germany 1880–1914', *Archiv für Sozialgeschichte*, 30 (1990), 99–100

  'German models for British social reform: compulsory insurance and the Elberfeld system of poor relief', in R. Muhs, J. Paulmann and W. Steinmetz (eds.), *Aneignung und Abwehr. Interkultureller Transfer zwischen Deutschland und Grossbritannien im 19. Jahrhundert. Veröffentlichung Nr. 32 des Arbeitskreises Deutsche England-Forschung* (Bodenheim, 1998)

  'Social policy under the Empire – myths and evidence', *German History*, 16 (1998), 58–74

  'Vaccination policy against smallpox, 1835–1914: a comparison of England with Prussia and Imperial Germany', *Social History of Medicine*, 11 (1998), 49–71

  'The urban sanitary movement in England and Germany, 1838–1914: a comparison', *Continuity and Change*, 15 (2000), 269–96

Henriques, U., *Before the welfare state* (London, 1979)

Hentschel, Volker, *Geschichte der deutschen Sozialpolitik 1880–1980. Soziale Sicherung und kollektives Arbeitsrecht* (Frankfurt, 1983)

Higgs, Edward, 'The struggle for the occupational census, 1841–1911', in Roy MacLeod (ed.), *Government and expertise* (Cambridge, 1988)

Hobhouse, L. T., *Liberalism* (London, 1911)

Hockerts, Hans Günther, *Sozialpolitische Entscheidungen im Nachkriegsdeutschland. Allierte und deutsche Sozialversicherungspolitik 1945 bis 1957* (Stuttgart, 1980)

  'German post-war social policies against the background of the Beveridge Plan: some observations preparatory to a comparative analysis', in W. J. Mommsen (ed.), *The emergence of the welfare state in Britain and Germany 1850–1950* (London, 1981)

  'Sicherung im Alter. Kontinuität und Wandel der gesetzlichen Rentenversicherung 1889–1979', in Werner Conze and M. Rainer Lepsius (eds.), *Sozialgeschichte der Bundesrepublik Deutschland. Beiträge zum Kontinuitätsproblem* (Stuttgart 1983)

Hofmann, Wolfgang, 'Aufgaben und Struktur der kommunalen Selbstverwaltung in der Zeit der Hochindustrialisierung', in Kurt G. A. Jeserich, Hans Pohl, Georg-Christoph von Unruh (eds.), *Deutsche Verwaltungsgeschichte* (Stuttgart, 1984), vol. 3

Hofmeister, Herbert, 'Austria', in Peter A. Köhler and Hans F. Zacher (eds.), *The evolution of social insurance 1881–1981: studies of Germany, France, Great Britain, Austria and Switzerland* (London and New York, 1982)

Hohmann, J. S., *Berufskrankheiten in der Unfallversicherung* (Cologne, 1984)

Hohorst, G., *et al.*, *Sozialgeschichtliches Arbeitsbuch II* (2nd edn, Munich, 1975)

Hollingworth, Clare, 'Potters' rot and plumbism: occupational health in the North Staffordshire potteries, 1890–1914' (unpublished PhD thesis, University of Liverpool, 1995)

Hollis, Patricia, *Ladies elect: women in English local government 1865–1914* (Oxford, 1987)

Honigmann, Paul, 'Zur Arbeiterkrankenversicherungsfrage', *Jahrbücher für Nationalökonomie und Statistik*, NF 6 (1883), 96

Howell, George, *Trade unionism, new and old* (London, 1891)

Huber, R. G., *Sozialer Wandel und politische Konflikte in einer süd-hessischen Industriestadt. Kommunalpolitik der SPD in Offenbach 1898–1914* (Darmstadt, 1985)

Huerkamp, Claudia, *Der Aufstieg der Ärzte im 19. Jahrhundert. Vom gelehrten Stand zum professionellen Experten: Das Beispiel Preussens* (Göttingen, 1985)
'The making of the medical profession, 1800–1914: Prussian doctors in the nineteenth century', in G. Cocks and K. H. Jarausch (eds.), *German professions, 1800–1950* (New York and Oxford, 1990)

Humphreys, Robert, *Sin, organised charity and the poor law in Victorian England* (London, 1995)

Hutchins, B. L., and Harrison, A., *A history of factory legislation* (2nd edn, London, 1911)

International Labour Office, *First comparative report on the administration of labour laws: inspection in Europe* (London, 1911)
Factory inspection: historical development and present organisation in certain countries (Zurich, 1923)

Jans, Hans Peter, *Sozialpolitik und Wohlfahrtspflege in Ulm 1870–1930* (Stuttgart, 1994)

Jefferys, J. B., *The story of the engineers 1800–1945* (London, 1946)

Johnson, Paul, *Saving and spending: the working-class economy in Britain 1870–1939* (Oxford, 1985)

Jones, D., 'Did friendly societies matter? A study of friendly society membership in Glamorgan, 1794–1910', *Welsh History Review*, 12 (1984–5), 337–8

Köhler, Peter, and Zacher, Hans (eds.), *Ein Jahrhundert Sozialversicherung in der Bundesrepublik Deutschland, Frankreich, Grossbritannien, Österreich, und der Schweiz* (Berlin, 1981) (translated as *The evolution of social insurance 1881–1981: studies of Germany, France, Great Britain, Austria and Switzerland* (London, 1982)) (eds.), *Beiträge zur Geschichte und aktueller Situation der Sozialversicherung. Schriftenreihe* (Berlin, c.1983)

Köllmann, Wolfgang, *Sozialgeschichte der Stadt Barmen im 19. Jahrhundert* (Tübingen, 1960)

Karl, Michael, *Fabrikinspektoren in Preussen. Das Personal der Gewerbeaufsicht 1854–1945* (Opladen, 1993)

Kaschke, Lars, 'Nichts als "Bettelgelder"? Wert und Wertschätzung der Alters- und Invalidenrenten im Kaiserreich', *Historische Zeitschrift*, 270 (2000), 345–87

Kaschke, Lars, and Sniegs, Monika, *Kommentierte Statistiken zur Sozialversicherung in Deutschland von ihren Anfängen bis in die Gegenwart* (Skt Katharinen, 2001)

Kaufhold, K. H., 'Gewerbefreiheit und gewerbliche Entwicklung im 19. Jahrhundert', *Blätter für deutsche Landesgeschichte*, 118 (1982), 73–114

Kaufmann, C., 'Vergleichende Übersicht über den gegenwärtigen Stand der Unfallgesetzgebung in den verschiedenen Ländern mit Berücksichtigung der die ärztliche Tätigkeit berührenden Verhältnisse', in *Verhandlungen des III. internationalen medizinischen Unfallkongresses zu Düsseldorf 1912* (Düsseldorf, 1912)

Kaufmann, F.-X., 'Der Begriff Sozialpolitik und seine wissenschaftliche Deutung', in *Geschichte der Sozialpolitik in Deutschland seit 1945* published by the Bundesministerium für Arbeit und Sozialordnung and Bundesarchiv, vol. 1 (Baden-Baden, 2001)

Kayser, Karl, *Die Stellung der ehrenamtlichen Organe in der Armenpflege, Schriften des deutschen Vereins*, vol. 49 (Leipzig, 1900)

Keith-Lucas, B., *The English local government franchise: a short history* (Oxford, 1952)

Kiehel, Constance A., *Unemployment insurance in Belgium: a national development of the Ghent and Liège systems* (New York, 1932)

Killian Weitensteiner, Hans, *Karl Flesch – Kommunale Sozialpolitik in Frankfurt* (Frankfurt, 1976)

Kitson Clark, G., 'Statesmen in disguise: reflection on the history of the neutrality of the civil service', *Historical Journal*, 2 (1959), 19–39

Kleeis, F., *Die Geschichte der sozialen Versicherung in Deutschland* (reprint of 1926 publication, Berlin and Bonn, 1981)

Knaack, Rudolf, and Schröder, Wolfgang, 'Gewerkschaftliche Zentralverbände, Freie Hilfskassen und die Arbeiterpresse unter dem Sozialistengesetz.' *Jahrbuch für Geschichte*, vol. 22 (Berlin, 1981)

Kocka, J., *Unternehmungsverwaltung und Angestelltenschaft am Beispiel Siemens, 1847–1914* (Stuttgart, 1969)

White collar workers in America 1890–1940 (London, 1980)

(ed.), *Angestellte im europäischen Vergleich* (Göttingen, 1981)

'Capitalism and bureaucracy in German industrialization before 1914', *Economic History Review*, 2nd Ser. 34 (1981), 453–68

Die Angestellten in der deutschen Geschichte 1850–1980 (Göttingen, 1981)

Kosellek, Reinhart, *Preussen zwischen Reform und Revolution* (Stuttgart, 1967)

Krabbe, W. R., 'Die Gründung städtischer Arbeitsschutzanstalten in Deutschland', in W. Conze and U. Engelhardt (eds.), *Arbeiterexistenz im 19. Jahrhundert* (Stuttgart, 1981)

Die deutsche Stadt im 19. und 20. Jahrhundert (Göttingen, 1989)

Kruedener, J. von, 'The Franckenstein paradox in the intergovernmental fiscal relations of imperial Germany', in P. C. Witt (ed.), *Wealth and taxation in central Europe* (Leamington Spa, 1987)

Labisch, A., 'From traditional individualism to collective professionalism: the state, compulsory health insurance, and the panel doctor question in Germany, 1883–1931', in M. Berg and G. Cocks (eds.), *Medicine and modernity: public health and medical care in nineteenth- and twentieth-century Germany* (Cambridge, 1997)

Labisch, A., and Spree, R. (eds.), *Krankenhaus-Report 19. Jahrhundert* (Frankfurt, 2001)

Land, A., Lowe, R., and Whiteside, N., *The development of the welfare state 1939–1951: a guide to documents in the Public Record Office* (London, 1992)

Langerbeins, I., *Lungenheilanstalten in Deutschland 1854–1945* (Cologne, 1979)

Lederer, Emil, *Die Pensionsversicherung der Privatangestellten* (Tübingen, 1911)

Lee, W. R., 'Germany', in W. R. Lee (ed.), *European demography and economic growth* (London, 1978)

Lerchenfeld-Koefering, Hugo Graf von, *Erinnerungen und Denkwürdigkeiten 1843–1929* (Berlin, 1935)

Levine, Daniel, *Poverty and society: the growth of the American welfare state in international comparison* (New Brunswick, 1988)

Lindert, Peter H., 'Poor relief before the welfare state: Britain versus the Continent, 1780–1880', *European Review of Economic History*, 2 (1998), 101–40

Growing public (Cambridge, 2004)

Lippmann, K., *Die Reichsversicherungsordnung in der Fassung der Bekanntmachung vom 15. Dezember 1924* (Berlin and Leipzig, 1925)

Litt, Renate, *Zwischen innerer Mission und staatlicher Sozialpolitik. Der protestantische Sozialreformer Theodor Lohmann (1831–1905)* (Heidelberg, 1997)

Lockwood, David, *The black-coated worker* (London, 1958)

Lohmann, T. (ed.), *Die Fabrik-Gesetzgebungen der Staaten des europäischen Kontinents* (Berlin, 1878)

Lube, Barbara, 'Mythos und Wirklichkeit des Elberfelder Systems', in Karl-Hermann Beeck (ed.), *Gründerzeit. Versuch einer Grenzbestimmung in Wuppertal* (Cologne, 1984)

Müller, Rainer, 'German occupational health statistics', in P. Weindling (ed.), *The social history of occupational health* (London, 1985)

Münsterberg, Emil, 'Die Armenstatistik', *Conrads Jahrbücher für Nationalökonomie und Statistik*, NF 12 (1886), 377–451

Die deutsche Armengesetzgebung und das Material zu ihrer Reform (Leipzig, 1887)

Das Landarmenwesen. Schriften des deutschen Vereins für Armenpflege und Wohlthätigkeit, vol. 56 (Leipzig, 1890)

Das Elberfelder System. Schriften des Deutschen Vereins, vol. 63 (Leipzig, 1903)

Generalbericht über die Tätigkeit des deutschen Vereins für Armenpflege und Wohltätigkeit während der ersten 25 Jahre seines Bestehens 1880–1905, nebst Verzeichnissen der Vereinsschriften und alphabetischen Register zu den Vereinsschriften. Schriften des deutschen Vereins, vol. 72 (Leipzig, 1905)

Machtan, Lothar, 'Risikoversicherung statt Gesundheitsschutz für Arbeiter. Zur Entstehung der Unfallversicherungsgesetzgebung im Bismarck-Reich', *Leviathan*, 13 (1985), 420–41

'Der Arbeiterschutz als sozialpolitisches Problem im Zeitalter der Industrialisierung', in Hans Pohl (ed.), *Staatliche, städtische, betriebliche und kirchliche Sozialpolitik vom Mittelalter bis zur Gegenwart. Vierteljahrschrift für Sozial- und Wirtschaftsgeschichte*, Beiheft 95 (Stuttgart, 1991)

'Von Kreissägen und anderen "Gefahren die das menschliche Leben überall bedrohen". Eine vielzitierte Quelle zur Bismarckschen Sozialpolitik in neueren Licht', in Karsten Linne and Thomas Wohlleben (eds.), *Patient Geschichte. Für Karl Heinz Roth* (Frankfurt, 1993)

'Der Gesellschaftsreformer Theodor Lohmann. Grundanschauung und Programm', in I. Marssolek and T. Schelz-Brandenburg (eds.), *Soziale Demokratie und sozialistische Theorie. Festschrift für Hans-Josef Steinberg* (Bremen, 1996)

Macnicol, John, *The politics of retirement in Britain 1878–1948* (Cambridge, 1998)

Maine, Henry, *Ancient law* (London, 1861)

Malone, Carolyn, 'The gendering of dangerous trades: government regulation of womens' work in the white lead trade in England, 1892–1918', *Journal of Women's History*, 8 (1996), 15–35

Mandler, Peter, 'The making of the new poor law redivivus', *Past and Present*, 117 (1987)

'Tories and paupers: Christian political economy and the making of the new poor law', *Historical Journal*, 33 (1990)

Matthöfer, H., Mühlhausen, W., and Tennstedt, F. (eds.), *Bismarck und die soziale Frage im 19. Jahrhundert* (Friedrichsruh, 2001)

May, Vicki, and Bird, Katherine, 'Berufskrankheiten in England und Deutschland. Historische Entwicklungen und Forschungsfragen', in D. Milles (ed.), *Gesundheitsrisiken, Industriegesellschaft und soziale Sicherungen in der Geschichte* (Bremerhaven, 1993)

McBriar, A. M., *An Edwardian mixed doubles: the Bosanquets versus the Webbs: a study in British social policy 1890–1929* (Oxford, 1987)

McFeely, M. D., *Lady inspectors* (Oxford, 1988)

Melton, Edgar, 'The decline of Prussian Gutsherrschaft and the rise of the Junker as rural patron', *German History*, 12 (1994), 334–50

Mess, H. A., *Factory legislation and its administration 1891–1924* (London, 1926)

Meyer, Adolf, *Schule und Kinderarbeit* (Hamburg, 1971)

Milles, Dietrich, 'Pathologie des Defektes oder Ökonomie der Arbeitsfähigkeit. Zur Dethematisierung arbeitsbedingter Krankheiten in der Soziogenese der Arbeitsmedizin', in Rainer Müller und Dietrich Milles (eds.), *Beiträge zur Geschichte der Arbeiterkrankheiten und der Arbeitsmedizin in Deutschland* (Dortmund, 1984)

'Zur Dethematisierung arbeitsbedingter Krankheiten durch die Gutachtermedizin in der Geschichte der Sozialversicherung', in Rainer Müller and Dietrich Milles (eds.), *Beiträge zur Geschichte der Arbeiterkrankheiten und der Arbeitsmedizin in Deutschland* (Dortmund, 1984)

'From worker's diseases to occupational diseases: the impact of experts' concepts on workers' attitudes', in P. Weindling (ed.), *The social history of occupational health* (London, 1985)

'Industrial hygiene: a state obligation? Industrial pathology as a problem in German social policy', in W. R. Lee and E. Rosenhaft (eds.), *The state and social change in Germany, 1880–1980* (Oxford, 1990)

'Medical opinion and sociopolitical control in the case of occupational diseases in the late nineteenth century', *Dynamis*, 13 (1993), 139–53

Milles, D., and Müller, R., 'Zur Dethematisierung sozialpolitischer Aufgaben am Beispiel des Gesundheitsschutzes für Arbeiter in historischen Rückblick', in F.-X. Kaufmann (ed.), *Staat, intermediäre Instanzen und Selbsthilfe. Bedingungen sozialpolitischer Intervention* (Munich, 1987)

Mitchell, B. R., and Deane, P., *Abstract of British historical statistics* (Cambridge, 1962)

Mommsen, W. J. (ed.), *The emergence of the welfare state in Britain and Germany 1850–1950* (London, 1981)

Mortimer, I., and Melling, J., 'The contest between commerce and trade, on the one side, and human life on the other: British government policies for the regulation of anthrax infection and the wool textile industries, 1880–1939', *Textile History*, 31 (2000), 222–36

Mowat, C. L., *The Charity Organisation Society 1865–1913* (London, 1961)

Muthesius, Hans (ed.), *Beiträge zur Entwicklung der deutschen Fürsorge. 75 Jahre Deutscher Verein* (Cologne and Berlin, 1955)

National Committee of Organised Labour, *Ten years' work for old age pensions 1899–1909* (London, 1909)

Neave, David, *Mutual aid in the Victorian countryside: friendly societies in the rural East Riding 1830–1914* (Hull, 1991)

'Friendly societies in Great Britain', in Marcel van der Linden (ed.), *Social security mutualism* (Berne, 1996)

Neuhaus, Rolf, *Arbeitskämpfe, Ärztestreiks, Sozialreformer. Sozialpolitische Konfliktregelung 1900 bis 1914* (Berlin, 1986)

O'Neill, J., 'Self-help in Nottinghamshire: the Woodborough Male Friendly Society, 1826–1954', *Transactions of the Thoroton Society*, 90 (1986)

'Friendly societies in Nottinghamshire 1724–1912' (unpublished PhD thesis, Nottingham Trent University, 1992)

Oliver, Thomas (ed.), *Dangerous trades* (London, 1902)

Orthband, Eberhardt, *Der Deutsche Verein in der Geschichte der deutschen Fürsorge* (Frankfurt, 1980)

Otruba, Gustav, 'Privat-, Handlungsgehilfen- und Angestelltenorganisationen. Ihr Beitrag zur Entstehung des österreichischen Angestelltenpensionsversicherungsgesetzes 1906 (unter besonderer Berücksichtigung der Diskussion über den Angestelltenbegriff)', in J. Kocka, (ed.), *Angestellte im europäischen Vergleich* (Göttingen, 1981)

Palmowski, Jan, *Urban liberalism in imperial Germany: Frankfurt, 1866–1914* (Oxford, 1999)

Pellew, Jill, *The Home Office 1848–1914* (London, 1982)

Petrie, Charles, *The life and letters of the Rt Hon. Sir Austen Chamberlain* (London, 1939)

Pflanze, Otto, *Bismarck and the development of Germany*, 3 vols. (Princeton, 1990)

Phelps Brown, E. H., and Browne, Margaret H., *A century of pay* (London, 1968)

Pierenkämper, Toni, *Arbeitsmarkt und Angestellte im Deutschen Kaiserreich 1880–1914* (Stuttgart, 1987)

Pinker, Robert, *English hospital statistics 1861–1938* (London, 1966)

Poerschke, Stephan, *Die Entwicklung der Gewerbeaufsicht in Deutschland* (2nd edn, Jena, 1913)

Political and Economic Planning, *Report on the British health services* (London, 1937)

Postgate, R. W., *The builders' history* (London, 1923)

Preller, Ludwig, *Sozialpolitik in der Weimarer Republik* (Stuttgart, 1949, reprinted Düsseldorf, 1978)

Price, George M., *The administration of labor laws and factory inspection in certain European countries* (Washington, 1914)

Prinz, Michael, 'Die Arbeiterbewegung und das Modell der Angestelltenversicherung', in Klaus Tennfelde (ed.), *Arbeiter im 20. Jahrhundert* (Stuttgart, 1991)

Prinzing, Friedrich, 'Die soziale Lage der Witwe in Deutschland', *Zeitschrift für Socialwissenschaft*, 3 (1900), 199–205

Prochaska, Frank, *Women and philanthropy in nineteenth-century England* (Oxford, 1980)

Recker, Marie-Luise, *Nationalsozialistische Sozialpolitik im Zweiten Weltkrieg* (Munich, 1985)

Rehm, Max, *Rudolf Schwander und Kurt Blaum, Wegbahner neuzeitlicher Kommunalpolitik aus dem Elsass* (Stuttgart, 1974)

Reininghaus, Wilfried, 'Das erste staatlich beaufsichtigte System von Krankenkassen: Preussen 1845–1869. Das Beispiel der Regierungsbezirke Arnsberg und Minden', *Zeitschrift für Sozialreform*, 29 (1983), 271–96
  'Die Unterstützungskassen der Handwerkgesellen und Fabrikarbeiter in Westfalen und Lippe (1800–1850)', *Westfälische Forschungen*, 35 (1985), 130–63

Reitzenstein, F. von (ed.), *Die ländliche Armenpflege und ihre Reform* (Freiburg, 1887)
  'Über Beschäftigung arbeitsloser Armer', in *Schriften des Deutschen Vereins für Armenpflege und Wohltätigkeit*, vol. 4 (Leipzig, 1887)

Reulecke, J., 'Das "Elberfelder System" als Reiseziel – Johann Hinrich Wichern (1857), William Rathbone (1871), Andrew Doyle (1871)', in *Reisen im Bergischen Land*, vol. II (Neustadt an der Aisch, 1984)
  Geschichte der Urbanisierung in Deutschland (Frankfurt, 1985)
  'Formen bürgerlich-sozialen Engagement in Deutschland und England im 19. Jahrhundert', in J. Kocka (ed.), *Arbeiter und Bürger im 19. Jahrhundert* (Munich, 1986)

Riley, J. C., *Sick, not dead: the health of British workingmen during the mortality decline* (Baltimore and London, 1997)

Rimlinger, G. V., *Welfare policy and industrialization in Europe, America and Russia* (New York, 1971)

Ritter, Gerhard A., *Sozialversicherung in Deutschland und England. Entstehung und Grundzüge im Vergleich* (Munich, 1983)

Social welfare in Germany and Britain (trans. Kim Traynor, New York and Leamington Spa, 1986)

Der Sozialstaat. Entstehung und Entwicklung im internationalen Vergleich (Munich, 1989)

Rolling, J. D., *Liberals, socialists and city government in imperial Germany: the case of Frankfurt 1900–1918* (Madison, 1979)

Rose, M. E., 'Settlement, removal and the new poor law', in Derek Fraser (ed.), *The new poor law in the nineteenth century* (London, 1976)

(ed.), *The poor and the city: the English poor law in its urban context 1834–1914* (Leicester, 1985)

Rosner, David, and Markovitz, Gerald, *Deadly dust: silicosis and the politics of occupational disease in twentieth century America* (Princeton, 1987)

Roth, Ralf, *Gewerkschaftskartell und Sozialpolitik in Frankfurt. Arbeiterbewegung vor dem ersten Weltkrieg zwischen Restauration und Liberaler Erneuerung* (Frankfurt, 1991)

Rothfels, Hans, 'Bismarcks Staatsanschauung', in Hans Rothfels, *Otto von Bismarck, Deutscher Staat* (Munich, 1925)

Theodor Lohmann und die Kampfjahre der staatlichen Sozialpolitik (1871–1905) (Berlin, 1927)

Rowntree, B. S., *Poverty: a study of town life* (London, 1901)

Rubner, H. (ed.), *Adolph Wagner. Briefe, Dokumente, Augenzeugenberichte, 1851–1917* (Berlin, 1978)

Rudloff, W., *Die Wohlfahrtsstadt. Kommunale Ernährungs-, Fürsorge- und Wohnungspolitik am Beispiel Münchens 1910–1933* (Göttingen, 1998)

Sachsse, Christoph, *Mütterlichkeit als Beruf. Sozialarbeit, Sozialreform und Frauenbewegung 1871–1929* (Frankfurt, 1986)

'Frühformen der Leistungsverwaltung: die kommunale Armenfürsorge im deutschen Kaiserreich', *Jahrbuch für europäische Verwaltungsgeschichte*, 5 (1993), 1–20

Sachsse Christoph, and Tennstedt, Florian, *Geschichte der Armenfürsorge in Deutschland*, 3 vols. (Stuttgart, 1980–92)

Saldern, A. von, 'Gewerbegerichte im Wilhelminischen Deutschland', in K.-H. Manegold (ed.), *Wissenschaft, Wirtschaft und Technik* (Munich, 1969)

Satre, Lowell J., 'After the match girls' strike: Bryant and May in the 1890s', *Victorian Studies*, 26 (1982), 7–31

Sauerteig, L., *Krankheit, Sexualität, Gesellschaft: Geschlechtskrankheiten und Gesundheitspolitik in Deutschland im 19. und frühen 20. Jahrhundert* (Stuttgart, 1999)

Saul, Klaus, *Staat, Industrie, Arbeiterbewegung im Kaiserreich. Zur Innen- und Sozialpolitik des Wilhelminischen Deutschland 1903–1914* (Düsseldorf, 1974)

'Repression or integration? The state, trade unions and industrial disputes in imperial Germany', in Wolfgang Mommsen and Hans-Gerhard Husung (eds.), *The development of trade unionism in Great Britain and Germany, 1880–1914* (London, 1985)

Scarpa, Ludovica, *Gemeinwohl und Lokale Macht. Honorationen und Gemeindewesen in der Luisenstadt im 19. Jahrhundert* (Munich, 1995)

Schäffle, Albert, *Aus meinem Leben* (Berlin, 1904)

Schinkel, Harald, 'Armenpflege und Freizügigkeit in der preussischen Gesetzgebung vom Jahre 1842', *Vierteljahrschrift für Sozial- und Wirtschaftsgeschichte*, 50 (1963), 459–79

Schlaudraff, Elsa, *Ein Vergleich zwischen dem Elberfelder, dem Strassburger und dem Frankfurter System in der Armenpflege* (Nürnberg-Zirndorf, 1932)

Schmitt, Sabine, *Der Arbeiterinnenschutz im deutschen Kaiserreich. Zur Konstruktion der schutzbedürftigen Arbeiterin* (Stuttgart, 1995)

Schröder, Wolfgang, 'Subjekt oder Objekt der Sozialpolitik? Zur Wirkung der Sozialgesetzgebung auf die Addressaten', in Lothar Machtan (ed.), *Bismarcks Sozialstaat* (Frankfurt, 1994)

Schumann, M., 'Die Armenlast im deutschen Reich', *Conrads Jahrbücher für Nationalökonomie und Statistik*, NF 16 (1887)

Schwedtman, F. C., and Emery, J. A., *Accident prevention and relief: an investigation of the subject in Europe with special attention to England and Germany* (New York, 1911)

Searle, G. R., *The quest for national efficiency* (Oxford, 1971)

Sheehan, James J., *The career of Lujo Brentano: a study of Liberalism and social reform in Imperial Germany* (Chicago, 1966)

German history 1770–1866 (Oxford, 1989)

Silbergleit, H. (ed.), *Finanzstatistik der Armenverwaltungen von 108 deutschen Städten. Schriften des deutschen Vereins für Armenpflege und Wohlthätigkeit*, Heft 61 (Leipzig, 1902)

(ed.), *Finanzstatistik der Armenverwaltungen von 130 deutschen Städten 1901–1905. Schriften des deutschen Vereins für Armenpflege und Wohltätigkeit*, Heft 78 (Leipzig, 1908)

Simons, Rolf, *Staatliche Gewerbeaufsicht und gewerbliche Berufsgenossenschaften: Entstehung und Entwicklung des dualen Aufsichtssystems im Arbeitsschutz in Deutschland von den Anfängen bis zum Ende der Weimarer Republik* (Frankfurt, 1984)

Smelser, R., *Robert Ley: Hitler's labor front leader* (Oxford, 1988)

Snell, K. D. M., *Annals of the labouring poor: social change and agrarian England 1660–1900* (Cambridge, 1985)

Soell, H. D., 'Die sozialdemokratische Arbeiterbewegung im Reichsland Elsass-Lothringen 1871–1918' (PhD thesis, Heidelberg University, 1963)

Sokoll, Thomas, '"Alte Armut". Unterstützungspraxis und Formen lebenszyklischer Armut unter dem Alten Armenrecht, 1780–1834', in Bernd Weisbrod (ed.), *'Victorian Values'. Arm und Reich im Viktorianischen England* (Bochum, 1988)

Sommerfeld, T., *Der Gewerbearzt* (Jena, 1905)

Spree, R., 'Krankenhausentwicklung und Sozialpolitik in Deutschland während des 19. Jahrhunderts', *Historische Zeitschrift*, 260 (1995), 95–102

Stadtverwaltung Wuppertal (ed.), *Hilfe von Mensch zu Mensch, 100 Jahre Elberfelder Armenpflegesystem 1853–1953* (Wuppertal-Elberfeld, 1953)

Statistisches Bundesamt (ed.), *Bevölkerung und Wirtschaft 1872–1972* (Stuttgart and Mainz, 1972)

Stead, F. H., *How old age pensions began to be* (London, n.d. [1909])

Steadman Jones, Gareth, *Outcast London* (Oxford, 1971)

Steinhilber, Wilhelm, '25 Jahre Strassburger System', *Deutsche Zeitschrift für Wohlfahrtspflege*, 7 (1931), 61–7

Steinmetz, George, *Regulating the social: the welfare state and local politics in imperial Germany* (Princeton, 1993)

Steinmetz, Willibald, *Begegnung vor Gericht. Eine Sozial- und Kulturgeschichte des englischen Arbeitsrechts (1850–1925)* (Munich, 2002)

Stollberg, Gunnar, 'Hilfskassen in nineteenth-century Germany', in Marcel van der Linden (ed.), *Social security mutualism* (Berne, 1996)

Stolleis, Michael, *Quellen zur Geschichte des Sozialrechts* (Göttingen, 1976)

Summers, Anne, 'A home from home – women's philanthropic work in the nineteenth century', in Sandra Burman (ed.), *Fit work for women* (London, 1979)

Supple, Barry, *The Royal Exchange Assurance* (Cambridge, 1970)

Syrup, F., and Neuloh, O., *Hundert Jahre staatliche Sozialpolitik 1839–1939* (Stuttgart, 1957)

Tamm, Ingo, *Ärzte und gesetzliche Krankenversicherung in Deutschland und England 1880–1914* (Berlin, 1998)

Teleky, L., 'Die Tuberkulose', in A. Gottstein *et al.* (ed.), *Handbuch der Sozialen Hygiene und Gesundheitsfürsorge* (Berlin, 1926), vol. III

Tennstedt, F., *Berufsunfähigkeit im Sozialrecht* (Frankfurt, 1972)

'Sozialgeschichte der Sozialversicherung', in Maria Blohmke *et al.* (eds.), *Handbuch der Sozialmedizin* (Stuttgart, 1976)

Geschichte der Selbstverwaltung in der Krankenversicherung von der Mitte des 19. Jahrhunderts bis zur Gründung der Bundesrepublik Deutschland. Soziale Selbstverwaltung (Bonn, 1977)

'Fürsorgegeschichte und Vereinsgeschichte. 100 Jahre Deutscher Verein in der Geschichte der deutschen Fürsorge', *Zeitschrift für Sozialreform*, 27 (1981), 72–100

Sozialgeschichte der Sozialpolitik in Deutschland (Göttingen, 1981)

'Vorgeschichte und Entstehung der Kaiserlichen Botschaft vom 7. November 1881', *Zeitschrift für Sozialreform*, 27 (1981), 663–710

'Fortschritte und Defizite in der Sozialversicherungsgeschichtsschreibung – komparative und sonstige Kurzsichtigkeiten nach 100 Jahren "Kaiserliche Botschaft"', *Archiv für Sozialgeschichte*, 22 (1982), 653–4

'Die Errichtung von Krankenkassen in deutschen Städten nach dem Gesetz betr. die Krankenversicherung der Arbeiter vom 15. Juni 1883', *Zeitschrift für Sozialreform*, 29 (1983), 297–338

'Sozialreform als Mission. Anmerkungen zum politischen Handeln Theodor Lohmanns', in J. Kocka, H.-J. Puhle and K. Tenfelde (eds.), *Von der Arbeiterbewegung zum modernen Sozialstaat. Festschrift für Gerhard A. Ritter zum 65. Geburtstag* (Munich, 1994)

'"Nur nicht privat mit Dividende und Konkurs". Der deutsche Weg zum Sozialstaat – auch eine Folge von Bismarcks Ansichten über private Unfallversicherungsgesellschaften', in M. Heinze and Jochem Schmitt (eds.), *Festschrift für Wolfgang Gitter* (Wiesbaden, 1995)

'Vorläufer der gesetzlichen Rentenversicherung', in Stefan Fisch and Ulrike Haerendel (eds.), *Geschichte und Gegenwart der Rentenversicherung in Deutschland* (Berlin, 2000)

'"Bismarcks Arbeiterversicherung" zwischen Absicherung der Arbeiterexistenz und Abwehr der Arbeiterbewegung', in H. Matthöfer *et al.* (eds.), *Bismarck und die Soziale Frage im 19. Jahrhundert* (Friedrichsruh, 2001)

'Glaubensgewissheit und Revolutionsfurcht. Zum sozialpolitischem Wirken Robert Bosses', *Zeitschrift für Sozialreform*, 49 (2003), 831–46

Tennstedt, Florian, and Winter, Heidi, '"Der Staat hat wenig Liebe – activ wie passiv". Die Anfänge des Sozialstaats im Deutschen Reich von 1871, Teil 1', *Zeitschrift für Sozialreform*, 38 (1993), 362–92

'"Jeder Tag hat seine eigenen Sorgen, und es ist nicht weise, die Sorgen der Zukunft freiwillig auf die Gegenwart zu übernehmen". (Bismarck) Die Anfänge des Sozialstaats im Deutschen Reich von 1871 Teil 2', *Zeitschrift für Sozialreform*, 41 (1995), 671–706

'Neues zur Kaiserlichen Sozialbotschaft vom 17 November 1881', *Zeitschrift für Sozialreform*, 48 (2002), 644

Thane, Pat, 'Contributory vs non-contributory old age pensions, 1878–1908', in Pat Thane (ed.), *Origins of British social policy* (London, 1978)

'Women and the poor law in Victorian and Edwardian England', *History Workshop Journal*, 6 (Autumn 1978), 29–51

The foundations of the welfare state (London, 1982)

Old age in English history (Oxford, 2000)

Thomas, M. W., *The early factory legislation* (Leigh-on-Sea, 1948)

Thomson, A. L., *Half a century of medical research*, vol. 1, *Origins and policy of the Medical Research Council (UK)* (London, 1973)

Thomson, David, 'Provisions for the elderly in England, 1830–1908' (unpublished PhD thesis, University of Cambridge, 1980)

'I am not my father's keeper: families and the elderly in nineteenth century England', *Law and History Review*, 2 (1984), 265–86

'The decline of social welfare: falling state support for the elderly since early Victorian times', *Ageing and Society*, 4 (1985), 451–82

Toft, Christian, 'Jenseits der Dreiweltendiskussion', *Zeitschrift für Sozialreform*, 46 (2000), 68–86

Turner, J. J., 'Friendly societies in South Durham and North Yorkshire c.1790–1914: studies in development, membership characteristics, and behaviour' (unpublished PhD thesis, Teesside Polytechnic, 1992)

Tweedale, G., *From magic mineral to killer dust: Turner & Newall and the asbestos hazard* (Oxford, 2000)

Tweedale, G., and Hansen, P., 'Protecting the workers: the medical board and the asbestos industry, 1930s–60s', *Medical History*, 42 (1998), 439–57

Ullmann, H.-P., 'Industrielle Interessen und die Entstehung der deutschen Sozialversicherung 1880–1889', *Historische Zeitschrift*, 229 (1979), 574–610

'German industry and Bismarck's social security system', in W. J. Mommsen (ed.), *The emergence of the welfare state in Britain and Germany* (London, 1981)

Verhandlungen des Dritten Deutschen Städtetags am 12. Sept. 1911 zu Posen zur Frage der Arbeitslosenversicherung (Berlin, 1911)

Vincent, David, *Poor citizens: the state and the poor in the twentieth century* (London and New York, 1991)

Vogel, W., *Bismarcks Arbeiterversicherung* (Braunschweig, 1951)

Volkmann, Heinrich, *Die Arbeiterfrage im preussischen Abgeordnetenhaus 1848–1869* (Berlin, 1968)

Wagner, Adolph, 'Der Staat und das Versicherungswesen', *Zeitschrift für die gesamte Staatswissenschaft*, 37 (1881), 102–72

Walker, Mack, *German home towns: community, state, general estate, 1648–1871* (Ithaca, 1971)

Webb, S., and Webb, B., *English poor law policy* (London, 1910)

The prevention of destitution (London, 1911)

Industrial democracy (London, 1920)

English prisons under local government (London, 1922)

Statutory authorities for special purposes (London, 1922)

English poor law history, Part II, *The last 100 years* (London, 1929)

Webster, Charles, *The health services since the war* (London, 1996)

Wehler, Hans-Ulrich, *Deutsche Gesellschaftsgeschichte* (Munich, 1987), vol. I

Deutsche Gesellschaftsgeschichte (Munich, 1989), vol. II

Weindling, P. (ed.), *The social history of occupational health* (London, 1985)

'Hygienepolitik als sozialintegrative Strategie im späten Kaiserreich', in A. Labisch and R. Spree (eds.), *Medizinische Deutungsmacht im sozialen Wandel des 19. und frühen 20. Jahrhunderts* (Bonn, 1989)

Weisbrod, Bernd, 'Wohltätigkeit und "symbolische Gewalt" in der Frühindustrialisierung. Städtische Armut und Armenpolitik im Wuppertal', in H. Mommsen and W. Schulze (eds.), *Vom Elend der Handarbeit. Probleme historischer Unterschichtenforschung* (Stuttgart, 1981)

Whiteside, Noel, 'Welfare legislation and the unions during the First World War', *Historical Journal*, 23 (1980), 857–74

Bad times (London, 1991)

'La protection du métier: l'organisation industrielle et les services des syndicats dans l'Angleterre de la fin du dix-neuvième siècle', *Les cahiers d'histoire de l'institut de recherches marxistes*, 51 (1993), 29–51

'Definir le chômage', in M. Mansfield , R. Salais and N. Whiteside (eds.), *Aux sources du chômage, 1880–1914* (Paris, 1994)

'Creating the welfare state in Britain, 1945–1960', *Journal of Social Policy*, 25 (1996), 83–103

'Mutuality and politics: state policy and trade union benefit systems in Britain, France and Germany in the late nineteenth century' (unpublished paper given at the European Social Science History Conference, May 1996)

'Regulating markets: the real costs of polycentric administration under the national health insurance scheme, 1912–46', *Public Administration*, 75 (1997), 464–85

'Accounting and accountability: an historical case study of a private–public partnership', in R. A. W. Rhodes (ed.), *Transforming British government*, vol. 2, *Changing roles and relationships* (London, 2000)

Wickenhagen, Ernst, *Geschichte der gewerblichen Unfallversicherung. Anlageband* (Munich, 1980)

Wilkinson, J. Frome, *Mutual thrift* (London, 1891)

Williams, Karel, *From pauperism to poverty* (London, 1981)

Wilson, A., and Levy, H., *Workmen's compensation* (London, 1939)

Witzleben, G. von, 'Die Vorschläge zur Reform der Invaliditäts- und Altersversicherung', *Schmollers Jahrbuch*, 23 (1899), 333–61

Woedtke, E. von, *Das Reichsgesetz, betr. die Krankenversicherung der Arbeiter* (11th edn by G. Euken-Addenhauser, Berlin, 1905)

Wohl, A. S., *Endangered lives* (London, 1983)

Worboys, Michael, 'The sanatorium treatment for consumption in Britain', in J. V. Pickstone (ed.), *Medical innovations in historical perspective* (London, 1992)

Wrigley, E. A., and Schofield, R. S., *The population history of England 1541–1871: a reconstruction* (London, 1981)

Zacher, Georg, *Die Arbeiterversicherung im Ausland*, 5 vols. (Berlin 1900–8)

Zacher, Hans (ed.), *Bedingungen für die Entstehung und Entwicklung von Sozialversicherung* (Berlin, 1979)

Zahn, F., 'Arbeiterversicherung und Armenwesen in Deutschland', *Zeitschrift d. Königl. Bayerischen Statistischen Landesamts*, 43 (1911)

Zimmermann, Bénédicte, 'Municipal innovations versus national wait-and-see attitudes: unemployment policies in Kaiserreich Germany (1871–1918)', in Michèle Dagenais *et al.* (eds.), *Municipal services and employees in the modern city: new historical approaches* (London, 2003)

BRITISH OFFICIAL PUBLICATIONS

Parliamentary papers

Doyle, Andrew, 'The poor law system of Elberfeld', in *Local Government Board, Report*, 1872 C.516 XXVIII

Royal Commission on Friendly and Benefit Building Societies, Fourth report, Appendix XVI, 1874 C.961-I XXIII

Royal Commission on Friendly Societies, George Young, *Report to the Royal Commission*, p. 2, 1874 C.997 XIII

Return of the number of registered burial societies, 1875 (34) XLII, p. 339

Chief Registrar of Friendly Societies, Report for 1874, 1875 (408) LXXI, p. 97

Royal Commission on Factory and Workshops Acts, Report, Appendix D, 1876 C.1443 XXIX

Select Committee on National Provident Insurance, Minutes of Evidence, Q.1483, 1884–5 (270) X

Return of paupers relieved, January 1885, 1886 (58B) LVI, p. 59

Local Government Board, Report for 1885–6, 1886 C.4844 XXXI

Davy, J. S., 'Report on the Elberfeld system of poor law relief in some German towns', in *Reports on the Elberfeld poor law system*, 1888 C.5341 LXXX, p. 313

Return . . . of the number of persons . . . in receipt of indoor relief and of outdoor relief aged over 60 returned in quinquennial groups on 1 August 1890 (Burt's Return), 1890–1 (36) LXVIII, p. 563

Return . . . of the number of persons . . . over 65 years and upwards . . . in receipt of indoor relief and outdoor relief on 1 January 1892 and at any time during the 12 months ended Lady Day 1892 (Ritchie's Return), 1892 Session 1 (265) LXVIII

Chief Registrar of Friendly Societies, Report for 1891, 1892 C.137-I LXXIII

Royal Commission on Labour, Minutes of Evidence, 1893–4 C.7063-I XXXIX

Chief Registrar of Friendly Societies, Report for 1892, 1893–4 (513) and (513-I) LXXXIV, pp. 447 and 591

Local Government Board, Report for 1892–3, 1893 C.7180 XLIII

Report on trade unions for 1891, 1893–4 C.6990 CII, p. 85

Committee on Old Age Pensions, Report, Appendix X, 1898 C.8911 XLV

Select Committee on the Aged Deserving Poor, Report, Appendix I, 1899 (296) VIII

Select Committee on the Aged Pensioners' Bill, Special report, 1903 (276) V, p. 393

Report of the Board of Trade on agencies and methods for dealing with the unemployed in certain foreign countries, ed. D. F. Schloss, 1905 Cd.2304 LXXIII, p. 471

Lowry, A., *Labour bureaux*, 1906 (86) CII, p. 363

Dangerous trades: action taken by the Home Office under the Factory and Workshop Acts, 1891, 1895 and 1901, 1906 Cd.3037 CX, p. 119

Return of numbers of paupers relieved, 1 January 1907 and 1 July 1907, 1907 (108) LXXII, p. 155

Bulstrode, H. Timbrell, *Report on sanatoria for consumption and certain other aspects of the tuberculosis question, Supplement to Local Government Board, annual report of the medical officer for 1905–6*, 1908 Cd.3657 XXVII

Return of the number of registered burial societies, 1875 (34) XLII, p. 339

Board of Trade, Cost of living of the working classes: German towns, by W. H. Dawson, 1908 Cd.4032 CVIII

Royal Commission on the Poor Laws and Relief of Distress Due to Lack of Employment, Report, 1909 Cd.4499 XXXVII

    Minutes of Evidence, Appendix, vol. III, 1909 Cd.4755 XL

    Minutes of Evidence, Appendix, vol. V, 1909 Cd.4888 XLI

    Minutes of Evidence, Appendix, vol. VII, 1910 Cd.5035 XLVII

Minutes of Evidence, Appendix, vol. VIII, 1910 Cd.5066 XLVIII
Minutes of Evidence, Appendix, vol. IX, 1910 Cd.5068 XLIX
Statistics relating to England and Wales, Appendix, vol. XXV, 1910 Cd.5077 LIII
Foreign and colonial systems of poor relief, Appendix, vol. XXXIII, 1910 Cd.5441 LV
Departmental Committee on Factory Accidents, Report, 1911 Cd.5535 XXIII
National Insurance Bill (Part II: Unemployment), Explanatory Memorandum, 1911 Cd.5991
National Insurance Bill (Part I: Health), Memorandum explanatory of the Bill as passed by the House of Commons, 1911 Cd.5995 LXXIII, p. 69
Unemployment insurance: Proceedings of the Board of Trade under Part II of the National Insurance Act 1911, 1913 Cd.6965 XXXVI, p. 677
Report of the labour correspondent of the Board of Trade for 1908–10, 1912–13 Cd.6109 XLVII, p. 655
Departmental Committee on Tuberculosis, Interim report, 1912–13 Cd.6164 LXVIII
Final report, vols. I and II, 1912–13 Cd.6641 and Cd.6654 XLVIII
Report of Chief Registrar of Friendly Societies for 1911, 1912–13 (123-I) LXXI
Chief Inspector of Factories and Workshops, Annual Report, 1914 Cd.7491 XXIX, p. 541
Administration of national health insurance: Report for 1913–14, 1914 Cd.7496 LXXXII
Statistics of compensation and proceedings under the Workmen's Compensation Act of 1906 ... during the year 1913, 1914–16 Cd.7669 LXI, p. 991
Chief Medical Officer, Ministry of Health, 1st Annual Report, 1919–20, 1920 Cmd.978 XVII, p. 577
Royal Commission on National Health Insurance, Report, 1926 Cmd.2596 XIV, p. 311

Other British official publications

Hansard, *Parliamentary Debates*

GERMAN OFFICIAL DOCUMENTS

Kaiserliches Statistisches Amt, *Statistik der öffentlichen Armenpflege im Jahre 1885, Statistik des Deutschen Reichs*, NF 29 (1887)
Prussian Population Census 1890, Statistik des Deutschen Reichs, NF 68 (Berlin, 1893)
Vierteljahrshefte zur Statistik des Deutschen Reichs (Berlin, 1897), vol. II
Die bestehenden Einrichtungen zur Versicherung gegen die Folgen der Arbeitslosigkeit im Ausland und im Deutschen Reich (3 vols., Berlin, 1906)
Gebiete und Methoden der amtlichen Arbeiterstatistik (Berlin, 1913)
'Statistik der Krankenversicherung der Arbeiter im Jahre 1891', in *Statistik des Deutschen Reichs*, NF vol. 65 (Berlin, 1893)

'Statistik der Krankenversicherung ... 1911', in *Statistik des Deutschen Reichs*, NF vol. 258 (Berlin, 1912)

Reichsversicherungsamt, *Statistik der Arbeiterversicherung des Deutschen Reichs 1885–1904* (Berlin, 1906)

Stenographische Berichte des Reichstags (SBRT)

Index